THE WAR AT SEA

ROYAL & DOMINION NAVY ACTIONS IN WORLD WAR 2

GORDON SMITH

LONDON

IAN ALLAN LTD

CONTENTS

First published 1989

ISBN 0 7110 1739 5

Published by Ian Allan Ltd, Shepperton, Surrey;
and phototypeset & printed by Ian Allan Printing Ltd
at their works at Coombelands in Runnymede, England

INTRODUCTION

Journeying through the immensity of World War 2, the main aim of this book is simply to answer the questions: what Royal Navy warships were lost, when, where and in what circumstances? And what else of significance was taking place in the naval and maritime, the military and political spheres. To balance this picture, German, Italian and Japanese losses due to the Royal Navy are also included.

There are two other aims:

● To acknowledge the part played by all the navies (and the other armed forces) of the then British Empire, now the Commonwealth of Nations, and especially the Royal Australian, Canadian, Indian and New Zealand Navies. Collectively they are referred to, as they often would have been at the time of World War 2, as the Dominion Navies.

● To ensure a more balanced account by summarising the operations of the US Navy in the Atlantic, European and Mediterranean areas, as well as their overwhelming role in the Pacific, the theatre most important to Australia and New Zealand.

FORMAT

To convey all this information, the background events and major warship losses on both sides are shown month-by-month, across the four main theatres of the world. The result is not so much a reference book as a framework within which the reader can better appreciate the overall war at sea, and place his own particular interests.

By major warships are meant capital ships, aircraft carriers, cruiser, destroyers and submarines. In the case of the Royal and Dominion Navies, most of the classes are introduced by a series of photographs, spread through the book, and accompanied by a brief summary of their main characteristics and losses. They are grouped in the order of the warships constructed in World War 1, the inter-war years, and finally World War 2.

To reflect the importance of the Battle of the Atlantic and in part, the role of the Royal Canadian Navy, losses in ocean escorts are also included in the text.

Although the emphasis is on warships sunk or so badly damaged that repair was not worthwhile, the greatest loss was in the men of the Royal and Dominion Navies killed in action. These totalled over 50,000, or nearly 50% of the prewar strength of the Service, and understanding how just one of these men was lost, in this case my father, gave me the reason for tackling this vast subject in this way.

ACKNOWLEDGEMENTS

Any book of this nature builds on the work of many others, and the main publications used are listed in the Bibliography. Some were more invaluable than others and to these a special debt of gratitude is due. On the naval side, Capt Roskill's monumental four volumes of *The War at Sea* set a standard for any writer on maritime matters, and Rohwer & Hummelchen's encyclopaedic *Chronology of the War at Sea* has no obvious equal. Understanding something of this great conflict is no easy task, and any guides through the maze are to be welcomed. Amongst these must be mentioned Simon Goodenough's *War Maps*, Basil Liddell Hart's *History of the Second World War* and *The Almanac of World War II* edited by Brigadier Young.

The Naval Historical Branch of the Ministry of Defence kindly allowed me to check the details of all major Royal Navy warship losses, and special thanks are offered for their help and patience. Finally, thanks are also due to Real Photographs Co Ltd for providing most of the photographs, unless otherwise credited.

After all these acknowledgements are made, there is still one more, and that is to accept that any errors or misinterpretations remain mine.

Gordon Smith
Penarth

GENESIS

Of course, World War 2 did not just 'happen' but resulted from many factors. If one is to start anywhere, why not with the end of World War 1 and the Treaty of Versailles? Some of the political and naval milestones on the way to the outbreak of war therefore serve as an introduction to the main events of the book.

Political	Naval
1919 Treaty of Versailles — Under its provisions, Germany is to be disarmed, the Rhineland occupied and reparations paid. At this time Poland is re-created from parts of Germany and Russia, as are other Central European states out of the Austro-Hungarian Empire. Japan is given a mandate over the ex-German islands in the Pacific. The League of Nations is formed.	**1921-22** Washington Naval Treaty — Britain, United States, Japan, France and Italy agree to limit the displacement and main armament of capital ships, aircraft carriers and cruisers, and total tonnage and age of the first two categories.
1922 Benito Mussolini and his Fascist Party come to power in Italy.	**1922** Japanese carrier *Hosho* completed.
1926 The German Weimar Republic joins the League of Nations.	**1927** The Geneva Naval Conference fails to reach agreement on total tonnage of cruisers, destroyers and submarines. Major warships completed are the RN battleships *Nelson* and *Rodney*, the French carrier *Bearn*, the US carriers *Lexington* and *Saratoga*, and the Japanese carrier *Akagi*.
	1928 Japanese carrier *Kaga* completed.
1930 Following the Wall Street Crash of 1929 the world moves into major economic depression.	**1930** London Naval Treaty — Britain, US and Japan agree on total tonnage, tonnage and armament limitations for cruisers, destroyers and submarines. Also no new capital ships to be laid down until 1937. Neither France or Italy are signatories.
1931 An incident in the Chinese province of Manchuria leads to the Japanese invasion which is completed by early 1932. The puppet state of Manchukuo is declared. By then Japanese forces have taken control of the Shanghai area in further fighting.	
1933 Following earlier Nazi Party election successes, Adolph Hitler becomes Chancellor of Germany in January. He takes the country out of the League of Nations later in the year, by which time the Japanese have already walked out over the Manchurian issue.	**1933** Major warships completed are the German pocket battleship *Deutschland* and the Japanese carrier *Ryujo*.

Political	Naval
1934 Russia joins the League. Meanwhile Hitler consolidates his power and in August proclaims himself Führer.	**1934** The 1932 Geneva Disarmament Conference finally breaks down and Japan announces its intention to withdraw from the 1922 and 1930 Naval Treaties when they expire in 1936. Planning starts on the giant battleships of the 'Yamato' class. Major warships completed are the US carrier *Ranger* and the German pocket battleship *Admiral Scheer*.
1935 **March** — Hitler introduces military conscription. **April** — The United States passes the Neutrality Act forbidding the supply of arms to belligerents in the event of war. **October** — Following border disputes between Italian Somaliland and Abyssinia, Italy invades. League of Nations sanctions have little effect and by May the country has been taken over by Mussolini's forces.	**1935** **June** — Anglo-German Naval Agreement — Germany is to be allowed to build a fleet up to 35% of British total tonnage and to 45% of submarines. Parity in the latter is allowed with notice.
1936 **March** — German troops are sent to re-occupy the Rhineland. **July** — The Spanish Civil War starts; eventually Italy and Germany are aligned on one side and Russia on the other.	**1936** **November** — London Protocol — The major powers including Germany agree to prohibit unrestricted submarine warfare against unarmed ships. **December** — The 1922 and 1930 Naval Treaties are allowed to lapse and the major powers move towards rearmament. In Britain this effectively starts with the 1936/37 Estimates. The German pocket battleship *Admiral Graf Spee* is completed.
1937 **July** — Further incidents in China, this time near Peking lead to Japan slowly extending its hold over northeastern China and the major port areas by the end of 1938.	**1937** French battlecruiser *Dunkerque* completed; US carrier *Yorktown* completed; Italian battleships *Littorio* and *Vittorio Veneto* launched; and Japanese carrier *Soryu* completed.
1938 **March** — German troops march into and annex Austria. **September** — In the Munich Crisis Czechoslovakia is forced to cede Sudetenland to Germany.	**1938** Germany draws up the major naval rearmament programme, the 'Z' plan, to bring the Navy closer to equality to Britain by the mid-1940s. Royal Navy carrier *Ark Royal* completed; French battlecruiser *Strasbourg* completed; US carrier *Enterprise* completed; and German battlecruiser *Gneisenau* completed and carrier *Graf Zeppelin* launched (but never completed).

1939
March — Germany completes its occupation of Czechoslovakia and takes back Memel on the Baltic coast from Lithuania. Now Britain and France guarantee Poland's independence.
    The Spanish Civil War comes to an end.
April — Italy invades Albania.
May — Britain re-introduces military conscription. Germany and Italy join forces in the Pact of Steel.
August — Following secret negotiations the Russian-German Non-Aggression Pact is signed in Moscow to the world's amazement. Its provisions include the dismemberment of Poland.
September — on the 1st, Germany invades Poland.
	1939
	April — Germany abrogates the 1935 Anglo-German Naval Agreement.
	June — The Reserve Fleet of the Royal Navy is manned.
	August — Full mobilisation of the Royal Navy is ordered and the Admiralty takes control of all merchant shipping. German U-boats and two pocket battleships sail for their war stations in the Atlantic.
	    Major warships to 3 September: Royal Navy battleships *King George V* and *Prince of Wales* and fleet carriers *Illustrious* and *Formidable* launched; French battleship *Richelieu* launched; US carrier *Wasp* launched; German battleships *Bismarck* and *Tirpitz* launched and battlecruiser *Scharnhorst* completed; Japanese carriers *Shokaku* launched and *Hiryu* completed.

ABBREVIATIONS

A	American (escort group)
AA	Anti-aircraft
ABDA	American, British, Dutch, Australian
ACM	Air Chief Marshal
Adm	Admiral
AMC	Armed merchant cruiser
ANZAC	Australian and New Zealand armed forces
A/S	Anti-submarine
ASDIC	Allied Submarine Detection Investigation Committee (submarine detection system)
ASV	Anti-surface vessel or air-to-surface radar
B	British (escort Group)
B-	Boeing
BEF	British Expeditionary Force
BPF	British Pacific Fleet
C	Canadian (escort group)
C-in-C	Commander-in-Chief
CAM	Catapult aircraft merchantman
Capt	Captain
CHOP	Change of operational control
Cdr	Commander
Cdre	Commodore
Col	Colonel
DEI	Dutch East Indies
Do	Dornier
E-boat	German motor torpedo boat
EG	Escort Group
FAA	Fleet Air Arm
Flg Off	Flag Officer
Flt Lt	Flight Lieutenant
Gen	General
He	Heinkel
HF/DF	High frequency direction finding
HMAS	His Majesty's Australian Ship
HMCS	His Majesty's Canadian Ship
HMS	His Majesty's Ship/Submarine
HMNZS	His Majesty's New Zealand Ship
Hs	Henschel
Ju	Junkers
LSI	Landing Ship, Infantry (converted merchantman)
LST	Landing Ship, Tank

Lt	Lieutenant
Lt-Cdr	Lieutenant-Commander
MAC	Merchant aircraft carrier
MAD	Magnetic anomaly detector
Maj	Major
Me	Messerschmitt
Med	Mediterranean Sea
MGB	Motor gun boat
MTB	Motor torpedo boat
Plt Off	Pilot Officer
PM	Prime Minister
POW	Prisoner of war
RAAF	Royal Australian Air Force
RAF	Royal Air Force
RAFVR	Royal Air Force Volunteer Reserve
RAN	Royal Australian Navy
RCAF	Royal Canadian Air Force
RCN	Royal Canadian Navy
RCNVR	Royal Canadian Naval Volunteer Reserve
RIN	Royal Indian Navy
RINR	Royal Indian Naval Reserve
RN	Royal Navy
RNR	Royal Naval Reserve
RNVR	Royal Naval Volunteer Reserve
RNZAF	Royal New Zealand Air Force
RNZN	Royal New Zealand Navy
S	*Schnellboot* or German MTB
ss	Steamship
SAAF	South African Air Force
SANF	South African Naval Force
Sub Lt	Sub Lieutenant
TA	*Torpedoboot Ausland* or torpedo boat captured by German Navy
TF	Task force
TT	Torpedo tubes
U	*Unterseeboot* or German submarine
UIt	Ex-Italian submarine in German service
UJ	*Unterseebootjäger* or German submarine chaser
US	United States
USAAF	United States Army Air Force
USN	United States Navy
VLR	Very long range
WRNS	Women's Royal Naval Service
Z	*Zerstörer* or German destroyer

MAJOR NAVAL EVENTS

THE ROYAL AND DOMINION NAVIES IN OUTLINE

In 1939, the heart of the Royal Navy is its centuries old traditions and 200,000 officers and men including the Royal Marines and Reserves. At the very top as professional head is the First Sea Lord, Admiral of the Fleet Sir Dudley Pound. The Royal Navy, still the largest in the world in September 1939, includes:

- 15 capital ships, of which only two are post-World War 1. Five 'King George V' class battleships are building.
- Seven aircraft carriers. One is new and five of the planned six fleet carriers are under construction. There are no escort carriers.
- 66 cruisers, mainly post-World War 1 with some older ships converted for AA duties. Including cruiser-minelayers, 23 new ones have been laid down.
- 184 destroyers of all types. Over half are modern, with 15 of the old 'V' and 'W' classes modified as escorts. Under construction or on order are 32 fleet destroyers and 20 escort types of the 'Hunt' class.
- 60 submarines, mainly modern with nine building.
- 45 escort and patrol vessels with nine building, and the first 56 'Flower' class corvettes are on order to add to the converted 'V' and 'Ws' and 'Hunts'. However, there are few fast, long-endurance escorts to start with.

Included in the totals are the Dominion navies:

- Royal Australian Navy — six cruisers, five destroyers and two sloops;
- Royal Canadian Navy — six destroyers;
- Royal Indian Navy — six escort and patrol vessels;
- Royal New Zealand Navy, until October 1941 the New Zealand Division of the Royal Navy — two cruisers and two sloops.

The Fleet is reasonably well-equipped to fight conventional surface actions with effective guns, torpedoes and fire control. But in a maritime war that will soon revolve around the battle with the U-boat, the exercise of air power, and eventually the ability to land large armies on hostile shores, then the picture is far from good.

ASDIC, the RN's answer to the submarine, has limited range and is of little use against surfaced U-boats, and the stern-dropped or mortar-fired depth charge is the only reasonably lethal anti-submarine weapon available. The Fleet Air Arm (FAA) recently returned to full control of the Navy, is equipped with obsolescent aircraft, and in the face of heavy air attack the Fleet has few, satisfactory anti-aircraft guns. Co-operation with the RAF is limited although three Area Combined Headquarters have been established in Britain. Coastal Command, the RAF's maritime wing, has only short range aircraft, mainly for reconnaissance. And there is little in the way of combined operations capability.

On the technical side, early air warning radars are fitted to a small number of ships. The introduction by the Germans of magnetic mines will find the RN equipped to sweep moored contact mines. Finally, the German Navy's B-Service can read the Navy's operational and convoy codes.

As the war progresses, so the Royal and Dominion Navies expand rapidly with large construction programmes, particularly of escort carriers, destroyers, corvettes, frigates and submarines. By mid-1944, 800,000 officers and men and 73,000 WRNS are in uniform. Vastly improved radars and anti-submarine weapons have been introduced and ship-borne and land-based aircraft are vital in the life and death struggle against the U-boat. Huge combined operations landings take place with air superiority usually assured. Magnetic, then acoustic and finally pressure mines are kept under control. And perhaps of greatest single significance, the 'Ultra' operation against the German Enigma codes allows the Allies to penetrate to the very heart of German and Axis planning and operations.

In short, in a war that starts with cavalry and ends with the atomic bomb, the Royal and Dominion Navies face each new threat and learn to deal with them technically and operationally — and, above all, successfully.

ATLANTIC AND EUROPEAN THEATRES — STARTING CONDITIONS

Strategic and Maritime Situation

Areas under direct Allied control include Canada and Newfoundland, Bermuda, many of the West Indies, British and French Guiana, islands in the Central and South Atlantic, much of the Atlantic seaboard of Africa, and Gibraltar. And, of course, the waters of Britain and France. The one major defensive gap is in the lack of bases in Eire to cover the Western Approaches further out into the Atlantic.

Germany is restricted to a short North Sea and Baltic coastline. Its exits to the Atlantic pass through the Allied controlled English Channel and North Sea. However, Britain's survival depends on the Atlantic trade routes; Germany's does not.

Primary Maritime Tasks

These are based on the assumption that Britain and France are actively allied against the European Axis powers of Germany and Italy. The RN is responsible for the North Sea and most of the Atlantic, although the French will contribute some forces. In the Mediterranean the task of defence is to be shared between both Navies. As it happens, Mussolini's 'Mare Nostrum' will not become a theatre of war for another nine months.

OBJECTIVES	INITIAL OPERATIONS
Defence of trade routes, and convoy organisation and escort, especially to and from Britain.	Until May 1940 the main threat is from U-Boats operating in the North Sea and South Western Approaches. For a few months two pocket battleships pose a danger in the broader reaches of the Atlantic.
	The first overseas convoys leave Britain via the South Western Approaches. From the Thames they go out through the English Channel (OA) and from Liverpool through the Irish Sea (OB). Later in September convoys leave Freetown, Sierra Leone (SL), Halifax, Nova Scotia (HX) and Gibraltar (HG) for the UK.
	In the North Atlantic anti-submarine escorts are provided from Britain out to 200 miles west of Ireland (15°W) and to the middle of the Bay of Biscay; also, for a few hundred miles from Halifax, cover is given by Canadian warships and from other overseas assembly ports. Cruisers and (shortly) armed merchant cruisers then

sometimes take over as ocean escorts. Particularly fast or slow ships sail as independents as do the many hundreds of vessels scattered across the rest of the world's oceans. Almost throughout the war it is amongst these and the stragglers from convoys that the mainly German warships, raiders, aircraft and above all the submarine find so many of their victims.

OBJECTIVES	INITIAL OPERATIONS
Detection and destruction of surface raiders and U-boats.	Patrols are carried out by RAF Coastal Command in the North Sea, and by Home Fleet submarines off southwest Norway and the German North Sea bases. RAF Bomber Command prepares to attack the warships in these bases.
	Fleet aircraft carriers are employed on anti-U-boat sweeps in the Western Approaches.
Maritime blockade of Germany and contraband control.	As German merchant ships try to reach home or neutral ports, units of the Home Fleet sortie into the North Sea and the waters between Scotland, Norway and Iceland. The Northern Patrol of old cruisers and, later, armed merchant cruisers has the unenviable task of covering the area between the Shetlands and Iceland. In addition, British and French warships patrol the North and South Atlantic.
	Closer to Germany the first mines are laid by RN destroyers in the approaches to their North Sea bases.
Defence of own coasts.	Right through until May 1940 U-boats operate around the coasts of Britain and in the North Sea. The Moray Firth is often a focus of their activities. They attack with both torpedoes and magnetic mines. Mines will also be laid by surface ships and aircraft.
	British East Coast convoys (FN/FS) commence between the Thames Estuary and the Firth of Forth in Scotland. Southend-on-Sea, the Thames seaside resort, will see over 2,000 convoys arrive and depart in the course of the war.
	Defensive minelaying begins on an anti-U-boat barrier in the English Channel across the Straits of Dover, and later on an East Coast barrier to protect the coastal convoy routes.
Escort troops to France and between Britain, the Dominions and other areas under Allied control.	An immediate start is made on transporting the British Expeditionary Force (BEF) to France. By the end of 1939 the first Canadian troops have arrived in Britain, and by early 1940 Australian, Indian and New Zealand forces are on their way to Egypt and the Middle East. Troop convoys are

always heavily escorted, and the Dominion Navies play an important part in protecting their men as they leave their home shores. Australian and New Zealand cruisers are particularly active in the Indian Ocean.

Major Naval Strengths

	ROYAL NAVY		FRENCH	GERMAN	
	Home Waters (a)	Atlantic (b)	Atlantic/Channel	European Waters	Atlantic on station
Battleships	9	—	2	3	2(c)
Carriers	4	—	1	—	—
Cruisers	21	14	3	7	—
Destroyers	82	13	20	22	—
Submarines	21	4	—	41(d)	16
Totals	137	31	26	73	18
	Plus escorts			Plus torpedo boats	

Notes:
Royal Navy is a mix of World War 1, modernised and recently completed ships. The French warships allocated to the Atlantic and the German are mainly modern.

(a) Home Fleet commanded by Adm Sir Charles Forbes with 7 capital ships, 2 carriers and 16 cruisers based at Scapa Flow and Rosyth; Channel Force with 2 battleships, 2 carriers and 3 cruisers; Humber Force with 2 cruisers; and various destroyer flotillas.
(b) North Atlantic Command based at Gibraltar with 2 cruisers and 9 destroyers; America and West Indies at Bermuda with 4 cruisers; and South Atlantic at Freetown with 8 cruisers and 4 destroyers.
(c) Pocket battleships *Admiral Graf Spee* in the South and *Deutschland* in the North Atlantic.
(d) Includes U-boats on patrol in the North Sea and British coastal waters.

DECLARATION OF WAR

3rd — *After Germany invades Poland on the 1st, Britain and France demand the withdrawal of German forces. The ultimatum expires and at 11.15 on the 3rd, Prime Minister Neville Chamberlain broadcasts to announce that Britain is at war with Germany. He forms a War Cabinet which includes Winston Churchill as First Lord of the Admiralty. France, Australia, New Zealand and India (through the Viceroy) declare war the same day. South Africa follows on the 6th and Canada on the 10th.*

ATLANTIC

SEPTEMBER

Battle of the Atlantic

The six-year battle starts on the 3rd with the sinking of liner *Athenia* by *U30* (Lt Lemp) northwest of Ireland. She has been mistaken for an armed merchant cruiser, and her destruction leads the Admiralty to believe that unrestricted submarine warfare has been launched. The full convoy plans are put into operation, but in fact Hitler has ordered his U-boats to adhere to international law and, after the *Athenia* incident, controls are tightened for a while.

Liverpool-out convoy OB4 is the first to be attacked, and *U31* sinks one ship on the 16th. Convoys actually suffer little harm over the next seven months, and most of the losses due to U-boats are among the independently routed and neutral merchantmen. In the period to March 1940 they sink 222 British, Allied and neutral ships in the Western Approaches, the North Sea and around the coasts of Britain. In the same time they lose 18 of their number, a third of all in commission in September 1939, and more than new boats entering service.

14th/17th — After an unsuccessful attack on carrier *Ark Royal* off the Hebrides, *U39* is sunk on the 14th by screening destroyers *Faulknor*, *Firedrake* and *Foxhound*. Three days later, to the southwest of Ireland, fleet carrier **COURAGEOUS** is sent to the bottom by *U29* with heavy loss of life. Carriers are withdrawn from anti-U-boat patrols as the lesson is slowly learnt that the best chance of sinking U-boats is to attract them to well-defended convoys when the escorts can hunt them down.

20th — After sinking trawlers off the northern Hebrides, *U27* is located and sunk by destroyers *Fortune* and *Forester*.

Pocket battleship *Admiral Graf Spee* sinks her first ship off Brazil on the 30th.

Battle of the Atlantic
Summary of Allied and Axis (Warship) Losses
- 20 British, Allied and neutral ships of 110,000 tons from all causes in the North and South Atlantic and 1 fleet carrier.
- 2 U-boats.

OCTOBER

The Pan-American Conference establishes a 300-mile and more security zone off the coasts of the Americas, within which all hostile action by the belligerent powers is forbidden.

Graf Spee claims four more merchant ships in the South Atlantic before heading into the southern Indian Ocean. To search for her, seven hunting groups are formed in the Atlantic and one in the Indian Ocean. In total the Royal and French Navies deploy three capital ships, four carriers and 16 cruisers.

EUROPE

SEPTEMBER

On the 4th, advance units of the British Expeditionary Force are carried by destroyers from Portsmouth to Cherbourg. A week later the main force starts landing in France. By June 1940 half a million men are carried in both directions without loss.

Aircraft of RAF Bomber Command make their first attack on German warships in Wilhelmshaven and Brunsbüttel on the 4th. The cruiser *Emden* is slightly damaged by a crashing aircraft.

10th — Home Fleet submarines on patrol off southwest Norway suffer their first casualty in tragic circumstances. **OXLEY** is torpedoed in error by the *Triton* and goes down off Obrestad.

The British Code & Cipher School moves to Bletchley Park, England, the site of its magnificent successes in breaking the German Enigma codes through the 'Ultra' programme. The school starts with the work of the Polish code-breakers. By April the first low level Luftwaffe codes are being deciphered. Many months follow before comparable progress is made with the Naval ones.

Polish Campaign — Conclusion

As the German advance into Poland continues, Russia invades from the east on the 17th. Warsaw surrenders to the German Army on the 28th, and next day the country is partitioned in accordance with the Soviet-German Pact. The last of the Polish Army surrenders on 5 October and Poland enters long dark years of brutality and oppression.

Merchant Shipping War
Summary of Allied Losses
- 33 British, Allied and neutral ships of 85,000 tons in UK waters.

OCTOBER

Most of the BEF is now in France just as Hitler orders the first plans to be prepared for the invasion of France and the Low Countries.

8th-24th — The anti-U-boat mine barrage in the Strait of Dover is completed and accounts for three U-boats — *U12* on the 8th, *U40* on the 13th, and *U16* on the 24th.
No more attempt the passage of the English Channel, and have to sail around the north of Scotland to reach the Atlantic.

ATLANTIC

Meanwhile the *Deutschland*, after accounting for two ships in the North Atlantic, has been ordered home. She reaches Germany in November and is renamed *Lützow*.

13th/14th — Two U-boats are sunk by escorting destroyers when they attack convoys to the southwest of Ireland. On the 13th *U42* is sent to the bottom by *Imogen* and *Ilex* with Liverpool-out convoy OB17. Next day *Icarus*, *Inglefield*, *Intrepid* and *Ivanhoe* with Kingston, Jamaica/UK convoy KJ3 destroy *U45*.

Battle of the Atlantic

The first UK/Gibraltar convoy, OG1, sails in October.

Partly because of the loss of *U42* and *U45*, only three of the intended nine U-boats are available for the first group attack on a convoy using an on-board tactical commander. Three ships out of the 27 in unescorted convoy HG3 are sunk, and the experiment is only repeated a few times. The first wolf-pack attacks conducted personally by Adm Dönitz from ashore do not occur for another year.

Losses
- 22 ships of 133,000 tons.
- 2 U-boats.

NOVEMBER

The United States Neutrality Act is amended to allow the supply of arms to belligerents on a 'cash and carry' basis. At the same time American shipping is banned from the war zones.

Graf Spee sinks a small tanker southwest of Madagascar and then heads back for the South Atlantic. More Allied hunting groups are formed.

23rd — Armed merchant cruiser **RAWALPINDI** (Capt E. C. Kennedy) on Northern Patrol is sunk by the 11in battlecruiser *Scharnhorst* as she and sister ship *Gneisenau* try to break out into the Atlantic. After the action, which takes place to the southwest of Iceland, they turn back and return to Germany, having avoided searching ships of the Home Fleet.

29th — *U35*, on patrol in the Orkneys area to support the battlecruisers, is found to the east of the Shetlands and sunk by destroyers *Kashmir*, *Kingston* and *Icarus*.

Battle of the Atlantic

RAF Coastal Command continues to patrol for U-boats on passage into the Atlantic. Equal priority is now given to attacking them, but the aircraft crews are not trained for these duties and their A/S bombs are ineffective. Their first success is a joint one with the RN at the end of January.

Losses
- 6 ships of 18,000 tons and 1 armed merchant cruiser.
- 1 U-boat.

EUROPE

Battlecruiser *Gneisenau* and other ships of the German Navy sortie on the 8th off Norway to draw the Home Fleet within U-boat and aircraft range. Capital ships *Hood*, *Nelson*, *Repulse*, *Rodney* and *Royal Oak*, together with the carrier *Furious*, cruisers and destroyers, sail for various positions, but there is no contact.

14th – Battleship **ROYAL OAK** returns to Scapa Flow after guarding the Fair Isle passage. There at anchor she is torpedoed and sunk by *U47* (Lt-Cdr Prien) in the early hours of the 14th.

Attacks by sea and air are stepped up in British waters against merchant shipping and the Royal Navy:
- Ju88s bomb ships in the Firth of Forth on the 16th and slightly damage cruiser **Southampton**. Next day more Ju88s strike at Scapa Flow and the old gunnery training battleship **Iron Duke** has to be beached.
- Destroyers, and later other surface vessels, start laying mines off the East Coast.
- Aircraft attack the East Coast convoy routes, but initially without success. It takes some months to arrange for effective sweeps by RAF Fighter Command, and there are few AA guns available for the arming of merchantmen.

Merchant Shipping War

Losses
- 24 ships of 63,000 tons.

NOVEMBER

The first HN/ON convoys between the Firth of Forth and Norway sail in November and are covered by the Home Fleet. They are discontinued in April.

U-boat and surface ship-laid mines continue to inflict heavy losses on merchant ships and warships alike:

13th – Cruiser minelayer **Adventure** and accompanying destroyer *Blanche* are both mined in the Thames Estuary. **BLANCHE** is a total loss.

21st – New cruiser **Belfast** is badly damaged in the Forth on a mine laid by *U21*. With her back broken she is out of action for three years.

21st – Destroyer **GIPSY** is lost on mines laid by destroyers off Harwich.

Seaplanes also lay the first magnetic mines off the East Coast, and early on drop one at Shoeburyness in the Thames Estuary. On the 23rd it is defused and recovered by Lt-Cdr Ouvry. This marks a vital step in the battle against these particular mines which are causing heavy losses and long delays. In November alone 27 ships of 121,000 tons are sunk, and for a time the Thames is virtually closed to shipping.

Home Fleet submarines gain their first success in the Heligoland Bight when *Sturgeon* sinks the German patrol ship *V209* on the 20th.

Russo-Finnish War

Negotiations between the two countries on border changes and the control of islands in the Gulf of Finland break down, and Russia invades on the 30th. Against fierce resistance by the Finns, the war drags on until March.

Merchant Shipping War
Losses
- 43 ships of 156,000 tons.

DECEMBER

The first Canadian troop convoy, TC1, sails from Halifax for Britain, heavily escorted and accompanied part of the way by Canadian destroyers.

13th — Battle of the River Plate — Now back in the South Atlantic, *Graf Spee* claims three more victims to bring her total to nine ships of 50,000 tons, before heading for the shipping lanes off the River Plate. Cdre Harwood with his Hunting Group G — 8in cruisers *Exeter* and *Cumberland* and 6in *Ajax* and the New Zealand *Achilles* — correctly anticipates that the 11in pocket battleship will make for this area. Unfortunately *Cumberland* is by now in the Falklands.

At 06.00 on the 13th, 150 miles east of the Plate Estuary, *Graf Spee* (Capt Langsdorff) is reported to the northwest of the three cruisers.

Faced by *Graf Spee's* heavier armament, Cdre Harwood has decided to split his force in two and try to divide her main guns. *Exeter* closes to the south while the two light cruisers work around to the north, all firing as they manoeuvre. *Graf Spee* soon concentrates her 11in guns on **Exeter** which is badly hit. By 06.50 all ships are heading west, *Exeter* with only one turret in action and on fire. She has to break off, and heads for the Falklands.

Now it is up to *Ajax* and *Achilles*. They continue to harry the pocket battleship from the north, but at 07.25 **Ajax** loses her two after turrets to an 11in hit. *Achilles* already has splinter damage, but still the German ship fails to press home its advantage. By 08.00, still with only superficial damage, it heads for Montevideo, the cruisers shadowing.

Graf Spee enters the port at midnight. As other Allied hunting groups head for the area, much diplomatic manoeuvring takes place to hold her there. Finally, on the 17th, Capt Langsdorff takes his ship out into the estuary where she is scuttled and blown up. Only *Cumberland* has arrived by this time. Langsdorff then commits suicide.

Battle of the Atlantic
Losses
- 7 ships of 38,000 tons.
- 1 pocket battleship.

DECEMBER

4th — Returning from the hunt for the German battle-cruisers after the sinking of *Rawalpindi*, **Nelson** is damaged by a mine laid by *U31* off Loch Ewe, northwest Scotland.

4th/13th — On patrol off the Heligoland Bight, submarine *Salmon* (Lt Cdr Bickford) sinks the outward bound *U36* on the 4th. Nine days later she torpedoes and damages cruisers *Leipzig* and *Nürnberg* as they cover a destroyer minelaying operation off the Tyne.

12th/28th — Battleship **Barham** is involved in two incidents. On the 12th in the North Channel she collides with and sinks one of her screening destroyers, **DUCHESS**. And later in the month she is damaged off the Hebrides by *U30* (Lt Cdr Lemp)

Trawlers are the main victims of the first successful attacks by German aircraft off the East Coast. By the end of March they have accounted for 30 vessels of 37,000 tons. Losses from mines remain high — 33 ships of 83,000 tons in December.

Merchant Shipping War
Losses
- 66 ships of 152,000 tons.

JANUARY

30th — In attacks on Thames-out convoy OA80 to the west of the English Channel, *U55* is destroyed by the joint action of an RAF Sunderland of No 228 Squadron, sloop *Fowey* and destroyer *Whitshed*. This is the first such successful action, which will not be repeated for another five months.

Battle of the Atlantic

Losses
- 9 British, Allied and neutral ships of 36,000 tons in the North and South Atlantic.
- 1 U-boat.

FEBRUARY

5th — *U41* sinks one ship from Liverpool-out convoy OB84 south of Ireland, and is then sent to the bottom by the lone escort, destroyer *Antelope*.

23rd — Destroyer *Gurkha* on passage south of the Faeroes encounters *U53* as she returns from operations in the Western Approaches. The U-boat is sunk.

Battle of the Atlantic

Losses
- 17 ships of 75,000 tons.
- 2 U-boats.

MARCH

Liner *Queen Elizabeth* sails independently on her maiden voyage from Scotland to New York to be converted into a troopship.

JANUARY

1st – AA cruiser **Coventry** is damaged in an air raid on the Shetlands.

7th/9th – Home Fleet submarines suffer heavy losses in the Heligoland area at the hands of minesweeper patrols — **SEAHORSE** and **UNDINE** on the 7th and **STARFISH** two days later. Submarine operations in the Bight are abandoned.

German plans for a western offensive (Operation 'Gelb') are postponed. Planning goes ahead for the invasion of Norway under the codename 'Weserübung'.

19th – As destroyer **GRENVILLE** returns from contraband control off the Dutch coast she is lost off the Thames on a destroyer-laid mine.

21st – Searching for a reported U-boat off the Moray Firth, destroyer **EXMOUTH** is torpedoed by *U22* and lost with all hands. U-boats are particularly active in this area and the rest of the North Sea through until March. In January alone they sink 14 ships — all neutrals.

Merchant Shipping War

Losses
- 64 British, Allied and neutral ships of 179,000 tons in UK waters.

FEBRUARY

Britain and France plan to send aid to Finland. This will allow them to occupy Narvik in northern Norway and help cut Swedish iron ore supplies to Germany.

12th – *U33* on a minelaying operation in the Firth of Clyde is sunk by minesweeper *Gleaner*.

16th – In the *Altmark* Incident, the *Graf Spee's* supply ship with Merchant Navy prisoners aboard is located off Norway and takes refuge in Jossingfiord, within territorial waters. In the evening the destroyer *Cossack* (Capt Vian) goes alongside, and after a short struggle a boarding party releases the prisoners with the cry: 'The Navy's here!'

18th/25th – In operations against Norway/UK convoys, HN12 is attacked on the 18th and the destroyer **DARING** sunk by *U23* to the east of the Pentland Firth. A week later it is the turn of HN14. *U63* is sighted by the escorting submarine *Narwhal* and sent to the bottom by destroyers *Escort*, *Imogen* and *Inglefield*.

22nd – In the North Sea German destroyers are attacked in error by their own aircraft and run into a minefield laid by RN destroyers. *Leberecht Maass* and *Max Schultz* are lost northwest of the German Frisian Islands. *U54* is presumed lost in the same field.

Merchant Shipping War

Losses
- 46 ships of 152,000 tons.

MARCH

U31 is bombed and sunk by a RAF Blenheim of Bomber Command in the Heligoland Bight on the 11th. She is salvaged and re-commissioned to be lost once and for all eight months later.

ATLANTIC

20th — Home Fleet battlecruisers to the north of the Shetlands cover a cruiser sweep into the Skagerrak. As they do, screening destroyer *Fortune* sinks *U44*.

William MacKenzie King, Prime Minister of Canada, is re-elected by a massive majority in support of his government's war policies.

German raider *Atlantis* sails for the Indian Ocean via the Cape of Good Hope. In 1941 she moves into the South Atlantic, and her operations last for a total of 20 months until her loss in November of that year.

She is the first of nine active raiders, seven of which go out in 1940. Only one ever breaks out for a second cruise. Their success is not so much due to their sinkings and captures — a creditable average of 15 ships of 90,000 tons for each raider — but to the disruption they cause in every ocean. At a time when the RN is short of ships, convoys must be organised and patrols instituted in many areas. In 1940 the raiders account for 54 ships of 370,000 tons, and the first is not caught until May the following year.

Battle of the Atlantic
U-boats start withdrawing from the Western Approaches in preparation for the German invasion of Norway.
Losses
- 2 ships of 11,000 tons.
- 1 U-boat.

EUROPE

Russo-Finnish War — Conclusion

On the 13th a peace treaty brings the war to a close with the cession of Finnish territory to the victor. Later in the month, and in spite of having to abandon plans to help Finland, Britain and France decide to disrupt Swedish iron ore traffic by mining Norwegian waters (Operation 'Wilfred'). Plans are also made to land troops at Stavanger, Bergen, Trondheim and Narvik to forestall German retaliation (Operation 'R4'). The entire operation is timed for 8 April.

16th — Home Fleet is bombed in its Scapa Flow base and Cruiser **Norfolk** damaged.

The RN slowly counters the magnetic mine with the introduction of ship-degaussing and 'LL' minesweeping gear. Since September, 430,000 tons of shipping have been sent to the bottom by mines around the coasts of Britain. This is a rate only second to the U-boats. Although mines remain a threat throughout the war, they are never again the danger they represented in the first few months.

Merchant Shipping War
Losses
- 43 ships of 96,000 tons.

DEFENCE OF TRADE — THE FIRST SEVEN MONTHS

Summary of Losses
In this period much of the Royal Navy's efforts have been directed to organising the protection of trade both to and from Britain and around the British Isles. The small number of U-boats operating in the South Western Approaches and North Sea have had their successes but mainly against independents. Losses in UK waters are high from both U-boats and mines. From now on the submarine will not appear in UK coastal areas until mid-1944.

North Atlantic	South Atlantic	UK waters
75 ships of 371,000 tons.	8 ships of 49,000 tons.	319 ships of 883,000 tons.

= 402 British, Allied and neutral ships of 1,303,000 tons: ie 186,000 tons per month.

Submarines	222 ships of 765,000 tons.
Mines	129 ships of 430,000 tons.
Warships	16 ships of 63,000 tons.
Aircraft	30 ships of 37,000 tons.
Other causes	5 ships of 8,000 tons.

Western Europe is about to erupt: there will be a lull in the Battle of the Atlantic as U-boats are withdrawn for the Norwegian campaign, and before the raiders start operations, and long-range aircraft and U-boats emerge from bases in France and Norway. Around the British Isles aircraft and mines will continue to account for merchant ships of all sizes, especially during the confused months of May, June and July. During this time German E-boats will commence attacks in coastal waters. (E-boat is the English term for German motor torpedo boats or S-boats, not to be confused with the heavily armed torpedo boats or small destroyers with their 'T' designation.)

The comparatively low monthly average of 186,000 tons of merchant shipping lost in the first seven months will not return for any more than a month or two for three long years.

ATLANTIC

APRIL

Raider *Orion* sails for the Pacific and Indian Oceans around Cape Horn. She is out for 16 months until her return to France.

10th — *U50*, on patrol off the Shetlands in support of the Norwegian invasion, is sunk by destroyer *Hero*.

EUROPE

APRIL

Just as the 'phoney' war ends in Europe (it had never existed at sea) so the end of the war is foreshadowed when the British government establishes the Maud Committee to oversee nuclear research. Similar steps have already been taken in the United States.

ATLANTIC

On the 13th an advance guard of Royal Marines is landed on the Faeroes with the eventual agreement of the Danish Governor.

Battle of the Atlantic
Losses
- 4 ships of 25,000 tons.
- 1 U-boat.

The 'Queen Elizabeth' class battleship HMS *Valiant* was one of a class of five, with *Malaya, Queen Elizabeth* and *Warspite*, plus *Barham* which was lost in November 1941. Completed in 1916 and of 31,000 tons standard displacement, *Valiant* could make 24kt, and carried a main armament of eight 15in guns and 1,120 crew. *Real Photos (S5181)*

HMS *Glowworm*, a 'G' and 'H' class destroyer, was sunk at around 09.00 on Monday 8 April 1940 at position 64°27N, 06°28E. Her opponent, the cruiser *Admiral Hipper*, picked up survivors, although she herself had been rammed by the *Glowworm*. *Real Photos (S1518)*

EUROPE

The Bletchley Park 'ULTRA' programme is now decoding some Luftwaffe low-level Enigma codes, partly because of the poor security procedures. There is little evidence that the information gleaned influences the war over the next two violent months.

Norwegian Campaign

3rd – The first German troop transports leave for Norway. Warships follow on the 7th.

8th – Operation 'Wilfred' — RN destroyers lay minefields, simulated and real, at three points off the Norwegian coast between Stadtlandet and Bodo. They are covered by battlecruiser *Renown* and other destroyers. One of the screen, the **GLOWWORM** (Lt-Cdr Roope), is detached to search for a man overboard, just as the 8in cruiser *Admiral Hipper* heads into Trondheim. They meet to the northwest of the port and the destroyer is soon sunk, but not before she rams and damages the *Hipper*. ✠ Lt-Cdr Gerard Roope RN is posthumously awarded the Victoria Cross.

7th-8th – In response to reported German movements, units of the Home Fleet including *Rodney, Valiant, Repulse*, four cruisers and 14 destroyers sail from Scapa Flow and Rosyth. Accompanying them is a French cruiser and two destroyers. Two more British cruisers and nine destroyers leave other duties and head for Norwegian waters. Next day, on the 8th, they are joined by the four troop-carrying cruisers of Operation 'R4', but *after* the soldiers have been disembarked back in Britain. More than 20 submarines, including three French and one Polish, take up positions.

9th – Germany invades Denmark and Norway in Operation 'Weserübung'. Copenhagen is soon occupied and Denmark surrenders. In Norway, troops land at Oslo, Kristiansand and Bergen in the south, Trondheim in the centre, and Narvik in the north. The southern forces and those from Trondheim push inland and join up by the end of April. They then move north to relieve Narvik, which has been isolated soon after the first landings.

German Navy forces include a pocket battleship, six cruisers and 14 destroyers for the landings at the five Norwegian ports, with battlecruisers *Scharnhorst* and *Gneisenau* covering the two most northerly ones. Thirty U-boats patrol off Norway and British bases, but throughout the campaign they suffer from major torpedo defects.
 Early in the morning *Renown* is in action with the two battlecruisers to the west of Vestfiord. *Gneisenau* is damaged and **Renown** slightly. The Germans withdraw.
 Around the same time the occupation forces heading for Oslo come under heavy fire from Norwegian coastal defences. Heavy cruiser *Blücher* is sunk by guns and torpedoes.
 A Home Fleet cruiser force is detached to attack the German warships in Bergen, but is soon ordered to withdraw. As they do they come under sustained air attack and destroyer **GURKHA** is bombed and sunk southwest of the port.
 That evening, on the 9th, German cruiser *Karlsrühe* leaves Kristiansand and is torpedoed by submarine *Truant*. She has to be scuttled next day.

10th — First Battle of Narvik – The 2nd Destroyer Flotilla (Capt Warburton-Lee with *Hardy, Havock, Hostile, Hotspur* and *Hunter*) enters Ofotfiord to attack the German ships assigned to the occupation of Narvik. These include 10 large destroyers. Several transports are sunk together with *Anton Schmitt* and *Wilhelm Heidkamp*. Others are damaged, but as the 2nd Flotilla

HM submarine *Seal* is seen as U-boat *UB* in German service in 1941. Previously a 'Porpoise' class minelaying submarine, she was captured in the Kattegat on Sunday 5 May 1940. *Real Photos (S1860)*

The 'Royal Sovereign' class battleship HMS *Royal Oak* was lost at Scapa Flow in October 1939, torpedoed by *U-47*. The class of five ships comprised *Ramillies*, *Resolution*, *Revenge* and *Royal Sovereign* (the Russian *Arkangelsk* from 1944). Photographed in 1936, *Royal Oak* was completed in 1916, displaced 29,000 tons, could make 21kt and carried eight 15in guns and 1,150 crew. *Real Photos (S573)*

retires, **HARDY** and **HUNTER** are sunk by the remaining German ships and **Hotspur** badly damaged. ✝ Capt Bernard Warburton-Lee RN is posthumously awarded the Victoria Cross.

Home Fleet is now reinforced by battleship *Warspite* and carrier *Furious*.

Still on the 10th, submarine **THISTLE** on patrol off Utsira fails in an attack on *U4*. Shortly after she is herself sunk by the same U-boat.

Cruiser *Königsberg*, damaged by shore batteries in the landings at Bergen, is sunk at her moorings by FAA Skuas of 800 and 803 Squadrons flying from the Orkneys. This is the first major warship to be sunk by air attack.

11th – Returning from the Oslo landings, pocket battleship *Lützow* is torpedoed and badly damaged by submarine *Spearfish* in the Skagerrak.

Cruiser **Penelope** is damaged when she runs aground in Vestfiord on her way into Narvik.

13th — Second Battle of Narvik – The *Warspite* and nine destroyers are sent into the Narvik fiords to finish off the remaining German ships. *U64* is first of all sunk by *Warspite's* Swordfish catapult aircraft scouting ahead. Then the surviving eight destroyers are all destroyed or scuttled — *Bernd von Arnim*, *Diether von Roeder*, *Erich Giese*, *Erich Koellner*, *Georg Thiele*, *Hans Lüdemann*, *Hermann Künne* and *Wolfgang Zenker*. The Royal Navy's *Eskimo* and *Cossack* are damaged.

The first British troop convoys have by now left the Clyde for Narvik, but some ships are diverted to Namsos. German forces are well-established in the south and centre of Norway and have control of the air.

14th – Submarine **TARPON** on patrol off southern Norway is sunk by German minesweeper *M6*.

The first Allied landings take place from the 14th to the 16th. In the north, British troops occupy Harstad in preparation for an attack on Narvik. They are later followed by French and Polish units through into May.

Royal Marines lead British and French troops into Namsos ready for an attack south towards Trondheim. The British alone go ashore in the Andalsnes area to try to hold on to central Norway with the Norwegian Army. Neither of these operations prove possible and on the 27th the decision is taken to pull out of central Norway.

15th – As the Harstad troopships approach the port, escorting destroyers *Brazen* and *Fearless* find *U49* and sink her. Southwest of Stavanger, *U1* is sent to the bottom after striking a mine.

RAF Bomber Command lays its first mines off the German and Danish coasts.

17th – Heavy cruiser **Suffolk** bombards installations at Stavanger, but as she returns is badly damaged by Ju88 bombers. She barely makes Scapa Flow.

18th – Four days after sinking the gunnery training ship *Brummer*, submarine **STERLET** is presumed lost in the Skagerrak to A/S trawlers.

24th – After four days of continuous AA duty off Andalsnes, cruiser **Curacoa** is badly damaged by bombs. Carrier *Glorious* flies off Gladiator biplanes for shore operations.

ATLANTIC	EUROPE

EUROPE (continued)

29th – Submarine **UNITY** is lost in collision with a Norwegian merchantman off the northeast coast of England.

30th – Sloop **BITTERN** is sunk by Ju87 dive-bombers off Namsos.

Merchant Shipping War

Losses
- 54 ships of 134,000 tons.

MAY

ATLANTIC

Raider *Widder* heads for central Atlantic operations before her return to France in six months time.

On her way into the Indian Ocean, *Atlantis* lays mines off South Africa.

On the 10th, Royal Marines are landed from two cruisers at Reykjavik, Iceland. More troops follow to set up air and sea bases that in time will become vital to Britain's defence of her Atlantic supply routes.

Soon after the attacks on Holland, Allied troops land on the Dutch West Indies islands of Aruba and Curacoa to protect oil installations.

Battle of the Atlantic

U-boats start returning to the Western Approaches. As they do, one of the first 'Flower' class corvettes, *Arabis*, is attacking one of their number in defence of a Gibraltar/UK convoy.

With the closure of the Mediterranean to Allied shipping, the trade routes around Africa and the ports to sustain them take on a new importance. Particularly vital is the West African base at Freetown, Sierra Leone.

Losses
- 10 ships of 55,000 tons.

MAY

EUROPE

Norwegian Campaign — Continued

After three days, and by the night of 2nd/3rd, the last British and French troops — a total of 10,000 — have been evacuated from Namsos and around Andalsnes. Others are later landed further north to try to block the German advance from Trondheim towards Narvik. The Allies continue to build up their forces for the attack on this port. ✠ Lt-Cdr Richard Stannard RNR, commanding officer of HM trawler *Arab* of the 15th A/S Striking Force, is awarded the Victoria Cross for gallantry under air attack during operations off Namsos.

3rd – Retiring northwest from Namsos, destroyers **AFRIDI** and the French *Bison* are sunk by Ju87s.

4th – As preparations continue in the north for the attack on Narvik, Polish destroyer *Grom* is bombed and sunk.

5th – Submarine **SEAL** successfully lays mines in the southern Kattegat on the 4th before being damaged by a German one herself. Trying to make for neutral Sweden on the surface, she is attacked and captured off the Skaw by German air and sea patrols.

German aircraft continue to mine the south and east coasts of Britain and, as the western offensive gets under way, the waters of Holland, Belgium and northern France.

Following a House of Commons debate on the Norwegian campaign, Prime Minister Neville Chamberlain resigns and Winston Churchill is appointed in his place on the 10th. Albert V. Alexander succeeds Churchill as First Lord of the Admiralty.

Western Front

On the 10th, Germany invades Holland, Belgium and Luxembourg — Operation 'Gelb'. Anglo-French troops cross into Belgium, but the main German thrust is in the centre through the Ardennes. By the 13th they have crossed into France at Sedan. They break through and German armour heads west for the Channel to trap the Allied armies in Belgium and northern France.

The Admiralty has already made plans to withdraw shipping from the Low Countries, to block the main ports and demolish installations, and to remove gold and diamonds. Most of these duties are carried out with the aid of the RN's destroyers, and they suffer almost crippling losses over the next few weeks.

By the 13th, Dutch Queen Wilhelmina and her Government are on their way to Britain by RN destroyer. Rotterdam is blitzed the next day, and the surrender of the Dutch Army follows on the 15th. This is the day when the British War Cabinet decides not

ATLANTIC	EUROPE

HMS *Effingham*, a 'Hawkins' class cruiser, was completed in 1925. She is shown here after reconstruction in 1938, with nine 6in guns. Approaching Bodo in Norway, late on Friday 17 May 1940, she ran aground between Briksvaer and Terra Islands. *Real Photos (S1094)*

The 'Repulse' class battlecruiser HMS *Repulse*, sister-ship to *Renown*, was lost in December 1941. Both were completed in 1916 and displaced 32,000 tons. The two ships could make 29kt and carried six 15in guns and a crew of c1,200 *Real Photos (S1110)*

to send any more RAF fighters to France and orders the strategic bombing of Germany. Raids are made on the Ruhr. As the Allies retreat from Belgium, German forces enter Brussels on the 17th.

15th/19th – Destroyers continue to support Allied land forces off the Dutch and Belgian coasts, and under heavy air attack, two are bombed and beached — **VALENTINE** on the 15th in the Scheldt Estuary and **WHITLEY** on the 19th near Nieuport on the Belgian coast.

On the 20th, German tanks reach the Channel near Abbeville and shortly advance north on the ports of Boulogne, Calais and Dunkirk. Destroyers carry troops to the first two, but by the 26th they have fallen. The BEF and French fall back on Dunkirk.

24th – During these operations, French destroyers *L'Adroit, Orage, Jaguar* and *Chacal* are lost off the ports. On the 24th it is the turn of destroyer **WESSEX**, bombed and sunk off Calais as she supports the defenders.

Norwegian Campaign — Continued

17th – Cruiser **EFFINGHAM** runs aground on an uncharted rock in Vestfiord as she carries troops to Bodo to help block the German advance on Narvik. She is later torpedoed and abandoned.

By the 23rd the carriers *Furious* and *Glorious* have flown ashore the first modern RAF fighters. Next day the Allies decide to pull out of Norway, but not before the port installations of Narvik have been destroyed.

26th/28th – During the attack on Narvik, AA cruiser **CURLEW** is bombed and sunk in Lavang Fiord. Two days later her sister-ship **Cairo** is badly damaged off the town of Narvik itself, just as French and Polish troops complete its capture.

Western Front — Continued

26th-31st — Dunkirk Evacuation: Operation 'Dynamo' – Initial plans are to lift off 45,000 men of the BEF over a two-day period under the direction of Vice-Adm B. H. Ramsey. The surrender of the Belgian Army on the 28th endangers the operation, yet in the last days and nights of May, first 8,000, then 18,000, 47,000, 54,000 and 68,000 men are carried to Britain.

'Dynamo' is subjected to heavy attack by air, sea and from the shore. Some 40 British, six French and a Polish destroyer take part, together with 800 other vessels, large and small. Losses are considerable. On the 29th, apart from those damaged, three RN destroyers are sunk off the beaches — **GRAFTON** torpedoed by *U62*, **GRENADE** by bombs, and **WAKEFUL** by a torpedo from E-boat *S30*. In the last two days of the month, French destroyers *Bourrasque* and *Sirocco* are lost. The evacuation continues into June.

31st – *U13* is believed sunk by sloop *Weston* off Lowestoft.

Merchant Shipping War
Losses
● 90 ships of 231,000 tons.

MEDITERRANEAN THEATRES
— STARTING CONDITIONS

Although the Mediterranean situation changes drastically for Britain in the space of two weeks from the entry of Italy into the war until the surrender of France, it is helpful to look at the circumstances on 10 June separately from those at the end of the month. In this way Britain's isolation becomes that much more obvious, as does the flexibility of her Naval power.

Strategic Situation

There are three main theatres — the Mediterranean itself, the oil production regions of the Middle East, and the Red Sea area.

Mediterranean – To the west, Britain and France control Gibraltar at the entrance from the Atlantic, southern France, Corsica, Algeria and Tunisia. Malta at the centre is a British colony. In the east, Britain maintains a hold on Egypt and the Suez Canal, Palestine and Cyprus. In the Levant, Lebanon and Syria are French.

Italy stands astride the central basin, with Italy itself, Sardinia and Sicily to the north and Libya with its provinces of Tripolitania and Cyrenaica to the south. The Dodecanese Islands in the southern Aegean and Albania on the Adriatic are Italian.

At one end of the Mediterranean, Spain is neutral, as are Greece and Crete, Yugoslavia and Turkey at the other.

Middle East – Iraq, Persia (Iran) and the Persian Gulf area are within the British sphere of influence and are surrounded by Allied or neutral countries.

Red Sea Area – To the east, Aden is a British colony and Saudi Arabia has close ties with Britain. On the west are Egypt and the Anglo-Egyptian Sudan, and further south French and British Somaliland. In between are the linked Italian colonies of Eritrea, Ethiopia (Abyssinia) and Italian Somaliland. Bordering them to the south is British Kenya.

Military and Maritime Circumstances

Even allied to France, Britain's position in the Mediterranean is not guaranteed. Gibraltar may be secure, assuming Spain's continued neutrality, but Malta is considered indefensible in the face of the Italian Air Force based in Sicily. As it happens, only the later arrival of the Luftwaffe turns this into a near reality. However, Malta's well-equipped base has to be abandoned by the Mediterranean Fleet for the poorer facilities at Alexandria.

Alexandria and the Suez Canal are threatened by a large Italian army in Libya, against which only a relatively small British and Dominion force can be fielded. Fortunately this has been reinforced earlier in the year by Australian and New Zealand troops.

ATLANTIC

JUNE

6th-15th — Three armed merchant cruisers on Northern Patrol are lost to U-boats in the waters between Ireland and Iceland — **CARINTHIA** on the 6th/7th to *U46*, **SCOTSTOUN** on the 13th to *U25*, and **ANDANIA** on the 15th to *UA*, an ex-Turkish boat.

Two more German raiders sail. *Thor* makes for the South Atlantic and returns to Germany after 11 months. *Pinguin* leaves for the Indian Ocean around the Cape of Good Hope. Later she goes into the Antarctic and is finally lost in May 1941.

Meanwhile the *Orion* is laying mines off New Zealand that account for the gold-bullion carrying liner *Niagara*.

Battle of the Atlantic

The loss of Norway brings German warships and U-boats many hundreds of miles closer to the Atlantic convoy routes and in time within close range of the Russian convoys that start after the invasion of June 1941. Britain's blockade line from the Orkneys to southern Norway is outflanked and a new one has to be established between the Shetlands and Iceland. The RN starts the massive task of laying a mine barrage along this line.

Within a matter of days the first U-boats are sailing from Bergen in Norway, while others are sent to patrol as far south as the Canary and Cape Verde Islands off northwest Africa. Italian submarines join them in this area, but without any early successes.

Towards the end of the month, *U122* and *U102* are lost off the North Channel, possibly on mines (according to German sources). It is in this area and throughout the North Western Approaches that such U-boat commanders as Endras, Kretschmer, Prien and Schepke enjoy their 'Happy Time' until early 1941. U-boat strength is no greater than at the beginning of the war, and there are never more than 15 boats on patrol out of the 25 operational; the rest are training or on trials. Yet from now until the end of December they account for most of the 315 ships of 1,659,000 tons lost in the Atlantic. Many of these are stragglers, independents or in unescorted convoys, but it is among the escorted convoys that

EUROPE

JUNE

'Ultra' is now breaking the Luftwaffe Enigma codes with some regularity, and early in the month has its first major breakthrough when supporting evidence for the Knickebein *navigation aid for bombers is obtained. Army codes are more secure because of the greater use of land-lines, and the Naval ones will not be penetrated until mid-1941.*

Western Front — Continued

1st – As the Dunkirk evacuation continues under heavy air attack, destroyers **KEITH**, **BASILISK** and **HAVANT** and the French *Le Foudroyant* are bombed and lost off the beaches.

On the 4th, the evacuation of the BEF and some of the French troops trapped with them comes to an end. In the first four days and nights of June, 64,000, 26,000, 27,000 and 26,000 men are saved to give an overall total of 340,000, including the bulk of Britain's army in northern France. Naval and civilian shipping loses are heavy. In destroyers alone the RN has lost six sunk and 19 badly damaged.

By early June the RN is taking steps to meet the threat of German invasion. The invasion fleet is to be attacked as it builds up and before it can reach British shores. Four destroyer flotillas with cruiser support move to the south, and escort and other vessels patrol offshore. The loss of these escorts from Atlantic convoy duties contributes to the sinking of many merchant ships, and eventually they return to these duties.

Norwegian Campaign — Conclusion

Between the 4th and the 8th, Allied forces amounting to 25,000 men are evacuated from the Narvik area, by which time Norwegian King Haakon VII and his Government are on their way to Britain in heavy cruiser *Devonshire*. On the 9th the remaining Norwegian troops surrender to the German Army.

From bases in Italian East Africa the Italian Air Force and Navy are capable of cutting Allied supply routes to Suez through the Red Sea. The Italian army is also powerful enough to take British and French Somaliland and pose a threat to the Sudan and Kenya. The Italians' one major problem however is the impossibility of supplying these forces other than by air from Libya.

These threats to Malta, Suez and the Red Sea depend on Italy taking and holding on to the initiative. She does not. Malta becomes a thorn in the side of Axis supply routes to Libya. And Libya and Italian East Africa in fact become endangered from the very Allied territories they threaten.

Over the next three years, Malta above all will be the pivot about which the whole Mediterranean campaign revolves — both the problems of its supply and its effectiveness as an offensive base. Later Axis plans to invade the island never come to anything.

Major Naval Strengths

The RN maintains a small force of destroyers at Gibraltar, largely for Atlantic convoy work, but the Western Mediterranean is primarily the responsibility of the French Navy — although RN reinforcements can soon be sent down from the Home Fleet as shortly happens. The Eastern Mediterranean is in the hands of the Mediterranean Fleet based at Alexandria with a small French squadron. It is up to strength in major units but still weak in cruisers, destroyers and submarines when compared with the Italian Navy. This is partly offset by the presence of the carrier *Eagle* to accompany the battleships *Malaya*, *Ramillies*, *Royal Sovereign* and *Warspite*.

What the Mediterranean Fleet lacks in numbers is more than made up by the aggressive fighting spirit of its Commander-in-Chief, Adm Sir Andrew B. Cunningham, and that of his officers and men and their training.

The Italian Navy maintains a small but useful force in the Red Sea. Against these can be deployed ships of the East Indies Command based at Trincomalee in Ceylon. But its overwhelming strength is in the Mediterranean.

	Western Med FRENCH	ITALIAN NAVY Mediterranean	Eastern Med RN MED FLEET	FRENCH	ALLIED total
Battleships	4	6 (b)	4	1	9
Carriers	—	—	1	—	1
Cruisers	10	21	9	4	23
Destroyers	37 (a)	52 (c)	25	3	65
Submarines	36	106	10	—	46
Totals	87	185 (d)	49	8	144

Notes:
(a) Plus 10 RN destroyers at Gibraltar.
(b) Includes 2 new battleships completing.
(c) Plus over 60 large torpedo boats.
(d) Based at Massawa in the Red Sea are another 7 destroyers, 8 submarines and 2 torpedo boats.

MEDITERRANEAN

JUNE

Italy Declares War

Italy declares war on Britain and France on the 10th. That same day, Australia, Canada, India, New Zealand and South Africa declare against Italy. Later in the month Italian forces invade southern France but with little success.

On the 11th, Italian aircraft carry out the first of the many raids on Malta. Next day, the RAF makes its first attacks on Italian mainland targets.

12th — The Mediterranean Fleet with *Warspite*, *Malaya*, *Eagle*, cruisers and destroyers sails from Alexandria for a sweep against Italian shipping in the Eastern basin. South of Crete, light cruiser **CALYPSO** is torpedoed and sunk by Italian submarine *Bagnolini*.

Mediterranean Fleet submarines operate out of Alexandria off Italian bases and soon lose three of their number. At the time mines are usually blamed, but it turns out that Italian anti-submarine forces are more effective than expected:

13th — **ODIN** in the Gulf of Taranto to the guns and torpedoes of destroyer *Strale*.

16th — **GRAMPUS** minelaying off Augusta, Sicily to torpedo boats *Circe* and *Clio*.

19th — **ORPHEUS** north of Tobruk in Libya to destroyer *Turbine*.

The many Italian submarines on patrol suffer far heavier losses. In the Red Sea area, four out of the eight submarines are soon accounted for:

The battlecruiser HMS *Hood* (lost in May 1941) was completed in 1920. She displaced about 42,000 tons, could make 31kt, carried eight 15in guns and 1,350 crew, and is shown with her aircraft catapult, added post-1929. *Real Photos (S584)*

ATLANTIC

U-boat tactics are particularly notable. Instead of attacking submerged where they can be detected by ASDIC, they are operating on the surface at night as 18kt torpedo boats, faster than most of the escorts — and in any case there are few enough of these as many are held on anti-invasion duties.

Losses
- 53 ships of 297,000 tons and 3 armed merchant cruisers.
- 2 U-boats, dates and causes of loss uncertain.

The fleet carrier HMS *Furious* was launched as a light battlecruiser in 1916 but fully reconstructed as a carrier in the early 1920s. At 22,400 tons, she retained a battlecruiser's speed of 30kt while carrying 36 aircraft and 1,200 crew *Real Photos (S2588)*

EUROPE

8th – At the end of the evacuation, fleet carrier **GLORIOUS** and escorting destroyers **ACASTA** and **ARDENT** sail for Britain independently of the other forces. West of Lofoten Islands they meet the 11in gun battlecruisers *Scharnhorst* and *Gneisenau* on their way to attack expected Allied shipping off Harstad. The British ships are soon overwhelmed and sunk, but not before *Acasta* hits *Scharnhorst* with a torpedo. Few of their crews survive. Five days later aircraft from *Ark Royal* attack the damaged battlecruiser in Trondheim but to little effect.

Losses on both sides have been heavy:

	Royal Navy	Allied	German
Carriers	1	—	—
Cruisers	2	—	3
Destroyers	7	2	10
Submarines	4	1	4

8th/20th – Allied submarines working with the RN continue to play a part in operations off Norway and have their share of losses. On the last day of the campaign the famous Polish *Orzel* is presumed mined. And on the 20th the Dutch *O13* is torpedoed in error by Polish *Wilk*. Both were on passage to their patrol areas.

20th – As the damaged *Scharnhorst* heads for Germany, *Gneisenau* makes a feint towards Iceland. West of Trondheim she is torpedoed and damaged by submarine *Clyde*. Both ships are out of action until the end of the year. By now, of the 23 German ships of destroyer size and larger that have taken part in the invasion of Norway, 17 have been sunk or damaged.

A heavily escorted convoy arrives in Britain with Australian and New Zealand troops, after setting out in early May.

Western Front — Conclusion

The battle for France begins on the 5th with a German advance south from the line River Somme to Sedan. The Germans enter Paris on the 14th.

Now the evacuation of British and Allied forces from the rest of France gets underway. Starting on the 10th, Operation 'Cycle' lifts off 11,000 from Le Havre. From the 15th, 'Aerial' begins with the evacuation of Cherbourg and continues for the next 10 days, moving right down to the Franco-Spanish border. The only major loss is on the 17th off St Nazaire, when the liner *Lancastria* is sunk with the death of nearly 3,000 men.

The French Government of Marshal Pétain requests armistice terms from Germany and Italy on the 17th. The Franco-German surrender document is signed on the 22nd, its provisions including German occupation of the Channel and Biscay coasts and demilitarisation of the French fleet under Axis control.

25th – The evacuation ends with over 215,000 servicemen and civilians saved, but Operations 'Aerial' and 'Cycle' never capture the public's imagination like the Dunkirk 'miracle'. On the last day, Canadian destroyer **FRASER** is rammed and sunk by AA Cruiser *Calcutta* off the Gironde Estuary.

On the 30th, the first German troops land on the Channel Islands, the only part of the British Empire occupied by them throughout the war.

Eastern Europe

Russia occupies Lithuania, Estonia and Latvia. In July these Baltic states are formally incorporated into the USSR. Russia also takes over parts of Roumania.

Merchant Shipping War
Losses
- 77 ships of 209,000 tons.

15th — *Macallé* runs aground and is a total loss.

19th — *Galileo Galilei* on patrol off Aden is captured by armed trawler *Moonstone*.

23rd — Off French Somaliland *Toricelli* is sunk by destroyers *Kandahar* and *Kingston* and sloop *Shoreham*. During this action, destroyer **KHARTOUM** suffers an internal explosion and sinks in shallow water off Perim Island. She is a total loss.

23rd/24th — *Galvani* sinks Indian patrol sloop **PATHAN** but next day off the Gulf of Oman she is accounted for by sloop *Falmouth*.

Six more are sunk in the Mediterranean, half by the RN.

20th — *Diamante* by submarine *Parthian* off Tobruk.

27th/29th — To the south and west of Crete a patrol of Mediterranean Fleet destroyers including *Dainty* and *Ilex* sink *Liuzzi* and *Uebi Scebeli*.

Of the remainder, *Provana* is sunk by a French sloop off Oran and *Argonauta* and *Rubino* by RAF Sunderlands.

The Franco-Italian Armistice is signed on the 24th, and includes provision for the demilitarisation of French naval bases in the Mediterranean.

28th — As the Mediterranean Fleet 7th Cruiser Squadron covers convoy movements in the Eastern Mediterranean, three Italian destroyers carrying supplies between Taranto and Tobruk are encountered. In a running gun battle, *Espero* is sunk by Australian cruiser *Sydney* to the southwest of Cape Matapan.

By the end of the month, Force H has assembled at Gibraltar from units of the Home Fleet. Vice-Adm Sir James Somerville flies his flag in battlecruiser *Hood* and has under his command battleships *Resolution* and *Valiant*, carrier *Ark Royal* and a few cruisers and destroyers. He reports directly to the Admiralty and not to the Commander, North Atlantic.

From Gibraltar, Force H can cover the Western Mediterranean and the Atlantic, as will happen in the hunt for the *Bismarck*. Units can also quickly transfer back to the Home Fleet and UK waters as shortly becomes necessary at the height of the German invasion scare. There can be no better example of the flexibility of British naval power.

Merchant Shipping War
Summary of Allied Losses

● 6 British, Allied and neutral ships of 45,000 tons in the Mediterranean. In general, losses will be low as most shipping for the Middle East is diverted around the Cape of Good Hope.

HMS *Wakeful*, a 'V' & 'W' class destroyer, was one of the first destroyers lost during the Dunkirk evacuation. Loaded with troops and sailing for Dover, she was torpedoed once by an E-boat off Nieuport, Belgium at 00.45 on Wednesday 29 May 1940, sinking rapidly. *Real Photos (S508)*

The aircraft carrier HMS *Argus* in her original dazzle camouflage. Completed in 1918 on a liner hull, she displaced 14,000 tons, could make 20kt and carried 20 aircraft and 370 crew plus aircrew. *Real Photos (S1007)*

STRATEGIC AND MARITIME SITUATION — ATLANTIC AND EUROPE

Britain's circumstances are transformed. From North Cape in Norway to the Pyrenees at the Spanish border, the coast of Europe is in German hands. With the occupation of the Low Countries and northern France, the south and east coasts of England are now in the front line. In addition to bases in Norway, German forces can dominate the South Western Approaches from the French Biscay ports. The British occupation of Iceland takes on a new and vital importance. The lack of bases in Eire becomes more evident.

In addition, the majority of French possessions on the Atlantic seaboards of Africa and the Americas are under the control of Vichy France, and thus denied to British forces. Worse still is the danger of them being occupied by the Axis.

The naval situation is similarly transformed. Not only is the French fleet denied to the Allies, but the fear is that it will be taken over by the German and Italian navies and totally alter the naval balance of power. The French Navy refuses to make for British ports and most of the modern ships sail for French North and West Africa. The uncompleted battleships *Jean Bart* and *Richelieu* reach Casablanca and Dakar respectively.

ATLANTIC

JULY

1st — Corvette *Gladiolus* claims the first success for one of the 'Flower' class when, with the support of an RAF Sunderland, she sinks *U26* southwest of Ireland.

5th — Detached from an outward-bound OB convoy to search for a reported U-boat, destroyer **WHIRLWIND** is lost to the west of Land's End to *U34*.

Carrier *Hermes* and cruisers *Dorsetshire* and the Australian *Australia* lay off Dakar on the 8th after negotiations are refused on the future of French battleship *Richelieu*. Attacks with depth-charges from a fast motorboat fail and a torpedo strike by Swordfish inflicts only minor damage.

No action is taken against *Richelieu's* sister ship *Jean Bart* at Casablanca. In the French West Indies, carrier *Bearn* and two cruisers are immobilised by mainly diplomatic means.

German raider *Komet* sails for the Pacific through the North East Passage across the top of Siberia with the aid of Russian icebreakers. She operates in the Pacific and Indian Oceans until her return to Germany in November 1941. She is the last of the first wave of raiders.

28th — Off the coast of Brazil, *Thor* badly damages armed merchant cruiser **Alcantara** in a gun duel.

Battle of the Atlantic

Convoys are now being re-routed through the North Western Approaches to the British Isles instead of to the south of Ireland and through the Irish Sea. North Channel and the sea lanes leading to it becomes a focal point for all shipping leaving or arriving in British waters.

The following convoys continue:

Liverpool out — OB
UK/Gibraltar — OG
Fast Halifax/UK — HX
Gibraltar/UK — HG
Sierra Leone/UK — SL

Thames-out OA convoys are now joining FN East Coast ships and passing around the north of Scotland before going out through the North West Approaches. They stop altogether in October.

Slow Sydney, Cape Breton/UK convoys start in August with SC1.

The limits of the few escorts available are only just pushed out from 15°W to 17°W where they stay until October. U-boats are patrolling well beyond this range and so many sinkings are taking place in unescorted convoys or when the ships have dispersed.

EUROPE

JULY

The two old French battleships *Courbet* and *Paris* and several destroyers and submarines, including the giant *Surcouf*, are in British ports. On the 3rd they are boarded and seized, but not before there are casualties on both sides.

Battle of Britain

Hitler decides that an invasion of Britain is possible and orders preliminary air attacks which start with Channel shipping and ports. Preparations for the landings — Operation 'Sealion' — start on the 16th and are scheduled to take place in mid-August. On the 19th Hitler offers to make peace with Britain, but his overtures are rejected three days later.

4th — In attacks on Thames-out convoy OA178 off Portland, Ju87 Stukas sink the auxiliary AA ship **FOYLE BANK** and four merchantmen. ✠ Leading Seaman Jack Mantle, gunner in the *Foyle Bank*, continues in action although mortally wounded. He is posthumously awarded the Victoria Cross.

6th — Home Fleet submarines carry out patrols off the coast of southwest Norway, but with heavy losses in July. Late on the 5th, **SHARK** is badly damaged by German aircraft and next morning has to be scuttled off Skudenses. A few days later **SALMON** is presumed lost on mines. Later still **THAMES** is also probably mined in the middle of the North Sea on passage to her patrol area.

16th — Cruiser *Glasgow* rams and sinks accompanying destroyer **IMOGEN** off the Pentland Firth.

Heavy attacks continue on shipping and four destroyers are bombed and lost:

20th – **BRAZEN** on convoy duty off Dover,

27th – **WREN** off Aldeburgh on the East Coast as she gives AA cover to minesweepers,

27th – **CODRINGTON** in Dover harbour,

29th – **DELIGHT** escorting a Channel convoy off Portland.

26th – As the damaged *Gneisenau* makes for Germany from Norway, submarine *Swordfish* carries out an attack and sinks escorting torpedo boat *Luchs*.

STRATEGIC AND MARITIME SITUATION — MEDITERRANEAN

With the fall of France, Italy continues to dominate the central basin, and the western end becomes more problematical as shipping between Gibraltar and Malta can no longer look to Algeria and Tunis for protection. At the other end, Lebanon and Syria go over to Vichy France and in time come to be a danger to Britain's position in the Middle East. At this stage Greece and Crete are fortunately neutral, otherwise the Mediterranean Fleet could be dominated by enemy aircraft as soon as it leaves Egyptian waters. This will happen when they are occupied by the Germans.

The comparatively healthy naval position overall also changes for the worse. In all except capital ships — 7 to 6 — the Royal Navy is distinctly inferior in numbers to the Italians, but has its two near-priceless fleet carriers: the *Ark Royal* based on Gibraltar, and *Eagle*, later joined by *Illustrious*, operating out of Alexandria, will come to dominate the Mediterranean for the next six months.

This is helped by the French Fleet staying neutral and out of Axis hands — that is, other than when its own sovereignty is under attack when the ships fight back fiercely. The arrival of Force H at Gibraltar goes some way to offsetting the loss of French naval power in the Western Mediterranean.

MEDITERRANEAN

JULY

East Africa

Italian forces from Ethiopia occupy British border posts in Kenya and the Sudan.

3rd — Action at Oran: Operation 'Catapult' — Adm Somerville arrives with Force H off the French Algerian base of Mers-el-Kebir near Oran. The French Adm Gensoul is offered a number of choices to ensure his fleet with its four capital ships stays out of Axis hands. All are turned down and, at around 18.00, Force H opens fire on the anchored ships. *Bretagne* blows up and the *Dunkerque* and *Provence*, together with other ships, are badly damaged. Battlecruiser *Strasbourg* and some destroyers manage to break out in spite of attacks by aircraft from *Ark Royal*. They reach Toulon.

Three days later the damaged *Dunkerque* is torpedoed at her moorings by *Ark Royal's* Swordfish. The unhappy episode is over as far as Oran is concerned.

On the 4th there is a more peaceful solution at Alexandria. Adm Cunningham is able to reach agreement with French Adm Godfrey on the demilitarisation of battleship *Lorraine*, four cruisers and a number of smaller ships.

No action is taken against the French warships at Algiers and Toulon.

Torpedo-carrying Swordfish from *Eagle's* squadrons fly from land bases for separate and successful attacks on Tobruk and area:

5th — Aircraft of 813 Squadron sink destroyer *Zeffiro* and a freighter at Tobruk.

20th — In the nearby Gulf of Bomba, 824 Squadron is responsible for sinking destroyers *Nembo* and *Ostro* and another freighter.

9th — Action off Calabria: Battle of Punto Stilo — On the 7th, Adm Cunningham sails from Alexandria with *Warspite*, *Malaya*, *Royal Sovereign*, *Eagle*, cruisers and destroyers to cover convoys from Malta to Alexandria and to challenge the Italians to action. Next day two Italian battleships, 14 cruisers and 32 destroyers are reported in the Ionian Sea covering a convoy to Benghazi. Italian aircraft now start five days of accurate high-level bombing (and against Force H out of Gibraltar) and cruiser **Gloucester** is hit and damaged. Mediterranean Fleet heads for a position to cut off the Italians from their base at Taranto.

The fleet carrier HMS *Eagle* was lost in August 1942. Completed in 1920 on a Chilean battleship hull, she displaced 22,600 tons and could make 24kt. Her complement was 20 aircraft and 750 crew plus aircrew
Real Photos (S1466)

ATLANTIC

Losses
- 34 ships of 173,000 tons and 1 destroyer.
- 1 U-boat.

AUGUST

A British scientific mission carries to the United States details of many important developments. Amongst these is the recently invented cavity magnetron, vital for short wavelength radar and the eventual defeat of conventional U-boats.

10th/28th — Two more AMCs of the Northern Patrol are lost to U-boats to the north of Ireland — **TRANSYLVANIA** to *U56* on the 10th and **DUNVEGAN CASTLE** to *U46* on the night of the 27th/28th.

20th — Submarine *Cachalot* on Bay of Biscay patrol sinks the returning *U51* off Lorient.

24th — An attack by *U37* on SC1 to the southeast of Greenland leads to the loss of a merchantman and sloop **PENZANCE**.

Battle of the Atlantic
Long range Focke Wulf Kondors start patrols off the coast of Ireland from a base near Bordeaux. As well as spotting for U-boats they attack and sink many ships, and continue to be a major threat until the introduction of ship-borne aircraft in late 1941 starts to counteract them.
Losses
- 39 ships of 190,000 tons, 2 armed merchant cruisers and 1 sloop.
- 1 U-boat.

EUROPE

Merchant Shipping War
With the Germans now so close to British shores, new convoy routes have to be established and meshed in with overseas ones. The Thames/Forth FN/FS convoys continue along the East Coast. Two additional ones are:

- Forth/Clyde, EN/WN, around the north of Scotland,
- Thames/English Channel, CW/CE, through the Strait of Dover.

Losses in the Channel are so heavy that the latter have to be stopped for a while. On the 25th and 26th, CW8 loses eight of its 21 ships to attacks by Stukas and E-boats. Four more merchantmen and two destroyers are damaged.
Losses
- 67 ships of 192,000 tons.

AUGUST

1st — Submarine **SPEARFISH** on patrol in the North Sea is torpedoed by *U34* and sunk. **NARWHAL** is paid off the same day. After leaving the Humber on 22 July for a minelaying mission off Norway, she fails to return.

3rd — Mines laid off the German North Sea coast by RN destroyers continue to claim victims. *U25* is lost as she heads out for Atlantic patrol.

The Germans start planning the invasion of Russia.

Battle of Britain

The Luftwaffe switches its attacks to RAF Fighter Command and on the 13th launches a major offensive — 'Adlertag' — especially against airfields. Damage to these and losses in aircraft on both sides are heavy. Bombs dropped on London on the 24th lead to RAF Bomber Command raiding Berlin the next night. By the end of the month the first possible date for 'Sealion' has been put back to late September.

RN codes are changed and for the first time operational signals are secure from German interception and decoding. It will be another three years before the convoy codes are made safe from the German B-Service.

31st/1st (September) — Destroyers of the 20th Flotilla sail to lay mines off the Dutch coast. They run into a German field northwest of Texel. **ESK** sinks, **IVANHOE** goes down the next day, and **Express** is badly damaged.

Merchant Shipping War
Losses
- 45 ships of 163,000 tons.

MEDITERRANEAN

On the 9th, *Eagle's* aircraft fail to find the Italians and first contact is made by a detached cruiser squadron which is soon under fire from the heavier ships. *Warspite* comes up and damages battleship *Giulio Cesare* with a 15in hit. As the Italian battleships turn away, the cruisers and destroyers engage but with little effect. Mediterranean Fleet pursues to within 50 miles of the Calabrian coast before withdrawing.

As Adm Cunningham covers the by now delayed convoys to Alexandria, *Eagle's* Swordfish attack Augusta harbour on the 10th. Destroyer *Pancaldo* is torpedoed, but later re-floated and re-commissioned.

11th — Force H, which has put to sea on receiving reports of the Italian fleet, is now returning to Gibraltar, when screening destroyer **ESCORT** is sunk by the submarine *Marconi*.

16th — Submarine **PHOENIX** attacks an escorted tanker off Augusta and is lost to depth charges from Italian torpedo boat *Albatros*.

19th — Action off Cape Spada — Australian cruiser *Sydney* and destroyers *Hasty*, *Havock*, *Hero*, *Hyperion* and *Ilex* on a sweep into the Aegean are sent to intercept two reported Italian cruisers. Off Cape Spada at the north west tip of Crete, *Bartolomeo Colleoni* is stopped by *Sydney's* gunfire and finished off with torpedoes from the destroyers. *Bande Nere* manages to escape.

Merchant Shipping War

Losses
- 2 ships of 7,000 tons.

AUGUST

1st — Submarine **OSWALD** on patrol south of the Strait of Messina reports Italian Navy movements. She is detected and later rammed and sunk by destroyer *Vivaldi*.

The decision is taken to reinforce Malta and, in Operation 'Hurry', carrier *Argus* flies off 12 Hurricanes from a position southwest of Sardinia.

This is the first of many reinforcement and supply operations, often bitterly fought to keep Malta alive and in the fight against Axis supply routes to their armies in North Africa. Now, as in the future, cover from the west is provided by Force H. The opportunity is taken for *Ark Royal's* aircraft to hit Sardinian targets.

In the middle of the month, Mediterranean Fleet battleships *Warspite*, *Malaya* and *Ramillies* bombard Italian positions around Bardia in Libya, just over the border from Egypt.

East Africa

Italian forces from Ethiopia invade British Somaliland. The capital of Berbera is evacuated on the 14th and the garrison carried across to Aden. Italians enter the town five days later, just as a British mission goes into Ethiopia to help organise uprisings against the Italians there.

22nd — Land-based Swordfish from *Eagle's* 824 Squadron repeat their July success with another torpedo strike in the Gulf of Bomba. Just as she prepares for a human torpedo attack on Alexandria, submarine *Iride* and a depot ship are sunk.

23rd — Heavy mining in the Strait of Sicily by Italian surface ships leads to the loss of destroyer **HOSTILE** on passage from Malta to Gibraltar. Extensive Italian fields in the 'Sicilian

The aircraft carrier HMS *Hermes* (lost in April 1942) was the first vessel designed as an aircraft carrier for the Royal Navy. Completed 1924 at around 10,800 tons and able to make 25kt, *Hermes* carried 15 aircraft and 660 crew plus aircrew. *Real Photos (S1467)*

HMS *Express* an 'E' class destroyer, was mined late on Saturday 31 August 1940 off the Dutch coast at 53°30N, 03°47E, with all before the bridge blown off and about 90 casualties. Nevertheless, she reached port, and in 1943 became HMCS *Gatineau*. *Real Photos (S312)*

SEPTEMBER

1st — Cruiser **Fiji** is torpedoed by *U32* off Rockall as she escorts troop transports for the Dakar expedition. Her place is taken by the heavy cruiser *Australia*.

After months of negotiations, an agreement is announced on the 5th for the transfer of 50 old but valuable US destroyers to the RN in exchange for bases in Newfoundland, Bermuda, the West Indies and British Guiana. The first of them arrive in Britain towards the end of the month.

6th — Escorting convoy OA205, corvette **GODETIA** is rammed and sunk by the merchantman *Marsa* north of Ireland. She is the first 'Flower' class to be lost.

15th — *U48* attacks convoy SC3 northwest of Ireland and sinks sloop **DUNDEE**. Both she and *Penzance*, lost in August, were long endurance ships used as A/S ocean escorts for the slow and vulnerable SCs.

23rd-25th — Dakar Expedition: Operation 'Menace' — Because of Dakar's strategic importance to the North and South Atlantic routes, an expedition is mounted to acquire the port for Allied use. Free French troops led by Gen de Gaulle are carried in ships escorted and supported by units of the Home Fleet and Force H under the command of Vice-Adm John Cunningham. They include battleships *Barham* and *Resolution*, carrier *Ark Royal*, three heavy cruisers and other smaller ships including Free French. Naval forces at Dakar include the unfinished battleship *Richelieu* and two of the cruisers recently arrived from Toulon.

Attempts to negotiate on the 23rd soon fail and as Vichy French ships attempt to leave harbour, shore batteries open fire, damaging heavy cruiser **Cumberland** and two destroyers. Shortly afterwards, the Vichy submarine *Persée* is sunk by gunfire and large destroyer *L'Audacieux* disabled by the *Australia* and beached. A Free French landing is beaten off.

Next day, on the 24th, Dakar is bombarded by the warships and *Richelieu* is attacked by *Ark Royal's* aircraft. Vichy submarine *Ajax* is sunk by destroyer *Fortune*.

The bombardment continues on the 25th, but **Resolution** is now torpedoed and badly damaged by submarine *Bévéziers* and **Barham** hit by *Richelieu's* 15in gunfire. At this point the operation is abandoned and the Anglo-French forces withdraw.

Battle of the Atlantic

Early in the month the first wolf-pack attacks are directed by Adm Dönitz against convoy SC2. Five of the 53 ships are sunk. A similar operation is mounted two weeks later against the 40 ships of HX72. The U-boats present include those commanded by the aces Kretschmer, Prien and Schepke. Eleven ships are lost, seven to Schepke's *U100* in one night. The German B-Service is instrumental in directing U-boats to many convoys, where they hold the advantage as they manoeuvre on the surface between the merchantmen and escorts. Radar is urgently needed to detect them, so the escorts can drive them down where they lose their speed advantage and ASDIC can come into its own.

Losses
● 53 ships of 272,000 tons and 2 escorts.

SEPTEMBER

Battle of Britain

By now heavy units of the Home Fleet have come south from Scapa Flow ready to oppose the expected German invasion. The Blitz on Britain gets under way on the 7th when major raids are launched against London. An attack on the 15th — subsequently known as Battle of Britain Day — leads to heavy Luftwaffe losses, but nowhere near the claimed 185 aircraft: the Luftwaffe loses some 60 in exchange for 26 RAF fighters. Operation 'Sealion' is shortly postponed until further notice and invasion shipping starts to disperse. The Blitz does not let up.

9th – Cruiser **Galatea** is damaged by an acoustic mine in the Thames Estuary.

18th – Major raids on Clydeside badly damage heavy cruiser **Sussex** as she refits.

Germany, Italy and Japan sign the Tripartite Pact in Berlin on the 27th. They agree to oppose any country joining the Allies at war — by which they mean the United States.

Merchant Shipping War
Losses
● 39 ships of 131,000 tons.

MEDITERRANEAN

Narrows' sink and damage many RN ships over the next three years.

Merchant Shipping War

Losses
● 1 ship of 1,000 tons.

SEPTEMBER

Reinforcements are sent to the Mediterranean Fleet right through until the end of the year. They are covered from Gibraltar by Adm Somerville and Force H, and then met in the central basin by Adm Cunningham. The opportunity is usually taken to run in supplies of men and material to Malta.

Early in September the new fleet carrier *Illustrious*, with its armoured flightdeck, battleship *Valiant* and two cruisers are transferred in this way in Operation 'Hats'. On passage with them, aircraft from *Ark Royal* attack Sardinian targets. *Illustrious*, having joined with *Eagle*, sends aircraft against Rhodes. The Italian Fleet sorties during these operations, but fails to make contact.

The arrival of *Illustrious* allows Adm Cunningham to go ahead with his plans to attack the Italian battlefleet at Taranto.

Three Vichy French cruisers with accompanying destroyers sail from Toulon and, on the 11th, pass through the Strait of Gibraltar. They are bound for French West Africa. All but one of the cruisers arrive at Dakar just as Operation 'Menace' is about to get underway. Adm Sir Dudley North, Flag Officer, North Atlantic, at Gibraltar, is somewhat unfairly held responsible for allowing their passage. He is relieved of his command and never officially cleared.

North Africa

From bases in Libya, Italy invades Egypt on the 13th. Sollum, just over the border, is occupied and Sidi Barrani reached on the 16th. There the Italian advance stops. Neither side makes a move until December.

17th — Units of the Mediterranean Fleet including *Valiant* sail with *Illustrious* for a raid on Benghazi. Swordfish torpedo the destroyer *Borea*, and mines laid by them off the port sink another, the *Aquilone*. On the return to Alexandria, heavy cruiser **Kent** is detached to bombard Bardia. She is torpedoed and badly damaged by Italian aircraft.

22nd — Submarine *Osiris* on patrol in the southern Adriatic attacks a convoy and sinks torpedo boat *Palestro*.

30th — Submarine *Gondar* approaches Alexandria with human torpedoes for an attack on the base. She is located by a RAF Sunderland of No 230 Squadron and sunk by Australian destroyer *Stuart*.

Merchant Shipping War

Losses
● 2 ships of 6,000 tons.

The fleet carrier HMS *Courageous*, lost September 1939, was sister-ship to the *Glorious*, sunk in June 1940. Completed as light battlecruisers in 1917, and reconstructed as carriers 1924-30. At 22,500 tons they carried 48 aircraft and 1,200 crew yet could still make a good speed. *Real Photos (S1362)*

HMS *Kent*, a 'County' class heavy cruiser, is photographed leaving Yokohama in 1935. At 23.30hrs on Tuesday 17 September 1940 she was hit by one aircraft torpedo to the northeast of Bardia, and extensively damaged. *Real Photos (S1234)*

ATLANTIC

OCTOBER

22nd — Canadian destroyer **MARGAREE** is lost in collision with merchantman *Port Fairy* as she escorts Liverpool-out convoy OL8 to the west of Ireland. This is the last of the short-lived fast OLs from Liverpool.

30th — Destroyers *Harvester* and *Highlander* sink *U32* northwest of Ireland during a convoy attack.

Pocket battleship *Admiral Scheer* sails from Germany for the Atlantic and later Indian Oceans. She gets back home in March.
   Raider *Widder* meanwhile arrives in France after six months of operations in the central Atlantic where she has sunk or captured 10 ships of 59,000 tons.

Battle of the Atlantic

Kondors continue to range the waters off Ireland and on the 26th one of them damages the 42,000-ton liner *Empress of Britain*. She is finished off two days later by *U32*, just before her own sinking.
   The Luftwaffe's long-range aircraft are now flying from bases in Norway. Inter-service rivalry between the Luftwaffe and Navy means the Kondor will never be fully integrated into the German effort in the Battle of the Atlantic.
   Escort limits are only now pushed out to 19°W. In a series of pack attacks on lightly-defended Canada/UK convoys, U-boats sink more than 30 ships from SC7 and HX79 between the 17th and 20th, a rate of loss that will soon bring Britain to her knees. Fortunately, a number of measures are being taken to ease the dire situation and provide some of the foundations from which Britain and her Allies will go on to defeat the U-boats:

● The old US destroyers are coming into service and the British building programme is starting to deliver the escorts needed.

● The need for permanent escort groups to develop and maintain expertise is being accepted and greater emphasis given to A/S training.

● Co-operation between RAF Coastal Command and Western Approaches Command is steadily improving.

However, there is still a long way to go, and vast areas of the Atlantic are without air or sea anti-submarine cover.
Losses
● 56 ships of 287,000 tons and 1 destroyer.
● 1 U-boat.

NOVEMBER

Franklin D. Roosevelt is elected to an unprecedented third term of office as President of the United States.

2nd — Attacking a convoy northwest of Ireland, *U31* is sunk for the second and final time, on this occasion by destroyer *Antelope* in co-operation with shore-based aircraft of Coastal Command: the first was by RAF Bomber Command in March.

3rd/4th — Two more armed merchant cruisers, **LAURENTIC** and **PATROCLUS**, are lost to the west of Ireland as they return from patrol — both to Kretschmer's *U99*.

5th — Loss of the *Jervis Bay* — Halifax/UK convoy HX84 of 37 ships and its solitary escort, the AMC *Jervis Bay* (Capt Fegen), is attacked by the 11in *Admiral Scheer* in mid-Atlantic. As the convoy scatters, **JERVIS BAY** heads for the *Scheer*, guns firing. The end is in no doubt and she goes down, but her sacrifice saves all but five of the merchant ships. ✛ Capt Edward Fegen RN is posthumously awarded the Victoria Cross.

EUROPE

OCTOBER

German troops occupy the Roumanian oilfields.

Battle of Britain

Birmingham, Liverpool and Manchester join London as targets for German bombers in the Blitz. On the 12th the planned invasion of Britain is postponed until the next spring.

Three ships of World War 1 vintage are lost:

18th — Submarine **H49**, on anti-invasion patrol off the Dutch coast, is lost to A/S trawlers.

19th — Destroyer **VENETIA** is sunk by a mine in the Thames Estuary while on patrol.

30th — Destroyer **STURDY**, local Western Approaches escort for Halifax/UK convoy SC8, runs aground off the west coast of Scotland, on Tiree Island. She is a total loss.

Merchant Shipping War
Losses
● 43 ships of 132,000 tons.

NOVEMBER

7th — A planned attack by German torpedo boats off the coast of Scotland ends when *T6* is mined on the East Coast barrage and goes down.

Former Prime Minister Neville Chamberlain dies on the 9th.

The Blitz continues with a particularly damaging raid on Coventry on the night of the 14th. Night-time attacks on London and other ports and cities carry on through to May. German cities also are targets for the RAF.

16th — Submarine **SWORDFISH**, setting out on Bay of Biscay patrol, strikes enemy mine off the Isle of Wight and sinks.

Hungary and Roumania join the Axis Tripartite Pact on the 20th and 23rd. Only Yugoslavia and Bulgaria hold out against German pressure to become members, and are the only countries in Eastern Europe and the Balkans not completely dominated by the Axis or Russia.

MEDITERRANEAN

OCTOBER

2nd — Destroyers *Havock* and *Hasty* sink submarine *Berillo* off Sollum.

12th/14th — From Alexandria a convoy safely reaches Malta covered by the Mediterranean Fleet with four battleships and carriers *Illustrious* and *Eagle*. On the 12th as it returns, attacks are made by Italian light forces southeast of Sicily. Cruiser *Ajax* sinks torpedo boats *Airone* and *Ariel* and badly damages destroyer *Artigliere*. The latter is sunk by heavy cruiser *York*.

The carriers launch air strikes against Leros in the Dodecanese and, on the 14th, as the Fleet heads for Alexandria, cruiser **Liverpool** is badly damaged by a torpedo hit from Italian aircraft.

15th — On patrol off Calabria in the Ionian Sea, submarine **RAINBOW** is lost in a gun action with the submarine *Enrico Toti*. At about this time **TRIAD** is mined (probably) off the Gulf of Taranto.

18th/20th — Air and sea patrols account for two Italian submarines to the east of Gibraltar. On the 18th *Durbo* goes down to attacks by destroyers *Firedrake* and *Wrestler* and RAF London flying boats of No 202 Squadron. Two days later it is the turn of *Lafolé* to destroyers *Gallant*, *Griffin* and *Hotspur*.

21st — Red Sea convoy BN7 is attacked by Italian destroyers from Massawa. The escorts, including New Zealand cruiser *Leander* and the destroyer *Kimberley*, drive *Nullo* ashore with their gunfire. Next day she is destroyed by RAF Blenheims.

Balkans

On the 28th, the Italians invade Greece from points in Albania. They are soon driven back and the fighting continues on Albanian soil until April.

Merchant Shipping War
Losses
● 1 ship of 3,000 tons.

HMS *Ajax*, a 'Leander' class light cruiser, was one of the River Plate victors. In the early hours of 12 October 1940 she sank two Italian large torpedo boats and damaged a destroyer. *Real Photos (S1086)*

The 'C' class light cruiser HMS *Curlew* (lost May 1940), was one of a class of 13 ships, of which six were lost and one not repaired. Completed 1917-22, eight of the vessels, including *Curlew*, were converted to anti-aircraft cruisers (starting in 1935): 4,200 tons, 29kt, five 6in or eight 4in AA guns, and 400 crew. *Real Photos (S1090)*

NOVEMBER

11th — Fleet Air Arm Attack on Taranto: Operation 'Judgement' — Early in the month a series of reinforcement and supply moves mounted from both ends of the Mediterranean lead up to the classic attack on the Italian battlefleet at Taranto.

From Alexandria, Adm Cunningham, with *Malaya*, *Ramillies*, *Valiant* and *Warspite*, carrier *Illustrious*, cruisers and destroyers, sails to cover convoys to Crete and Malta. *Eagle* has to be left behind because of defects caused by earlier bombing. Force H, in a separate operation called 'Coat', supports the passage of battleship *Barham*, two cruisers and three destroyers through from the west to reinforce the Mediterranean Fleet. Troops are also carried to Malta at this time from Gibraltar.

Mediterranean Fleet meets its new members and covers the return of an empty ship convoy from Malta. On the 11th a cruiser force is detached for what turns out to be a successful attack on Italian shipping in the Strait of Otranto. *Illustrious* meanwhile, escorted by cruisers and destroyers, heads for a position 170 miles to the southeast of Taranto. All six

ATLANTIC

It is in this action that the tanker *San Demetrio* is damaged by gunfire and abandoned. Later re-boarded, a few of her crew get her into port. *Scheer* now heads for the central and later South Atlantic.

In separate North Atlantic operations, submarines *U104* and the Italian *Faa di Bruno* are lost. In both cases the circumstances are uncertain, but *U104* is claimed by corvette *Rhododendron* and the Italian by destroyer *Havelock*. *U104* is the last German U-boat lost until March although the Italians have casualties. By the end of the month they have 26 submarines operating out of Bordeaux, but they are never as successful as their ally.

Battle of the Atlantic

Outward bound OB244 and UK-bound SC11 are attacked by two groups of U-boats west of North Channel. Fifteen merchant ships are sunk, including seven from SC11 by Schepke's *U100* on the night of the 22nd/23rd.

Important steps are taken in the air war when an RAF Sunderland equipped with 1½m wavelength anti-surface vessel (ASV) radar locates a U-boat. This is the first success of its kind with a system that is mainly effective by day as contact is lost when within two miles of the target. It is the addition of the Leigh light that will turn it into a powerful night-time weapon as well. Now Coastal Command is using depth charges instead of its ineffective A/S bombs.

Losses
- 38 ships of 201,000 tons and 3 armed merchant cruisers.
- 2 German and 1 Italian U-boats.

DECEMBER

1st — Armed merchant cruiser **Carnarvon Castle** is badly damaged in action with raider *Thor* off Brazil, her second and equally successful fight with an AMC.

Kormoran is the first of the second wave of raiders to leave for operations. She starts in the central Atlantic and later moves to the Indian Ocean, where she is lost in November 1941.

Much further afield in the South West Pacific, *Komet* and *Orion* share in the sinking of five ships near the phosphate island of Nauru. Later in the month *Komet* shells the installations.

2nd — *U99* claims her third armed merchant cruiser when **FORFAR** is sent to the bottom west of Ireland. At the same time nearby convoy HX90 is attacked just before the Western Approaches escorts arrive. Eleven ships are lost to the U-boats.

15th — Italian submarine *Tarantini* is torpedoed and sunk by submarine *Thunderbolt* in the Bay of Biscay as she returns from North Atlantic patrol.

EUROPE

Merchant Shipping War
Losses
- 48 ships of 93,000 tons.

DECEMBER

Adm Sir John Tovey succeeds Adm Forbes as C-in-C, Home Fleet.

5th — The ex-American destroyer **CAMERON** is bombed and badly damaged in Portsmouth harbour as she refits. Not worth repairing, she is used for experimental purposes.

17th — Following repairs to bomb damage, destroyer **ACHERON** is carrying out trials off the Isle of Wight when she detonates a mine and goes to the bottom.

Hitler orders detailed planning for Operation 'Barbarossa' — the invasion of Russia.

Merchant Shipping War
Losses
- 34 ships of 83,000 tons.

battleships of the Italian Navy are at anchor there.

That night *Illustrious* launches two waves of Swordfish, some of which belong to *Eagle*. Under the command of Lt-Cdrs K. Williamson and J. W. Hale, the total of no more than 20 aircraft of 813, 815, 819 and 824 Squadrons hit *Conte di Cavour* and *Caio Diulio* with one torpedo each and the brand new *Littorio* with three. All three battleships sink at their moorings and *Cavour* is never recommissioned, all for the loss of just two Swordfish. The Japanese Navy studies the attack carefully.

Balkans

As the Greek Army pushes back the Italians into Albania, RAF squadrons are sent from Egypt to Greece and the RN carries over the first Australian, British and New Zealand troops by cruiser.

Mediterranean Fleet establishes an advance base at Suda Bay on the northcoast of Crete.

27th — Action off Cape Spartivento, Southern Sardinia

— A fast convoy under the codename Operation 'Collar' sails from Gibraltar with ships for Malta and Alexandria. Cover as usual is provided by Force H with *Renown, Ark Royal,* cruisers *Despatch* and *Sheffield.*

Meanwhile, units of the Mediterranean Fleet including *Ramillies* and cruisers *Newcastle, Berwick* and *Coventry* head for a position south of Sardinia to meet them. Others accompany the two Mediterranean Fleet carriers in separate attacks on Italian targets — *Eagle* on Tripoli and *Illustrious* on Rhodes. These take place on the 26th.

Next day, on the 27th, south of Sardinia, *Ark Royal's* aircraft sight an Italian force with two battleships and seven heavy cruisers. Force H, now joined by *Ramillies,* sails to meet them. In an hour-long exchange of gunfire *Renown* and the cruisers are in action, during which time **Berwick** is damaged and an Italian destroyer badly hit. The slower *Ramillies* has not come up by the time the Italians have turned back for home. Adm Somerville pursues them but as he approaches their shores has to turn back himself. The convoys arrive safely.

Adm Somerville is later subjected to a board of enquiry for not continuing after the Italians. He is soon exonerated.

Merchant Shipping War
Losses
● There are no British or Allied shipping losses in November.

DECEMBER

Submarines **REGULUS** and **TRITON** are lost in late November or early December, possibly mined in the Strait of Otranto area. *Regulus* may have been sunk by Italian aircraft on 26 November.

3rd — At anchor in the poorly defended Suda Bay, cruiser **Glasgow** is hit by two torpedoes from Italian aircraft and badly damaged.

North Africa

Gen Wavell launches the first British offensive on the 9th against the Italian forces in Egypt. Sidi Barrani is captured on the 10th and by the end of the month British and Dominion troops have entered Libya for the first time. The offensive continues on until February by which time El Agheila, half way across Libya and well on the way to Tripoli, has been reached. Italian losses in men and material are considerable.

13th/14th — Units of the Mediterranean Fleet including the

The German battlecruiser *Scharnhorst*. With her sister-ship *Gneisenau* she broke out into the Atlantic in January 1941 for a raiding cruise in which the two ships sank 22 merchant ships.
Imperial War Museum (IWM HU1042)

small ship Inshore Squadron and the Australian Destroyer Flotilla play an important part in supporting and supplying the land campaign. On the 13th, cruiser **Coventry** is torpedoed by Italian submarine *Neghelli*, but she carries on. On the 14th, destroyers *Hereward* and *Hyperion* sink the submarine *Naiade* off Bardia.

The German X Fliegerkorps of the Luftwaffe — including its Ju87 Stukas — is ordered to Sicily and southern Italy to bolster the Italian Air Force.

22nd — Another series of convoy and offensive operations are carried out by the Mediterranean Fleet with battleships *Warspite* and *Valiant* and carrier *Illustrious*. On the 17th the carrier's aircraft attack Rhodes and on the night of the 18th/19th the two battleships bombard Valona, Albania.

At the same time, battleship *Malaya* passes through to the west. On the way, one of her escorting destroyers, **HYPERION**, hits a mine near Cape Bon on the 22nd and has to be scuttled. *Malaya* carries on and is met by Force H.

ATLANTIC

25th — Earlier in the month the 8in cruiser *Admiral Hipper* leaves Germany and passes into the Atlantic through the Denmark Strait. On Christmas Day, 700 miles to the west of Cape Finisterre, she encounters Middle East troop convoy WS5A, one of 'Winston's Specials', escorted by cruisers and accompanied by carrier *Furious* ferrying aircraft to Takoradi. In an exchange of gunfire the heavy cruiser **Berwick** and two merchantmen are slightly damaged. *Hipper* retires and soon reaches Brest.

Hipper is the first of the German big ships to reach the French Biscay ports. From there she and her companions will pose a major threat to the Atlantic convoy routes right up until the Channel Dash of February 1942.

Battle of the Atlantic

Losses
- 42 ships of 239,000 tons and 1 armed merchant cruiser.
- 1 Italian U-boat.

MEDITERRANEAN

By year's end, nine RN submarines have been lost since June in the Mediterranean, a poor exchange for the 12 Italian merchantmen of 45,000 tons. Most of them are the large, older boats transferred from the Far East and unsuited to the waters of the Mediterranean. In the same time the Italians have lost 18 submarines from all causes throughout the Mediterranean and Red Sea areas.

So far the Mediterranean has not turned out to be Mussolini's own preserve. In spite of the loss of French naval power, Force H and the Mediterranean Fleet have been more than able to hold the Italian Navy in check. Malta has been supplied and reinforced, and the British offensive in North Africa is underway. To the south a start is about to be made on ending the Italian East African Empire, and the Greeks are driving the Italians back into Albania.

It is now only a matter of months and even weeks before the Luftwaffe appears in Sicily, Rommel in North Africa and the German Army in Greece, followed by their paratroops in Crete.

Merchant Shipping War

Losses
- There are no shipping losses in December.

DEFENCE OF TRADE — NINE MONTHS FROM APRIL TO DECEMBER 1940

Summary of Losses

U-boats and now long-range aircraft have exacted a heavy toll of British, Allied and neutral shipping, mainly in the North Western Approaches to the British Isles. Further afield surface raiders have sunk, captured and disrupted shipping as far away as the Pacific. U-boats have also operated with success off West Africa.

In UK waters, heavy attacks by aircraft and E-boats have been added to the continuous danger from mines. Over half of the ships and 40% of tonnage lost have been close to home. Vital as the Battle of the Atlantic may be, there can be no let up in the equally important battle for the UK coastal routes. Only heavily escorted transports will use the Mediterranean until 1943.

The monthly loss rate in these months is twice that of the first seven months of the war, and each form of attack requires a different technical and operational response from the Royal Navy and its allies.

The 1940 patterns of assault against the trade routes will continue throughout 1941, although the U-boats will move further out into the Atlantic: by year's end they will have reached the coasts of America.

North Atlantic	UK waters	Mediterranean	Indian Ocean
321 ships of 1,683,000 tons.	497 ships of 1,367,000 tons.	13 ships of 64,000 tons.	24 ships of 173,000 tons.

South Atlantic			Pacific Ocean
8 ships of 55,000 tons.			15 ships of 99,000 tons.

= 878 British, Allied and neutral ships of 3,441,000 tons: ie 382,000 tons per month.

Submarines	363 ships of 1,842,000 tons.
Aircraft	172 ships of 546,000 tons.
Raiders	54 ships of 367,000 tons.
Mines	151 ships of 342,000 tons.
Other causes	99 ships of 201,000 tons.
Warships	16 ships of 95,000 tons.
Coastal forces	23 ships of 48,000 tons.

ATLANTIC	EUROPE

JANUARY

7th — Italian submarine *Nani* attacks a convoy west of North Channel and is sunk by corvette *Anemone*.

Pocket battleship *Admiral Scheer* operates in the South Atlantic, while *Scharnhorst* and *Gneisenau* in Germany and heavy cruiser *Hipper* in Brest prepare to go out. At the end of the month the two battlecruisers head into the Atlantic for two months until their return to Brest.

Six raiders of the original seven are still at sea — *Orion* and *Komet* in the Pacific, *Atlantis* at Kerguelen in the southern Indian Ocean, *Kormoran* in the central and *Thor* in the South Atlantic, and finally *Pinguin* in the Antarctic. All move to different areas over the next few months.

Up until June, German warships sink 37 ships of 188,000 tons and raiders 38 ships of 191,000 tons. Thereafter neither type inflicts many losses as world-wide convoys are organised and the raiders' supply ships are sunk.

Battle of the Atlantic

For the next few months the U-boat's 'Happy Time' continues in the Western Approaches against the poorly defended convoys. Bad weather in January and February fortunately keeps the level of sinkings down. Approximately 22 U-boats are operational out of the 90 in commission, and long-range aircraft including the Kondors still roam the waters off Ireland spotting for U-boats and sinking ships.

Losses
- 59 British, Allied and neutral merchant ships of 273,000 tons in the North and South Atlantic.
- 1 Italian U-boat.

JANUARY

The Blitz on Britain continues with attacks on Bristol, Cardiff, London and Portsmouth during the month.

15th – Cruiser minelayer **Adventure** is damaged for the second time on a mine while on passage from Milford Haven to Liverpool.

Merchant Shipping War

Losses due to air attack and mines remain a major problem. Aircraft and E-boats have now added acoustic to the magnetic and moored contact mines in their armoury, but these are never the threat that magnetic mines were a year earlier.

Losses
- 15 British, Allied and neutral ships of 37,000 tons in UK waters.

The 'Hawkins' class cruiser HMS *Hawkins* was one of a class of four surviving ships including the rearmed nine 6in gun *Effingham* (lost in May 1940), the *Frobisher*, and the repair ship *Vindictive*. Completed 1918-25, they displaced c9,800 tons, could make 30kt, carried seven 7.5in guns and had a crew of 710. *Real Photos (S1097)*

MEDITERRANEAN

JANUARY

North Africa

As the British advance into Libya continues, Bardia is taken on the 5th. Australian troops capture Tobruk on the 22nd and Derna by the end of the month.

The Inshore Squadron plays an important part in the campaign — bombarding shore targets, carrying fuel, water and supplies, and evacuating wounded and prisoners of war.

Hurricane fighters, transported to Takoradi in West Africa, start to arrive in Egypt after flying right across the continent. They too play their part in the offensive.

RAF Wellingtons raid Naples and damage the battleship *Giulio Cesare.*

6th-11th — Malta Convoy: Operation 'Excess' — Another complex series of convoy movements around Malta lead to carrier *Illustrious* being badly damaged and the RN losing its comparative freedom of operation in the Eastern Mediterranean. This follows the arrival of the Luftwaffe in Sicily.

On the 6th, 'Excess' leaves Gibraltar for Malta and Greece covered by Force H. At the same time the Mediterranean Fleet from Alexandria prepares to cover ships to Malta and bring empty ones out. Mediterranean Fleet cruisers *Gloucester* and *Southampton* carry troops to Malta and then carry on west to meet 'Excess'. Force H returns to Gibraltar.

By the 10th, 'Excess' has reached the Strait of Sicily and is attacked by Italian torpedo boats. *Vega* is sunk by escorting cruiser *Bonaventure* and destroyer *Hereward*. As the Mediterranean Fleet meets the convoy off Pantelleria, one of the screening destroyers, **GALLANT**, hits a mine. Towed back to Malta, she is not re-commissioned and is finally wrecked by bombing in April 1942.

Still to the west of Malta, heavy attacks by German and Italian aircraft are launched. **Illustrious** is singled out and soon hit six times by Ju87 and Ju88 bombers. She struggles into Malta with 200 casualties. There, under continual attack, she is repaired temporarily and leaves on the 23rd for Alexandria. Her sister-ship *Formidable* is sent out via the Cape of Good Hope, but it is some weeks before she reaches the Eastern Mediterranean.

On the 11th, as the return Malta/Alexandria convoy proceeds eastwards, *Gloucester* and *Southampton* sail to join it. Both are attacked by German aircraft to the east of Malta and **SOUTHAMPTON** sunk and **Gloucester** damaged.

All merchantmen reach their destinations safely, but at a cost of a cruiser and destroyer, and the loss of *Illustrious'* vital airpower.

19th — Destroyer *Greyhound*, escorting a convoy to Greece, sinks Italian submarine *Neghelli* in the Aegean.

East Africa

The British and Dominion campaign to oust the Italians from East Africa starts. Eritrea in the north is invaded from the Sudan by largely Indian forces, while East African and South African troops attack Italian Somaliland from Kenya to the south.

Merchant Shipping War

Losses

● No British, Allied or neutral merchant ships are lost in the Mediterranean.

HMS *Furious*, responsible for bringing south many of the aircraft landed at Takoradi in late 1940/early 1941. *Real Photos (S1558)*

The 'S' class destroyer HMS *Stronghold*, lost in March 1942. Five of the class were lost, all but one in the Far East. The similar 'R' and 'S' classes were completed 1918-24, displacing 900 tons, armed with one to three 4in guns, with a crew of c90 and able to make 36kt. *Real Photos (S567)*

ATLANTIC	EUROPE

FEBRUARY

At the beginning of the month, *Admiral Hipper* sails from Brest. On the 12th, far to the west of Gibraltar, she sinks seven ships from unescorted convoy SLS64 bound for Britain from Sierra Leone. She then returns to Brest, and in March heads back to Germany via the Denmark Strait to take no further part in independent commerce raiding.

On the 8th, *Scharnhorst* and *Gneisenau* sight convoy HX106 escorted by battleship *Ramillies* south of Greenland. They do not attack. Later, on the 22nd, they sink five unescorted ships east of Newfoundland before heading for the Sierra Leone routes. Meanwhile pocket battleship *Admiral Scheer* operates successfully off Madagascar before preparing to return to Germany.

22nd — Italian submarine *Marcello* is believed sunk to the west of the Hebrides by ex-US destroyer *Montgomery* and other escorts of Liverpool-out convoy OB287. The convoy is reported by Kondors which sink two and damage four merchantmen, but no other U-boats are able to make attacks.

Battle of the Atlantic
Adm Sir Percy Noble takes over as C-in-C, Western Approaches, just as the command moves from Plymouth to Liverpool.
Losses
● 69 ships of 317,000 tons.
● 1 Italian U-boat.

FEBRUARY

The submarine **SNAPPER**, after leaving her escort off Lands End for Bay of Biscay patrol, is not heard from again. She fails to rendezvous on the 12th, possibly lost on mines.

25th – Escort destroyer **EXMOOR** is the first of the 'Hunt' class to be lost. She is torpedoed off Lowestoft by E-boat *S30* while escorting Thames/Forth convoy FN417.

Merchant Shipping War
Losses
● 26 ships of 51,000 tons.

The 'V' & 'W' class destroyer HMS *Whirlwind* was lost in July 1940. Similar classes of a total of 58 ships, many of the 'V' & 'W' destroyers were converted to escorts. Sixteen were lost and two not repaired. Completed 1917-24, they displaced 1,100 tons, had a maximum speed of 34kt, and carried two to four 4in or 4.7in guns and 125 crew. Three of the four RAN ships were lost — HMA Ships *Vampire*, *Voyager* and *Waterhen. Real Photos (S1150)*

MARCH

7th-23rd — With better weather the spring U-boat offensive starts, and they sink 41 ships of 243,000 tons. However, in the space of a few days they suffer their first major defeat at the hands of the escorts and lose three of their aces. From now on, escort versus wolf-pack battles will predominate in the North Atlantic.

In attacks on Liverpool-out convoy OB293, *U70* is sunk by corvettes *Arbutus* and *Camellia*, and *U47* (Cdr Prien) by destroyer *Wolverine*, on the 7th and 8th respectively.

On the 17th against Halifax/UK HX112, *U99* (Lt-Cdr Kretschmer) and *U100* (Lt-Cdr Schepke) are sunk by the 5th EG commanded by Cdr MacIntyre. Destroyers *Vanoc* and *Walker* are mainly responsible.

Then, on the 23rd, armed trawler *Visenda* accounts for *U551*.

All losses take place to the south of Iceland; they are the first German ones since the previous November.

The United States Lend-Lease Bill is passed into law. In time Britain and her Allies will be able to receive American arms and supplies without immediate payment.

MARCH

Bulgaria joins the Tripartite Pact on the 1st and German troops enter the country. In the Balkans only Yugoslavia stays outside.

A successful commando raid is carried out on the Lofoten Islands, and installations destroyed and shipping sunk. Escort is provided by destroyers and cover by units of the Home Fleet.

Merchant Shipping War
Motor gun-boats are entering service to combat E-boat attacks on East Coast convoys. Improved MTBs are also being built to attack German coastal shipping. This marks the first step in the building up of Coastal Forces.
Losses
● 73 ships of 153,000 tons.

FEBRUARY

North Africa

British armoured forces cross the Libyan desert to a point south of Benghazi and cut off the retreating Italians. The resulting Battle of Beda Fomm, starting on the 5th, inflicts heavy losses on them. Australian troops capture the major port of Benghazi at the same time, and by the 9th El Agheila is reached. There the advance stops. Large numbers of British and Dominion troops are now withdrawn for transfer to Greece, just as the first units of the Afrika Korps under Gen Rommel arrive in Tripoli.

Force H with *Ark Royal*, *Renown* and *Malaya* sails into the Gulf of Genoa. The big ships bombard the city of Genoa, while carrier aircraft bomb Leghorn and lay mines off Spezia, all on the 9th. An Italian battlefleet sorties but fails to make contact.

24th — Destroyer **DAINTY**, escorting supplies to Tobruk with the Inshore Squadron, is sunk off the port by German Ju87 Stukas.

25th — On patrol off the east coast of Tunisia, submarine *Upright* torpedoes and sinks Italian cruiser *Armando Diaz* as she covers a convoy from Naples to Tripoli.

East Africa

In the north the Indian advance into Eritrea is held up for most of February and March by the Battle for Keren. In the south, the Italian Somaliland capital of Mogadishu is captured on the 25th, after which the British forces advance northwest into Ethiopia.

The East Indies Command under Vice-Adm R. Leatham continually supports the land campaign.

27th — After breaking out of Massawa, Italian armed merchant cruiser *Ramb I* is located off the Maldives and sunk by New Zealand cruiser *Leander*.

Merchant Shipping War
Losses
● 2 ships of 8,000 tons.

MARCH

Greece

In the space of three weeks in March, 60,000 British and Dominion troops are carried from North Africa to Greece, escorted by the RN (Operation 'Lustre').

6th — Italian submarine *Anfitrite* attacks a troop convoy east of Crete and is sunk by escorting destroyer *Greyhound*.

26th — At anchor in Suda Bay, heavy cruiser **YORK** is badly damaged by Italian explosive motor boats. Beached, she is later wrecked by bombing and abandoned when Crete is evacuated in May.

28th — Battle of Cape Matapan — As ships of the Mediterranean Fleet cover troop movements to Greece, 'Ultra' intelligence is received that an Italian battlefleet with one battleship, six heavy and two light cruisers plus destroyers is sailing to attack the convoy routes. On the 27th, Vice-Adm Pridham-Wippell with cruisers *Ajax*, *Gloucester*, *Orion* and the

HMS *Ramillies*, the 'Royal Sovereign', class battleship. In February 1941 she protected HX106 against the two raiding German battlecruisers, *Scharnhorst* and *Gneisenau*. *Real Photos (S1130)*

Scharnhorst and *Gneisenau* are sighted by the aircraft of battleship *Malaya* then escorting convoy SL67 off the Cape Verde Islands. They return to the Newfoundland area where on the 15th and 16th they sink or capture 16 unescorted ships. Returning to Brest on the 22nd, they are never again successfully used for commerce raiding. On this cruise they have accounted for 22 ships of 116,000 tons.

20th — *Malaya* is now with convoy SL68 off the west coast of Africa. Torpedoed and damaged by *U106*, she becomes the first British ship repaired in the United States under Lend-Lease arrangements. The convoy loses seven merchantmen to the U-boats.

Battle of the Atlantic

On 6 March, faced with the mortal threat of the German U-boat and aircraft offensive in the Atlantic, Winston Churchill issues his famous Battle of the Atlantic directive. Catapult armed merchantmen (CAM) are to be fitted out, merchant ships to be given AA weapons as a first priority, and more Coastal Command squadrons formed and fitted with radar. Port and dockyard congestion is to be dealt with and the defence of ports greatly improved.

These and numerous other matters are to be dealt with as a matter of the very highest priority. The survival of Britain depends on them. Overall direction is to be exercised by a Battle of the Atlantic Committee chaired by the Prime Minister himself.

Losses

● 63 ships of 365,000 tons.
● 5 German U-boats — including three of the U-boat arm's most experienced Commanders.

The 'Town' class destroyer HMS *Broadway* was one of 50 US flushdeckers transferred to Britain in 1940, with nine lost and one not repaired. Completed around 1918, the class displaced 1,050 tons, could make 35kt, carried one to three 4in guns and three torpedo tubes, plus 145 crew. Many served in the RCN and some in the Norwegian and, later, the Russian navies. Losses included HMCS *St Croix*, the Norwegian-manned *Bath* and the Russian *Deyatelnyi*. IWM (A829)

MEDITERRANEAN

Australian *Perth* and destroyers sails from Greek waters for a position south of Crete. Adm Cunningham with *Formidable*, *Warspite*, *Barham* and *Valiant* leaves Alexandria on the same day to meet the cruisers.

Around 08.30 on the 28th, south of Crete, Adm Pridham-Wippell is in action with an Italian cruiser squadron. Just before noon he finds himself between them and the battleship *Vittorio Veneto* which has now come up. An attack by Swordfish from *Formidable* fails to hit the Italian battleship, but enables the RN cruisers to extricate themselves. The Mediterranean Fleet heavy units arrive, but their only chance of action is to slow down the Italians before they can reach Italy.

A second Swordfish strike at around 15.00 hits and slows down the *Veneto*, but only for a short while. At 19.30 a third strike southwest of Cape Matapan stops heavy cruiser *Pola*. All this time, RAF aircraft are attacking but without success. Later that evening (still on the 28th), two more heavy cruisers — *Fiume* and *Zara* with four destroyers are detached to help *Pola*. Before they reach her, Adm Cunningham's ships detect them and *Fiume*, *Zara* and the destroyers *Alfieri* and *Carducci* are crippled by the close range gunfire of *Barham*, *Valiant* and *Warspite*. They are finished off by four destroyers led by the Australian *Stuart*. Early next morning *Pola* is found, partly abandoned. After taking off the remaining crew, destroyers *Jervis* and *Nubian* sink her with torpedoes.

The Royal Navy loses one aircraft.

31st — Cruiser **BONAVENTURE** with a Mediterranean Fleet cruiser force escorts a convoy from Greece to Egypt and is sunk to the southeast of Crete by Italian submarine *Ambra*.

East Africa

British forces are carried from Aden to Berbera in British Somaliland on the 16th. They follow this with an advance southwest into Ethiopia. To the north, Keren falls to the attacking Indian troops, and the road is opened to the Eritrean capital of Asmara and port of Massawa.

Late in the month a small convoy sails for Malta from the east covered by the Mediterranean Fleet. These are the first supplies to arrive since the January 'Excess' operation. In the intervening two months Malta has been heavily attacked by the Axis air forces, which hope to neutralise the island as a base for air and sea attacks against the supply routes to Libya.

North Africa

In command of German and Italian troops, Gen Rommel starts his first offensive with the capture of El Agheila on the 24th. Within three weeks the British and Dominion forces are back in Sollum on the Egyptian side of the border.

Yugoslavia

On the 25th Yugoslavia joins the Tripartite Pact, but two days later an anti-Nazi coup topples the Government.

28th/31st — Mines laid by submarine *Rorqual* west of Sicily on the 25th sink two Italian supply ships next day and torpedo boat *Chinotto* on the 28th.

Then, on the 31st, off northeast Sicily, she torpedoes and sinks submarine *Capponi*.

Merchant Shipping War
Losses
● 2 ships of 12,000 tons.

The 'Shakespeare' class destroyer HMS *Broke* (lost on 8 November 1942 during Operation 'Torch') was one of three surviving ex-flotilla leaders completed 1919-22. At 1,480 tons, they had a maximum speed of 36kt, and carried five 4.7in guns and 160 crew. *Real Photos (S478)*

German aircraft attacks

In April, aircraft sink 116 ships of 323,000 tons, the highest rate for any month of the whole war. In the first six months of 1941 alone the losses total 294 ships of 811,000 tons. These are not only due to the long-range aircraft operating off Ireland from bases in France and Norway, but to attacks in coastal waters where the defences are still weak.

More AA weapons are needed for merchantmen, more and better controlled shore-based fighters in coastal areas, and ship-borne aircraft are vital out to sea. The needs are recognised as the Battle of the Atlantic Directive makes clear, but will take many months to meet.

APRIL

4th-13th — Armed merchant cruisers again suffer heavy losses at widely scattered locations and in different circumstances. On the 4th **VOLTAIRE** is sunk in a gun duel with raider *Thor* west of the Cape Verde Islands. Two days later **COMORIN** catches fire and finally goes down west of Ireland — the rescue of her crew and passengers in raging seas is an epic in its own right. Then, on the 13th, **RAJPUTANA** on Northern Patrol is lost to *U108* in the Denmark Strait.

Thor returns to Germany after an absence of 11 months, having accounted for 11 ships of 83,000 tons and the *Voltaire*.

Pocket battleship *Admiral Scheer* also gets back to Germany after five months in the Atlantic and Indian Oceans. Her score is 16 ships of 99,000 tons plus the *Jervis Bay*.

5th/28th — Slow Halifax/UK convoy SC26 is attacked by U-boats for two days and loses 10 merchantmen. On the 5th, escorting destroyer *Wolverine* and sloop *Scarborough* sink *U76*. Towards the end of the month faster convoy HX121 loses four ships but corvette *Gladiolus* destroys *U65*. Both actions take place south of Iceland.

Battle of the Atlantic

Over the next few months a number of long awaited new ship types and weapons start to be introduced. These will contribute significantly to the eventual defeat of the U-boat.

The first fighter catapult ships flying the White Ensign and equipped with a 'one-way' Hurricane are ready in April. They shoot down their first Kondor in August. In May a Hurricane is successfully launched from a Red Ensign CAM, but they do not claim their first victim until November. CAM-ships are eventually superseded in 1943 by merchant aircraft carriers (MACs) — merchantmen with full flightdecks, but sailing under the Red Ensign and also carrying oil or grain.

The final step in the introduction of ship-borne aircraft into the Battle of the Atlantic comes in June when the first escort carrier is ready for service. HMS *Audacity*, converted from a German prize, has a short life, but will prove the great value of these vessels.

New scientific developments also start to play their part. In May the first high definition, 10cm radar (Type 271) is installed in a corvette. Later still, high frequency, direction finding (HF/DF or 'Huff-Duff') is introduced to supplement the work of the shore stations. It is many months before either system is widely in service, and not until 1942 do they claim their first U-boats. Finally, inter-service co-ordination is further improved when RAF Coastal Command is placed under operational control of the Admiralty.

Losses

- 48 ships of 282,000 tons and 3 armed merchant cruisers.
- 2 U-boats.

APRIL

The arrival of the German battlecruisers *Scharnhorst* and *Gneisenau* in Brest marks the start of a long series of heavy RAF raids. These will not end until the Channel Dash in February 1942. During this time both ships will sustain varying amounts of damage. On the 6th *Gneisenau* is torpedoed and badly damaged by an RAF Beaufort of No 22 Squadron, Coastal Command. ✠ Flg Off Kenneth Campbell RAFVR, Canadian pilot of the Beaufort, is posthumously awarded the Victoria Cross.

Merchant Shipping War

Losses

- 40 ships of 99,000 tons.

MEDITERRANEAN

APRIL

East Africa

In the north, the capture of Eritrea is completed when Asmara is occupied on the 1st and the Red Sea base at Massawa on the 8th. Two days before that, Addis Ababa, capital of Ethiopia, has been taken. Italian resistance continues mainly in the north of the country.

3rd/8th — Leading up to the capture of Massawa, the remaining eight Italian destroyers and torpedo boats are lost or scuttled. On the 3rd, five seaworthy destroyers sail to attack Port Sudan. Shore-based Swordfish from carrier *Eagle* sink the *Manin* and *Sauro*.

Before the final scuttling, Italian MTB *MAS213* torpedoes and damages cruiser **Capetown** on the 8th as she escorts a convoy off Massawa.

Four Italian submarines do manage to escape and eventually reach Bordeaux in France.

Middle East

A pro-German coup in Iraq on the 1st threatens Allied oil supplies. British and Indian units are entering the country through the Persian Gulf by the middle of the month.

In the first week of April, *Ark Royal*, escorted by Force H, flies off 12 Hurricanes for Malta. Three weeks later the operation is repeated with 20 more.

Yugoslavia and Greece

Germany invades both countries on the 6th. By the 12th they have entered Belgrade and within another five days the Yugoslav Army has surrendered. Greek forces in Albania and in Greece itself follow suit. Starting on the 24th and over a period of five days, 50,000 British, Australian and New Zealand men are evacuated to Crete and Egypt in Operation 'Demon'. The Germans occupy Athens on the 27th.

27th — As units of the Mediterranean Fleet carry out the evacuation, destroyers **DIAMOND** and **WRYNECK** rescue troops from the bombed transport *Slamat*. Shortly afterwards, both are sunk by more German bombers off Cape Malea at the southeast tip of Greece. There are few survivors from the three ships.

North Africa

Germans enter Benghazi on the 4th and by mid-month have surrounded Tobruk and reached the Egyptian border. Attacks on the British and Australian troops defending Tobruk are unsuccessful, and an eight-month siege begins.

16th — Action off Sfax, Tunisia — Capt P. J. Mack with destroyers *Janus*, *Jervis*, *Mohawk* and *Nubian* from Malta intercept a German Afrika Korps convoy of five transports escorted by three Italian destroyers off Kerkennah Islands, east of Tunisia. All Axis ships are sunk including the destroyers *Baleno* (foundered next day), *Lampo* (later salvaged) and *Tarigo*. In the fighting **MOHAWK** is torpedoed by *Tarigo* and has to be scuttled.

Battleships *Barham*, *Valiant* and *Warspite* together with carrier *Formidable* cover the movement of fast transport *Breconshire* to Malta. On their return to Alexandria they bombard Tripoli on the 21st.

Merchant Shipping War
Losses
● 105 ships of 293,000 tons.

The 'Scott' class destroyer HMS *Malcolm* was one of a class of seven surviving ex-flotilla leaders, including HMAS *Stuart* and also the *Bruce*, sunk as a target in November 1939. Completed 1918-19, they displaced 1,530 tons, could make 36kt, and carried two to five 4.7in guns, plus 160 crew. *Real Photos (N1076)*

HMS *Mohawk*, a 'Tribal' class destroyer. She served in the Mediterranean, including the Action off Calabria, Malta convoy 'Excess' and the Battle of Cape Matapan. She was hit by two Italian torpedoes early on Wednesday, 16 April 1941 with the loss of 40 men. She is seen arriving at Portsmouth from her builders, in 1938. *Real Photos (S1103)*

MAY

8th — On patrol north of the Seychelles in the Indian Ocean, heavy cruiser *Cornwall* finds and sinks the raider *Pinguin*. This is the first raider to be hunted down, having accounted for 28 ships of 136,000 tons.

9th — The Capture of *U110* and Enigma — South of Iceland, *U110* (Lt-Cdr Lemp of the *Athenia* sinking) attacks Liverpool out convoy OB318 protected by ships of Capt A. J. Baker-Creswell's escort group. Blown to the surface by depth charges from corvette *Aubretia* on the 9th, *U110*'s crew abandon ship, but she fails to go down. A boarding party from destroyer *Bulldog*, led by Sub-Lt Balme, manages to get aboard. In a matter of hours they transfer to safety *U110*'s entire Enigma package — coding machine, code books, rotor settings and charts. The destroyer *Broadway* stands by.

Two days later *U110* sinks on tow to Iceland, knowledge of her capture having been withheld from the crew and Lt-Cdr Lemp having died at the time of the boarding. The priceless Enigma material represents one of the greatest intelligence coups ever and is a major naval victory in its own right.

U110 is far and away the most successful of the attempts to capture Enigma codes. In the March raid on the Lofoten Islands, spare coding rotors were found. Then two days before the *U110* triumph, a cruiser force had tried to capture the weather trawler *München* off Iceland. At the end of June a similar operation is mounted against the *Lauenberg*. In both cases useful papers are taken but the real breakthrough only comes with *U110*. Included with the material are all rotor settings until the end of June.

A number of codes are used with Enigma. The U-boat one is 'Hydra', also used by all ships in European waters. From the end of June, Bletchley Park is able to decipher 'Hydra' right through until the end of the war. Unfortunately the U-boats move off this version to the new 'Triton' in February 1942. The big ship 'Neptun' and Mediterranean 'Sud' and 'Medusa' codes will also soon be broken.

13th — Armed merchant cruiser **SALOPIAN** on passage to Halifax after escorting convoy SC30 is torpedoed a total of six times by *U98*. Eventually she goes down southeast of Cape Farewell, the sadly named but appropriate southern tip of Greenland.

Hunt for the *Bismarck*

18th — New German 15in battleship *Bismarck* and heavy cruiser *Prinz Eugen* sail from Gdynia for the Atlantic via Norway. A simultaneous sortie by the two battlecruisers from Brest is fortunately prevented by the damage inflicted by the RAF.

21st — In the evening the German ships are sighted in a fiord south of Bergen. Two of the Home Fleet's capital ships, *Hood* and *Prince of Wales* (the latter new and still working up), sail from Scapa Flow towards Iceland to support the cruisers on Northern Patrol.

22nd — *Bismarck* is reported at sea and the main body of the Home Fleet under Adm Tovey leaves Scapa Flow and heads west. Battleship *King George V*, fleet carrier *Victorious*, cruisers and destroyers are later joined by battlecruiser *Repulse*. *Victorious* is also working up.

23rd — In the early evening, heavy cruisers *Suffolk* and shortly *Norfolk* sight the German ships north west of Iceland and shadow them southwestwards through the Denmark Strait. *Hood* and *Prince of Wales* press on to intercept west of Iceland.

MAY

Heavy raids on Belfast, the Clyde, Liverpool and especially London on the night of the 10th/11th mark the virtual end of the Blitz. The bulk of the Luftwaffe is now transferring east for the attack on Russia. RAF raids on Germany continue, and will grow as a major plank in British and Allied strategy for the defeat of Germany.

Rudolf Hess, Hitler's deputy, flies to Britain on his self-appointed peace mission.

Merchant Shipping War
Losses
● 99 ships of 101,000 tons.

The German heavy cruiser *Prinz Eugen*, which joined the *Bismarck* on her breakout in May 1941. *Real Photos (S1731)*

MEDITERRANEAN

MAY

In late April or early May, two submarines operating out of Malta are lost, possibly due to mines — **USK** in the Strait of Sicily area and **UNDAUNTED** off Tripoli. *Usk* may have been sunk by Italian destroyers west of Sicily while attacking a convoy.

2nd — Returning to Malta with cruiser *Gloucester* and other destroyers from a search for Axis convoys, **JERSEY** is mined and sunk in the entrance to Grand Harbour.

Middle East

British bases in Iraq are besieged as other British and Dominion forces advance on Baghdad from Jordan and the Persian Gulf. An armistice is signed on the 31st and Baghdad occupied the next day.

Early in the month, Force H and the Mediterranean Fleet carry out another series of complicated supply, reinforcement and offensive operations. Five fast transports sail from Gibraltar with tanks and supplies urgently needed for the Army of the Nile (Operation 'Tiger'). Four arrive safely. On the way they are accompanied by battleship *Queen Elizabeth* and two cruisers sailing to join the Mediterranean Fleet. Two small convoys are escorted from Egypt to Malta. Other units of the Mediterranean Fleet shell Benghazi on the night of the 7th/8th.

After covering 'Tiger', *Ark Royal*, joined by carrier *Furious*, is once again south of Sardinia and flying off a further 48 Hurricanes to Malta on the 21st. Five days later, *Ark Royal's* Swordfish are crippling the *Bismarck* in the North Atlantic!

The transfer of many German aircraft from Sicily for the attack on Russia brings some relief to Malta.

North Africa

A British offensive starts from the Sollum area on the 15th in an attempt to relieve Tobruk (Operation 'Brevity'). Two weeks later both sides are back to their original positions.

The first of many supply trips to besieged Tobruk are made by Australian destroyers *Voyager* and *Waterhen* and other ships of the Inshore Squadron.

25th — Sloop **GRIMSBY** and the supply ship she is escorting on the Tobruk run are both sunk by bombers northeast of the port.

Battle for Crete

18th — On patrol south of Crete, AA cruiser *Coventry* is heavily attacked from the air. ✠ Petty Officer Alfred Sephton continues to carry out his duties in the director after being mortally wounded. He is posthumously awarded the Victoria Cross.

21st — In the opening stages of the attack on Crete, cruiser minelayer *Abdiel* lays mines off the west coast of Greece, which sink the Italian destroyer *Mirabello* and two transports.

Most of the Mediterranean Fleet with its four battleships, one carrier, 10 cruisers and 30 destroyers fight the Battle for Crete. For the Navy there are two phases, both of which take place under intense air attack, mainly German, from which all losses result.

Phase one is from the German airborne invasion on the 20th until the decision is take on the 27th to evacuate the island. During this time the Mediterranean Fleet manages to prevent the sea-borne reinforcement of the German paratroops, but at heavy cost. Most of these losses happen as the ships try to

The battleship HMS *Queen Elizabeth*, having completed her major reconstruction earlier in the year, sailed in May 1941 to join the Mediterranean Fleet, later hoisting the flag of Adm Cunningham. *IWM (A9829)*

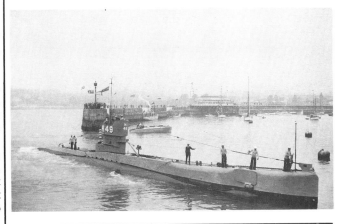

The 'H' class submarine *H49* was lost in October 1940. Of the class of nine boats, she and *H31* were sunk. Completed 1918-20, they displaced 410/500 tons, could make 13/10kt, and carried 22 crew. *Real Photos (S462)*

ATLANTIC

24th — That morning the big ships meet and open fire. Around 06.00, after firing two or three salvos, *Bismarck* hits **HOOD** which blows up with only three survivors. Now it is **Prince of Wales** turn to be the target. After being hit several times she turns away but not before damaging *Bismarck* and causing her to lose fuel oil to the sea. German Adm Lütjens then decides to make for St Nazaire in France and heads southwest and later south out of the Denmark Strait. The two RN cruisers, and for a while the damaged *Prince of Wales*, continue to shadow. Adm Tovey hurries west with the rest of Home Fleet.

With *Hood's* loss, Force H (Adm Somerville) with battle-cruiser *Renown*, carrier *Ark Royal* and cruiser *Sheffield* is sailing north from Gibraltar. Battleship *Ramillies*, released from convoy escort duties, and *Rodney*, then to the west of Ireland, head towards *Bismarck's* expected track. *Ramillies* does not play a part in later operations.

At 18.00, still on the 24th, *Bismarck* feints north towards her shadowers for long enough to allow *Prinz Eugen* to get away. (The cruiser goes south, later refuels from a tanker and cruises for three days before reaching Brest on 1 June. There she joins the two battlecruisers under heavy RAF attack until the Channel Dash of February 1942.)

Around midnight, southeast of Cape Farewell, Swordfish from Adm Tovey's *Victorious* get one hit on *Bismarck* after she has resumed her southerly course. The damage is negligible. Shortly after in the early hours of the 25th, she alters course to the southeast for France and the cruisers lose contact. At this point Adm Tovey's heavy ships are only 100 miles away.

25th — *Bismarck* holds her southeasterly course, but breaks radio silence. Unfortunately the British direction-finding service puts her on a *north*easterly heading. Adm Tovey sails in that direction for a while before turning to the southeast in pursuit. Now he is well astern of his quarry. Only by slowing her down can her destruction become possible. In the meantime, Force H continues to sail north to take up a blocking position between *Bismarck* and her new goal of Brest.

26th — After a 30-hour interval, *Bismarck* is once more sighted, this time by a RAF Catalina of No 209 Squadron, and only 30hr from home. In the afternoon a Swordfish strike from Force H's *Ark Royal* attacks the *Sheffield* in error. She is not hit. A second strike takes place in the evening by 810, 818 and 820 Squadrons with 15 Swordfish led by Lt-Cdr Coode. They torpedo *Bismarck* twice and one hit damages her propellers and jams the rudder. As *Bismarck* circles, destroyers of the 4th Flotilla (Capt Vian) come up around midnight, and make a series of torpedo and gun attacks but with uncertain results. The *Cossack, Maori, Sikh, Zulu* and Polish *Piorun* have been detached from troop convoy WS8B, an indication of the seriousness of the *Bismarck's* threat.

By this time Adm Tovey's force of heavy ships has lost *Repulse* to refuel, but been joined by *Rodney*. They now come up from the west but do not attack just yet.

27th — *King George V, Rodney* and *Bismarck* all open fire around 08.45. Only the German ship is hit and by 10.15 she is a blazing wreck. Heavy cruiser *Dorsetshire*, having left convoy SL74 the previous day, fires torpedoes to finish her off. *Bismarck* sinks at 10.36 to the southwest of Ireland. The *Norfolk* is there at the end.

28th — The many warships deployed from all parts of the North Atlantic return to other duties. As they do, heavy attacks by German aircraft sink destroyer **MASHONA** off the west coast of Ireland.

EUROPE

HMS *Prince of Wales*, the 'King George V' class battleship, had been completed only on 31 March 1941 before joining the hunt for the *Bismarck*. In August 1941 she carried Winston Churchill across the Atlantic to meet President Roosevelt, and before 1941 was out, was lost off Malaya after being hit by four Japanese torpedoes.
Real Photos (S1779)

withdraw from night-time patrols north of the island out of range of enemy aircraft.

Phase two is from 27 May to 1 June when over 15,000 British and Dominion troops are evacuated. Ten thousand have to be left behind — and again the losses are heavy.

21st — In the morning destroyer **JUNO** is sunk and cruiser **Ajax** slightly damaged as they withdraw southeast of Crete. Later that evening *Ajax*, with *Dido*, *Orion* and four destroyers, savage a German troop convoy of small craft. More such vessels are sunk over the next few days off the north coast.

22nd — Early that morning another force of four cruisers and three destroyers sweeps to the north and is attacked on the return. Cruisers **Naiad** and **Carlisle** are damaged, and as they reach their support force to the northwest, **Warspite** is badly hit.

Later on, destroyer **GREYHOUND** is caught on her own in the same area and soon sent to the bottom. Other destroyers go to rescue her survivors, covered by cruisers *Gloucester* and *Fiji*. As the cruisers withdraw, first **GLOUCESTER** is sunk northwest of Crete by Ju87s and Ju88s, and then three hours later **FIJI** is caught by a single Me109 fighter-bomber and sinks to the southwest. All ships are very short of AA ammunition by this stage.

23rd — Withdrawing from the usual night-time patrols leads to the loss of two more destroyers. Capt Lord Louis Mountbatten's five ships are attacked to the south and **KASHMIR** and **KELLY** sunk.

Over the next few days the north coast sweeps continue and supplies and reinforcements are brought into Crete.

26th/27th — Carrier *Formidable*, accompanied by *Barham* and *Queen Elizabeth*, flies off aircraft on the 26th from a position well to the south for an attack on the Scarpanto Island airfields. In the counter-attack **Formidable** and destroyer **Nubian** are damaged. Next day, as **Barham** covers a supply mission, she is hit to the northwest of Alexandria.

28th/29th — The decision to evacuate is made, and cruisers and destroyers prepare to lift off the troops. On the 28th as they approach, **Ajax** and destroyer *Imperial* are damaged to the southeast. Early in the morning of the 29th, 4,000 men are evacuated from Heraklion on the north side. As they do, so the damaged **IMPERIAL** has to be scuttled. **HEREWARD** is hit and left behind to go down off the eastern tip of Crete. Shortly, **Dido** and **Orion** are badly damaged to the southeast.

30th — Early in the day, more troops are lifted from the southern port of Sphakia by another cruiser force. Well to the south the Australian cruiser **Perth** is bombed and damaged.

1st (June) — As the last men are carried from Crete, cruisers *Calcutta* and *Coventry* sail from Alexandria to provide AA cover. **CALCUTTA** is sunk north of the Egyptian coast.

Some 15,000 troops are saved but at a cost to the RN of 2,000 men killed. Total warship casualties are:

	Sunk	Badly damaged
Battleships	—	2
Carriers	—	1
Cruisers	3	5
Destroyers	6	5

The 'L' class submarine *L27* was one of just three boats remaining of the class: none was lost. Completed in 1919 at 760/1,080 tons and able to make 17/10kt, the vessels had four torpedo tubes, a 4in gun and 40 crew. *Real Photos (N1047)*

Battle of the Atlantic

Total U-boat strength is now over 100 with 30 operational and the rest undergoing training or trials. Most are active in the North Atlantic, but a small number are concentrated against the weakly-defended shipping off Freetown and between there and the Canaries. In this area *U107* (Lt-Cdr Hessler) sinks 14 ships of 87,000 tons on one patrol. Other U-boats do almost as well.

RN escort groups can provide cover from UK bases out to 18°W, and those from Iceland the mid-Atlantic gap to 35°W. With the opening of a Newfoundland Escort Force base at St John's by the Royal Canadian Navy, the rest of the North Atlantic convoy routes can now receive protection. However, continuous escort is not yet available. Then, around the 20th, unescorted convoy HX126 from Halifax is attacked at 40°W and loses heavily. Steps are immediately taken and HX129 sailing at the end of the month is the first of the UK-bound convoys to receive regular and continuous cover.

Losses

- 60 ships of 336,000 tons, 1 battlecruiser, 1 destroyer and 1 armed merchant cruiser.
- *Bismarck* and *U110*.

JUNE

2nd — Destroyer *Wanderer* and corvette *Periwinkle* sink *U147* northwest of Ireland during a convoy attack.

Following the capture of the *U110* material, the Royal Navy tracks down the supply ships already in position to support the *Bismarck* as well as other raiders and U-boats. In 20 days, six tankers and three other ships are sunk or captured in the North and South Atlantic. From now, distant water U-boats will have to be supplied by U-boat 'Milchcows' although the first purpose-built ones will not be ready until 1942.

18th — As Force H heads into the Atlantic to help search for the German vessels, they come across one of the U-boats concerned off the Strait of Gibraltar. Screening destroyers *Faulknor, Fearless, Forester, Foresight* and *Foxhound* share in the destruction of *U138*.

In the middle of the month, pocket battleship *Lützow* attempts to break out. Attacked on the 13th off the Norwegian coast by an RAF Beaufort, she is hit by one torpedo and only just makes it back to Germany.

27th — Italian submarine *Glauco* is scuttled west of Gibraltar after being damaged by destroyer *Wishart*.

27th/29th — A total of 10 U-boats attack Halifax/UK convoy HX133 south of Iceland. Five ships are lost but the convoy escort sinks two U-boats. Corvettes *Celandine, Gladiolus* and *Nasturtium* account for *U556* on the 27th, and destroyers *Scimitar* and *Malcolm*, corvettes *Arabis* and *Violet* and minesweeper *Speedwell* sink *U651* on the 29th.

The escort had been reinforced to a total of 13 ships as a result of 'Ultra' intercepts. This, the first of the big convoy battles, leads to the development of additional support groups.

Russian Convoys

The invasion of Russia soon leads to the introduction of the Russian or Arctic convoys with their dreadful conditions and, after some months have elapsed, their high losses in men and ships. However, the RN's presence in the Arctic is first made known in August when submarines start operating, with some success, against German shipping supporting the Axis attack from Norway towards Murmansk. The port is never captured.

Conditions with these convoys are at the very least difficult. Both summer and winter routes are close to good German

JUNE

The report on nuclear research by the Maud Committee leads to the setting up of a development programme by Imperial Chemical Industries. Code named 'Tube Alloys', it will oversee both bomb and reactor work.

10th – Patrol sloop **PINTAIL** is mined off the Humber while escorting Thames/Forth coastal convoy FN477.

Eastern Front

On the 22nd the German attack on Russia (Operation 'Barbarossa') starts with the eventual aim of destroying the Russian Armies and occupying the whole of the country west of the line Archangel in the Arctic to the Caspian Sea. Germany and its Axis partners invade from the Baltic to the Black Sea:

- *North through the Baltic States to Leningrad. Further north still Finland will regain its lost territories;*
- *In the centre through Minsk and Smolensk and on to Moscow;*
- *And in the south towards Kiev and the Crimea Peninsular in the Ukraine, and then to Kharkov and Rostov before heading for Stalingrad and the oilfields of the Caucasus.*

Italy and Roumania declare war on Russia on the 22nd. Finland follows on the 26th and Hungary on the 27th.

Merchant Shipping War

Losses
- 34 ships of 86,000 tons.

MEDITERRANEAN

East Africa

The remaining major Italian forces in northern Ethiopia surrender at Amba Alagi on the 19th. Some resistance continues until November.

Submarine *Upholder* (Lt-Cdr Wanklyn) attacks a strongly escorted troop convoy off the coast of Sicily on the 24th and sinks the 18,000-ton *Conte Rosso*. ✠ Lt-Cdr Malcolm Wanklyn RN is subsequently awarded the Victoria Cross for this and other successful patrols as commander of *Upholder*.

Merchant Shipping War
Losses
● 19 ships of 71,000 tons.

JUNE

With German forces now in Greece and Crete the problems of supplying Malta are even greater. From airfields in Crete as well as Libya they are as close to the eastern basin convoy routes as Sardinia and Sicily are to the western ones. Nevertheless, the men and material are fought through for the defence of Malta and its use as an offensive base.

In the one month of June, *Ark Royal*, once on her own, at other times accompanied by *Furious* or *Victorious*, flies off more than 140 aircraft for Malta. Meanwhile submarines are carrying in urgently needed fuel and stores.

Middle East

Concerned about German influence in Vichy French Lebanon and Syria, British, Dominion and Free French forces invade on the 8th from points in Palestine, Jordan and later Iraq. The Free French enter Damascus on the 21st, but strong resistance continues into July.

16th/25th — During the campaign a RN cruiser and destroyer force, including Australian *Perth* and New Zealand *Leander*, provide close support on the Army's flank. They also fight a series of actions with Vichy French warships as well as German aircraft. A number of destroyers are damaged, but a French destroyer and submarine are sunk.

On the 16th, Fleet Air Arm torpedo-bombers flying from Cyprus sink the large destroyer *Chevalier Paul*, and on the 25th submarine *Parthian* torpedoes submarine *Souffleur*.

North Africa

Another unsuccessful British offensive to relieve Trobruk starts from Sollum on the 15th (Operation 'Battleaxe'). Within two days the operation is called off.

24th/30th — A heavy price has to be paid for the supply of besieged Tobruk by the Royal and Royal Australian Navy ships involved. All trips take place under German and Italian aircraft attack. On the 24th, sloop **AUCKLAND** is lost off Tobruk, and later, on the 30th, Australian destroyer **WATERHEN** of Bardia.

27th — Submarine *Triumph* on patrol off the Egyptian coast sinks the Italian submarine *Salpa*.

Merchant Shipping War
Losses
● 3 ships of 9,000 tons.

HMS *Ark Royal* sinking 30 miles east of Gibraltar on Friday 14 November 1941, one of the many major warships of the Royal Navy lost or damaged worldwide in that month and the next. In June 1941 she had ferried yet more aircraft to Malta. *IWM (A6332)*

ATLANTIC

bases in Norway from which U-boats, aircraft and surface ships can operate. In the long winter months there is terrible weather and intense cold, and in summer, continual daylight. Many consider that no ships will get through.

The first convoy sails in August and, by the end of the year, over 100 merchantmen have set out in both directions. Only one is lost to a U-boat. In 1942 the picture changes considerably.

Battle of the Atlantic
Losses
- 70 ships of 329,000 tons.
- 4 German and 1 Italian U-boats.

JULY

US forces land in Iceland to take over the defence of the island and surrounding seas from Britain.

Battle of the Atlantic
Continuous escort is now being provided for convoys to North America and from West Africa. Three new convoys are introduced — UK/North America fast ONF and slow ONS to replace the OBs and UK/Sierra Leone OS.

Air cover from Ireland, Iceland and Newfoundland is improving, but Coastal Command lacks the aircraft to cover the mid-Atlantic gap. It is in this area, some 800 miles long, that the U-boats are now concentrating.

Until the end of 1941, North Atlantic losses are considerably down on those for the first six months — 104,000 tons as against 300,000 tons per month. The change is due to various reasons. Amongst them are evasive convoy routeing and more effective aircraft deployment from the 'Ultra' work, introduction of radars and HF/DF, and more escorts and continuous escort. Losses due to German aircraft are also well down as many of them transfer to the Russian front.
Losses
- 23 ships of 98,000 tons.

AUGUST

3rd — Southwest of Ireland, ships of the 7th EG escorting Sierra Leone/UK convoy SL81 — destroyers *Wanderer* and Norwegian *St Albans* and corvette *Hydrangea* — sink *U401*.

7th — Submarine *Severn*, on patrol for U-boats attacking HG convoys west of Gibraltar, torpedoes and sinks Italian submarine *Bianchi*.

Winston Churchill travels across the Atlantic in battleship Prince of Wales to meet President Roosevelt off Argentia, Newfoundland between the 9th and 12th. Together they draft the Atlantic Charter setting out their aims for war and peace. This is signed by the United States and 14 Allied governments

EUROPE

JULY
Eastern Front

German forces advance in all sectors, and in the centre capture Minsk, capital of Byelo-Russia and surround Smolensk on the road to Moscow. Russian losses in men and material are immense.

On the 12th, an Anglo-Soviet Mutual Assistance Pact is signed in Moscow. Both countries agree not to seek separate peace negotiations with the Axis powers.

19th – Submarine **UMPIRE**, working up and on passage north with an East Coast convoy, is rammed and sunk off Cromer by an armed trawler escorting a southbound convoy.

RAF Bomber Command badly damages *Scharnhorst* at La Pallice on the 24th. Heavy cruiser *Prinz Eugen* is also damaged in July. With *Gneisenau* in Brest and *Lützow* back in Germany, both undergoing repairs, the main big ship threat is from the new battleship *Tirpitz*.

Merchant Shipping War
Losses
- 18 ships of 15,000 tons.

AUGUST
Eastern Front

The attack north on Leningrad continues. In the centre Smolensk is taken, but the drive on Moscow is halted. Instead, the forces are directed south to help with the capture of Kiev in the Ukraine.

Merchant Shipping War
Losses
- 11 ships of 20,000 tons.

The 'Nelson' class battleship HMS *Rodney* was sister-ship to the *Nelson*. Completed in 1927 and the only British battleships built between the wars, they displaced 34,000 tons, had a relatively low maximum speed of 23kt, but were well armed with nine (sometimes unreliable) 16in guns grouped forward. They had complements of c1,300. *Real Photos (S1131)*

JULY

5th — Submarine *Torbay* on patrol in the Aegean sinks Italian submarine *Jantina*.

11th — On the Tobruk Run, destroyer **DEFENDER** is bombed by German or Italian aircraft and goes down off Sidi Barrani.

Middle East

An Allied/Vichy French armistice signed in the middle of the month brings the fighting in Lebanon and Syria to an end.

20th/30th — Two more submarines fall victim to Italian anti-submarine forces during convoy attacks — **UNION** to torpedo boat *Circe* off Pantellaria on the 20th, and **CACHALOT** 10 days later while on passage from Malta to Alexandria, rammed by torpedo boat *Papa*.

21st-24th — Malta Convoy: Operation 'Substance' — 'Substance' sets out from Gibraltar with six transports covered by Force H with *Ark Royal*, battlecruiser *Renown*, cruisers and destroyers. Battleship *Nelson*, three cruisers and more destroyers reinforce Force H from the Home Fleet. On the 23rd, south of Sardinia, sustained Italian air attacks start. Cruiser **Manchester** is hit and destroyer **FEARLESS** sunk by aircraft torpedoes. Next day the transports reach Malta safely.

On the 26th the Italians launch an attack on Grand Harbour with explosive motor-boats, human torpedoes and aircraft, but fail to reach the recently arrived ships. By the 27th, Force H and a return empty convoy are in Gibraltar. During this operation, Mediterranean Fleet has been carrying out diversionary manoeuvres in the eastern basin.

Merchant Shipping War
Losses
● 2 ships of 8,000 tons.

AUGUST

2nd — Early in the month, two cruisers, cruiser-minelayer *Manxman* and two destroyers successfully carry reinforcements and supplies from Gibraltar to Malta (Operation 'Style'). On the way, cruiser *Hermione* rams to destruction Italian submarine *Tembien* southwest of Sicily on the 2nd.

18th — Submarine **P32** is lost on mines off Tripoli as she attempts to attack a convoy entering the port. **P33** is also lost around the same time in this area, possibly on mines.

26th — As an Italian battlefleet returns from a sortie against Force H, submarine *Triumph* torpedoes and damages heavy cruiser *Bolzano* north of Sicily.

in September. Discussion also takes place on US Navy involvement in the Battle of the Atlantic, which will initially revolve around the supply of US forces in Iceland.

12th — Corvette **PICOTEE** with the 4th EG accompanying convoy ONS4 is detached to search for a reported U-boat south of Iceland. She is sunk without trace by *U568*.

19th/23rd — In a series of attacks on UK/Gibraltar convoy OG71, a total of nine merchantmen are lost. Of the ships with the 5th EG Norwegian destroyer **Bath** is sunk on the 19th by *U204* or *U201*, and corvette **ZINNIA** by U564 to the west of Portugal on the 23rd.

Raider *Orion* returns to France from the Indian Ocean via the Cape of Good Hope. In 16 months she has accounted for 9½ ships of 60,000 tons, some in co-operation with *Komet*.

25th — South of Iceland, armed trawler *Vascama* and a RAF Catalina of No 209 Squadron sink *U452*.

27th — *U570* on patrol south of Iceland surfaces and is damaged by depth charges from an RAF Hudson of No 269 Squadron, piloted by Sqn Ldr Thompson. She soon surrenders and is towed into Iceland. After refitting, *U570* is commissioned into the RN as HMS *Graph*.

The first Russian convoy, 'Dervish', sails from Iceland with seven ships and arrives safely. Carrier *Argus* accompanies them to fly off Hurricanes for Kola.

Battle of the Atlantic

Losses
- 25 ships of 84,000 tons and 3 escorts.
- 3 German and 1 Italian U-boats.

SEPTEMBER

8th — As Italian submarines patrol to the west of Portugal for HG convoys, *Baracca* is depth charged and rammed by destroyer *Croome*. Later in the month, on the 21st, destroyer *Vimy* claims to have sunk *Malaspina* in operations against HG73; she may in fact have been lost earlier through unknown causes.

Escort carrier *Audacity* sails with UK/Gibraltar convoy OG74. Her American-built Martlet fighters shoot down the first Kondor to fall victim to an escort carrier, but U-boats still manage to sink five merchantmen.

10th-19th — Attacks on Halifax/UK convoys southwest of Iceland lead to the first success and loss by Royal Canadian Navy forces in the Battle of the Atlantic. Against SC42, *U501* is sunk by Canadian corvettes *Chambly* and *Moosejaw* on the 10th. Next day RN destroyers *Leamington* and *Veteran* of 2nd EG sink *U207*. SC42 loses 16 of its 64 merchantmen. A few days later, on the 19th, Canadian corvette **LEVIS** with SC44 is lost to *U74* southeast of Cape Farewell.

The USN starts to escort HX and ON convoys between Newfoundland and Mid Ocean Meeting Point, south of Iceland, where the RN takes over. Five US destroyers begin on the 17th with HX150 (50 ships). Earlier on the 4th, the first incident occurs when US destroyer *Greer* on passage to Iceland is in action with *U652*. There is no result.

SEPTEMBER
Eastern Front

In the north the siege of Leningrad is about to start, and will not be lifted completely until early 1944. Kiev in the south is captured and the Centre Army Group released to continue the Moscow offensive. Further south still, the Crimea is cut off and the German forces drive on towards Rostov-on-Don.

Merchant Shipping War

Losses
- 13 ships of 55,000 tons.

MEDITERRANEAN

27th — Covering the transport of troops into and out of besieged Tobruk, cruiser **Phoebe** is hit by an aircraft torpedo.

Middle East

The possibility of a pro-Axis coup d'état leads to Anglo-Soviet forces going into Persia on the 25th from points in Iraq, the Persian Gulf and Russia. A ceasefire is announced within four days, but later violations lead to Tehran being occupied in the middle of September.

With the exception of small parts of Ethiopia, the whole of the Middle East with its vital oilfields and pipelines together with East Africa are now under Allied control.

The landings in Persia from the Gulf are made from a small force of British, Australian and Indian warships of the East Indies Command.

Merchant Shipping War
Losses
● 2 ships of 6,000 tons.

HMS *Sirius*, a 'Dido' class AA cruiser and sister-ship to *Phoebe*, which was torpedoed on 27 August 1941. *IWM (A12798)*

SEPTEMBER

Ark Royal and *Furious* between them fly off over 50 Hurricanes for Malta in two separate operations.

The 10th Submarine Flotilla is formed at Malta with the smaller 'U' class boats which are more suited to Mediterranean conditions. On the 18th, Lt-Cdr Wanklyn in *Upholder* sinks the 19,500-ton transports *Neptunia* and *Oceania*. Between June and the end of September, submarines will have sunk a total of 49 ships of 150,000 tons. Added to the losses inflicted by the RAF this represents a high proportion of Axis shipping bound for Libya.

24th-28th — Malta Convoy: Operation 'Halberd' — 'Halberd' sails from Gibraltar with nine transports. Force H (Adm Somerville), reinforced from the Home Fleet, includes *Nelson*, *Rodney* and *Prince of Wales* and the usual air cover from *Ark Royal*. On the 26th the Italians sail to intercept but return to base the next day. South of Sardinia on the 27th, **Nelson** is damaged by an Italian aircraft torpedo, and at the end of the day Force H turns back for Gibraltar.

Convoy and escort (Rear-Adm H. M. Burrough) go on to reach Malta on the 28th minus one transport lost to air attack.

30th — As Force H returns, screening destroyers *Gurkha* and *Legion* sink Italian submarine *Adua* off the coast of Algeria.

Three major convoys have now reached Malta in 1941 — 'Excess' in January, 'Substance' in July and now 'Halberd'. Nearly 40 merchantmen have got through with only one sunk.

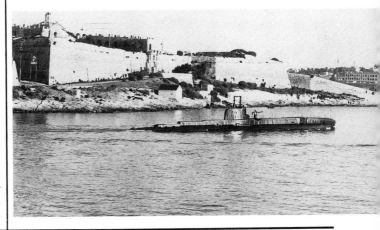

HM Submarine *Sealion*, a prewar 'S' class boat, is seen in Valetta harbour, Malta, which became home of the newly-formed 10th Submarine Flotilla. *Real Photos (S1503)*

Russian convoy PQ1 and the return QP1 both set out in September. A total of 24 ships are passed through without loss by early October.

Battle of the Atlantic

The increased number of U-boats available to Adm Dönitz (approaching 200 with 80 operational) allows him to establish patrol lines. It is into these that the two SCs, 42 and 44, have stumbled with such heavy losses. Convoys SL87 and HG73 also lose badly and the four convoys between them see a total of 36 merchant ships go down.

Losses

- 53 ships of 200,000 tons and 1 escort.
- 2 German and 2 Italian U-boats.

OCTOBER

4th — Supply U-boat *U111* returning from the Cape Verde area is sunk off the Canaries by armed trawler *Lady Shirley*.

14th–27th — Two escorts and two U-boats are lost in attacks on the UK/Gibraltar convoy routes. In operations against Gibraltar-bound OG75, *U206* sinks corvette **FLEUR DE LYS** off the Strait of Gibraltar on the 14th. In the same area on the 19th, *U204* is lost to patrolling corvette *Mallow* and sloop *Rochester*. Six days later Italian submarine *Ferraris* is damaged by a RAF Catalina of No 202 Squadron and sent to the bottom by the gunfire of escort destroyer *Lamerton*.

UK-bound HG75 loses five ships, and on the 23rd the famous destroyer **COSSACK** is torpedoed by *U563*. After struggling in tow for four days she founders to the west of Gibraltar.

16th/18th — In mid-Atlantic, convoy SC48 of 39 ships and 11 stragglers is reinforced by four US destroyers. On the 16th corvette **GLADIOLUS** is torpedoed by *U553* or *U568* and goes down. There are no survivors. Next day the US *Kearny* is damaged by a torpedo from *U568*, and on the 18th destroyer **BROADWATER** is lost to *U101*. Nine merchantmen are sunk.

Convoy HX156 is escorted by another US group, and on the 31st the destroyer **Reuben James** is sunk by *U552*. This first US loss in the Battle of the Atlantic comes only two weeks after the torpedoing of *Kearny*. The United States is virtually at war with Germany.

The six merchant ships of Russian convoy PQ2 get through to Archangel without loss.

Battle of the Atlantic

By now the pattern of escort in the North Atlantic and the involvement of the rapidly growing RCN and the USN is becoming established. With UK-bound convoys, for example, the RCN provides escort from Halifax to the Western Ocean Meeting Point south of Newfoundland. From there, as far as the Mid Ocean Meeting Point at 22°W, the USN escorts HX, and joint RN/RCN groups the slower SC, convoys. RN ships based in Iceland then take over until the convoys are met by Western Approaches escorts operating out of Londonderry and the Clyde.

US Navy and Army Air Force aircraft are now adding to the efforts of the RAF and RCAF by flying escort and patrols from Newfoundland and Iceland. The mid-Atlantic air-gap is narrowing.

Losses

- 33 ships of 160,000 tons and 5 escorts, including US *Reuben James*.
- 2 German and 1 Italian U-boats.

OCTOBER

Eastern Front

As the German forces in the centre approach Moscow, a state of siege is declared, but the offensive is temporarily halted at the end of the month. In the south, Kharkov, east of Kiev in the Ukraine, falls.

Merchant Shipping War

Losses

- 12 ships of 36,000 tons.

A prewar picture of the US battleship *New York*. As the United States waged undeclared war in the North Atlantic in late 1941, ships of the Atlantic Fleet, including *New York*, were on active patrol and covering convoys to Iceland. *IWM (DS595-4)*

MEDITERRANEAN

The RN's losses have been one cruiser and a destroyer sunk, and a battleship, carrier and two cruisers damaged.

27th — Submarine *Upright* sinks Italian torpedo boat *Albatros* off Messina, northeast Sicily.

28th — Corvette *Hyacinth* on patrol off Jaffa, Palestine, sinks Italian submarine *Fisalia*.

Merchant Shipping War
Losses
● 4 ships of 16,000 tons.

OCTOBER

20th — Mines previously laid by submarine *Rorqual* in the Gulf of Athens sink Italian torpedo boats *Aldebaran* and *Altair*.

Force K is formed at Malta to add to the offensive against Axis shipping by submarines and aircraft. Under the command of Capt W. G. Agnew are cruisers *Aurora* and *Penelope* and destroyers *Lance* and *Lively*.

25th — Over a period of 10 days, cruiser-minelayers *Abdiel* and *Latona* transport troops and supplies into besieged Tobruk and carry out Australian units. On the last mission **LATONA** is bombed and sunk north of Bardia by Ju87s.

Late in the month, submarine **TETRARCH** sails from Malta for Gibraltar but fails to arrive, presumed lost on mines in the Strait of Sicily.

Merchant Shipping War
Losses
● 6 ships of 22,000 tons.

HMS *Barham* turns over with her magazines exploding after being hit by three torpedoes to the north of Sidi Barrani on Tuesday 25 November 1941. Over 800 men were killed but many others were saved — but *Barham* is another of the heavy losses in men and ships of the Royal Navy to come in November and December 1941. *IWM (FLM1984)*

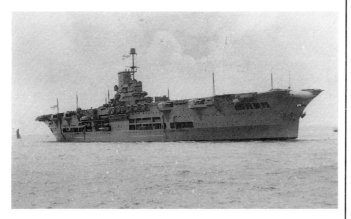

An early picture of the fleet carrier HMS *Ark Royal* (lost in November 1941). The only carrier built between the wars for the Royal Navy, completed in 1938, she displaced 22,000 tons, carried 60 aircraft and 1,570 crew, and could make a speed of 31kt *Real Photos (S1468)*

ATLANTIC

NOVEMBER

3rd — The recently completed fleet carrier **Indomitable** runs aground and is damaged off Kingston, Jamaica. She is due to accompany the *Prince of Wales* and *Repulse* to the Far East.

19th — Far across the Indian Ocean off Western Australia, the Australian cruiser *Sydney* comes across German raider *Kormoran*. Apparently caught unawares, **SYDNEY** is mortally damaged and lost without trace. *Kormoran* also goes down. In a cruise lasting 12 months she has sunk or captured 11 other ships of 68,000 tons.

22nd/24th — While replenishing *U126* north of Ascension Island, raider *Atlantis* is surprised and sunk by heavy cruiser *Devonshire*. The raider's operations in the Atlantic and Indian Oceans have cost the Allies 22 merchantmen of 146,000 tons.

On her way to rescue *Atlantis* survivors, *U124* encounters cruiser **DUNEDIN** on patrol off the St Paul's Rocks, half way between Africa and South America. The cruiser is sunk on the 24th with heavy loss of life.

Komet returns to Germany through the Atlantic having reached the Pacific across the top of Siberia some 17 months earlier. Her score is just 6½ ships, some of them with *Orion*.

As the completed *Tirpitz*, sister-ship to *Bismarck*, prepares for operations, units of the Home Fleet sail for Iceland waters to cover any possible breakout. They are supported by a US battle squadron.

RAF aircraft of Coastal Command are now flying regular patrols in the Bay of Biscay equipped with effective airborne depth charges and the long wavelength ASV radar. The first success is by a Whitley of No 502 Squadron on the 30th. *U206* on passage to the Mediterranean is detected and sunk.

In November Russian convoys PQ3/4/5 and return convoys QP2/3 with a total of 45 ships set out. Three turn back but the rest get through without loss.

Battle of the Atlantic

There is a considerable drop in U-boat sinkings in the North Atlantic in the last two months of the year; again the reasons are varied. On one hand there is the increasing number of escorts, the help given by the US Navy, and the increasing effectiveness of land-based aircraft. Escort carrier *Audacity* is also proving her worth. On the other the Allies are helped by Hitler's orders to Adm Dönitz to transfer large numbers of U-boats to the Mediterranean. These are needed to shore up the Italians and help secure the supply lines to the Axis armies in North Africa.

This movement has led to a concentration of U-boats off Gibraltar, and to the need to strengthen the HG/SL convoy escorts. After the attacks on HG75 in October, the next HG does not sail until December when *Audacity* is available to close the Britain/Gibraltar air gap.

Losses
- 11 ships of 55,000 tons and 1 cruiser.
- 2 raiders, 1 German U-boat and 1 Italian (cause unknown).

EUROPE

NOVEMBER
Eastern Front

The German advance on Moscow is restarted and soon troops are on the outskirts of the Russian capital. In the south they have driven right into the Crimea. Only Sevastopol holds out and the siege lasts until June. Further east Rostov-on-Don is captured, but the Russians re-take the city.

Merchant Shipping War
Losses
- 20 ships of 30,000 tons.

INDIAN AND PACIFIC OCEANS — STARTING CONDITIONS

Events until November 1941

Since November 1939 when the *Graf Spee* first entered the Indian Ocean, German raiders have hunted there and in the Pacific. The Royal and Dominion Navies have not only been busy tracking them down, but also escorting troops of Australia, India, New Zealand and other members of the British Empire to the theatres of war. All this time Japan has manoeuvred to complete the conquest of China.

By the end of 1938, northeast China as far south as Shanghai, together with the major ports, is in Japanese hands. In February 1939 it occupies the large island of Hainan in the South China Sea. By early 1940, events are moving inexorably towards a total world war:

1940

March – Japan establishes a Chinese puppet-government in Nanking.

June/July – With its possession of the Chinese ports, Japan wants to close the remaining entry points into the country. Pressure is put on France to stop the flow of supplies through Indo-China, and on Britain to do the same with the Burma Road. Both comply, but Britain does so only until October, when the road is re-opened.

September – Vichy France finally agrees to the stationing of Japanese troops in the north of Indo-China.

1941

April – Five Year Neutrality Pact between Japan and Russia benefits both powers. Russia can free some troops for Europe and Japan concentrate on expansion southwards.

July – The demand for bases in southern Indo-China is now conceded. Britain, Holland and the United States protest and

NOVEMBER

9th — Action off Cape Spartivento, Southwest Italy — RAF reports of an Italian convoy in the Ionian Sea making for North Africa leads to Force K sailing. The convoy consists of seven transports escorted by six destroyers and with a distant cruiser covering force. Early in the morning every one of the transports and destroyer *Fulmine* are sent to the bottom. Later, while rescuing survivors, destroyer *Libeccio* is sunk by submarine *Upholder*.

13th/16th — As Force H returns to Gibraltar after flying off more Hurricanes from *Ark Royal* and *Argus* for Malta, **ARK ROYAL** is hit by one torpedo from *U81*. Next day she founders in tow only a few miles east of her base. One man is killed.

U81 is one of four U-boats that have just passed into the Mediterranean. A second one, *U433*, is sunk in the same area by corvette *Marigold* on the 16th. Then, towards the end of the month, Dutch submarine *O21* sinks *U95*. Between late September and December, 26 U-boats break through into the Mediterranean and for many months take a heavy toll of RN ships.

North Africa

A major British offensive (Operation 'Crusader') starts on the 18th, again from the Sollum area, and by January has reached El Agheila. Axis forces around Sollum and Bardia are by-passed in the drive on Tobruk. The first link-up with the besieged garrison is made by New Zealand troops on the 27th.

27th — Australian sloop **PARRAMATTA** escorting an ammunition ship on the Tobruk Run is sunk by *U559* off the port. Since the siege started destroyers and other warships have been carrying in men and supplies almost nightly. As it comes to an end the cost can be counted — 25 warships of all sizes and five merchantmen lost.

25th — Force K hunts for Italian convoys to North Africa supported by the Mediterranean Fleet with battleships *Barham*, *Queen Elizabeth* and *Valiant*. In the afternoon, north of Sidi Barrani, **BARHAM** is hit by three torpedoes from *U331* and explodes as she capsizes. Over 800 men are lost with her.

Just before this tragedy, Force K has sunk two more Axis supply ships west of Crete. At this stage 60% of Axis North African supplies are being lost to attacks by British aircraft, submarines and warships.

East Africa

The last Italian forces surrender at Gondar in the north of Ethiopia on the 27th. The Italian East African empire ceases to exist.

Merchant Shipping War
Losses
● 4 ships of 19,000 tons.

---

freeze Japanese assets, but the troops go in. The Dutch East Indies cancels oil delivery arrangements and the Americans shortly impose their own oil embargo. Japan has lost most of its sources of oil.
September – Japan and the US continue to negotiate over their differences, but as its oil stocks rapidly decline Japan accelerates preparations for war.
October – War Minister Gen Tojo becomes Japanese Prime Minister. (Following the resignation of Australian Prime Minister Robert Menzies in August, his Country Party falls in October. John Curtin and the Labour Party come to power.)
November – As talks drag on and the United States demands the departure of Japan from China as well as French Indo-China, the Pearl Harbor Strike Force sails into the North Pacific. Vice-Adm Nagumo commands the fleet carriers *Akagi*, *Hiryu*, *Kaga*, *Soryu*, *Shokaku* and *Zuikaku*, plus two battleships, cruisers and destroyers.

Britain's limited naval deterrent to Japanese expansion, capital ships *Prince of Wales* and *Repulse* meet at Colombo on the 28th, en route to Singapore. Without the *Indomitable* they have no carrier aircraft support.

Strategic and Naval Background

Britain and Dominions – Responsible for defending India, Ceylon, Burma, Malaya, northern Borneo, Hong Kong, Australia, New Zealand, the Papua, New Guinea/Bismarck Archipelago/Solomon Islands chain, and numerous island groups throughout the Indian Ocean and Central and South Pacific.

Few forces can be spared from existing war zones to protect this vast spread of territory and its supply routes. Britain's main base is at Singapore with its two recently arrived big ships. Three old cruisers and some destroyers are in Malayan waters, and a few old destroyers at Hong Kong. By now the surviving seven cruisers and smaller ships of the Royal Australian and New Zealand Navies are back in the area.

United States – Apart from the defence of its Western seaboard, Panama Canal Zone, Alaska and the Aleutians, Hawaiian Islands and various islands in the Central Pacific, the US has responsibilities towards the Philippines. In the event of attack, they are expected to hold out until relieved by the US Pacific Fleet fighting its way from the main base at Pearl Harbor, a distance of 4,500 miles.

In the Philippines is the Asiatic Fleet with three cruisers, 13 destroyers and 29 submarines. The Pacific Fleet itself consists of eight battleships, three fleet carriers, 21 cruisers, 67 destroyers and 27 submarines.

Dutch – Naval forces allocated to the defence of the many islands of the Dutch East Indies include three cruisers, seven destroyers and fifteen submarines.

Japan – Already established in Korea, Manchuria, northeast China, its main ports and Hainan, Formosa, and the Mariana, Caroline and Marshall Island groups, Japan now has the whole of French Indo-China. Japan's main aim is still the conquest of China, for which the oilfields of the Dutch East Indies (DEI) are indispensable. Also important is the closing of the Burma Road over which Allied supplies continue to roll.

Both moves mean war with Britain and the US, and a vital part of the Japanese strategy is the establishment of a huge defence perimeter stretching from Burma right around to the Aleutians. Only in this way can it hope to hold off the United States once its manpower and industrial resources are mobilised.

Japan goes to war with both the strategic and military advantages:
● Strategically she is well placed to occupy the territory needed for the defence lines:
In the north, much of China is occupied and the Neutrality Pact with Russia, coupled with the German invasion means Japan has little to fear for now from this direction. Hong Kong can be taken easily from adjacent occupied China.

To the west, Thailand and Malaya will soon fall to the invading forces from Hainan and Indo-China. Thereafter the capture of Burma can proceed smoothly. The Burma Road will be cut, India threatened, and that perimeter is secured.

In the south lay the oilfields of the DEI and the protection offered by the island chain of Sumatra, Java and Bali through to Timor. Java, the main island is the target of two massive pincer movements:

West
From Indo-China to northern Borneo, and later direct to Sumatra and Java.

East
From bases in Formosa and the Carolines to the Philippines. From there to southern Borneo, Celebes and Moluccas, and on to Timor and Bali. Then to eastern Java.

Southeastwards, landings in north New Guinea, the Bismarck Archipelago and northern Solomons will protect the Japanese Carolines. From there, forces can strike Australia and its supply routes.

Finally, to the east are the vast distances of the Pacific. By taking the US islands of Guam and Wake, and some of the British Gilberts, the mandated islands are further protected. America is also kept at bay.

Only when Japan seeks to extend the last two parts of its perimeter in mid-1942 does it suffer the first defeats. America's growing power will then make Allied victory inevitable.

● Militarily, Allied and Japanese naval forces are about balanced in numbers:

| | ALLIES | | | | | JAPAN |
	Royal Navies	Dutch East Indies	US Asiatic Fleet	US Pacific Fleet	Totals	Total
Battleships	2	—	—	8	10	10
Carriers	—	—	—	3	3	11
Cruisers	10	3	3	21	37	40
Destroyers	13	7	13	67	100	112
Submarines	—	15	29	27	71	63
Totals	25	25	45	126	221	236

ATLANTIC

DECEMBER

7th — Canadian corvette WINDFLOWER with Halifax/UK convoy SC58 is lost in collision with the ss *Zypenburg* east of Newfoundland.

15th-21st — Battle for Convoy HG76 — Gibraltar/UK convoy HG76 (32 ships) is escorted by the 36th EG (Cdr F. J. Walker) and with a support group that includes the escort carrier *Audacity*. In advance of the convoy leaving Gibraltar, destroyers of Force H, including the Australian *Nestor*, locate and destroy *U127* on the 15th. In the four days from the 17th, four more U-boats are sunk for the loss of two of the escorts and two merchantmen. The battle takes place to the far west of Portugal, north of Madeira and the Azores:

17th — *U131* to destroyers *Blankney*, *Exmoor* and *Stanley*, corvette *Pentstemon* and sloop *Stork*, together with Grumman Martlets from *Audacity*.

18th — *U434* to *Blankney* and *Stanley*.

19th — STANLEY is sunk by *U574*, which is then sent to the bottom by *Stork* through ramming.

21st — AUDACITY is torpedoed by *U751* and lost, but in the general counter-attack *U567* is sunk by corvette *Samphire* and sloop *Deptford*.

The sinking of five U-boats in exchange for two merchant ships is a significant victory for the escorts, and proves beyond any doubt the value of escort carrier aircraft against the submarine — and against the patrolling Kondors, two of which are shot down.

Three Russian convoys — PQ6/7/7B — and one return — QP4 — with a total of 31 ships set out in December. All but PQ6 arrive at their destinations in January, with two returns and one lost to U-boats.

Battle of the Atlantic
Losses
● 11 ships of 57,000 tons, 1 escort carrier and 2 escorts.
● 5 German U-boats, and two transferring to the Mediterranean.

EUROPE

DECEMBER
Eastern Front

As the Germans halt outside Moscow, the Russians launch a major counter-offensive from near Leningrad in the north to as far south as Kharkov. By April 1942 they have regained much lost territory, but few major cities. The siege of Leningrad itself continues.

In a series of diplomatic moves, numerous declarations of war are made:
5th/6th – Britain, Australia, Canada, New Zealand and South Africa on Finland, Hungary and Roumania.
11th-13th – Germany, Italy, Roumania, Bulgaria and Hungary on the United States.
28th-14th (January) – Britain, Australia, New Zealand and South Africa on Bulgaria.

Separate commando raids take place in northern Norway on the Lofoten Islands and further south on Vaagsö Island. Their aim is to destroy installations and sink and capture shipping. The first force is led by cruiser *Arethusa* with limited results. The second with cruiser *Kenya* is more successful. On the 27th **Arethusa** is damaged by bombing.

26th – By this date the old submarine **H31** is overdue, possibly lost on mines during her Bay of Biscay patrol.

Merchant Shipping War
Losses
● 19 ships of 57,000 tons.

There the comparison ends. The Imperial Japanese Navy has far more carriers, its surface task forces are well trained, espcially in night-fighting, and they have no command or language difficulties. They also introduce the Allies to a secret and powerful weapon in the 24in Long Lance torpedo. In contrast, the Allied ships are scattered and have no central command. Their main bases at Singapore and Pearl Harbor are 6,000 miles apart, and most of the strength is concentrated with the US Pacific Fleet.

For its conquests, the Japanese Army fields only slightly more troops, but these are usually better trained, and also experienced in amphibious operations. They have air superiority both overall and locally. Only the US Pacific Fleet poses an immediate danger to Japanese plans. Hence the decision to attack it in Pearl Harbor rather than wait for it to try to fight through to the Philippines.

The Japanese choose the time and place of their landings, all well escorted by cruiser and destroyer forces. Air cover is maintained by land-based aircraft or from carriers and seaplane carriers as necessary, and battleships and cruisers provide distant support. By this time the annihilation of the Allied capital ships will make their presence unnecessary.

The few Allied sorties — some surface, but mainly by aircraft and submarine — have few successes against the invasion fleets. And in return they suffer heavy losses.

MEDITERRANEAN

DECEMBER

1st — Force K, out searching for Axis shipping, encounters Italian destroyer *Da Mosto* north of Tripoli. She is sunk by cruisers *Aurora* and *Penelope* and destroyer *Lively*. By now Force K has been reinforced by cruisers *Ajax* and *Neptune* and two more destroyers.

6th — Submarine **PERSEUS** on patrol off the west coast of Greece goes down on a mine off Zante Island. One man escapes to the surface and reaches the shore.

11th — Submarine *Truant* sinks Italian torpedo boat *Alcione* north of Crete. On the same day escort destroyer *Farndale*, on passage, sights the submarine *Caracciolo* on a supply trip from Bardia and sinks her.

11th/21st — As more German U-boats transfer to the Mediterranean, two are lost. Corvette *Bluebell* sinks *U208* as she leaves her Atlantic patrol area to the west of Gibraltar. Ten days later, Swordfish of 812 Squadron flying from Gibraltar sink *U451* in the Strait. These aircraft managed to get away from the sinking *Ark Royal* and play an important part in patrolling the waters in which their ship went down.

13th — Action off Cape Bon, Tunisia — Destroyers *Legion*, *Maori*, *Sikh* and Dutch *Isaac Sweers* under the command of Cdr G. H. Stokes sail from Gibraltar to join the Mediterranean Fleet at Alexandria. Off Cape Bon they come across two Italian 6in cruisers, *Da Barbiano* and *Di Giussano*, which have turned back from trying to carry a deck cargo of petrol to Tripoli. In a short night action and without being seen the destroyers quickly sink both cruisers with gunfire and torpedoes. Loss of life is heavy.

North Africa

As fighting continues around Tobruk, Rommel decides to pull back to Gazala. Besieged Tobruk is completely relieved on the 10th. Under pressure, the Afrika Korps subsequently withdraws to El Agheila and on the 25th British forces enter Benghazi.

INDIAN & PACIFIC OCEANS

DECEMBER

Because of the International Dateline, events that take place on the 7th in Hawaii, as far as Washington and London are concerned, are already into the 8th in Hong Kong and Malaya. By the 8th:

● *Japan has declared war on Britain and the US;*

● *Britain, Australia, Canada, New Zealand, South Africa, Holland, the United States and a number of Central American and Caribbean states have declared against Japan;*

● *China declares against the Axis powers.*

Hong Kong

The territory is invaded from mainland China on the 8th, and within five days the defenders have withdrawn to Hong Kong Island. Fighting carries on until Christmas Day when the British and Dominion troops surrender.

Destroyer **THRACIAN** is bombed in defence of the colony and later beached and abandoned. She is re-commissioned into the Japanese Navy as a patrol boat.

West — Thailand, Malaya and Burma

Japanese forces land on the Kra Isthmus of Thailand as well as northeast Malaya on the 8th. From there they start the drive down the west coast towards Singapore, outflanking the defences by land and sea. Follow-up landings take place later in the month and in January.

By the 13th they have crossed from Thailand into the southern tip of Burma, but stay there for the time being.

10th — Sinking of Force Z — By the 8th, *Prince of Wales* and *Repulse* have assembled at Singapore as Force Z under the command of Adm Sir Tom Phillips. That evening they sail with four destroyers to attack the Japanese landing on the northeast coast. Fighter cover is requested but is not readily available.

In the evening of the 9th, Force Z is well up into the South China Sea. Japanese aircraft are spotted and Adm Phillips decides to return. Around midnight he receives a false report of landings at Kuantan, well down the Malay Peninsular, and sets course for there. The ships have by now been reported by a submarine, and a naval aircraft strike force is despatched from Indo-China. Attacks start around 11.00 on the 10th, and in less than three hours **PRINCE OF WALES** and **REPULSE** have been hit by a number of torpedoes and sent to the bottom. Nearly a thousand men are lost, but 2,000 are picked up by the destroyers.

With this tragedy and the Pearl Harbor attack, not one of the Allies' 10 battleships in the Pacific area remain in service.

South — Northern Borneo and Philippines

The first landings in northern Borneo take place in Sarawak and Brunei on the 16th, and continue through until late January.

In the Philippines, the island of Luzon is the main target. Between the 10th and 22nd, landings take place in the north, the south and at Lingayen Gulf in the west. The Japanese all drive on the capital of Manila, which is declared an open city. They enter there on 2 January, by which time preparations are being made to attack Gen MacArthur's US and Filipino troops now withdrawn into the Bataan Peninsular just to the west of Manila. The southern island of Mindanao is invaded on 20 December.

MEDITERRANEAN

14th-19th — First Battle of Sirte and Related Actions —
Italian convoy operations to Libya lead directly or indirectly to major RN losses over just a few days.

An Axis convoy for Benghazi sets out on the 13th, covered by an Italian battlefleet. On receiving this news, Rear-Adm Vian leaves Alexandria with a cruiser force to join up with Force K. On the evening of the 14th, submarine *Urge* torpedoes and damages battleship *Vittorio Veneto* off the Strait of Messina and the Italians cancel that operation. The cruiser forces return to their bases and as they do, Adm Vian's **GALATEA** is hit by three torpedoes from *U557* and goes down off Alexandria late that night.

Adm Vian goes out again later on the 15th to escort fast supply ship *Breconshire* to Malta. On the 17th they are met by Force K off the Gulf of Sirte, and shortly encounter Italian battleships covering another convoy to Tripoli. The combined cruisers attack and the Italians withdraw in what becomes known as the First Battle of Sirte.

Breconshire reaches Malta on the 18th and Force K leaves harbour to search for the Italian convoy still making for Tripoli. Early on the 19th, off the port the ships run into a minefield. Cruiser **NEPTUNE** hits three or four and sinks with only one man surviving. *Aurora* is badly damaged and **Penelope** slightly. Trying to reach *Neptune*, destroyer **KANDAHAR** is mined and has to be scuttled the following day. Only three destroyers escape damage.

Still in the morning of the 19th, three Italian human torpedoes from submarine *Sciré* (Cdr Borghese) penetrate Alexandria harbour. Their charges badly damage **Queen Elizabeth** with Adm Cunningham on board and **Valiant**. They both settle to the bottom and the Mediterranean Fleet battle squadron ceases to exist, although news of the sinking is kept from the Italians.

23rd-28th — A sizeable number of German U-boats are now
operating off the coasts of Egypt and Libya and attacking convoys, with losses to both sides. On the 23rd, escorting destroyers *Hasty* and *Hotspur* sink *U79* off Tobruk. Next day off Mersa Matruh, corvette **SALVIA** is lost to *U568*. Four days later, in the same area, destroyer *Kipling* accounts for *U75*.

Merchant Shipping War
Losses
- 9 ships of 37,000 tons.

INDIAN & PACIFIC OCEANS

East — Hawaii, Guam, Wake and Gilberts

On the morning of the 7th, local time (shortly after the Malayan landings), the Japanese Strike Force aircraft hit Pearl Harbor. Battleships Arizona and Oklahoma are total losses, three more sink but are later re-commissioned, and the remaining three damaged. Many are killed and a considerable number of aircraft destroyed. Although the Pacific battlefleet ceases to exist, the three fleet carriers are very fortunately absent and the large oil stocks and important repair installations left virtually untouched.

By the 10th, Guam in the Mariana Islands is captured and Makin and Tarawa in the British Gilberts occupied. Tarawa is then abandoned until the following September.

Wake Island is attacked on the 11th, but the Japanese are driven off by the US Marine defenders and two of their destroyers sunk. A later attempt on the 23rd succeeds.

Merchant Shipping War
Summary of Allied Losses
- Indian Ocean — 5 British, Allied and neutral merchant ships of 800 tons.
- Pacific — 241 ships of 432,000 tons.

DEFENCE OF TRADE — JANUARY TO DECEMBER 1941

Summary of Losses

North Atlantic 496 ships of 2,423,000 tons.	*UK waters* 350 ships of 740,000 tons.	*Mediterranean* 158 ships of 501,000 tons.	*Indian Ocean* 20 ships of 73,000 tons.
South Atlantic 29 ships of 134,000 tons.			*Pacific Ocean* 246 ships of 458,000 tons.

Submarines	432 ships of 2,172,000 tons.
Aircraft	371 ships of 1,017,000 tons.
Other causes	272 ships of 421,000 tons.
Mines	111 ships of 231,000 tons.
Raiders	44 ships of 227,000 tons.
Warships	40 ships of 202,000 tons.
Coastal forces	29 ships of 59,000 tons.

= 1,299 British, Allied and neutral ships of 4,329,000 tons: ie 361,000 tons per month.

ATLANTIC

JANUARY

Arcadia Conference

In late December and early January, Winston Churchill and President Roosevelt with their Chiefs of Staff meet in Washington DC. They agree to the setting up of a Combined Chiefs of Staff Committee and to the defeat of Germany as the first priority. On 1 January the United Nations Pact embodying the principles of the Atlantic Charter is signed in Washington by 26 countries.

The German big ships give the Admiralty much cause for concern. *Scharnhorst*, *Gneisenau* and *Prinz Eugen*, all now repaired, are ready for a possible break-out from Brest into the Atlantic. At the same time the new battleship *Tirpitz* moves to Trondheim in the middle of the month from where she can prey on the Russian convoys. In fact Hitler has ordered the Brest squadron back to Germany. By early February the Admiralty has got wind of the proposed Channel Dash and prepares accordingly.

Raider *Thor* sails from France for her second cruise. She is the only raider to do so successfully. Operations in the South Atlantic and Indian Ocean continue until her loss in November. No German raiders have been at sea since the previous November, and *Thor* is the first of three to break out in 1942. In the first six months of the year they sink or capture 17 ships of 107,000 tons.

15th — Destroyer *Hesperus* escorting convoy HG78 sinks *U93* north of Madeira.

17th — Destroyer **MATABELE** escorting Iceland/Russia convoy PQ8 is sunk off Murmansk by *U454*. Only two men survive. None of the eight merchantmen in the convoy are lost although one is damaged by a U-boat torpedo. In two return convoys in the month — QP5 and QP6 — 10 ships set out to arrive safely.

31st — Canadian troop convoy NA2 sailing for Britain is attacked by *U82* southeast of Nova Scotia. Destroyer **BELMONT** is lost with all hands.

31st — Ex-US Coast Guard cutter **CULVER** is sunk by *U105* west of the Bay of Biscay as she escorts Sierra Leone convoy SL93.

Battle of the Atlantic

U-boat strength is up to 250 with 90 operational. Two-thirds are spread across the Atlantic, nearly a quarter in the Mediterranean, and a few on patrol in the Arctic for Russian convoys. It is at this time that Adm Dönitz, with never more than 10 or 12 U-boats at a time, launches Operation 'Paukenschlag' ('Drumroll') off the coasts of America. The U-boat commanders enjoy their second 'Happy Time', especially against the unescorted ships sailing in virtually peace-time conditions off the United States. Warship patrols are started, but the USN finds it hard to accept the long, hard-fought lessons of the RN and establish convoys immediately.

Atlantic convoys still start and end at Nova Scotia so the first U-boats operate off the Canadian coast south of there. Over 40 merchantmen are lost in this area alone in January and February. By this time U-boats are also sinking many ships off the US east coast.

On the weapons front, the forward-firing Hedgehog with its 24 A/S mortar bombs starts to enter RN service. Its first success does not come until late in the year.

Losses, including Russian Convoys

- 48 British, Allied and neutral ships of 277,000 tons in the North and South Atlantic, and 3 escorts.
- 1 U-boat

EUROPE

JANUARY

RAF Bomber Command carries on its offensive against Germany and occupied Europe. Attacks are made in January on Bremen, Emden and Hamburg and the big ships in Brest.

The 'Final Solution' for the extermination of all European Jews is presented to Hitler. As large-scale transportation gets underway, a number of main camps, including Auschwitz, are prepared for this foul work. By war's end, 6,000,000 men, women and children will have been killed.

First United States' troops land in Northern Ireland.

Eastern Front

The Russian advance continues to make headway. In the centre it reaches to within 70 miles of Smolensk. To the south the forces drive a deep salient into the German lines south of Kharkov. German resistance grows as the Russians begin to over-extend themselves.

Merchant Shipping War

E-boats and aircraft continue to attack coastal convoy routes directly and with magnetic and acoustic mines. Convoy escorts and minesweepers fight back, supported by RAF Fighter Command, but they have their losses:

9th – Escorting a southbound East Coast convoy, destroyer **VIMIERA** is mined and sunk in the Thames Estuary.

Losses

- 14 ships of 19,000 tons in UK waters.

MEDITERRANEAN

JANUARY

Submarine **TRIUMPH** sails from Alexandria on 26 December for a cloak-and-dagger landing near Athens before patrolling in the Aegean. She reports the landing on the 30th, but fails to rendezvous back there on the 9th and is presumed mined off the island of Milo, southeast of the Greek mainland.

Three Axis submarines fall victim to their RN counterparts in different patrol areas:

5th — Italian *Saint-Bon* north of Sicily to Lt-Cdr Wanklyn's *Upholder*.

12th — German *U374* off the east coast of Sicily to *Unbeaten* (Lt-Cdr E. A. Woodward).

30th — Italian *Medusa* to *Thorn* in the Gulf of Venice, right up in the Adriatic.

17th — During the month, Malta is resupplied by three small convoys coming from the east. In the second one, four fast transports leave Alexandria covered by Adm Vian's Mediterranean Fleet cruiser force. On the 17th one of the close escorting destroyers, **GURKHA (2)**, is torpedoed north of Sidi Barrani by *U133* and is scuttled. Next day the surviving ships are met by *Penelope* of Force K from Malta, and get there on the 19th.
   During this period the Italian Navy has been able to escort two substantial convoys to North Africa in time for Rommel's next offensive. Malta continues to be heavily bombed for many months by the German and Italian Air Forces.

North Africa

By the 6th the British advance has reached the German and Italian lines at El Agheila. Just two weeks later, on the 21st, Rommel starts his second campaign. The first of two phases takes him as far as Gazala, just to the west of Tobruk.
   El Agheila soon falls and Benghazi is occupied before the month is out. On 1 February Eighth Army withdraws to Gazala and within a week Rommel has come up. There he stays until May.

Merchant Shipping War
Losses
● 1 ship of 7,000 tons.

A German 'T' type escort torpedo boat operating in the English Channel during 1942. *Real Photos (S1855)*

INDIAN & PACIFIC OCEANS

JANUARY

Early in the month, Gen Wavell is appointed to command ABDA (American, British, Dutch, Australian) forces responsible for holding Malaya and the DEI.

West — Malaya and Burma

In their drive on Singapore, the Japanese capture Kuala Lumpur on the 11th. To the north they cross into southern Burma from the Kra Isthmus on the 15th, and on the 20th start the invasion proper of Burma from central Thailand. Thailand shortly declares war on Britain and the United States.
   On the last day of January, the retreating British, Australian and Indian troops withdraw into Singapore Island, having been driven down the length of the Malay Peninsula.

27th — Two old destroyers, the *Thanet* and Australian *Vampire*, attack well-protected troop transports off Endau, southeast Malaya. **THANET** is sunk by the 5.5in cruiser *Sendai* and a number of destroyers.
   Around this time *Indomitable* flies off 48 Hurricanes for Singapore via Java.

17th — Japanese submarine *I60* tries to pass through the Sunda Strait for the Indian Ocean. She is located and sunk by destroyer *Jupiter* escorting a convoy to Singapore.

South — Philippines and Dutch East Indies

As the US and Filipinos are slowly pushed into Bataan, the Japanese begin the invasion of the Dutch East Indies from southern Philippines. First landings take place on the 11th at Tarakan in Borneo and in the Celebes. More follow later in the month, but which time they have reached the Moluccas in the drive south towards Java.

20th — Submarine *I124*, minelaying off Darwin, northern Australia, is sunk by Australian minesweepers *Deloraine*, *Katoomba* and *Lithgow* and US destroyer *Edsall*.

Southeast — Bismark Archipelago

The Japanese's first move towards the southeast takes place on the 23rd with landings at Kavieng (New Ireland) and Rabaul (New Britain). Rabaul will become the major Japanese base in the South West Pacific and help dictate the whole strategy of Allied moves in the next two years.

Merchant Shipping War
Losses
● Indian Ocean — 13 ships of 46,000 tons.
● Pacific — 30 ships of 71,000 tons.

ATLANTIC

FEBRUARY

2nd — As she attacks a damaged troopship sailing from the Azores, *U581* is sunk by the escorting destroyer *Westcott*.

6th — Returning from the American coast where she sank the *Belmont*, *U82* encounters UK/Sierra Leone convoy OS18 north of the Azores and is destroyed by corvette *Tamarisk* and sloop *Rochester*.

5th/11th — *U136* on patrol off Rockall sinks two escorts. On the 5th, corvette **ARBUTUS** is detached with destroyer *Chelsea* from UK/Halifax convoy ONS63 to hunt for a U-boat and is sunk by *U136*. Less than a week later Canadian corvette **SPIKENARD** falls victim to her while escorting Halifax/UK convoy SC67.

23rd — Following the Channel Dash, *Prinz Eugen* sails with pocket battleship *Admiral Scheer* to join *Tirpitz* in Norway. Off Trondheim, submarine *Trident* torpedoes and heavily damages the heavy cruiser.

In four Russian convoys — PQ9, PQ10 and PQ11 and the return QP7 — 31 merchantmen arrive safely at their destination without loss.

Battle of the Atlantic
U-boats extend Operation 'Paukenschlag' to the Caribbean and start by shelling installations and sinking tankers off Aruba, Curacoa, Trinidad and other oil ports. However, they are still active elsewhere in the Atlantic, and east of Newfoundland five of them attack convoy ON67 (36 ships). Eight ships are lost, six of them tankers.

The RN suffers a setback when U-boats in the Atlantic change from the Enigma 'Hydra' code to 'Triton', which will not be broken until December. But all is not lost as they still use 'Hydra' in European waters. This, together with signals traffic analysis and the vast amount of experience built up to date, means that remarkably accurate pictures can be drawn of U-boat operations and intentions.

Losses
- 73 ships of 430,000 tons, 2 corvettes and 2 US destroyers off Newfoundland and the US east coast.
- 2 U-boats.

EUROPE

FEBRUARY

11th–13th — The Channel Dash – The Brest Squadron (Vice-Adm Ciliax) with *Scharnhorst*, *Gneisenau* and *Prinz Eugen*, heavily escorted by air and other naval forces, leaves late on the 11th for Germany (Operation 'Cerberus'). The aim is to pass through the Strait of Dover around noon the next day. A number of unfortunate problems conspire to prevent the RAF standing patrols detecting their departure.

The first intimation of them comes with a RAF report around 10.45 on the 12th as they steam towards Boulogne. This leaves little time for attacks to be mounted. Soon after midday the first are made by five motor torpedo boats from Dover and six Swordfish of 825 Squadron (Lt-Cdr Esmonde), but without any hits. All Swordfish are shot down. ✠ Lt-Cdr Eugene Esmonde is posthumously awarded the Victoria Cross.

From then on, events move swiftly. At 14.30 off the Scheldt, *Scharnhorst* is slightly damaged by a mine. An hour later, torpedo attacks by six destroyers from Harwich are unsuccessful. Twenty minutes later a heavy attack by the RAF fails. The German ships continue, and in the early evening off the Dutch Frisian Islands, first *Gneisenau* and then *Scharnhorst* (for the second time) hit mines. Both are damaged, but together with *Prinz Eugen* reach German ports in the early hours of the 13th.

The escape proves embarrassing to the British Government, but a tactical victory for the German Navy is a strategic one for the RN, as the Brest Squadron no longer directly threatens the Atlantic convoy routes. And two weeks later *Gneisenau* is badly damaged in a RAF raid on Kiel. A start is made on repairing her, but in early 1943 she is laid up, never to go to sea again.

Operation 'Sealion', the planned German invasion of Britain, is finally cancelled.

Air Marshal Harris is appointed C-in-C RAF Bomber Command for the all-out bombing campaign against Germany. This will be Britain's main weapon in the war on the German homeland itself until late 1944.

Commandos carry out a raid on Bruneval in northern France to capture radar equipment. They are lifted off by Royal Navy coastal forces.

Merchant Shipping War
Losses
- 5 ships of 11,000 tons.

MEDITERRANEAN

FEBRUARY

12th — Heavy air attacks continue on Malta; and the destroyer **MAORI**, based on the island and at anchor in Grand Harbour, is bombed and sunk by German aircraft.

Three escorted merchantmen covered by cruisers and destroyers leave Alexandria on the 12th for Malta. One is disabled and the other two sunk by aircraft. There is to be little relief for the island.

13th/23rd — Two RN submarines are lost and a third saved by the gallantry of her crew. Italian torpedo boat *Circe* is central to both of the sinkings:

On the 13th **TEMPEST** torpedoes a supply ship off the Gulf of Taranto but is depth-charged, brought to the surface and soon sinks. Ten days later **P38** attacks a heavily defended convoy off Tripoli and she too is lost to the escorts' counter-attack.

Thresher is also hit back at by the escorts of a convoy off northern Crete on the 16th. Two unexploded bombs lodge between the casing and hull, and at great risk of being drowned should she have to submerge, two of the boat's crew manage to remove them. ✠ Lt Peter Roberts RN and Petty Officer Thomas Gould are awarded the Victoria Cross.

Merchant Shipping War
Losses
● 4 ships of 19,000 tons.

Left:
The US heavy cruiser *Houston* at Southampton in 1930. She sailed in company with HMS *Exeter* in the Battle of the Java Sea and, early on the morning of Sunday 1 March 1942, in the Battle of the Sunda Strait, she went to the bottom at 05°50S, 105°55E, with HMAS *Perth*.
Real Photos (S1072)

INDIAN & PACIFIC OCEANS

FEBRUARY

West — Malaya, Singapore and Burma

On the 8th, Japanese forces start crossing over to Singapore Island. Heavy fighting takes place, but by the 15th Singapore surrenders and over 80,000 mainly Australian, British and Indian troops are doomed to captivity. Many will not survive. The Allies have lost the key to South East Asia and the South West Pacific.
In Burma the Japanese push on towards Rangoon.

12th — Light cruiser **Durban** is damaged in bombing attacks off Singapore.

✠ Lt Thomas Wilkinson RNR, commanding officer of auxiliary patrol ship **Li Wo** (single 4in gun), is posthumously awarded the Victoria Cross. Escaping to Batavia he attacks a troop convoy south of Singapore on the 14th and is soon sunk by a Japanese cruiser.

Aircraft from four of the Pearl Harbor Strike carriers raid Darwin on the 19th. One American destroyer and a number of valuable transports are lost.

South — Dutch East Indies

The two-pronged advance on Java continues with airborne landings on Palembang in southern Sumatra on the 14th, followed up by landings from the sea one day later launched from Indo-China. A few days later the islands of Bali and Timor are invaded from the Celebes and Moluccas respectively. The scene is set for the conquest of Java.

27th-1st (March) — **Battles of the Java Sea** — ABDA's main naval force is commanded by the Dutch Adm Doorman and consists of a mixed squadron of cruisers and destroyers for the defence of Java:

● Heavy cruisers *Exeter* and the US *Houston*.

● Light cruisers *Perth* (Australian), *De Ruyter* and *Java* (both Dutch).

● Destroyers *Electra*, *Encounter*, *Jupiter*, plus two Dutch and four American.

They put to sea on the 26th on the news that invasion convoys are approaching. Failing to find them they head back to Surabaya the next day, but before getting in, more reports arrive and the Allied force goes out again towards a position to the northwest.

The main battle starts on the 27th at around 16.00 against the two heavy and two light cruisers and 14 destroyers covering the Japanese transports. Both Allied heavies open fire at long range, but **Exeter** is soon hit and her speed reduced. In the resulting confusion one of the Dutch destroyers is torpedoed and sunk. As *Exeter* returns to Surabaya with the second Dutch destroyer, the RN ones go in to attack and **ELECTRA** is sunk by gunfire.

Adm Doorman heads back towards the Java coast and sends off the US destroyers to refuel. He then turns to the north with his remaining four cruisers and two RN destroyers. By now it is late evening and **JUPITER** is lost on what is probably a Dutch mine. *Encounter* picks up survivors from the first Dutch destroyer and shortly follows the Americans to Surabaya.

The four cruisers, now without any destroyers, are in action sometime before midnight and both **De Ruyter** and **Java** are

MARCH

German raider *Michel* sails for the South Atlantic and later Indian and Pacific Oceans.

1st-12th — Russian Convoy PQ12 and Return QP8 — By now *Tirpitz*, the ship that will for so long dictate the Royal Navy's policies in northern waters, has been joined in Norway by *Admiral Scheer*. The next convoys therefore set out on the same day, the 1st, so they can be covered by the Home Fleet with *Duke of York*, *Renown*, *King George V* and carrier *Victorious*. On the 4th, cruiser **Sheffield** is damaged on a mine off Iceland as she sails to join the cover force.

The two convoys pass to the southwest of Bear Island and, with *Tirpitz* reported at sea, the Home Fleet tries to place itself between her and the convoys. There is no contact between the surface ships, but on the 9th, aircraft from *Victorious* attack but fail to hit the *Tirpitz* off the Lofoten Islands. Of the 31 merchantmen in two convoys, only one straggler from QP8 is lost to the German force.

20th-3rd (April) — Russian Convoy PQ13 and Return QP9 — These next two convoys set out around the 20th, again covered by the Home Fleet. Off North Cape on the 24th *U655* is rammed and sunk by minesweeper *Sharpshooter* escorting QP9. Of the 19 merchantmen in this convoy all reach Iceland in safety.

PQ13 and its escort, including cruiser *Trinidad* and destroyers *Eclipse* and *Fury*, are scattered by severe gales and heavily attacked. On the 29th three German destroyers encounter the escort north of Murmansk. *Z26* is sunk, but in the action **Trinidad** is disabled by one of her own torpedoes. As she limps towards Kola Inlet an attack by *U585* fails and the U-boat is herself sunk by *Fury*. Five of the 19 ships with PQ13 are lost — two to submarines, two to aircraft, and one by the destroyers. *Trinidad* reaches Russia.

MARCH

Lord Louis Mountbatten is promoted Vice-Adm and appointed Chief of Combined Operations as planning continues for the raids on St Nazaire and later Dieppe.

15th – Destroyer **VORTIGERN**, escorting Forth/Thames convoy FS749, is torpedoed and sunk by E-boat *S104* off Cromer on the east coast of England.

28th — Raid on St Nazaire – Concerned about the possibility of *Tirpitz* breaking out into the Atlantic, the decision is made to put out of action the only dry-dock in France capable of taking her — the 'Normandie' at St Nazaire. Ex-US destroyer *Campbeltown* is to be loaded with high explosives and rammed into the lock gates, while commandos, carried over in motor launches, are to land and destroy installations.

The force sails from southwest England on the 26th, and by a number of ruses penetrates the heavily defended port early on the 28th. In the face of intense fire, *Campbeltown* is placed exactly in position and many of the commandos get ashore to carry out their mission. Losses in men and coastal forces' craft are heavy, but when **CAMPBELTOWN** does go up, the lock gates are put out of commission for the rest of the war.

The Victoria Cross is awarded to three of the RN men taking part,

✠ Cdr Robert Ryder RN, Commanding Officer, Naval Forces. He and his staff are aboard *MGB314*.

✠ Lt-Cdr Stephen Beattie RN, Commanding Officer, HMS *Campbeltown*.

✠ Able Seaman William Savage, gunner on *MGB314*, posthumously for great gallantry under heavy fire.

MEDITERRANEAN

MARCH

The RN submarine service wins another Victoria Cross and sinks three more Axis submarines, all Italian, in the space of four days.

4th — *Torbay* (Cdr Miers) carries out a difficult attack on shipping off Corfu and torpedoes two merchantmen. This is only the latest of a number of successful patrols.
✠ Cdr Anthony Miers RN is awarded the Victoria Cross.

14th — *Millo* is sunk off Calabria in the Ionian Sea by *Ultimatum*.

17th — *Guglielmotti* also off Calabria, by *Unbeaten* (Lt-Cdr Woodward).

18th — *Tricheco* off Brindisi in the southern Adriatic by *Upholder* (Lt-Cdr Wanklyn).

Carriers *Eagle* and *Argus* fly off the first Spitfires for Malta from a position south of the Balearics.

11th — Adm Vian's cruiser force returns to Alexandria after searching for Axis shipping and covering the passage of cruiser *Cleopatra* from Malta. North of Sidi Barrani, the flagship *NAIAD* is torpedoed by *U565* and does down.

22nd — Second Battle of Sirte — Adm Vian sails on the 20th from Alexandria with four fast supply ships for Malta escorted by cruisers *Cleopatra, Dido, Euryalus* and *Carlisle* plus destroyers. Seven 'Hunts' come from Tobruk and, as they carry out anti-submarine sweeps ahead of the convoy, *HEYTHROP* is sunk off Sidi Barrani by *U652*.
The remaining six join the convoy to bring the total number of destroyers to 16.

INDIAN & PACIFIC OCEANS

blasted apart by the big Japanese torpedoes. *Perth* and *Houston* make for Batavia, further west along the north coast of Java.
The next evening, on the 28th, *Perth* and *Houston* leave Batavia for the Sunda Strait to break through to the Indian Ocean. From Surabaya the US destroyers go east and eventually reach safety through the shallow Bali Strait. *Exeter's* draught is too great for this route and the damaged cruiser has to make for the Sunda Strait accompanied by destroyer *Encounter* and another US destroyer, the *Pope*.

28th/1st (March) — Battle of the Sunda Strait — Late that evening **PERTH** and **Houston** run into the Japanese invasion fleet in the Strait and attack the transports. Before long they are overwhelmed by the gunfire and torpedoes of the covering cruisers and destroyers and sink in the opening minutes of the 1st. A Dutch destroyer following astern suffers the same fate.

Later that morning **EXETER, ENCOUNTER** and **Pope** fight a lengthy action with a cruiser force to the northwest of Surabaya before they too succumb.

The ANZAC Squadron is formed in the South West Pacific from Australian cruisers *Australia, Canberra* and the old light *Adelaide*, New Zealand light cruisers *Achilles* and *Leander*, and the American *Chicago*.

Merchant Shipping War
Losses
- Indian Ocean — 18 ships of 38,000 tons.
- Pacific — 54 ships of 181,000 tons.

MARCH

West — Burma

Rangoon, the entry port for the Burma Road, falls on the 8th. Towards the end of the month the Andaman Island group flanking the south of Burma is occupied.

South — Philippines and Dutch East Indies

As the US and Filipinos struggle to hold on to Bataan, Gen MacArthur is order to leave for Australia. There he assumes the post of Supreme Commander, South West Pacific. US Adm Nimitz is to command the rest of the Pacific.
The Java landings go ahead on the 1st and Batavia, the capital of all the DEI, falls. The Allied surrender is agreed on the 9th. On the 12th, northern Sumatra is occupied and the rest of March is spent consolidating the Japanese hold throughout the many islands.
Japan's southern perimeter has been secured in less than four months.

2nd/4th — Strong naval forces patrol the Indian Ocean south of Java to stop the escape of Allied shipping. On the 2nd, destroyer **STRONGHOLD** is sunk in action with the 8in cruiser *Maya* and two destroyers. Two days later Australian sloop **YARRA** and the ships she is escorting are also destroyed.

South East — Bismarck Archipelago, New Guinea and Solomons Islands

The Bismarck Sea is secured with two series of landings. To the north the Japanese take Manus and other parts of the Admiralty Islands. In northern New Guinea, they land in the Huon Peninsula at Lae, Salamaua and Finschhafen.

ATLANTIC

27th — UK/Middle East troop convoy WS17 is on passage southwest of Ireland. As *U587* heads for American waters her sighting report is detected and she is sunk by the convoy escort including destroyers *Aldenham*, *Grove*, *Leamington* and *Volunteer*. This is the first success using ship-borne, high frequency direction-finding — HF/DF.

Battle of the Atlantic

Losses continue at a high rate in US and West Indian waters with over 40 ships sunk in March, many of them the valuable tankers. Over the next few months RN and RCN escorts and a RAF Coastal Command squadron are loaned to the Americans. Ten corvettes are also transferred.

Losses
- 98 ships of 547,000 tons.
- 1 destroyer and 5 U-boats, including 2 by US aircraft off Newfoundland.

EUROPE

Merchant Shipping War

Losses
- 8 ships of 15,000 tons.

The heavy cruiser HMS *York*, lost in March 1941, was a close sister-ship to *Exeter*, sunk a year later. They were completed in 1930/31, displaced 8,300 tons, could make 32kt, were armed with six 8in guns and had a crew of c600. *Real Photos (S1268)*

APRIL

14th — U252 attacks UK/Gibraltar convoy OG82 southwest of Ireland and is sunk by sloop *Stork* and corvette *Vetch* of the 36th EG (Cdr Walker). This is one of the first successful attacks using 10cm Type 271 radar. From now on the new radar and HF/DF will play an increasing part in the sinking of U-boats.

On the 14th, the USN claims its first warship success against U-boats when destroyer *Roper* sinks *U85* off the east coast of America.

During the month, Russian convoy PQ14 sets out from Iceland with 24 ships. Only seven arrive. One is sunk by a U-boat and

APRIL

Following a successful RAF attack on the old city of Lübeck in March, the 'Baedeker' raids are carried out at Hitler's orders against such historic British cities as Bath and York.

Eastern Front

By now the Russian offensive in the north and centre has come to a halt. Territory has been regained but few cities. The Russians maintain their hold on the Kharkov salient in the south.

MEDITERRANEAN

Early on the 22nd, Italian battleship *Littorio* with two heavy and one light cruisers plus destroyers sets out for the British force. In the early afternoon they are sighted to the north, just off the Gulf of Sirte. Now joined by *Penelope* and destroyer *Legion* from Malta, Adm Vian has prepared for their arrival. The supply ships with an escort of five 'Hunts' are to stand off to the south, protected by smoke laid by *Carlisle* and the sixth 'Hunt'. The remaining ships will split into five divisions and hold off the Italians with guns, torpedoes and smoke.

The four main phases of the battle last for a total of four hours. For much of this time the convoy is heavily attacked from the air. Starting at around 15.00:

1. The three Italian cruisers are driven off in a long-range gunnery duel with the RN 5.25in cruisers.

2. They return, this time with *Littorio*. A series of attacks out of the smoke by cruisers and destroyers holds them off.

3. Contrary to Adm Vian's expectations, the Italians work around the smokescreen to the *west*, suddenly appearing only eight miles away. Torpedo attacks by four destroyers are unsuccessful, and **Havock** is disabled by a 15in shell. Then *Cleopatra* and *Euryalus* come out of the smoke firing their 5.25s and launching more torpedoes.

4. The Italian force continues trying to get round the smoke and, in another destroyer torpedo attack, **Kingston** this time receives a 15in hit. As the Italians turn north and away, the cruisers go in for a last time.

By 19.00 the battle is over. The supply ships escorted by 'Hunts' make their separate ways to Malta, followed by damaged *Havock* and *Kingston*. Adm Vian's force returns to Alexandria.

24th/26th — Unfortunately all four transports, including the renowned *Breconshire*, are lost to air attack, two off Malta and two in harbour before much of their cargo can be off-loaded. As the 'Hunt' **SOUTHWOLD** stands by *Breconshire* on the 24th, she hits a mine and sinks off the island. And on the 26th the returned **LEGION** and submarine **P39** are lost in air-raids.

Just after the battle, severe storms damage ships of both sides and on the 23rd two of the returning Italian destroyers founder east of Sicily.

26th — As destroyer **JAGUAR** escorts a tanker to Tobruk, both are sunk by *U652* off Sidi Barrani.

Merchant Shipping War
Losses
- 4 ships of 20,000 tons.

APRIL

Adm Cunningham relinquishes his position as C-in-C Mediterranean Fleet, and Adm Sir Henry Harwood shortly takes over. Adm Cunningham is to become the RN's permanent representative on the Combined Chiefs of Staff Committee in Washington DC. He returns to his old post in February 1943 by way of commander of the naval forces for Operation 'Torch'.

1st — Submarine *Urge* sinks the Italian cruiser *Bande Nere* north of Sicily. This is a welcome success as RN losses are heavy in April, including *Urge* herself.

INDIAN & PACIFIC OCEANS

When they occupy the northern island of Bougainville, the scene is being set for the fierce Solomons Islands battles to come.

Merchant Shipping War
Losses
- Indian Ocean — 65 ships of 68,000 tons.
- Pacific — 98 ships of 184,000 tons.

APRIL

5th/9th — Japanese Carrier Attacks on Ceylon — By now a new Eastern Fleet has been assembled under the command of Adm Sir James Somerville, recently of Force H. The variety of ships are split into two groups. The fast one includes battleship *Warspite*, carriers *Indomitable* and *Formidable*, heavy cruisers *Cornwall* and *Dorsetshire*, two light cruisers plus destroyers. In the slower one are four 'R' class battleships, old carrier *Hermes* and some cruisers and destroyers. Two Australian destroyers accompany each group. As the Ceylon bases of Colombo and Trincomalee are poorly defended and too far forward, Adm Somerville is working out of the secret base of Addu Atoll in the Maldives.

another 16 have to turn back because of the weather. Return convoy QP10 loses four of its 16 ships around the same time — two each to U-boats and aircraft.

30th — Towards the end of the month convoys PQ15 and QP11 sail. Both have cruisers in close support and PQ15 is covered by units of the Home Fleet including *King George V* and the American battleship *Washington*. On the 30th the QP11 cruiser **Edinburgh** is torpedoed twice by *U456* and has to turn back for Murmansk. The story of the two convoys is taken up in May.

Battle of the Atlantic
Losses
- 74 ships of 439,000 tons and 1 US destroyer mined off Florida.
- 2 U-boats.

Merchant Shipping War
Losses
- 14 ships of 55,000 tons.

Below:
The Japanese fleet carrier *Hiryu*. In April 1942 she was in action in the Indian Ocean off Ceylon and was sunk later at the Battle of Midway. *IWM (MM6491)*

Bottom:
The 'Leander' class light cruiser HMS *Achilles*. The five ships of the class included *Neptune* (lost in December 1941), and *Achilles* and *Leander* serving in the RNZN. The class was completed 1933-35, displacing 7,200 tons, able to make 32kt, and carrying eight 6in guns and 550 crew. *Real Photos (S1136)*

MEDITERRANEAN

Malta

In a month that will see the bombing of Malta reaching a peak, the island is awarded the George Cross on the 16th by King George VI. At this time Malta has almost ceased to be a base for attacks on Rommel's supply lines, and most of his transports are getting through.

The German and Italian bombing leads to the loss, directly and indirectly, of numerous ships. They concentrate on the *Penelope* in dry dock and the *Havock* and *Kingston* (damaged in the Battle of Sirte):

1st — Submarines **P36** and **PANDORA** sunk and others of the 10th Flotilla damaged. *Pandora* has only recently arrived from Gibraltar on a supply trip.

4th — Greek submarine **Glavkos** sunk.

5th — Destroyer **Gallant** wrecked. She was badly damaged in January 1941 and not repaired.

6th — **HAVOCK** tries to reach Gibraltar but runs aground near Cape Bon. Wrecked, she is later torpedoed by an Italian submarine.

Penelope, by now nicknamed HMS 'Pepperpot', gets away on the 8th to reach Gibraltar two days later.

9th — Destroyer **LANCE** in dry dock is badly damaged and never repaired.

11th — **KINGSTON** sunk.

27th — By this time the 10th Flotilla has been ordered to leave Malta. **URGE** sails for Alexandria on the 27th, but fails to arrive.

President Roosevelt lends the US carrier *Wasp* to ferry nearly 50 Spitfires to the Island. Escort is provided by battlecruiser *Renown*, cruisers *Cairo* and *Charybdis* and six destroyers including two American. Sadly most of the aircraft are destroyed soon after they land on the 20th.

14th — 10th Flotilla loses its most famous boat when **UPHOLDER** (Lt-Cdr Wanklyn VC) is lost. She attacks a convoy northeast of Tripoli and is presumed sunk in the counter-attack by destroyer escort *Pegaso*.

Merchant Shipping War
Losses
● 6 ships of 13,000 tons.

INDIAN & PACIFIC OCEANS

Early in April, two Japanese forces head into the Indian Ocean. One under Adm Ozawa with carrier *Ryujo* and six cruisers makes for the Bay of Bengal and east coast of India. In a matter of a few days 23 ships of 112,000 tons are sunk. At the same time Japanese submarines sink a further five off the west coast. Bad as this threat is, the real one comes from the carrier strike force of Adm Nagumo with his five Pearl Harbor carriers — *Akagi, Hiryu, Soryu, Shokaku* and *Zuikaku* — plus four battleships and three cruisers.

The fleet is first sighted on the 4th south of Ceylon, and shipping is cleared from the ports. In the morning of the 5th a heavy raid on Colombo sinks destroyer **TENEDOS** and armed merchant cruiser **HECTOR**. At this time **CORNWALL** and **DORSETSHIRE** are to the southwest, sailing from Colombo to rejoin the main fleet. Found at noon they soon go to the bottom under a series of aircraft attacks. Adm Nagumo has not yet finished.

As Adm Somerville's two squadrons search for the Japanese from a position between Addu Atoll and Ceylon, they circle round to the east. From there, on the 9th, Japanese aircraft find the shipping cleared from Trincomalee and back on its way in. **HERMES**, Australian destroyer **VAMPIRE** and corvette **HOLLYHOCK** are amongst those that soon go down. The Japanese ships leave the Indian Ocean, never again to return in force. Not knowing this, the surviving ships of the RN withdraw — the slow group to Kilindini in East Africa and the other to the Bombay area.

6th — Indian sloop **INDUS** is bombed and sunk off Akyab on the Arakan coast of Burma.

Philippines — Conclusion

Japanese units make their final push on Bataan and on the 9th the defenders surrender. The island fortress of Corregidor holds out until its fall on 6 May. Some resistance continues on other Philippines islands.

The Doolittle Raid — B-25 bombers under the command of Col Doolittle take off from the US carrier Hornet for the first ever raid on Japan on the 18th. Damage is slight, but the strategic implications are to prove fatal to the Japanese.

Merchant Shipping War
Losses
● Indian Ocean — 31 ships of 154,000 tons.
● Pacific — 7 ships of 14,000 tons.

Strategic and Maritime Situation

To the north and the south the Japanese are now secure as planned. To the west they soon will be, as the British, together with the Chinese in the northeast, are steadily driven out of Burma. The debate is now whether or not to push out to the southeast towards Australia and New Zealand, and eastwards to the United States.

All their gains have been at little cost, not least on the naval side, as can be seen from the losses up until the end of April from all causes:

MAY

On the 22nd, Mexico joins most of the Central American and Caribbean republics by declaring war on the Axis powers.

26th (April)-7th — Russian Convoy PQ15 and Return QP11 — As *Edinburgh* limps back to Russia, three German destroyers attack QP11, but only manage to sink a straggler. On the 2nd they find the cruiser. In a series of confused fights amidst snow showers and smokescreens, *Edinburgh* disables the *Hermann Schoemann*, but is then torpedoed for a third time by either *Z24* or *Z25*. Escorting destroyers *Forester* and *Foresight* are also damaged. Both **EDINBURGH** and *Schoemann* have to be scuttled. The rest of QP11's 12 merchantmen get through to Reykjavik.

PQ15 meanwhile suffers misfortune twice. On the 1st, *King George V* rams one of her escorting destroyers, the **PUNJABI**, and is damaged by the latter's depth charges as she goes down with heavy loss of life. Then on the 2nd, minesweeper *Seagull* and Norwegian destroyer *St Albans* in error sink Polish submarine **Jastrzab**. Three of the convoy's merchant ships are lost to torpedo aircraft but the remaining 22 reach Murmansk.

14th/15th — After *Trinidad* is damaged escorting PQ13 in March, she is patched up at Murmansk ready for the homeward journey. Escort is provided by four destroyers and cover by more cruisers, but on the 14th she is heavily attacked from the air and hit by a Ju88 bomb. Fires start, get out of control and **TRINIDAD** is scuttled the next day in the cold waters north of North Cape.

In addition to aircraft and U-boats, the Germans now have *Tirpitz*, *Scheer*, *Lützow*, *Hipper* and nearly a dozen of the big destroyers at Narvik and Trondheim. With by now continuous

MAY

13th — German raider *Stier* leaves Rotterdam for the Channel and operations in the South Atlantic. Off Boulogne she and her escorts are attacked by RN coastal forces. One MTB is lost, but German torpedo boats *Iltis* and *Seeadler* are torpedoed and sunk. *Stier* is free for four months until her eventual sinking.

Eastern Front

In the south, Russian forces attack from their salient below Kharkov. They make some progress, but the Germans start their own counter-attack and soon encircle and capture the Russians. They push on beyond Kharkov ready for their main spring offensive.

On the last night of the month, RAF Bomber Command scrapes together enough aircraft for its first 1,000-bomber raid. Cologne is the target, and Essen and Bremen follow in June.

Merchant Shipping War
Losses
- 14 ships of 59,000 tons.

MEDITERRANEAN

Left:
The 'Perth' class light cruiser HMAS *Perth*. The class of three all served with the RAN, with both *Perth* and *Sydney* sunk and only *Hobart* surviving. Completed 1935-36 at 6,900 tons, they could steam at 32kt. They were armed with eight 6in guns and had a crew of 550.
Real Photos (S1015)

Above:
HM Submarine *Oberon*, an 'O' class submarine and sister to *Olympus* (lost on 8 May 1942). *Real Photos (S1105)*

MAY

2nd/28th — Two U-boats are lost to the RN. On the 2nd, east of Gibraltar, *U74* is sunk by destroyers *Wishart* and *Wrestler* and RAF aircraft of No 202 Squadron. In attacks on Tobruk supply traffic, *U568* is hunted down and sunk by destroyers *Hero*, *Eridge* and *Hurworth* on the 28th.

8th — Submarine **OLYMPUS** sails from Malta for Gibraltar with many passengers including the crews of *P36* and *P39*. Just off Grand Harbour she hits a mine laid by German E-boats and goes down with heavy loss of life.

USS *Wasp* and the *Eagle* fly a further 60 Spitfires to Malta on the 9th. More are ferried in by *Eagle* and *Argus* a week or so later. This time they are kept safe on arrival.

11th/12th — Destroyers *Jackal*, *Jervis*, *Kipling* and *Lively* leave Alexandria to search for reported Axis shipping bound for Benghazi. There is no fighter cover. On being sighted they turn back, but north of Sidi Barrani (yet again) are attacked by a specially trained anti-ship group of German Ju88s. **KIPLING** and **LIVELY** are sent to the bottom that evening, and **JACKAL** has to be scuttled on the 12th. Only *Jervis* with 630 survivors reaches Alexandria.

North Africa

From Gazala, Rommel starts the second phase of his advance towards Egypt on the 26th with a main attack around Bir Hakeim. Shortly aftwards, heavy fighting breaks out between there and Gazala around the areas known as the 'Cauldron' and 'Knightsbridge'.

INDIAN & PACIFIC OCEANS

	Allied					Japanese
	Royal Navy	Royal Australian Navy	Dutch	United States Navy	Total	Total
Battleships	2	—	—	2*	4	—
Carriers	1	—	—	—	1	—
Cruisers	3	1	2	1	7	—
Destroyers	7	1	7	5	20	5
Submarines	—	—	8	4	12	7
Total:	13	2	17	12	44	12

Note: *plus 6 battleships sunk at their moorings or damaged.

Now it is the Allies' turn to establish a defence perimeter, running from the Hawaiian Islands around to Australia and New Zealand. With most of the ANZAC forces in North Africa, it is left to the Americans to garrison many of the islands needed to protect the supply routes from the US to the two Dominions. By now they are occupying the Line Islands south of Hawaii as well as Samoa, Tonga, New Hebrides and New Caledonia. The Australians are reinforcing Port Moresby in Papua New Guinea and New Zealanders landing in Fiji.

The Doolittle Raid is decisive to Japanese thinking. To keep the Allies away from their homeland, they will extend both the southeast and eastern conquests. Landings will be made at Port Moresby to bring Australia within bomber range, the southern Solomons and beyond will be taken to cut the US Australia supply lines, and Midway and the Aleutians occupied to isolate Pearl Harbor.

Each of these three moves will lead to famous battles — Coral Sea, Guadalcanal, and Midway. Thereafter the Japanese will be on the defensive.

MAY

5th — Landings at Diego Saurez, Madagascar: Operation 'Ironclad' — Concerned about the Japanese carrier sorties into the Indian Ocean and the vulnerability of the Cape of Good Hope/Middle East convoy routes, Britain decides to take Diego Saurez at the north end of Vichy French Madagascar. Under the command of Rear-Adm E. N. Syfret (recently appointed to Force H), a large force of ships including battleship *Ramillies* and carriers *Indomitable* and *Illustrious* assemble at Durban towards the end of April.

The assault takes place on 5 May in Courrier Bay to the west of Diego Saurez. As usual the Vichy French forces resist strongly. Submarine *Bévéziers* is sunk, but the only RN casualty is the corvette **AURICULA** mined on the 5th. The advance on Diego Saurez is held up and next day a Royal Marine unit storms the town from the sea. By the 7th the fighting is over and the important anchorage is in British hands. On the 7th and 8th the two French submarines *Le Héros* and *Monge* are sunk by joint air and sea attacks.

By September the complete occupation of Madagascar becomes necessary.

30th — That night, Japanese submarines *I16* and *I20* launch midget submarines for attacks on Diego Saurez. **Ramillies** is torpedoed and badly damaged and a tanker sunk.

Burma

On 29 April Lashio is captured and the Burma Road cut in the north. After this, supplies for China have to be flown over high mountains known as the 'Hump' for nearly three years until a new road is finally completed in early 1945. Mandalay falls on the 1st and by mid-month the retreating British Army is crossing the border into India. The Chinese are also back in

daylight throughout the journey, the Admiralty presses for the convoys to be discontinued until the days shorten. For political reasons they go ahead.

PQ16 and QP12 pass through in May. PQ16 starts out with 35 ships but one returns, six are lost to heavy aircraft attack and one to U-boats. QP12 has one return but the other 14 reach Iceland.

Battle of the Atlantic

U-boat strength approaches 300 with over 100 operational. A fairly complete convoy system is being introduced off the US east coast from Florida north, but the submarines are now concentrating in the Caribbean and Gulf of Mexico. They can now spend more time on station assisted by the 'Milchcow' supply boats. The result is that Allied losses continue at a high rate, especially among tankers.

In the North Atlantic, convoy ONS92 loses seven ships in one night to a pack attack.

Losses

- 122 ships of 585,000 tons, 2 cruisers, 1 destroyer and 1 submarine.
- 1 U-boat by US Coast Guard off east coast of America and 1 destroyer.

The US carrier *Lexington* after being mortally hit during the May 1942 Battle of the Coral Sea. *IWM (OEM1566)*

JUNE

Winston Churchill flies to Washington DC for another series of meetings with President Roosevelt. They agree on the sharing of nuclear research and to concentrate the work in the United States. The resulting 'Manhattan Project' will be put under military control in September. Agreement does not come so easily on the question of where to open a second front in 1942.

The Americans want to land in France to take pressure off the Russians, but the British consider this to be impossible at present and propose the invasion of French North Africa. Not until the following month does the President come to accept this. Planning then starts on what soon becomes known as Operation 'Torch'.

17th — As destroyer **WILD SWAN** heads for Gibraltar/UK convoy HG84 she is attacked and sunk off south west Ireland by German Ju88s, but not before she has shot down a number of them. The convoy loses five ships to U-boats.

21st — Ex-US submarine **P514** on passage around the coast of Newfoundland from Argentia to St Johns is rammed and sunk in error by Canadian sloop *Georgian*.

Russian convoys PQ17 and QP13 set sail towards the end of the month.

Battle of the Atlantic

In the first six months of 1942, submarines worldwide have sunk 585 ships of over 3,000,000 tons, mostly in the Atlantic — and a large proportion of these in American waters where losses remain high in the Caribbean and Gulf of Mexico. At the same time the 108 new U-boats entering service far outweigh the 13 sunk in the Atlantic in this period.

Losses

- 128 ships of 650,000 tons, 1 destroyer and 1 submarine.
- 2 U-boats by US forces off Cuba and Bermuda.

JUNE

Reinhard Heydrich, German 'Protector' of Czechoslovakia, dies following an assassination attempt in May. In part reprisal, the village of Lidice is wiped out and its people murdered.

Eastern Front

Towards the end of the month the Russians start to evacuate Sevastopol. By early July all the Crimea is in German Hands.

By this time the Germans have started their spring attack. The aim is to take Rostov-on-Don and push south towards the vital oilfields of the Caucasus. Meanwhile, from the area of Kursk and Kharkov, a second army group will move on Stalingrad to protect the left flank of what is initially the main thrust to the south. Stalingrad later dictates the outcome of the entire campaign.

Merchant Shipping War

Losses
- 5 ships of 3,000 tons.

MEDITERRANEAN

29th — In a series of attacks on convoys bound for North Africa, submarine *Turbulent* (Cdr Linton) sinks three transports in the month. On the 29th she torpedoes and sinks escorting destroyer *Pessagno* northwest of Benghazi.

Merchant Shipping War
Losses
- 6 ships of 21,000 tons.

JUNE

Early in the month *Eagle* ferries over 50 Spitfires to Malta in two operations. By now the Germans have transferred many of their aircraft to Russia. This, together with the arrival of yet more RAF fighters, eases the terrible burden Malta has suffered for so long.

North Africa

After more than two weeks of fierce attack and counter-attack, British forces pull out of 'Knightsbridge'. Tobruk is surrounded by the 18th and three days later has surrendered. Another two days and the Axis forces are back in Egypt. Mersa Matruh falls on the 28th and Eighth Army prepares to make its last stand at El Alamein, just 60 miles from Alexandria.

With this threat to Suez and the Mediterranean Fleet's main base, warships and supplies start to be withdrawn from the immediate danger area.

2nd/12th — Attacks on Allied shipping to Tobruk before its fall bring further losses to both sides. Aircraft of FAA 815 Squadron and RAF No 203 Squadron damage *U652* off Sollum on the 2nd and she has to be finished off with a torpedo from *U81*. On the 12th, off Sidi Barrani, escort destroyer **GROVE** is sunk by *U77*.

12th-16th — Malta Convoys 'Harpoon' from Gibraltar and 'Vigorous' from Alexandria — Six escorted merchantmen pass through the Strait of Gibraltar covered by battleship *Malaya*, carriers *Argus* and *Eagle*, cruisers *Kenya*, *Charybdis* and *Liverpool* and destroyers — this is the force comprising Operation 'Harpoon'. Attacks by Italian aircraft on the 14th lead to the first merchant ship going down south of Sardinia. **Liverpool** is also damaged and has to return. Later that day, at the entrance to the Strait of Sicily, the cover force turns back.

In the morning of the 15th, south of Pantellaria, an Italian two-cruiser squadron in conjunction with Italian and German

INDIAN & PACIFIC OCEANS

their own country as well as India. With the conquest of Burma, Japan's western defence line is in place.

Papua, New Guinea and the Solomons

Battle of the Coral Sea — Sailing from Rabaul, a Japanese invasion force heads for Port Moresby covered by light carrier *Shoho* and cruisers. Distant cover is given by a carrier strike force of two fleet carriers. From the Coral Sea, the aircraft of US carriers *Lexington* and *Yorktown*, with a support group that includes Australian cruisers *Australia* and *Hobart*, search for them. First success goes to the Americans when on the 7th their planes sink *Shoho* off the eastern tip of New Guinea. Next day, on the 8th, more aircraft strikes put *Shokaku* out of action on one side and sink *Lexington* and damage *Yorktown* on the other. A draw in naval terms, the battle is a strategic defeat for the Japanese as their invasion ships turn back, leaving Port Moresby safe for now. Throughout the battle, neither side's ships have sighted each other — the first time in naval history a major action has occurred in this way.

Before the battle starts, the Japanese have taken the opportunity to occupy the small island of Tulagi, off Guadalcanal in the southern Solomons.

Merchant Shipping War
Losses
- Indian Ocean — 4 ships of 22,000 tons.
- Pacific — 5 ships of 17,000 tons.

JUNE

Midway and the Aleutians

Battle of Midway — Adm Yamamoto, with over 130 ships in a number of separate groups, sets out to seize Midway, occupy the western Aleutians and attack the eastern end, and draw out the Pacific Fleet for destruction. At the heart of the armada is the First Carrier Fleet (Adm Nagumo) with four of the Pearl Harbor carriers. The Americans have far fewer ships, but these include carriers *Enterprise*, *Hornet* and the barely repaired *Yorktown*.

On the 3rd, Dutch Harbor, close to Alaska, is attacked from two light carriers. But the main battle is far to the south off Midway between the carrier aircraft of both sides. There, on the 4th/5th in a close run action, all four Japanese carriers — *Akagi*, *Hiryu*, *Kaga* and *Soryu* go down. *Yorktown* is badly damaged and finished off by a Japanese submarine on the 7th. The Japanese forces retreat, Midway is spared, and the Allies have their first major strategic victory of World War 2. However, the Japanese Navy is still strong, with more carriers left in the Pacific than the Americans.

The occupation at this time of Attu and Kiska in the Aleutians is of little consequence.

The US Pacific Fleet is reorganised in June. Task Force 44 is allocated to Australian and New Zealand waters with Australian cruisers *Australia*, *Canberra* and *Hobart*, and the American *Chicago* under Rear-Adm V. A. C. Crutchley RN. Until the arrival of the British Pacific Fleet in early 1945, Australian and New Zealand ships are almost the only representatives of the White Ensign in the Pacific.

Merchant Shipping War
Losses
- Indian Ocean — 18 ships of 90,000 tons.
- Pacific — 6 ships of 31,000 tons.

The 'Arethusa' class light cruiser HMS *Penelope*. Both *Galatea* and *Penelope* were lost in the Mediterranean, and *Arethusa* and *Aurora* survived the war. Completed in 1935-37 at 5,200 tons, they could make 32kt and carried six 6in guns and 450 crew.   *Real Photos (S989)*

JULY

27th (June)-28th July — Destruction of Russian Convoy PQ17 — Convoy PQ17 and return QP13 both set out on 27 June. PQ17 leaves Reykjavik with 36 ships of which two return. The close escort under Cdr J. E. Broome includes six destroyers and four corvettes. Two RN and two US cruisers with destroyers are in support (Rear-Adm L. H. K. Hamilton), and distant cover is given by the Home Fleet (Adm Tovey) with battleships *Duke of York* and the US *Washington*, carrier *Victorious*, cruisers and destroyers.

The Admiralty believes the Germans are concentrating their heavy ships in northern Norway. In fact pocket battleship *Lützow* runs aground off Narvik, but this still leaves *Tirpitz*, *Admiral Scheer* and *Hipper* which reach Altenfiord on the 3rd. At this time PQ17 has just passed to the north of Bear Island, after which aircraft sink three merchantmen.

Fear of attack by the German ships leads the First Sea Lord, Adm Pound, far away in London, to decide the fate of the convoy. In the evening of the 4th the support cruisers are

JULY

The first USAAF aircraft join RAF Bomber Command in an attack on occupied Europe.

Eastern Front

By the end of the month the Germans have taken Rostov, crossed the Don on their way south into the Caucasus, and are approaching Stalingrad.

Merchant Shipping War

Losses
● 9 ships of 23,000 tons.

aircraft attack what is now a lightly defended convoy. The five fleet destroyers head for the Italians, but *Bedouin* and **Partridge** are disabled by gunfire. Three more ships are lost to bombing attacks and Italian torpedo aircraft finish off **BEDOUIN**. Later that evening, as the depleted convoy approaches Malta, it runs into a minefield. Two destroyers and the fifth supply ship are damaged, but Polish escort destroyer **Kujawiak** is sunk. Just two of 'Harpoon's six ships reach Malta for the loss of two destroyers and serious damage to three more and a cruiser.

Meanwhile, the Operation 'Vigorous' force of 11 ships and their escorts sail from Haifa and Port Said, and are met on the 13th off Tobruk by Adm Vian with seven light cruisers and 17 destroyers. By the 14th, two ships have been lost to air attack and two more damaged. That evening Vian learns of an Italian battlefleet with two battleships, two heavy and two light cruisers plus destroyers has sailed south from Taranto. The chances of fighting them off are slim.

Early on the 15th the first of five course reversals are made as 'Vigorous' tries to break through to Malta. As the convoy now heads back, German E-boats from Derna launch torpedo strikes. Cruiser **Newcastle** is damaged by *S56* and destroyer **HASTY** sunk by *S55*. At around 07.00, when the Italian fleet is 200 miles to the northwest, the convoy turns back for Malta. Attacks by Malta-based aircraft are made on the main Italian fleet without serious effect, although they disable heavy cruiser *Trento* which is finished off by submarine *Umbra*.

Between 09.40 and noon on the 15th, two more course reversals are made so that once again the convoy is bound for Malta. All afternoon air attacks are mounted; and south of Crete, cruiser **Birmingham** is damaged and escort destroyer **AIREDALE** sunk by Ju87 Stukas. The convoy is now down to six ships when the Australian destroyer *Nestor* is badly damaged. That evening 'Vigorous' finally turns back for Alexandria.

Now into the early hours of the 16th, cruiser **HERMIONE** is torpedoed and sunk by *U205* and **NESTOR** has to be scuttled. At around this time, as the Italian fleet makes for Taranto, a RAF Wellington from Malta torpedoes and damages the battleship *Littorio*.

None of the 'Vigorous' ships reach Malta. One cruiser, three destroyers and two merchant ships have been lost in the attempt.

Merchant Shipping War

Losses
- 16 ships of 60,000 tons.

JULY

North Africa

On the 1st, in the First Battle of El Alamein, Rommel's German and Italian army starts its assault on the defences. In three weeks of tough fighting, British, Australian, New Zealand, South African and other units of Eighth Army manage to hold on. Both sides then dig in.

9th/11th — Two Italian submarines are lost on patrol against Allied shipping off Beirut. On the 9th *Perla* is captured by corvette *Hyacinth*, the second time an Italian boat has ended up in the RN's hands. Two days later *Ondina* is sunk by South African armed trawlers *Protea* and *Southern Maid* working with a FAA Walrus flying boat of 700 Squadron.

Eagle once again flies off Spitfires for Malta. Shortly afterwards *Unbroken* is the first submarine of 10th Flotilla to return to the Island.

The pocket battleship *Lützow* in 1944/5. In July 1942 she was based with other German big ships in Norway at the time of the Russian convoy PQ17. *Real Photos (S1950)*

JULY

Papua, New Guinea

The Japanese plan to capture Port Moresby by landing on the north coast at Buna and Gona and advancing overland by way of the Kokoda Trail. They land on the 21st and move forward, just as the Australians are preparing to defend Kokoda itself and push on to Buna. Kokoda is captured on the 29th, and through August the Australians are pushed slowly back towards Port Moresby.

Merchant Shipping War

Losses
- Indian Ocean — 9 ships of 47,000 tons.
- Pacific — 6 ships of 32,000 tons.

ordered to withdraw and the convoy to scatter. Unfortunately Adm Hamilton takes the six escorting destroyers with him. The merchantmen are now to the north of North Cape.

Thirty-one of them try to make for Novaya Zemlya and then south to the Russian ports. Between the 5th and 10th, 20 are lost, half each to aircraft and U-boats as they are hunted down. Some shelter for days off the bleak shores of Novaya Zemlya. Eventually 11 survivors and two rescue ships reach Archangel and nearby ports between the 9th and 28th.

As it happens, *Tirpitz* and the other ships did not leave Altenfiord until the morning of the 5th, *after* the 'convoy is to disperse' order. They abandoned their sortie that same day. History suggests the vital decision on the future of PQ17 should have been left to the commanders on the spot. The US reacts strongly to the RN apparently leaving its merchantmen to their fate.

Meanwhile all has gone well with QP13's 35 ships from Murmansk, until the 5th. Approaching Iceland through the Denmark Strait they run into a British minefield. Escorting minesweeper **NIGER** and five merchant ships are lost. The rest get in.

No more Russian convoys run until September.

3rd — *U215* sinks an escorted ship south of Nova Scotia and is lost in the counter-attack by armed trawler *Le Tiger*.

11th — Northwest of the Canaries, UK/West Africa convoy OS.33 is attacked and *U136* is sunk by frigate *Spey*, sloop *Pelican* and Free French destroyer *Léopard*.

14th — Damaged in action with the cutter *Lulworth* and other escorts, Italian submarine *Pietro Calvi* is scuttled south of the Azores.

24th — Canadian destroyer *St Croix*, with the Canadian C2 group escorting UK/North America convoy ON113, sinks *U90* off Newfoundland.

Pending the setting up of support Escort Groups later in the year, mainly convoy escorts are designated by their nationality — A for American, B for British and C for Canadian.

31st — In mid-Atlantic, Canadian destroyer *Skeena* and corvette *Wetaskiwan* of the C3 group with ON115 sink *U588*.

31st — On passage out, *U213* stumbles across a convoy west of the Bay of Biscay, where she is sunk by the escort including sloops *Erne*, *Rochester* and *Sandwich*.

Battle of the Atlantic

The American convoy system is now being extended into the Caribbean and Gulf of Mexico, and merchantmen sinkings go down as U-boat losses start to mount. Nevertheless, with 140 operational U-boats out of a total of 330, the Germans have more than enough to continue the offensive in the North Atlantic and to maintain concentrations off Sierra Leone, Venezuela and Brazil. For some months to come it is again the tankers that lose heavily off Venezuela and Trinidad.

On the 1st of the month, the Change of Operational Control (CHOP) line is introduced for Atlantic convoys. Shipping to the east of 26°W is controlled by the British Admiralty and to the west by the US Navy from Washington. In November it is moved to 47°W.

Losses
- 101 ships of 511,000 tons.
- 11 German and 1 Italian U-boats, including 2 by RAF Bay of Biscay patrols; 1 by RCAF off Nova Scotia; and 3 by US forces in the Caribbean and off the east coast of America.

HMS *Duke of York*, the 'King George V' class battleship. In July 1942 she was flagship, Home Fleet, and part of the covering force for PQ17. *Real Photos (S2935)*

Right:
The 'Belfast' class light cruiser HMS *Belfast* was a sister-ship to the *Edinburgh*, lost in May 1942. Both were completed 1939, displacing 10,000 tons, and could make 32kt; they carried 12 6in guns and a crew of 850. *Belfast* is moored in London's River Thames as a museum ship. *Real Photos (S1012)*

Merchant Shipping War

Losses

● 3 ships of 6,000 tons.

The 'Southampton' class light cruiser HMS *Sheffield* in 1937. Of a class of eight ships, *Southampton*, *Gloucester* and *Manchester* were all sunk in the Mediterranean. Completed 1937-39 with 12 6in guns and 700 crew, they displaced over 9,000 tons and could make a maximum 32kt. *Real Photos (S1114)*

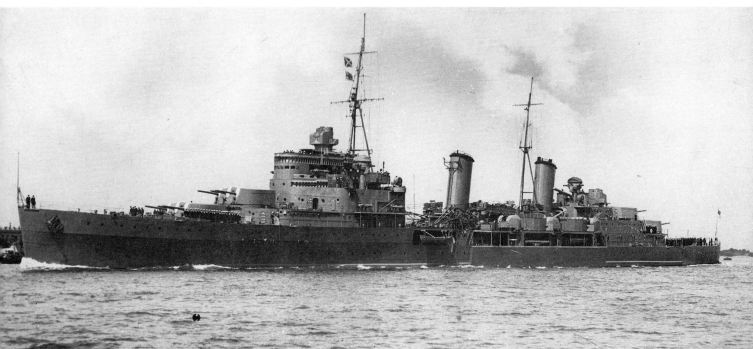

ATLANTIC

AUGUST

3rd — On patrol between the Shetlands and Norway, submarine *Saracen* torpedoes *U335* on passage out.

6th/8th — In the space of five days slow Halifax/UK convoy SC94 (33 ships) is attacked by a total of 17 U-boats and loses 11 merchant ships. Southeast of Greenland two U-boats are sunk by ships of the Canadian C1 group. On the 6th, Canadian destroyer *Assiniboine* shells and rams *U210*. Two days later RN corvette *Dianthus* depth charges and also rams *U379* to destruction. Four more U-boats are damaged.

The sinking of five Brazilian ships off their own coast in the middle of the month finally drives Brazil to declare war on Germany and Italy on the 22nd. Bases in the country extend Allied control of the South Atlantic.

28th — *U94* attacks Trinidad/Cuba convoy TAG15 off Jamaica. Damaged by a US Navy Catalina, she is finished off by Canadian corvette *Oakville*.

Battle of the Atlantic

For some time now aircraft of RAF Coastal Command have been using the Leigh light searchlight in conjunction with radar to illuminate and attack U-boats at night on the surface. The Germans now introduce the Metox detector which enables U-boats to pick up the 1.5m wavelength transmissions of the existing ASV sets in time for them to submerge. They have moved one step ahead of the Allies in the scientific war, and the RAF's Bay of Biscay patrols lose effectiveness accordingly.

Losses

- 106 ships of 544,000 tons and 1 US destroyer by collision off Nova Scotia.
- 9 U-boats including 1 by RAF Bay of Biscay patrols; 3 by US aircraft in Gulf of Mexico, Caribbean and off Iceland; 1 Italian by unknown causes, possibly by RAF Bay of Biscay patrols.

EUROPE

AUGUST

19th — Raid on Dieppe: Operation 'Jubilee' – Unable to open a second front in Europe, the Allies seek other ways to make their presence felt on the continent of Europe and to take some of the pressure off the Russians. A largely Canadian raid supported by British commandos is therefore planned on the defended port of Dieppe in northern France. Over 200 ships and landing craft, including escort destroyers and coastal forces under the command of Capt J. Hughes-Hallett, sail from south coast of England ports on the 18th, with 6,000 troops.

The attempted landings take place early on the 19th against heavy defensive gunfire. One flanking attack by commandos achieves some success, but the other and the frontal assault with tanks are total failures. By noon the decision has been taken to withdraw: as this proceeds under continuous air attack, escort destroyer **BERKELEY** is bombed and sunk, and others damaged. Canadian casualties in dead, wounded and prisoners are high, and Dieppe proves to have been an expensive but valuable lesson in the problems of landing in occupied Europe.

Eastern Front

The south continues to be the main focus of this long and bitterly contested front and will remain so until January. In the Stalingrad area the Germans have reached the River Volga and are within a few miles of the city. They break into the suburbs in September and the fighting increases in intensity as the Russians struggle to hold on to the west bank of the Volga. Further south still, the German invaders get to the Caucasus mountains, but thereafter progress is slow.

Merchant Shipping War

Losses

- For the first time since the war started, no merchant ships are lost in UK waters in August.

The 'B' class destroyer HMS *Basilisk*, which was sunk in June 1940. The 'A' and 'B' classes were the first class of post-World War 1 destroyers built for the Royal Navy, consisting of 20 ships including leaders. Eleven were lost and two not repaired. Completed 1930-31, they displaced 1,350 tons, could make 35kt, and carried four 4.7in guns, eight torpedo tubes, plus 140 crew. The programme included HMC Ships *Saguenay* and *Skeena*, both lost in the North Atlantic. *Real Photos (S348)*

MEDITERRANEAN

AUGUST

4th/10th — Two more Axis submarines are lost at the far east end of the Mediterranean, this time off Palestine. *U372* is sunk near Jaffa on the 4th by destroyers *Sikh* and *Zulu*, 'Hunts' *Croome* and *Tetcott* and a RAF Wellington of No 203 Squadron. Back in June this U-boat had sunk submarine depot ship *Medway* off Alexandria.

The Italians continue their underwater warfare and submarine *Scire* prepares to launch human torpedoes against Haifa. On the 10th she is found by armed trawler *Islay* and destroyed.

6th — Submarine **THORN** attacks a tanker off southwest Crete and is presumed sunk in the counter-attack by Italian escort destroyer *Pegaso*.

10th-15th — Malta Convoy: Operation 'Pedestal' — Malta's survival makes it essential to fight through another convoy, and the biggest operation ever is mounted from the Gibraltar end. Thirteen merchantmen, including two American, plus the British-manned tanker *Ohio* (Capt D. W. Mason), are given a massive escort. Close in under Rear-Adm Harold Burrough are cruisers *Nigeria*, *Kenya*, *Manchester* and *Cairo* and 12 destroyers. Covering are the three fleet carriers *Eagle*, *Indomitable* and *Victorious* each with their accompanying cruiser *Charybdis*, *Phoebe* and *Sirius*, battleships *Nelson* and *Rodney*, and another 12 destroyers. Eight more destroyers are with the force.

The opportunity will be taken for *Furious* to fly off 38 Spitfires for Malta, and the Mediterranean Fleet will try to distract the enemy at the other end of the Mediterranean. In overall command of 'Pedestal' is Vice-Adm E. N. Syfret.

The convoy passes Gibraltar on the 10th and from the next day is subjected to increasingly intense attacks by submarines, aircraft and, later, coastal forces. Early on the afternoon of the 11th, *Furious* sends off her Spitfires and later that day heads back for Gibraltar. On the 12th one of her escorting destroyers, *Wolverine*, rams and sinks Italian submarine *Dagabur* off Algiers.

Still on the 11th and by now north of Algiers, **EAGLE** is torpedoed four times by *U73* and goes down.

Air attacks take place later that day and early on the 12th, but it is not until noon, south of Sardinia, that they gain their first success. Italian and German aircraft slightly damage **Victorious** and hit a merchantman which later sinks. More submarines then appear and the Italian *Cobalto* is rammed to destruction by destroyer *Ithuriel*. From north of Bizerta, submarine, aircraft and Italian MTB attacks come fast and furiously.

At 18.30, still on the 12th, aircraft badly damage **Indomitable**, putting her out of action, and destroyer **FORESIGHT** is torpedoed by an Italian bomber and scuttled next day. The main force next turns back at the entrance to the Straits. The convoy carries on, still with 13 merchantmen and its close escort of four cruisers and 12 destroyers.

Disaster strikes soon after 20.00 to the northwest of Cape Bon. Italian submarines *Axum* and *Dessié* hit cruisers **Nigeria** and *Cairo* and tanker *Ohio*, and *Alagi* torpedoes the **Kenya**. **CAIRO** has to be scuttled and *Nigeria* sent back to Gibraltar. Around this time, aircraft sink two transports. *Charybdis* and two destroyers are dispatched from the main force to replace the lost ships.

In the early hours of the 13th, the convoy is hugging the coast south of Cape Bon when Italian MTBs strike. Four merchantmen are sent to the bottom and cruiser **MANCHESTER** hit. She has to be scuttled.

Air attacks later that morning account for one more merchantman, disable another which is finished off in the

INDIAN & PACIFIC OCEANS

AUGUST

Guadalcanal, Solomon Islands

The Japanese are now extending their hold in the southern Solomons and building an airfield on Guadalcanal. From there they can move against the New Hebrides, New Caledonia and other islands along the supply routes to Australia and New Zealand.

After the Japanese presence on Guadalcanal is discovered, the US 1st Marine Division is landed on the 7th, soon capturing the airstrip, which is renamed Henderson Field. Close cover is provided by a force of Australian and American cruisers.

9th — Battle of Savo Island — In the early hours of the 9th a Japanese force of seven cruisers and a destroyer heads for Savo Island to the north of Guadalcanal to get at the US transports. Instead they stumble on five patrolling cruisers. Taken completely by surprise, heavy cruisers **CANBERRA** and the American *Astoria*, *Quincy* and *Vincennes* are hit by a torrent of gunfire and torpedoes and sink in what will become known as Ironbottom Sound. *Australia* and *Hobart* are close by but take no part in the action. The transports are untouched.

From now on, as both sides try to bring in supplies and reinforcements, numerous naval battles are fought in and around the southern Solomons.

Battle of the Eastern Solomons — On the 24th, Japanese and American carrier groups covering supply operations to Guadalcanal are in action to the east of the island chain. Light carrier *Ryujo* is sunk and the *Enterprise* damaged.

From now on the Japanese rely increasingly on 'Tokyo Express' destroyers to bring in supplies by night down 'The Slot' between the islands of the Solomons.

Adm Somerville's Eastern Fleet carries out diversionary moves in the Indian Ocean at the time of the Guadalcanal landings. But he is continually losing ships to other theatres and by month's end is down to *Warspite*, *Valiant*, *Illustrious* and a few cruisers and destroyers; he also has too few escorts. By this time Japanese submarines are appearing in the Indian Ocean and taking a steady toll of Allied shipping. Until the end of 1944 they will be joined for various periods by German U-boats, sometimes direct from Europe and at other times operating out of Penang.

Papua, New Guinea

In their move on Port Moresby, Japanese troops land at Milne Bay at the extreme southeast tip of Papua on the 25th. The mainly Australian resistance is strong and, by the 30th, the invaders are starting to evacuate. By early September they have gone — the first major setback Japanese forces have experienced on land.

29th — Japanese submarine *RO33* attacks Australian troop reinforcements bound for Port Moresby and is sunk off the harbour by Australian destroyer *Arunta*.

Merchant Shipping War
Losses
- Indian Ocean — 1 ship of 5,000 tons.
- Pacific — 3 ships of 1,500 tons.

The 'C' class destroyer HMS *Cygnet*. The 'C' and 'D' classes of 14 ships (including leaders) lost nine ships. Completed 1932-33, they were otherwise similar to the 'A' and 'B' classes. *Cygnet* later served in the RCN as HMCS *St Laurent*, together with *Fraser*, *Margaree* and *Ottawa* (all three sunk), *Assinboine*, *Restigouche* and *Kootenay*.
Real Photos (S1355)

SEPTEMBER

2nd-26th — Russian Convoy PQ18 and Return QP14 — PQ18 leaves Loch Ewe in Scotland on the 2nd with over 40 merchantmen. The hard learnt lessons of PQ17 and previous convoys are not forgotten. Close escort is provided by 17 warships plus escort carrier *Avenger* and two destroyers. Two separate forces are in support — close in is cruiser *Scylla* and 16 fleet destroyers under Rear-Adm R. L. Burnett, and further out three heavy cruisers. Cover is given by Vice-Adm Sir Bruce Fraser with battleships *Anson* and *Duke of York*, a light cruiser and destroyers to the northeast of Iceland. Submarines patrol off the Lofoten Islands and northern Norway.

German heavy ships move to Altenfiord but do not sortie. Instead the attacks are mounted by bombers and torpedo aircraft as well as U-boats. On the 13th, aircraft torpedo nine ships, but next day *Avenger's* Hurricanes ensure only one more ship is lost to air attack. In total over 40 aircraft are shot down by the convoy's defences. U-boats sink three merchantmen but lose three of their number to Adm Burnett's forces. Destroyers *Faulknor*, *Onslow* and *Impulsive* sink *U88*, *U589* and *U457* respectively between the 12th and 16th in the Greenland and Barents Seas, but some sources reverse the identity of *U88* and *U589*. *Avenger's* Swordfish from 825 Squadron help with the destruction of *Onslow's* kill on the 14th. Out of the original 40 ships, 27 reach Archangel on the 17th.

Meanwhile return convoy QP14 with 15 ships has sailed on

SEPTEMBER

Merchant Shipping War
Losses
● 1 ship of 2,000 tons.

evening, and damage *Ohio* yet again with bombs and a crashing Stuka. Including the one tanker, five ships are left.

Now into the afternoon, three of them reach Malta. The fourth struggles in the next day, but the crippled *Ohio*, lashed to destroyer *Penn*, does not get there until the 15th. (Capt Mason is awarded the George Cross.) By now the close escort has just got back to Gibraltar.

Earlier on, an Italian cruiser force has set out to add to the convoy's miseries, but has turned for home. North of Sicily on the 13th it is sighted by submarine *Unbroken* (Lt A. C. G. Mars). Heavy cruiser *Bolzano* and the light *Attendolo* are both torpedoed and damaged.

Only five ships have got through for the loss of one carrier, two cruisers and a destroyer sunk, and a carrier and two cruisers badly damaged. But the supplies delivered — and especially the *Ohio's* vital oil — are enough to sustain Malta as an offensive base at a time critical to the coming Battle of El Alamein. More is still needed however, and only two days after *Ohio's* arrival, *Furious* flies off more Spitfires while submarines carry on with their supply trips.

22nd — Italian torpedo boat *Cantore* is lost on mines laid by submarine *Porpoise* northeast of Tobruk.

North Africa

Just after Gen Montgomery assumes command of Eighth Army, Rommel makes his last attempt to get round the El Alamein defences. In the Battle of Alam Halfa his attack breaks on the ridge of that name 15 miles behind the main lines. By early September he is back to his starting position.

29th — As escort destroyer **ERIDGE** returns from bombarding Axis positions west of El Alamein, she is torpedoed and badly damaged by a German E-boat, and declared a constructive total loss.

Merchant Shipping War

Losses
● 13 ships of 110,000 tons.

SEPTEMBER

13th/14th — Raid on Tobruk: Operation 'Agreement' — To help relieve the pressure on Eighth Army, a combined operations' raid is to be made on Tobruk to destroy installations and shipping. Simultaneously an attack will be launched from the landward side by the Long Range Desert Group. Destroyers *Sikh* and *Zulu* together with coastal forces' craft are to land Royal Marine and army units, while AA cruiser *Coventry* and 'Hunts' provide cover.

In the night of the 13th/14th, a few troops get ashore but **SIKH** is soon disabled by shore batteries. She goes down early in the morning of the 14th off Tobruk. As the other ships withdraw, heavy attacks by German and Italian aircraft sink **COVENTRY** and **ZULU** to the northwest of Alexandria. The land attack also fails.

Submarine **TALISMAN** leaves Gibraltar on the 10th with stores for Malta. She reports a U-boat off Philippeville on the 15th, but is not heard from again — presumed mined in the Strait of Sicily.

Merchant Shipping War

Losses
● 4 ships of 800 tons.

HMS *Sikh*, the 'Tribal' class destroyer, was sunk off Tobruk on Monday 14 September 1942 with 23 killed and the rest of the ship's company taken prisoner. *Real Photos (S1117)*

SEPTEMBER

Madagascar

Britain decides to occupy the rest of this Vichy French island. Starting on the 10th, British, East African and South African troops are landed through the month at points in the northwest, east and southwest. By the 23rd the capital, Tananarive, is captured but fighting continues into October. The Vichy French do not surrender until early November, by which time they have been driven down into the extreme southeast corner.

Papua, New Guinea

In mid-month the Japanese reach their furthest point down the Kokoda Trail, within 30 miles of Port Moresby. Now the Australian troops go over to the attack and slowly drive on towards Kokoda.

Guadalcanal, Solomon Islands

As the two sides struggle to build up their forces, more fighting takes place for possession of Henderson Field.

An old friend of the RN and Malta is lost when US carrier *Wasp* is torpedoed by submarine *I19* on the 15th. She is yet another casualty of the attempts to reinforce the island. Only *Hornet*

the 13th to gain the protection of *Avenger* and Adm Burnett's force. On the 20th, to the west of Bear Island, minesweeper **LEDA** is sunk by *U435* and support group destroyer **SOMALI** torpedoed by *U703*. After struggling for four days in tow towards Iceland a gale blows up and she founders to the north of her destination. Three merchant ships are lost to U-boats and the survivors reach Loch Ewe on the 26th.

In late 1941, escort carrier *Audacity* closed the Gibraltar air-gap for the first time. *Avenger* has now done the same for the Russian route. However, further convoys have to be postponed as ships are transferred in preparation for the North African landings.

3rd — *U162* attacks destroyer *Pathfinder* north of Trinidad and is then sunk by her and accompanying destroyers *Quentin* and *Vimy*.

11th — Canadian corvette **CHARLOTTETOWN** on passage with a minesweeper in the Gulf of St Lawrence is sunk by *U517*.

14th — *U91* sends Canadian destroyer **OTTAWA** to the bottom, east of Newfoundland. She is with the Canadian C4 group protecting UK/North American convoy ON127, which loses seven ships to U-boats.

Off West Africa, *U156* sinks the liner *Laconia* with 1,800 Italian POWs aboard on the 12th. Her CO calls for assistance in clear and other U-boats come to the rescue. Unfortunately an American aircraft attacks them and Dönitz subsequently forbids U-boats to help ships' survivors. He is indicted for the 'Laconia order' at the Nürnberg trials.

26th — U-boats attack convoy RB1 of Great Lakes steamers bound for the UK. In mid-Atlantic, escorting destroyer **VETERAN** is lost to *U404*. There are no survivors and her fate is not determined until after the war, from German records.

After sinking just three ships, German raider *Stier* encounters the American freighter *Stephen Hopkins* in the South Atlantic on the 27th. The *Hopkins* is sunk, but not before her single 4in gun damages the raider so severely that she has to be abandoned.

Battle of the Atlantic

U-boats continue to operate off Sierra Leone and the northern coast of South America where Allied losses remain high. Off Trinidad alone 29 ships of 143,000 tons go down in September. However, the interlocking convoy system is well on the way to being established off the Americas, and is increasing in effectiveness. In September the western termini for Atlantic convoys are moved from Halifax (Nova Scotia) and Sydney (Cape Breton) to New York. In time, pressure on the port becomes so great that some convoys are moved back to Halifax in March.

A long felt need starts to be met when Adm Noble forms the first support groups. These highly trained flotillas are to be used to reinforce the escorts of convoys under heavy attack, and although called Escort Groups should not be confused with the groups of 1941, often temporary in nature and with a diversity of ship types. Some of the new Escort Groups are formed around the new escort carriers that are entering service — the first since *Audacity*. Unfortunately none of these will be available to fight the Battle of the Atlantic for another six months: they are needed for the invasion of French North Africa.

Losses

● 102 ships of 531,000 tons and 5 escorts.

● 1 raider and 9 U-boats including 3 by US and RAF aircraft in the North Atlantic; 1 by RAF Bay of Biscay patrols; 1 on an RAF-laid mine in the Bay of Biscay.

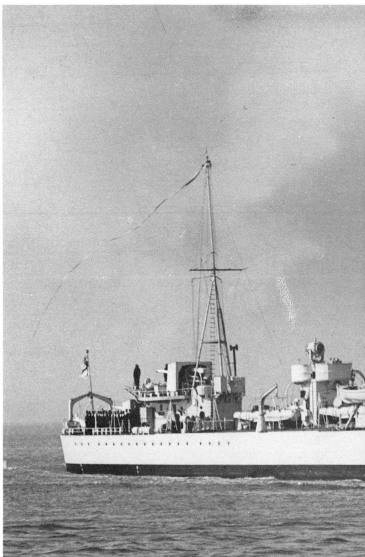

remains in the South Pacific, but she is joined by the repaired *Enterprise* in October.

Gilbert Islands

After their brief landing in December, Japanese forces re-occupy the atoll of Tarawa and start to fortify it.

23rd — Australian troops are carried to the occupied island of Timor in Australian destroyer **VOYAGER** to reinforce a guerilla unit known as Sparrow Force. She runs aground on the south coast of the island, is bombed by the Japanese and has to be destroyed.

Merchant Shipping War
Losses
- Indian Ocean — 6 ships of 30,000 tons.
- Pacific — 1 ship of 3,000 tons.

Left:
The 'F' class destroyer HMS *Faulknor*. The 'E' and 'F' classes, of 18 ships (including leaders) lost nine with one not repaired. They were completed 1934-35 with main characteristics similar to the 'A' and 'B' classes. Three were transferred to the RCN later in the war as HMC Ships *Gatineau*, *Qu'Appelle* and *Saskatchewan*. *Real Photos (S1096)*

Below:
The 'G', 'H' and 'I' class destroyers are represented here by HMS *Hero*. From the total of 27 ships, including leaders, 20 were sunk. Completed 1936-38, they were again very similar to the original 'A' and 'B' classes. *Hero* served as HMCS *Chaudiere* from 1943, together with *Griffin* as *Ottawa* (2). *Real Photos (S1098)*

ATLANTIC

OCTOBER

2nd — Off northwest Ireland the 81,000-ton liner *Queen Mary*, sailing as a fast unescorted troopship, meets her Western Approaches escort AA cruiser **CURACOA** and then accidentally rams and sinks her with the loss of over 300 men.

8th — *U179* sinks a merchantman off Cape Town and is then depth-charged and rammed to destruction by destroyer *Active*. Four other U-boats have preceeded *U179* to South African waters and in just four weeks sink over 20 ships.

15th/16th — Halifax/UK convoy SC104 (47 ships escorted by the British B6 group) loses eight merchantmen to U-boats. However, in mid-Atlantic on the 15th, destroyer *Viscount* rams and sinks *U619*, and next day destroyer *Fame* accounts for *U353*, also by ramming. (Note: the identity of *U619* is sometimes reversed with *U661* sunk in the vicinity by the RAF.)

Submarine **UNIQUE** on passage from Britain to Gibraltar is last reported on the 9th off Land's End. She is never heard from again.

23rd — Two U-boats are on patrol off the Congo Estuary, and *U161* torpedoes and badly damages cruiser **Phoebe** on passage to French Equatorial Africa.

Battle of the Atlantic
Losses continue high in the North Atlantic, many of them in the air-gaps on the trans-Atlantic and Sierra Leone routes which aircraft cannot reach from Newfoundland, Iceland, Northern Ireland, Gibraltar or Freetown. For example, Atlantic convoys HX212 and SC107 lose six and 15 ships, and Sierra Leone convoy SL125 as many as 13. Apart from escort carriers, more very long range (VLR) aircraft are still needed by RAF Coastal Command. Only one squadron — No 120 — is equipped with the VLR B-24 Liberators.

In October there are nearly 200 operational U-boats out of a total of 365. Their losses are increasing as the effectiveness of the air and sea escorts and patrols improves, but nowhere near enough to offset new construction.

Losses
- 82 ships of 548,000 tons and 1 cruiser.
- 15 U-boats including 6 by RAF in North Atlantic; 1 by RAF Bay of Biscay patrols; 1 by RAF-laid mine in the Bay of Biscay; 2 by RCAF off Newfoundland; 1 by US aircraft off French Guiana; 1 by unknown causes, possibly by US aircraft.

NOVEMBER

New fast (F) and slow (S) convoys start in October and November between the UK and North African ports:

- UK out — KMF and KMS.
- Home to UK — MKF and MKS.

From April these convoys sail to and from the Gibraltar area mainly with the OS and SL ships.

15th — The Germans react to the 'Torch' landings by concentrating U-boats off Morocco and to the west of Gibraltar. A number of empty transports are sunk, and on the 15th escort carrier **AVENGER** sailing with return convoy MKF1 is torpedoed by *U155* and goes down off the Strait of Gibraltar. Only 12 men survive. That same day, destroyer *Wrestler*, also with MKF1 sinks *U411*. Over the next few days US destroyers account for *U173* and the RAF for *U98*.

EUROPE

OCTOBER

14th — German raider *Komet* attempts to pass down the Channel on the way out to her second cruise. A force of RN escort destroyers and MTBs attack off Cherbourg, and in spite of her strong escort, she is torpedoed and sunk by *MTB236*.

Eastern Front

The Germans make little progress in the Caucasus. By November they are being worn down and the Russians start to go over to the offensive.

Hitler decides to concentrate on taking Stalingrad and major attacks are started in October and then November. Neither attack succeeds during vicious house-to-house, factory-to-factory, fighting.

Merchant Shipping War
Losses
- 6 ships of 13,000 tons.

The light cruiser HMAS *Adelaide*, served after February 1942 with the ANZAC Squadron in the South West Pacific and Indian Ocean areas. *Real Photos (S1486)*

NOVEMBER

11th — Submarine **UNBEATEN**, on patrol in the Bay of Biscay for U-boats on passage to and from Atlantic operations, is lost in an attack by a RAF Wellington.

Eastern Front

As the Germans in the Caucasus and within Stalingrad are slowly ground down, the Russians start their long-planned major offensive to relieve the city and trap the invaders in the Caucasus. Along 50-mile fronts to the north and the south, two large armies break through the largely Roumanian defenders. Before the month is out they have joined up, and the Sixth Army under Gen Paulus is surrounded.

Merchant Shipping War
Losses
- 5 ships of 6,000 tons.

MEDITERRANEAN

OCTOBER

French North Africa

In preparation for Operation 'Torch', US Gen Mark Clark lands in Algeria from submarine Seraph to help persuade the Vichy French authorities to support the coming Allied landings. Gen Giraud is to be smuggled from unoccupied France, again in Seraph, to head pro-Allied Frenchmen.

19th — South of Pantellaria, submarine *Unbending* attacks an Axis convoy bound for Tripoli. She sinks a transport and Italian destroyer *Da Verazzano*.

North Africa: The Second Battle of El Alamein

Gen Montgomery starts the final and decisive British offensive against the Axis forces in Egypt. On the night of the 23rd a massive bombardment precedes the advance of first infantry and then armour through the German and Italian lines in the centre. Progress is at first slow and the battle becomes a straight slogging match. Australian troops play an important part with a thrust in the north near the sea.

In the build-up to the battle, RN submarines and RAF aircraft, especially those based in Malta, are sinking more than a third of Axis supplies setting out for North Africa. As the offensive gets underway, the Inshore Squadron will continue to support and supply Eighth Army along its right flank.

At the end of the month, carrier *Furious* flies off Spitfires to Malta. The island even now is short of supplies and what little is getting through is carried by submarines and cruiser-minelayers.

30th — Destroyers *Pakenham*, *Petard* and *Hero*, escort destroyers *Dulverton* and *Hurworth* and RAF aircraft of No 47 Squadron sink *U559* north of Port Said.

Merchant Shipping War
Losses
● No Allied merchant ships are lost in October.

NOVEMBER

North Africa

By the 4th the Second Battle of El Alamein has been won by Eighth Army. Rommel's losses in men and material are so great he withdraws, first to Fuka and then Mersa Matruh. The British get there by the 7th. New Zealand troops enter Sidi Barrani on the 9th and two days later have reached the Libyan border. As the remaining Axis troops continue to fall back, Eighth Army enters Tobruk on the 12th and Benghazi a week later.

Rommel has moved back to the old 'start/finish' line of El Agheila by the end of the month. Montgomery halts Eighth Army after a 600-mile advance in 14 days.

8th — French North African Landings: Operation 'Torch'
— *By July the Allies have accepted that a cross-Channel assault on German-occupied Europe is not yet possible, and instead opt to land an expeditionary force in French North Africa. For political reasons the main landing forces will be American. Their arrival will be timed to coincide with Eighth Army's offensive.*

INDIAN & PACIFIC OCEANS

OCTOBER

Burma

In the first Arakan campaign a limited offensive is launched from India to take Akyab. By year's end the British and Indian forces are still short of their objective.

Papua, New Guinea

The Australians continue to push their way up the Kokoda Trail against the usual Japanese resistance, as US troops take a parallel track to reach the coast south of Buna. Landings also take place up the north coast from Milne Bay in preparation for the coming assault on Buna and Gona.

Guadalcanal, Solomon Islands

As the struggle carries on for the island's one airfield, supply and support operations lead to two more major naval battles:

Battle of Cape Esperance — Off the north tip of Guadalcanal on the night of the 11th/12th, a US cruiser force is in action with a similar Japanese force. Both sides lose a destroyer, and the Japanese a heavy cruiser.

Battle of Santa Cruz — From Truk, a large Japanese carrier and battleship task force approaches the southern Solomons to support a major land attack on Henderson Field. On the 26th they are in action with a much smaller US carrier group north of the Santa Cruz Islands. *Hornet* is lost and *Enterprise* put out of action in exchange for heavy damage to the carrier *Shokaku*.

The damaged *Enterprise* is now the only US carrier in the South Pacific. Adm King, US Navy Commander-in-Chief, asks for the loan of a fleet carrier from the RN. Some bad feeling is generated when problems are raised about the need to re-equip with US aircraft. Nevertheless, *Victorious* is ordered out in December.

Merchant Shipping War
Losses
● Indian Ocean — 11 ships of 64,000 tons.
● Pacific — 2 ships of 14,000 tons.

NOVEMBER

11th — Action of the *Bengal* and *Ondina* — Two Japanese raiders armed with 6in guns attack the Dutch tanker *Ondina* (one 4in) and her escort, the Royal Indian minesweeper *Bengal* (single 12pdr) commanded by Lt-Cdr W. J. Wilson RINR, to the southwest of the Cocos Islands in the Indian Ocean. *Bengal* hits *Hokoku Maru* which shortly blows up. The other raider soon disappears. Both Allied ships are damaged and separated, but reach port safely after this small ship action that ranks with the sinking of the *Stier* by the *Stephen Hopkins* just two months earlier.

Papua, New Guinea

Kokoda is captured on the 2nd, and by mid-month Australian and American troops are attacking the strongly fortified positions around Buna and Gona. Fierce fighting carries on throughout November and December.

15th — Canadian destroyer **SAGUENAY**, escorting an iron ore convoy off Cape Race, Newfoundland, is badly damaged in collision, and is not repaired.

18th/20th — UK/North America convoy ONS144 is heavily attacked in the mid-Atlantic and loses five ships. Escort is provided by the British B6 group largely composed of Norwegian corvettes. On the 18th the **Montbretia** is lost to *U624* or *U262*, but two days later her Norwegian sister-ship *Potentilla* sinks *U184*.

21st — Aircraft of 817 Squadron from fleet carrier *Victorious* account for *U517* southwest of Ireland.

Archangel to Loch Ewe convoy QP15 with 28 ships loses two to U-boat attack.

Battle of the Atlantic

World-wide losses in tonnage due to Axis aubmarines are the highest of any month of the war — 119 ships of 729,000 tons, mostly in the Atlantic. By year's end, submarines in 1942 will have accounted for 1,160 ships of 6,266,000 tons or a monthly average of 522,000 tons. Losses in the North and South Atlantic will not be far short of this total. To deal with this grave threat, a Cabinet Anti-U-boat Warfare Committee (*not* the 1941 Battle of the Atlantic Committee) is formed under the chairmanship of Winston Churchill. It sees the first need as closing the mid-Atlantic gap once and for all. Steps are taken to further expand Coastal Command and speed up the introduction of VLR aircraft into the fray.

Adm Sir Max Horton, commander of home-based submarines since 1940 and a World War 1 submariner himself, succeeds Adm Noble as C-in-C, Western Approaches.

Losses

● 93 ships of 567,000 tons, 1 escort carrier, 1 destroyer and 1 corvette.

● 7 U-boats including one by US aircraft off Iceland, and one possibly by the RAF in the North Atlantic.

Below:
The 'Tribal' class destroyer HMS *Ashanti*. These were relatively heavily armed destroyers, with a first group of 16 ships of which 12 were lost. Completed 1938-39 and displacing 1,870 tons with a speed of 36kt, they carried eight 4.7in guns and 190 crew. The second group included seven ships completed for the RAN and RCN between 1942 and the war's end, with HMCS *Athabaskan* lost and HMCS *Haida* now preserved in Canada. *Real Photos (S1017)*

Far right:
The still incomplete French battleship *Jean Bart* at Casablanca in 1941 with members of the Disarmament Commission. By the time of the North African landings on 8 November 1942, the forward 15in turret had been mounted and returned the fire of US warships.
Real Photos (S1858)

MEDITERRANEAN

Plans are formally approved in October, by which time the large amounts of shipping needed have been organised and assembled. To provide them, Russian convoys and those to and from Britain and Gibraltar/West Africa have been suspended and the Home Fleet stripped bare. The Allies' greatest concern is the hundred or more U-boats at sea.

Outline order of battle is:

Allied Commander-in-Chief
US Gen Dwight D. Eisenhower

Allied Naval Commander Expeditionary Force
Adm Sir Andrew Cunningham

Landing areas:	Casablanca, Morocco	Oran, Algeria	Algiers, Algeria
Departure from: Forces landing:	United States 35,000 US	Britain 39,000 US	Britain 33,000 US and British
Naval Task Forces and Commanders:	*Western* Rear-Adm H. K. Hewitt USN	*Centre* Cdre T. H. Troubridge	*Eastern* Vice-Adm Sir Harold Burrough
Battleships	3	—	—
Carriers	5	2	2
Cruisers	7	2	3
Destroyers	38	13	13
Other warships	16	41	40
Troop and supply transports, tankers, etc	36	47	33
Totals	105 USN	105 RN	91 RN

Most of the task force carriers are escort carriers, and the US totals include their cover force. In the Mediterranean Force H, reinforced by Home Fleet and under the command of Vice-Adm Sir Neville Syfret, covers the Algerian landings. The force's main task is to hold off any attack by the Italian fleet. Strength includes three capital ships, three fleet carriers, three cruisers and 17 destroyers. Various other forces add to the number of Allied ships in the area.

Over 300 ships are therefore directly involved in what is at that time the greatest amphibious operation in history, and the forerunner of even greater ones to come before the war is won. Throughout October and early November convoys sail for the landings on Vichy French soil in the early hours of the 8th. Negotiations with the French are not completed in time to avoid resistance. There is bloodshed on both sides.

Casablanca — US troops are landed at three points along a 200-mile stretch of coastline. By the 10th they prepare to attack Casablanca itself, but this is made unnecessary when the French forces stop fighting. Before this happens the Western Task Force has fought a series of fierce actions with Vichy French warships. Battleship *Jean Bart* is seriously damaged and a cruiser and several destroyers and submarines sunk or beached.

Oran — The landings to the west and east of the city are followed by an attempt to smash through the harbour boom, and land troops directly from ex-US Coast Guard cutters **WALNEY** (Capt Peters) and **HARTLAND**. Both are disabled by ship and shore gunfire and soon sink. Cruiser *Aurora* (Capt Agnew) and destroyers fight off an attack by French destroyers outside the port. The large *Epervier* is driven ashore and *Tornade* and *Tramontane* disabled. In addition, destroyers *Achates* and *Westcott* account for the submarines *Actéon* and *Argonaute*. (✠ Capt Frederick Peters RN of the *Walney* is awarded the Victoria Cross for his gallantry. Five days later he is killed in an aircraft accident.)

US troops fight their way into Oran, which falls on the 10th.

INDIAN & PACIFIC OCEANS

Guadalcanal, Solomon Islands

Three more naval battles take place as US forces start to push the Japanese away from the airfield towards Cape Esperance.

First Battle of Guadalcanal — On the night of the 12th/13th a large Japanese troop convoy approaches accompanied by two battleships to bombard Henderson Field. A US cruiser force sets out to meet them in Ironbottom Sound. They lose two cruisers and four destroyers, and the Japanese two destroyers in the fighting. Also, the Japanese battleship *Hiei* is disabled by gunfire and later finished off by aircraft attack.

Second Battle of Guadalcanal — Two nights later the Japanese again try to bring in troop transports. This time a battleship action results and *Kirishima* is sunk by the *Washington*.

Battle of Tassafaronga — At the end of the month, on the 30th and in the same area, an eight-destroyer 'Tokyo Express' is intercepted by US cruisers and destroyers. One of the Japanese is sunk but at the cost of one cruiser lost and three severely damaged as the 24in Long Lance torpedoes tear through the US lines.

On the 30th, German raider *Thor* is destroyed in Yokohama when a supply ship laying alongside catches fire and blows up. Since leaving France in January she has sunk or captured 10 ships of 56,000 tons.

Merchant Shipping War

A few Japanese submarines continue to operate in the Indian Ocean and now are joined by a number of German U-boats off the east coast of South Africa.

Losses
● Indian Ocean only — 23 ships of 131,000 tons.

Top:
Ex-Brazilian and Turkish destroyers including HMS *Inconstant* (shown here) and seven others taken over by RN. *Havant, Harvester* and *Hurricane* were sunk and *Ithuriel* not repaired. Completed 1940-41, they were similar to the 'G' to 'I' classes. *Real Photos (S1562)*

Above:
The 'O' class submarine *Otway*. The class of nine boats included *Oxley* (lost off Norway) and four more which were lost in the Mediterranean. Completed in 1927-30 at 1,400/1,900 tons, they could make 16/9kt. They were armed with eight torpedo tubes and a 4in gun, and had a crew of 55 *Real Photos (S354)*

Algiers — A similar opening attack is mounted with the old destroyers *Broke* and ***Malcolm***. The latter is badly damaged but ***BROKE*** eventually breaks through the boom to land her troops. Hard hit by shore batteries, she gets away to founder next day, on the 9th. Algiers is soon in Allied hands and Adm Darlan, C-in-C Vichy French forces, captured.

It is not Gen Giraud, but Adm Darlan who broadcasts the ceasefire on the 10th. Resistance is stopped, but confusion reigns for a number of days as the Vichy French authorities are pressurised by both the Allies and Axis. However, before long the forces of France are fighting on the Allied side in French North Africa. Adm Darlan is assassinated in late December and Gen Giraud takes his place.

On receiving news of the 'Torch' landings, Hitler orders his troops into unoccupied France on the 11th. On the 27th, SS units try to capture the French fleet at Toulon. They are too late to stop the scuttling of three battleships, seven cruisers, 30 destroyers, 16 submarines and many other smaller vessels. The first German troops also land in Tunisia on the 9th and within two days start their build-up.

Throughout all these events Spain fortunately stays neutral. There is therefore no threat to Gibraltar directly from Spanish troops, or from the Germans passing through the country. And the Americans in Morocco are safe from attack by the Spanish in Spanish Morocco.

9th — Off Oran the Corvette ***GARDENIA*** is lost in collison with armed trawler *Fluellen*.

9th/24th — In RN submarine operations off northwest Sicily, *Saracen* sinks Italian submarine *Granito* on the 9th. On the 24th ***UTMOST*** is lost to Italian destroyer escort *Groppo*.

In addition to the Atlantic approaches to Gibraltar, a large number of German and Italian submarines are concentrated in the Western Mediterranean to attack the 'Torch' follow-up convoys. Transports and escorting warships are sunk and damaged, but losses are never great, and seven submarines are sunk in exchange:

10th — Off Algiers, destroyer ***MARTIN*** is sunk by *U431*. Italian submarine *Emo* is scuttled after an attack by armed trawler *Lord Nuffield*.

12th-15th — *U660* is sunk by escorting corvettes *Lotus* and *Starwort* northeast of Oran on the 12th. Next day *Lotus*, this time with *Poppy*, accounts for *U605* off Algiers. On the 14th and 15th respectively, *U595* and *U259* are sunk by aircraft.

13th — *U431* sends Dutch destroyer ***Isaac Sweers*** to the bottom northwest of Algiers.

17th — *U331* is damaged by RAF Hudsons of No 500 Squadron and tries to surrender. Aircraft of 820 Squadron from carrier *Formidable* then torpedo her in error off Algiers.

28th — North of Bône the Italian *Dessié* is sunk by destroyers *Quentin* and the Australian *Quiberon*, now part of cruiser Force Q operating out of Bône.

On the 11th and 12th, troops are landed at Bougie and Bône. There is little air cover, and attacks on these and other Algerian ports by German aircraft sink or damage a number of ships:

10th — Sloop ***IBIS*** is torpedoed and goes down off Algiers.

20th — Cruiser ***Delhi*** is damaged by bombs in Algiers Bay.

28th — Destroyer ***ITHURIEL*** in harbour at Bône is badly damaged and not repaired.

18th/20th — The Relief of Malta — At the beginning of the month, cruiser-minelayer *Welshman* runs vitally needed stores

HMS *Achates*, an 'A' class destroyer. She took part in the Battle of the Barents Sea, and on New Year's Eve, Thursday 31 December, 1942, sank some 240 miles northwest of the Kola Inlet with 80 survivors being picked up. *Real Photos (N1039)*

The French battlecruiser *Strasbourg* firing at Force H off Oran in July 1940. She was one of the many major warships scuttled at Toulon on 27 November 1942 as the occupying German forces approached. *Real Photos*

DECEMBER

The world's first atomic reactor goes critical at Chicago University. By now problems have arisen over the sharing of the US work with Britain.

16th — In attacks on UK/North America convoy ON153, *U211* sinks destroyer **FIREDRAKE** in mid-Atlantic on the night of the 16th/17th.

26th — Outward bound *U357* is detected by HF/DF to the northwest of Ireland. Destroyers *Hesperus* and *Vanessa* of the British B2 group (Cdr MacIntyre) with convoy HX219 locate and sink her.

27th — *U356* attacks slow convoy ONS154 escorted by the Canadian C1 group to the north of the Azores. Destroyer *St Laurent* and corvettes *Battleford*, *Chilliwack* and *Napanee* all share in her sinking. Unfortunately the convoy loses 13 of its 45 ships.

31st — Battle of the Barents Sea and Russian Convoys JW51A and JW51B — After a three-month gap the first of the JW convoys set out. JW51 sails in two sections. Part A leaves Loch Ewe on the 15th with 16 ships for Kola Inlet. All arrive safely on Christmas Day accompanied by supporting cruisers *Jamaica* and *Sheffield*.

JW51B (14 ships) leaves on the 22nd escorted by six destroyers, a minesweeper and four smaller vessels under the command of Capt St. V. Sherbrooke in *Onslow*. Adm Burnett with *Jamaica* and *Sheffield* joins the convoy south west of Bear Island on the 29th to provide close cover through the Barents Sea.

By now, *Tirpitz*, pocket battleship *Lützow*, heavy cruiser *Admiral Hipper*, light cruisers *Köln* and *Nürnberg* and a number of 5in and 5.9in gun destroyers are in Norwegian waters. The Admiralty assumes they are there to attack Russian convoys. In fact, their presence is due to Hitler's fear that the Allies are about to invade Norway.

The convoy is reported on the 30th and the 8in *Hipper* (Adm Kummetz), 11in *Lützow* and six destroyers put to sea from

DECEMBER

3rd — Escort destroyer **PENYLAN**, with Portsmouth/Bristol Channel convoy PW257, is sunk by E-boat *S115* in the English Channel off Start Point.

The 'Cockleshell Heroes' — Maj H. G. Hasler leads Royal Marine Commandos in canoes up the Gironde Estuary in southwest France and damages several blockade runners with limpet mines on the 7th.

Eastern Front

A scratch German force tries to reach Stalingrad from the southwest, but is soon driven back. Further north, the Russians resume their push and annihilate an Italian army.

By now the Germans in the Caucasus are under heavy pressure and fear the Russians will reach Rostov and trap them. They begin to withdraw from the oilfields considered so important by Hitler.

Merchant Shipping War
Losses
- 10 ships of 9,000 tons

MEDITERRANEAN

to Malta. On the 11th, her sister-ship *Manxman* makes a similar dash from Alexandria. Then on the 17th a convoy of four ships, escorted by three cruisers and 10 destroyers, leaves Alexandria (Operation 'Stoneage'). Although cruiser **Arethusa** is badly damaged by German torpedo aircraft on the 18th and has to return with over 150 casualties, the convoy gets through on the 20th. Its arrival marks the effective lifting of the long and bloody siege of Malta.

Since Operation 'Excess' in January 1941, two aircraft carriers, four cruisers, 16 destroyers and five submarines have been lost in the many attempts to supply and reinforce the island, and in the heavy air attacks it has received.

French North Africa

After the Bougie and Bône landings, British paratroops land in the north and the advance begins on Bizerta and Tunis. US paratroops further south move on to Gafsa from where they threaten to take Gabes and cut Tunisia in half. Fighting takes place as the Allies close in, but by the time the main offensive starts on the 25th, the Germans have built up their forces around Bizerta and Tunis. They have also occupied the east coast towns of Sousse, Sfax and Gabes. Nevertheless, by month's end, units of the British First Army are within 12 miles of the capital.

Merchant Shipping War
Losses
- 13 ships of 103,000 tons.

DECEMBER

French North Africa

German forces counter-attack in the north, driving back the Allies. Much of the fighting takes place around Longstop Hill near Medjez el Bab. By the end of the year the Axis forces have established strong defence lines around Bizerta and Tunis, and are holding on to the eastern side of the country. The Allies have lost the race for Tunis.

Throughout January both sides attack along the line, but without much success. As this happens more and more German and Italian troops are drawn into the country. When the Axis command eventually surrenders in May, it will be found that it has drained Sicily and Italy of some of its best men.

2nd/14th — Cruiser Force Q from Bône and a new Malta-based cruiser force take turns attacking Axis shipping bound for North Africa. On the 2nd, Force Q with *Aurora*, *Argonaut* and *Sirius* and two destroyers goes into action in the Strait of Sicily. All four transports in a convoy and Italian destroyer *Folgore* are sunk by gunfire. As the Force returns, destroyer **QUENTIN** is lost to Italian torpedo aircraft north of Cape Bon. Two weeks later **Argonaut** is badly damaged by Italian submarine *Mocenigo* northeast of Bône.

Attacks on Allied shipping off Algeria lead to more losses. In return, one Italian submarine is sunk:

9th — Destroyer **PORCUPINE** escorts submarine depot ship *Maidstone* from Gibraltar to Algiers. Torpedoed off Oran by *U602* and badly damaged, she is not repaired. On the same day corvette **MARIGOLD** is sunk by torpedo aircraft to the west of Algiers while escorting North Africa/UK convoy MKS3.

11th — Escort destroyer **BLEAN** sailing with fast North Africa/UK convoy MKF4 is lost to *U443* west of Oran.

INDIAN & PACIFIC OCEANS

Admiral Hipper was one of the two German heavy ships taking part in the Battle of the Barents Sea on 31 December 1942.   *IWM (MA1009)*

Left:
The 'P' class submarine *Perseus* was lost in December 1941. Of a total of nine 'P' and 'R' class boats, only *Proteus* and *Rover* survived. The remaining seven were all lost in the Mediterranean. Completed in 1930-32 at 1,480/2,050 tons, they could make 17/9kt and were armed with eight torpedo tubes and a 4in or 4.7in gun, and had a crew of 55. *Real Photos (S308)*

DECEMBER

Guadalcanal, Solomon Islands

After four months of struggle, the US 1st Marine Division is relieved by the Army. Japanese destroyers continue to run in supplies by nightly 'Tokyo Express', but by the end of the month High Command in Tokyo has decided to evacuate its forces. Meanwhile US forces push west from Henderson Field.

Merchant Shipping War
Losses
- Indian Ocean only — 6 ships of 29,000 tons.

ATLANTIC

Altenfiord to intercept north of North Cape.

Early on the 31st, New Year's Eve, the British force is split into four parts. The main convoy with its five remaining 4in or 4.7in destroyers *Achates*, *Onslow*, *Obdurate*, *Obedient* and *Orwell* heads due east. (Some of the escort and merchantmen have been scattered by gales and never regain the convoy.) Adm Burnett's two 6in cruisers cover to the north. Further north still are a merchant ship and escorting trawler trying to reach the convoy. Finally, minesweeper *Bramble* is northeast of the convoy having been detached to search for missing ships.

Capt Sherbrooke plans to use the same tactics as those of Adm Vian in the Second Battle of Sirte and head for the enemy while the convoy turns away under smoke. Unfortunately Adm Kummetz divides his force and plans to attack from astern on both sides — *Hipper* and three destroyers on the north and *Lützow* with the other three on the south.

At around 09.30 the action starts when *Hipper's* three destroyers, heading north across the rear of the convoy, open fire on *Obdurate*. The convoy later turns south as planned, but towards *Lützow*. Then *Onslow*, *Orwell* and *Obedient* sight *Hipper* and hold her off until, at 10.20, **Onslow** is hit and Capt Sherbrooke badly wounded.

Adm Burnett's cruisers meanwhile have been diverted north by the straggler. They only head towards the action at 10.00.

Still to the north of the convoy, *Hipper* and her destroyers come across the hapless **BRAMBLE** and send her to the bottom at around 10.40. They head south, and 40min later the 8in cruiser approaches JW51B, opens fire and hits **ACHATES** which sinks after the battle is over.

Lützow has already come up on the convoy but does not join battle until 11.45. She is driven off by the remaining destroyers. By now *Jamaica* and *Sheffield* have arrived on the scene. They quickly damage *Hipper* and sink destroyer *Friedrich Eckoldt*. *Hipper* tries to get back to the convoy but again the destroyers skilfully keep her at bay.

By midday the German ships are withdrawing with the two cruisers in pursuit. Contact is shortly lost. None of the merchantmen are more than lightly damaged and all 14 reach Kola on the 3rd January.

Return convoy RA51 leaves Kola on the 30th. After being supported part of the way by *Jamaica* and *Sheffield*, its 14 ships are safely delivered to Loch Ewe on the 11th January.

When Hitler learns that his big ships have been driven off by light cruisers and destroyers he flies into a rage and orders all of them to be paid off. Grand-Adm Raeder resigns in protest and is succeeded as C-in-C, German Navy, in January by Adm Dönitz. The paying-off order is revoked.

✠ Capt Rupert St. V. Sherbrooke RN is awarded the Victoria Cross for gallantry.

Battle of the Atlantic

Total U-boat strength at year's end approaches 400 compared to 250 in January, and this is in spite of 86 having been destroyed in 1942. Of the total, over 200 are operational. Many of these are on passage but the numbers on patrol are still great and increasing. Most are in the North Atlantic or west of Gibraltar although groups operate off West Africa and South America with some success. The Allies can deploy 450 escort vessels of all types against the U-boats: this is a large number but still not enough to curb the menace and go over to the offensive.

In December the RN and its Allies regain an old advantage when, after a 10-month gap, the U-boat 'Triton' code for Atlantic operations is broken.

Losses
- 54 ships of 305,000 tons and 3 escorts.
- 1 destroyer and 5 U-boats including 1 each by US and indirectly by RAF aircraft in attacks on HX217; 1 by US Coast Guard in mid-Atlantic.

MEDITERRANEAN

13th — Sloop *Enchantress* sinks the Italian submarine *Corallo* off Bougie.

18th — *Porcupine's* sister-ship **PARTRIDGE** is torpedoed by *U565* while carrying out an A/S sweep with Force H. She goes down off Oran.

In the first USAAF raids on Italy, Italian light cruiser *Attendolo* is sunk and others damaged at Naples on the 4th.

Throughout the month, RN submarines are on patrol in the Western Mediterranean and lose four of their number. In return they sink several Axis ships including two Italian warships:

TRAVELLER leaves Malta on 28 November for the Gulf of Taranto. Overdue by the 8th, she is presumed mined in her patrol area.

6th — *Tigris* sinks submarine *Porfido* north of Bône.

12th — In the Gulf of Naples **P222** is lost to torpedo boat *Fortunale* while attacking a convoy.

17th — North of Bizerta, *Splendid* sinks destroyer *Aviere* escorting a convoy to North Africa.

25th — As a convoy heads into Tunis, **P48** attacks and is sunk by destroyer escorts *Ardente* and *Ardito*.

At the end of the month **P311** sails for Maddalena, Sardinia with Chariot human torpedoes for an attack on the cruisers based there. Her last signal is on the 31st and she is presumed lost on mines in the approaches to the port.

15th — Destroyers *Petard* and Greek *Queen Olga* sink Italian submarine *Uarsciek* south of Malta.

North Africa

On the 11th, Gen Montgomery resumes his advance. Under direct and flanking attack, Rommel abandons El Agheila and withdraws to defence lines at Buerat on the approaches to Tripoli. By now he has decided to make his main stand on the Mareth line in southern Tunisia. Eighth Army reaches Buerat by year's end.

19th — Escorting a convoy to Benghazi, corvette **SNAP-DRAGON** is bombed and sunk off there by German aircraft.

Merchant Shipping War

Losses
- 3 ships of 6,000 tons.

ATLANTIC

JANUARY

Russian convoy JW52 and return RA52 both set out in January. Out of the 25 ships in the two convoys, one of JW52's returns and one of RA52's is lost to U-boat attacks.

Battle of the Atlantic

Severe weather and evasive convoy routeing keeps losses down in January. However, south of the Azores, out of range of air cover, Trinidad/Gibraltar tanker convoy TM1 loses seven of its nine ships to U-boats.

Losses, including Russian Convoys

- 30 British, Allied and neutral ships of 189,000 tons in the North and South Atlantic.
- 4 U-boats including 1 by RAF in North Atlantic; 2 by US aircraft off Brazil; 1 by unknown causes.

Below:
HMS *Argus* operating off the Algerian coast. In late 1942/early 1943 she escorted KMF and MKF convoys as the French North Africa campaign continued. *IWM (A12882)*

EUROPE

JANUARY

RAF Bomber Command by night and increasingly the USAAF by day mount a growing attack on Germany and occupied Europe. As agreed at the Casablanca Conference, U-boat bases and their production centres are to be major targets in 1943. Yet in the first six months, not one U-boat is destroyed in air-raids and their construction programmes are hardly affected. Throughout the war no U-boats are lost in the incredibly strong, reinforced concrete shelters the Germans build at their main bases.

Eastern Front

The Russians are now strong enough to attack along parts of their front other than in the south. In the north they manage to open a narrow corridor through to Leningrad. The siege is partially lifted, but another year is needed to complete its liberation.

The offensive continues in the centre/south with the Russians aiming for Kursk, Kharkov and Rostov-on-Don. At the same time the pressure on the trapped Germans at Stalingrad is increased. A powerful attack early in the month leads to Gen Paulus and the remnants of the Sixth Army surrendering on the 31st and the last troops giving in on the 2 February. Further south still the German forces in the Caucasus start to retreat as the Russian attacks gather momentum. Those who can escape, do so through Rostov before its inevitable fall.

Merchant Shipping War

By now the attack is being carried into the waters of occupied Europe by coastal forces, the strike aircraft of RAF Coastal Command and minelayers of Bomber Command.

German aircraft, E-boats and mines continue to threaten shipping around the coasts of Britain, but few are now being lost — the minesweepers, convoy escorts and RAF fighters see to this.

Losses

- 4 ships of 16,000 tons in UK waters.

PROSPECTS FOR ALLIED VICTORY

The Russians have gained a famous victory with the German surrender at Stalingrad. Together with the British Battle of El Alamein and the American Battle of Midway, these three are usually considered as marking the turning point in the war against the Axis powers. However, 30 and more months of struggle and bloodshed must be endured before victory is certain.

And there is still one other battle that has to be won — the Battle of the Atlantic, which reaches a peak over the next four months.

MEDITERRANEAN

JANUARY

Axis attacks continue against Allied ships in Algerian ports and convoys off the coast. There are losses on both sides:

1st — Cruiser **Ajax** is severely damaged in Bône harbour by Ju87s.

13th/19th — Canadian corvettes carrying out convoy escort duties account for two submarines. *Ville de Quebec* sinks *U224* west of Algiers and *Port Arthur* the Italian *Tritone* by gunfire off Bougie.

30th — As corvette **SAMPHIRE** escorts Gibraltar/North African ports convoy TE14 she is torpedoed by Italian submarine *Platino* near Bougie.

Attempts by the Italian Navy to supply the Axis armies in Tunisia lead to heavy losses, especially on mines laid between Sicily and Tunis by minelayers *Abdiel* and *Welshman* and submarine *Rorqual*:

9th — Destroyer *Corsaro* hits one of *Abdiel's* mines northeast of Bizerta.

17th — Returning from Tunisia, destroyer *Bombardiere* is sunk off western Sicily by submarine *United*.

31st — Torpedo boat *Prestinari* and corvette *Procellaria* go down on mines laid by *Welshman* in the Strait of Sicily.

Casablanca Conference

Prime Minister Churchill and President Roosevelt with their Chiefs of Staff meet for this important conference. Major areas for discussion include the European invasion in 1944, landings in Sicily and Italy after the Tunisian campaign, the bombing of Germany and the continuation of the war in Burma and the Pacific. Losses due to U-boats and the shortage of shipping will prove to be significant constraints on Allied plans. At this time the two Allied leaders announce the policy of unconditional surrender of the Axis powers.

Final supply trips to Tripoli by Italian submarines lead to more losses north of the capital of Libya:

14th — *Narvalo* is attacked by a RAF Beaufort and finished off by destroyers *Pakenham* and *Hursley*, escorts to Malta/Alexandria convoy ME15.

20th — *Santarosa* is torpedoed off Tripoli by *MTB 260*, one of the growing number of coastal forces operating along the North African coast.

North Africa

Montgomery resumes the advance on the 15th, and Bueret, outflanked by British armour and New Zealand troops, is soon taken. The defences in front of Tripoli are similarly outflanked and on the 23rd the victorious Eighth Army enters the town.

21st — Submarine *Sahib* on patrol off western Corsica sinks *U301*.

Merchant Shipping War
Losses
● 14 British and Allied ships of 48,000 tons.

INDIAN & PACIFIC OCEANS

JANUARY

Burma

The first Arakan campaign continues as Indian troops try to move on Akyab.

Guadalcanal, Solomon Islands

Unknown to the Americans the Japanese have been ordered to evacuate. However, they still resist strongly as they are pushed back towards Cape Esperance.

5th — Operating off the Solomons with a US cruiser force, the New Zealand **Achilles** is badly damaged in a bombing attack off New Georgia Island.

29th — The Japanese still carry supplies to Guadalcanal by submarine, and *I1* is caught by New Zealand armed trawlers *Kiwi* and *Moa* to the north. In a fiercely fought action they manage to drive the 2,000-ton boat ashore just to the west of Cape Esperance and destroy her there.

Papua, New Guinea

The Buna and Gona area is slowly wrested from the Japanese, and by the 21st is in Allied hands. Papua, New Guinea has now been liberated. The first phase of the New Guinea campaign is over. Next is to clear the coast opposite New Britain and take the airfield at Lae. In preparation for this, Australian troops have already been airlifted to Wau, inland from Salamaua. Capturing the Huon Peninsula will take most of 1943.

Merchant Shipping War
Losses
● Pacific only — 2 ships of 9,000 tons.

ATLANTIC

FEBRUARY

4th/7th — Slow Halifax/UK convoy SC118 escorted by the British B2 group is heavily attacked in mid-Atlantic. A total of 20 U-boats sink 13 of the 63 merchantmen. However, on the 4th *U187* is detected by HF/DF, hunted down and sunk by destroyers *Beverley* and *Vimy*. Then three days later, Free French corvette *Lobélia* sinks *U609* and a RAF B-17 Flying Fortress *U624*.

17th — Slow UK/North America convoy ONS165 and the escorting British B6 group are attacked east of Newfoundland. Destroyer *Fame* accounts for *U201* and *Viscount* for *U69*. Only two merchantmen are lost.

22nd — U-boats attack ON166 and its American A3 group in mid-Atlantic and sink 14 ships in the course of four days. In exchange *U606* is depth-charged to the surface by Polish destroyer *Burza* and Canadian corvette *Chilliwack* and finished off by US Coast Guard cutter *Campbell* ramming her.

22nd — Mines laid by *U118* in the Strait of Gibraltar sink three merchantmen and on the 22nd the Canadian corvette **WEYBURN** as she escorts North Africa/UK convoy MKS8.

23rd — UK/Caribbean tanker convoy UC1 loses badly to U-boats, but southwest of Madeira, *U522* is sent to the bottom by cutter *Totland*.

Russian convoy JW53 sails with 28 merchantmen. Six turn back because of the weather, but the rest reach Kola Inlet on the 27th. Return convoy RA53 with 30 ships loses three to U-boats in March. These are the last convoys to or from Russia until November because of the pressure of events in the North Atlantic.

Battle of the Atlantic
Losses
- 50 ships of 310,000 tons and 1 corvette.
- 15 U-boats including 5 by RAF in North Atlantic and off Portugal and Gibraltar; 2 by RAF and US aircraft on Bay of Biscay patrols; 1 by US Navy in North Atlantic.

EUROPE

FEBRUARY

On or around the 23rd, submarine **VANDAL** is lost (cause unknown) as she works up in the Firth of Clyde area of Scotland.

Eastern Front

By mid-month in the centre/south the Russians have liberated their cities of Kursk, Kharkov and Rostov-on-Don, but within a matter of days German forces start a successful counter-attack around Kharkov.

With the capture of Rostov in the south, those Germans left in the Caucasus are driven back towards the Taman Peninsula opposite the Crimea.

Merchant Shipping War
Losses
- 2 ships of 5,000 tons.

The 'Thames' class submarine *Severn*. Her sister-ship *Thames* was sunk around July 1940 and *Clyde* survived the war. Completed 1932-35 at 1,850/2,700 tons and with a crew of 60, the class could make 22/10kt and carried six torpedo tubes and a 4in gun. *Real Photos (S1113)*

MEDITERRANEAN

FEBRUARY

1st — As cruiser-minelayer **WELSHMAN** sails from Malta to Alexandria after her minelaying operations in the Strait of Sicily, she is sunk by *U617* north of Bardia.

3rd — Italian destroyer *Saetta* and destroyer escort *Uragano*, supplying Axis forces in Tunisia, sink on *Abdiel's* mines northeast of Bizerta.

North Africa

As Rommel prepares his Mareth line defences in southern Tunisia, Eighth Army units cross the border from Libya on the 4th. All of Libya is now in Allied hands and the Italian North African Empire ceases to exist.

From Mareth, Rommel can switch his forces to the northwest or east as he wishes. His supply lines are also much shorter. The battle for the rest of North Africa is not yet over.

Leaving much of his forces to hold Mareth, in mid-month he launches an attack against the US Second Corps to the northwest. The aim is to break through the Allied lines around Gafsa and reach the sea near Bône. Gafsa soon falls and the Allies are pushed back through the Kasserine Pass and other passes. After a week of struggle the Axis forces are held. They withdraw to concentrate on the Mareth defences as the bulk of Eight Army approaches.

German and Italian operations against Allied shipping off Algeria lead to further losses:

6th — Canadian corvette **LOUISBERG** escorting UK/North Africa convoy KMS8 is torpedoed by German aircraft off Oran.

8th — The Royal Canadian Navy takes its revenge when corvette *Regina* sinks the Italian *Avorio* off Philippeville.

17th/23rd — A patrol of escort destroyers *Bicester, Easton, Lamerton* and *Wheatland* share in the sinking of two submarines. The Italian *Asteria* goes down off Bougie and six days later *U443* to the northwest of Algiers.

As the Mediterranean Fleet Inshore Squadron continues to support the advancing Eighth Army, ships are lost on both sides:

9th — Corvette **ERICA** on escort duty sinks on a British mine off Benghazi.

17th — *U205* attacks Tripoli/Alexandria convoy TX1 northwest of Derna. She is sunk by South African aircraft of No 15 Squadron and destroyer *Paladin*.

19th — Combined air and sea attacks also account for *U562* northeast of Benghazi. This time the convoy is Alexandria/Tripoli XT3, the warships destroyers *Isis* and *Hursley*, and the aircraft from No 38 Squadron RAF.

Adm Sir Andrew Cunningham resumes his old post as C-in-C, Mediterranean Fleet, on the 20th.

Merchant Shipping War

Losses
- 14 ships of 53,000 tons.

INDIAN & PACIFIC OCEANS

FEBRUARY

Burma

Col Wingate mounts the first Chindit operation behind the Japanese lines, northwest of Lashio. Success is limited, losses heavy and the survivors start to withdraw in late March. The Arakan offensive fails to make any progress.

Guadalcanal, Solomon Islands — Conclusion

By the 8th, Japanese destroyers have quietly evacuated over 10,000 troops from the Cape Esperance area. This marks the end of one of the most intense struggles ever for a single island. In the seven main naval battles alone, US losses have been one carrier, six cruisers and eight destroyers plus the *Wasp* and Australian *Canberra*. Japanese losses are two battleships, one carrier, a cruiser and six destroyers.

Merchant Shipping War

Losses
- Indian Ocean — 3 ships of 16,000 tons.
- Pacific — 4 ships of 19,000 tons.

ATLANTIC

MARCH

4th — In operations against the US/Gibraltar routes, *U87* is sunk off Portugal by Canadian destroyer *St Croix* and corvette *Shediac*.

11th — North American/UK convoy HX228 (60 ships), escorted by the British B3 group, loses a total of four ships. Destroyer *Harvester* rams *U444* but is disabled and the U-boat has to be finished off by French corvette *Aconit*. **HARVESTER**, later at a standstill, is sunk by *U432* which is in turn brought to the surface in mid-Atlantic by *Aconit's* depth charges and finally destroyed by gunfire and more ramming.

Battle of the Atlantic

Throughout the war a large proportion of the losses due to U-boats are among independently routed merchantmen and stragglers from convoys. In March 1943 they come close to overwhelming well escorted convoys. Between the 7th and 11th, slow convoy SC121 loses 13 ships. Worse is to come between the 16th and 20th in the largest convoy battle of the war — around HX229 and SC122. Over 40 U-boats are deployed against these two as they slowly coalesce in the mid-Atlantic air gap until there are 100 ships and their escort. Twenty submarines attack and sink 21 before additional air and surface escorts finally manage to drive them off. A RAF Sunderland accounts for the one U-boat lost. Again the German B-Service is responsible for providing Dönitz packs with accurate convoy details and routeing.

These losses take place during another turning point, in the secret war around Enigma. Early in the month the U-boats change from the three-rotor to the far more complex four-rotor 'Triton' code. Yet by month's end this has been broken by the men and women of Bletchley Park and their electro-mechanical computers. The Allies' tremendous advantage is restored. This happens just as a number of other developments come together to bring about a complete reversal in the war against the U-boats.

The first five RN support groups with their modern radars, anti-submarine weapons and HF/DF are released for operation in the North Atlantic. Two are built around Home Fleet destroyers, two around Western Approaches escorts, including Capt Walker's 2nd EG, and one with escort carrier *Biter*. *Archer* and the American *Bogue* are also ready, but *Dasher* is unfortunately lost in UK waters. Nevertheless, the mid-Atlantic air gap is about to be finally closed.

Another major breakthrough is again in the air war. Aircraft are now being fitted with the 10cm wavelength radar which is undetectable by the U-boat's Metox receivers. This radar and the Leigh light make a powerful weapon against the surfaced submarines, especially as they try to break out through the Bay of Biscay air patrols. More VLR aircraft are also joining Coastal Command to extend further the Allies' grip on the convoy routes throughout their length.

Losses
- 90 ships of 538,000 tons and 1 destroyer.
- 12 U-boats including 4 by the RAF in North Atlantic; 1 by RAF Bay of Biscay patrols; 1 by US aircraft off Barbados; 2 by US forces off the Azores and Canary Islands; 1 by unknown causes.

APRIL

2nd/18th — *U124* on passage to the Freetown area encounters UK/West Africa convoy OS45 to the west of Portugal. She sinks two ships but is attacked by sloop *Black Swan* and corvette *Stonecrop* of the 37th EG and is sunk in turn. To the south of Freetown on the 18th, *U123* torpedoes and sinks **P615** (ex-Turkish) on passage to the South Atlantic Command to provide anti-submarine training.

6th — In attacks on Halifax/UK convoy HX231 southwest of Iceland, two U-boats are lost — *U635* to frigate *Tay* of the British B7 group and *U632* to a RAF Liberator. Six of the

EUROPE

MARCH

RAF Bomber Command starts the Battle of the Ruhr, a four-month long campaign against the cities and factories of Germany's main industrial centre.

27th – Escort carrier **DASHER** works up in the Firth of Clyde after repairs to damage sustained during the February Russian convoy JW53. An aviation gasoline explosion leads to her total destruction.

Eastern Front

Until now the Germans have held on to their salients in the Moscow area left over from the Russian winter offensive of 1941/42 in the north/centre. Under attack they pull back and straighten their lines.

Back to the centre/south, the Germans retake Kharkov, but the Russian Army holds on to the salient around Kursk. As the front stabilises both sides prepare for the coming Battle of Kursk — the greatest tank battle of the war.

Merchant Shipping War
Losses
- 2 ships of 900 tons.

APRIL

The site of the massacre of Polish officers is found at Katyn near Smolensk: the Russians and Germans accuse each other of the atrocity.

In Poland itself the surviving Jews of the Warsaw Ghetto rise up against the Germans. SS troops are called in and by May the struggle is over. Those Jews not killed in the fighting are sent to extermination camps.

Eastern Front

To the south in the Caucasus the Russians squeeze the

MEDITERRANEAN

MARCH

The RN loses three of its 'T' class submarines:

TIGRIS sets out from Malta on 18 February for a patrol off Naples. She fails to return to Algiers on the 10th, possibly mined off the Gulf of Tunis as she returns.

12th — **TURBULENT** (Cdr Linton) attacks an escorted ship off Maddalena, Sardinia and is presumed sunk in the counter-attack by Italian MTB escorts. ✝ Cdr John Linton RN is awarded the Victoria Cross for his record as commanding officer of *Turbulent*. The award is not gazetted until May.

14th — **THUNDERBOLT** is lost off the north entrance of the Strait of Messina to Italian corvette *Cicogna*.

Tunisia

In the south, before his final recall from Africa, Field Marshal Rommel attacks Eighth Army positions in front of the Mareth Line, but is easily held. On the 20th the main Eighth Army offensive starts with British and Indian forces going in near the sea, as the New Zealanders once again move up to outflank. Meanwhile, from the northwest, the US Second Corps alongside the British First Army is attacking towards Gafsa and Gabes, endangering the Axis rear. By the 29th the Mareth Line is broken and the Germans and Italians have retreated to a strong position north of Gabes at Wadi Akarit. The Inshore Squadron is still in attendance on Eighth Army.

8th/24th — Minelayer *Abdiel* lays more mines in the Axis supply routes to Tunisia. North of Cape Bon, destroyer escort *Ciclone* is sunk on the 8th and destroyers *Ascari* and *Malocello* on the 24th.

12th — In a sortie against Axis shipping bound for Tunisia, Force Q destroyer **LIGHTNING** is torpedoed and sunk off Bizerta by German E-boat *S55*.

19th — Attacks by German aircraft on Tripoli harbour sink two supply ships and damage escort destroyer **DERWENT** so badly that she is not fully repaired. This is the Germans' first success with circling torpedoes.

Merchant Shipping War
Losses
● 16 ships of 86,000 tons.

APRIL

Tunisia

The battle of Gabes starts on the 5th when Eighth Army attacks the Wadi Akarit defences. Within two days the Axis is retreating. On that same day, the 7th, US troops of Second Corps meet Eighth Army units near Gafsa — the long awaited link-up at last.

By the 10th Sfax has fallen to Eighth Army, but a British First Army breakthrough at Fondouk is too late to cut off the retreating Germans and Italians. The 14th sees them well established in their main defence lines running around Tunis

INDIAN & PACIFIC OCEANS

MARCH

Burma

In the Arakan the Japanese go over to the attack and push back the British and Indian forces. By mid-May they are back in India. The first of three Allied Arakan campaigns has been a failure.

PACIFIC — STRATEGIC AND MARITIME SITUATION

At the Casablanca Conference in January, the Allied strategy for the South West Pacific was agreed. Twin offensives are to be mounted up the Solomons and along the New Guinea coast (and thence across to New Britain), leading to the capture of the main Japanese base at Rabaul — later by-passed. Breaking through the Bismarck Archipelago in this way will open the route to the Philippines. American strategy is subsequently revised to allow for a parallel push through the mandated islands to the north.

Gen MacArthur, C-in-C, South West Pacific, has full responsibility for the New Guinea area, and Adm Halsey as C-in-C, South Pacific, tactical command of the Solomons. This overlapping causes some complications. Japanese resistance in both Papua and on Guadalcanal points to many bloody battles in the months and years ahead.

The US Seventh Fleet has been formed to support Gen MacArthur's campaigning in New Guinea. For some time to come its main component (Task Force 74, previously 44) will be the cruisers *Australia* and *Hobart*, some US destroyers and the Australian 'Tribals' *Arunta* and *Warramunga*. Main US naval strength will remain with Adm Halsey's Third Fleet in the South Pacific Command area to which the New Zealand cruiser *Leander* is assigned.

New Guinea

Battle of the Bismarck Sea — Between the 2nd and 4th, US and Australian land-based aircraft annihilate a troop convoy bound for Lae from Rabaul. All eight transports and four escorting destroyers are sunk.

Aleutians

Battle of Komandorski Islands — Japanese supply operations to Kiska on the 26th lead to a cruiser gun action in which both sides have a cruiser damaged. The Japanese turn back.

Merchant Shipping War
Losses
● Indian Ocean — 10 ships of 62,000 tons.
● Pacific — 2 ships of 6,000 tons.

APRIL

New Guinea

Australian troops make limited moves from Wau towards the coast south of Salamaua.

Adm Yamamoto, Commander of the Japanese Combined Fleet, is killed when his aircraft is shot down over Bougainville in the northern Solomons. His travel plans are known in advance through decoded intercepts: since 1940 the Americans have been able to read the Japanese 'Purple' diplomatic and command ciphers.

ATLANTIC

convoy's merchantmen are lost to the 15-boat pack. (Note: the identity of these two U-boats is sometimes reversed.)

7th — Submarine *Tuna* on Arctic patrol sinks *U644* northwest of Narvik.

11th — Destroyer **BEVERLEY** of the British B6 group escorting convoy ON176 is sunk south of Greenland by *U188*.

23rd/25th — Slow UK/North America convoy ONS4 (renumbered from March) is escorted by the British B2 group (Cdr MacIntyre) and reinforced by the 5th EG with escort carrier *Biter*. On the 23rd *U191* is detected to the south of Greenland by HF/DF and sunk by destroyer *Hesperus* using her Hedgehog A/S mortar. Two days later one of Biter's Swordfish from 811 Squadron finds *U203*; destroyer *Pathfinder* finishes the job.

Battle of the Atlantic

U-boat strength is up to 425 with 240 operational, and over half of them on passage through or on patrol throughout the North Atlantic. However, there is somewhat of a lull until the end of the month with the start of the ONS5 battle. A group also operates once again in the weakly defended Sierra Leone area. In just one night *U515* sinks seven of the 18 ships in Takoradi/Sierra Leone convoy TS37.

Changes are again made in the Allies' responsibility for the North Atlantic routes. As agreed at the March Atlantic Convoy Conference in Washington:

● Royal Canadian Navy is to exercise full control of the northerly routes to the west of the 47°W CHOP line.

● Royal Navy is to take over to the east of 47°W.

● US Navy is to look after the southerly convoys, but to include the CU/UC tanker routes between the West Indies and the UK.

With these changes, the far more effective convoy Escort Groups and the developments described in March, the scene is set for the decisive convoy battles of May 1943.

Losses
● 40 ships of 242,000 tons, 1 destroyer and 1 submarine.
● 14 German and 1 Italian U-boats including 3 by the RAF in the North Atlantic and off the Canaries; 1 by RAF Bay of Biscay patrol; 1 by RAF-laid mine in the Bay of Biscay; 1 by RAAF north of the Faeroes; 3 to US forces in the North and South Atlantic, including the Italian one.

MAY

Trident Conference

Winston Churchill travels in the Queen Mary *together with 5,000 German POWs for his third Washington conference. The invasion of Sicily has now been agreed and he presses for follow-up landings in Italy. The cross-Channel invasion of Europe continues to be a major topic of discussion and D-day is set for May 1944.*

Battle of the Atlantic
The May 1943 Convoy Battles — Victory of the Escorts

At the beginning of the month, over 40 U-boats are deployed in three patrol lines off Greenland and Newfoundland. Another group operates to the far west of the Bay of Biscay. A number are passing through the northern transit area and over 30 on passage between their Biscay bases and the North Atlantic. More still are on patrol in the South Atlantic or passing through. There are numerous Allied convoys crossing the North Atlantic alone as suitable targets:

● *Slow UK/North America ONS5* — On 21 April the convoy with 42 ships sails from Liverpool. Escort is provided by the British B7 group (Cdr P. W. Gretton) with two destroyers, a frigate, four corvettes and two trawlers. Well before April is out *U710* is sunk by an escorting RAF B-17 Flying Fortress south of Iceland.

EUROPE

Germans further into the Taman Peninsula where they hold out until October.

Merchant Shipping War
Losses
● 5 ships of 10,000 tons.

MAY

After 2½ years in the post of C-in-C Home Fleet, Adm Tovey moves to command of The Nore. He is succeeded by Adm Sir Bruce Fraser.

The Dambusters' Raid — On the night of the 16th/17th, Wg Cdr Guy Gibson leads No 617 Squadron in the famous raid on the Ruhr dams. Two are breached by Barnes Wallis' bouncing bombs, but the damage to German industry is not great.

In occupied Europe, Tito's partisan armies continue to hold down large numbers of German troops in Yugoslavia. In France the various resistance groups meet to co-ordinate anti-German activities.

Merchant Shipping War
Losses
● 1 ship of 1,600 tons.

MEDITERRANEAN

and Bizerta from Enfidaville in the south, through Longstop Hill and to the sea west of Bizerta. For the rest of April heavy fighting takes place as the Allies slowly close in.

16th — Destroyers *Pakenham* and *Paladin* out of Malta encounter an Italian convoy north of Pantellaria. In a running gun battle with the four escorting torpedo boats, *Cigno* is sunk and one other damaged, and **PAKENHAM** disabled. She has to be scuttled.

Numerous Axis supply ships on the Tunisian route and elsewhere, and an Italian warship, fall victim to RN submarines. In return three are lost:

21st — **SPLENDID** to German destroyer *Hermes* (ex-Greek) south of Capri.

24th — After sinking a transport off northeast Sicily, **SAHIB** is counter-attacked by the escorts including a German Ju88 and finally sunk by corvette *Gabbiano*.

28th — *Unshaken* sinks torpedo boat *Climene* off Sicily as she escorts a convoy.

REGENT on patrol in the Strait of Otranto may have attacked a small convoy near Bari on the 18th. There is no response from the escorts. She fails to return to Beirut at the end of the month and is presumed lost on mines in her patrol area.

'The Man Who Never Was' — Submarine *Seraph* releases the body of a supposed Royal Marine officer into the sea off Spain. His false papers help to persuade the Germans that the next blows will fall on Sardinia and Greece as well as Sicily.

Merchant Shipping War
Losses
● 6 ships of 14,000 tons.

INDIAN & PACIFIC OCEANS

Merchant Shipping War
Losses
● Indian Ocean — 6 ships of 43,000 tons.
● Pacific — 7 ships of 35,000 tons.

HMS *Biter*, the 'Archer' class escort carrier in the Clyde, Scotland, before departing for Oran and Operation 'Torch'. In May 1943 she was the Senior Officer's ship of the 5th Escort Group and about to help turn the tide in the Battle of the Atlantic. *Real Photos*

MAY

North Africa and Tunis — The End for the Axis

The Allied Armies continue to push on, and on the 7th Tunis is taken by the British and Bizerta by the Americans. The Axis surrender comes on the 12th and nearly 250,000 Germans and Italians are taken prisoner. All of North Africa — French and Italian — is under Allied control after nearly three years of offensive and counter-offensive.

4th — As the Tunisian campaign ends, destroyers *Nubian*, *Paladin* and *Petard* sink Italian torpedo boat *Perseo* and a supply ship near Cape Bon.

In the first five months of 1942 Allied forces have sunk over 500 Axis merchantmen of 560,000 tons throughout the Mediterranean.

Six Axis submarines are lost in May — two German to the RAF, two Italian to US forces, and two to the Royal Navy:

21st — Submarine *Sickle* on patrol south of Toulon torpedoes *U303*.

MAY

Adm Somerville's Eastern Fleet has now lost its remaining carrier, two battleships and many smaller vessels to other theatres. An inadequate anti-submarine and escort force is left to deal with the submarines active in the Indian Ocean. The Japanese are being joined again by German U-boats, and right through until December not many more than a dozen German and Japanese boats inflict quite heavy losses throughout the length and breadth of the Indian Ocean. Between June and year's end they sink over 50 merchantmen.

After re-equipping with American aircraft and working-up out of Pearl Harbor, fleet carrier *Victorious* joins the Third Fleet under Adm Halsey. From now until August, she and *Saratoga* will be the only Allied big carriers in the South Pacific. While she is there, there will be no carrier battles to follow the four starting with Coral Sea.

Aleutians

US troops land on Attu on the 11th. As usual the Japanese fight ferociously and the island is not secured until the end of the month. A few wounded are captured; the rest die in the fighting or by their own hands.

The real battle starts in early May to the south of Greenland as the three U-boat groups close in. Before they arrive the escort is reinforced by the 3rd EG from St John's, Newfoundland. Rough seas make refuelling difficult and some of the escorts have to leave. The 1st EG, also from St John's, sails to replace them.

Over the next few days 13 merchantmen are lost, but at a cost of a further six U-boats. All go down in often confused fighting to the south of Greenland or northeast of Newfoundland. More still are damaged.

4th — *U630* to a RCAF Canso (Catalina).

5th — Corvettes *Pink* and *Loosestrife* of B7 sink *U192* and *U638* respectively.

6th — *U125* goes down to destroyer *Vidette* of B7. Destroyer *Oribi*, detached from convoy SC127 to join B7, together with corvette *Snowflake*, accounts for *U531*. (Note: the identity of these two U-boats is sometimes reversed.) Finally, *U438* is sunk by sloop *Pelican* of the 1st EG.

Type 271 radar plays a large part in the escort's successes. The surviving U-boats are regrouped for attacks on other convoys, but in this area as well as throughout the North Atlantic, sinkings go down as U-boat losses mount alarmingly for the Germans. Much of this is due to the way the supporting escort groups move from one convoy to another to help the existing escorts.

The number of convoys crossing the North Atlantic in both directions is truly impressive and the main movements in May, together with the U-boat sinkings associated with them, are summarised:

● *North America/UK HX236* — 46 ships, British B1 group, 2nd EG, no merchant ship losses.

11th — *U528* is damaged by US aircraft in an earlier attack on ONS5. Now southwest of Ireland, she is sunk by sloop *Fleetwood* and RAF aircraft of No 58 Squadron.

● *Convoy ONS6* — 31 ships, British B6 group, 4th EG with escort carrier *Archer*, no losses.

● *Convoy HX237* — 46 ships, Canadian C2 group, 5th EG with escort carrier *Biter*. Three stragglers sunk in exchange for possibly three U-boats in mid-Atlantic:

12th — *U89* to destroyer *Broadway* and frigate *Lagan*, both of C2, assisted by Swordfish of 811 Squadron from *Biter*.

12th — RAF B-24 Liberator of No 120 Squadron damages either *U456* or *U753*, which may then have been finished off by destroyer *Pathfinder* of the 5th EG. Alternatively, the U-boat involved may have gone missing on the 15th. (Sources vary.)

13th — One or other of *U456* or *U753* is then detected by RCAF Sunderlands of No 423 Squadron which bring up frigate *Lagan* and Canadian corvette *Drumheller* to sink the U-boat.

● *North America/UK SC129* — 26 ships, British B2 group, 5th EG from HX237 on the 14th. Two merchant ships lost in mid-Atlantic for two U-boats:

12th — *U186* to destroyer *Hesperus* of B2 (Cdr MacIntyre).

14th — *U266* to a RAF B-24 Liberator of No 86 Squadron.

● *UK/North America ON182* — 56 ships, Canadian C5 group, 4th EG from ONS6, no losses.

● *Convoy HX238* — 45 ships, Canadian C3 group, no losses.

● *Convoy ONS7* — 40 ships, British B5 group, 3rd EG after ONS5. One ship lost for two U-boats destroyed in the vicinity of the convoy to the southeast of Greenland and south of Iceland:

14th — *U657* to a US Navy Catalina.

17th — *U640* to frigate *Swale* of B5. (Note: the identity of this U-boat is sometimes reversed with *U657*.)

● *Convoy ON183* — 32 ships, British B4 group, no losses.

● *Convoy SC130* — 38 ships, British B7 group, 1st EG after ONS5. No ships lost for four more U-boats to the south of Greenland:

19th — *U954* to a RAF Liberator; *U209* to frigates *Jed* and *Sennen* of 1st EG; and *U381* to destroyer *Duncan* and corvette *Snowflake* of B7.

20th — *U258* to a RAF Liberator.

The Liberators are VLR aircraft from the very successful No 120 Squadron.

● *Convoy ON184* — 39 ships, Canadian C1 group, US 6th EG with escort carrier *Bogue*, no losses for one U-boat:

22nd — *U569* in mid-Atlantic to *Bogue's* Avengers.

● *Convoy HX239* — 42 ships, British B3 group, 4th EG with *Archer* after ON182, no losses, but one more U-boat:

23rd — *U752* in mid-Atlantic is badly damaged by rockets from *Archer's* Swordfish of 819 Squadron, and scuttled as the escorts approach. This is the first success with aircraft rockets.

23rd — As Italian submarine *Da Vinci* returns from a successful patrol off South Africa, she is detected and sunk northeast of the Azores by destroyer *Active* and frigate *Ness*.

By the 24th, U-boat losses are so heavy and the attacks so fruitless that Adm Dönitz orders them from the North Atlantic. They either return home or concentrate on the US/Gibraltar routes. It is some time before the Allies realise that the North Atlantic is almost free of them. The air and sea escorts are well and truly winning.

26th — *U436* is sunk to the west of Cape Ortegal, Spain by frigate *Test* and Indian corvette *Hyderabad*.

● *Convoy SC131* — 31 ships, British B6 group, 3rd and 40th EGs, no losses.

● *Convoy ONS8* — 52 ships, Canadian C4 group, 2nd EG (Capt Walker) after HX236, no losses.

● *Convoy HX240* — 56 ships, Canadian C5 group, 2nd EG from ONS8, no losses for one U-boat:

28th — *U304* to a RAF Liberator of No 120 Squadron south of Greenland.

Losses
● 40 ships of 204,000 tons.
● 37 German and 1 Italian U-boats. In addition to those lost in or around the convoy battles: 3 by RAF in North Atlantic; 6 by RAF and RAAF Bay of Biscay patrols; 4 by US forces in the North Atlantic, off Florida and off Brazil; 2 by collision in North Atlantic.

Right:
HMS *Nelson*. In May 1943 she was operating out of Gibraltar, and soon to take part in the July 1943 invasion of Sicily as Force 'H' flagship. *IWM (A16062)*

MEDITERRANEAN

25th — Escorting corvette *Vetch* sinks *U414* northeast of Oran.

By the middle of the month minesweepers have cleared a channel through the Strait of Sicily, and the first regular Mediterranean convoys since 1940 are able to sail from Gibraltar to Alexandria (GTX). Return XTGs start in June. The long haul around the Cape of Good Hope to the Middle East is no longer necessary, and the WS troop convoys are soon discontinued. The opening of the Mediterranean is equivalent to commissioning a large amount of merchant ship tonnage.

Merchant Shipping War
Losses
- 6 ships of 32,000 tons.

INDIAN & PACIFIC OCEANS

Merchant Shipping War
Losses
- Indian Ocean — 6 ships of 28,000 tons.
- Pacific — 5 ships of 33,000 tons.

DEFENCE OF TRADE — JANUARY 1942 TO MAY 1943

Summary of Losses

North Atlantic	UK waters	Mediterranean	Indian Ocean		
1,234 ships of 6,808,000 tons.	105 ships of 248,000 tons.	129 ships of 598,000 tons.	230 ships of 873,000 tons.		
South Atlantic			Pacific Ocean		
97 ships of 611,000 tons.			234 ships of 654,000 tons.		

Submarines	1,474 ships of 8,048,000 tons.
Aircraft	169 ships of 814,000 tons.
Other causes	228 ships of 348,000 tons.
Raiders	31 ships of 202,000 tons.
Mines	71 ships of 172,000 tons.
Warships	31 ships of 130,000 tons.
Coastal forces	25 ships of 78,000 tons.

= 2,029 British, Allied and neutral ships of 9,792,000 tons: ie 576,000 tons per month.

ATLANTIC

JUNE

1st — After supporting convoys ONS8 and HX240, Capt Walker's group locates *U202* south of Greenland, where she is sunk by *Starling*.

Aircraft of Coastal Command continue their Bay of Biscay patrols and now are joined by surface escort groups covered by cruisers. At the same time U-boats are being fitted with heavy AA armament to enable them to fight their way out on the surface in groups. Sinkings go down as aircraft losses mount, but four U-boats are destroyed:

1st — *U418* to a rocket-firing Beaufighter.

14th — *U564* to a RAF Whitley.

24th — The 2nd EG accompanied by cruiser *Scylla* accounts for two submarines northwest of Cape Ortegal. Tanker *U119* is brought to the surface and rammed by *Starling*. With her ASDIC out of action, the sinking of *U449* is left to *Wren*, *Woodpecker*, *Kite* and *Wild Goose*.

4th/11th — Submarine *Truculent* on anti-U-boat patrol between Norway and Iceland sinks *U308* north of the Faeroes. A week later an RAF Fortress accounts for *U417* in the same northern transit area.

14th — In the North Atlantic *U334* and other U-boats simulate the radio transmissions of large wolf packs. She is located and sunk by frigate *Jed* and sloop *Pelican* of the 1st EG.

Battle of the Atlantic

The RN has finally changed the convoy codes and made them secure against the work of the German B-Service. In contrast, the British 'Ultra' work is fully integrated into the Admiralty U-boat Tracking Room, and an almost complete picture of German Navy and U-boat operations is available.

Not one North Atlantic convoy is attacked during the month although U-boats are operating around the Azores. As Allied air and sea forces grow in strength and effectiveness, especially through the use of 10cm radar and 'Ultra', Adm Dönitz seeks other ways to regain the initiative, which in fact never returns to his U-boats. Nevertheless, right through until the last day of the war, the Allies cannot relax their efforts, and introduce new weapons, detection systems and tactics.

Against numerous, well-trained and effectively-used escorts, the day of the conventional submarine is drawing to a close. The Germans place much faith in the Walther hydrogen peroxide boat, now under development, which, with its long underwater endurance and high speed, could prove a formidable foe. It does not get beyond the experimental stage by war's end. An interim step on the road towards the 'true' submarine starts at the end of 1943 with the design and building of Type XXI ocean and XXIII coastal boats. Using the streamlined hull of the Walther and high capacity batteries, their underwater speed will make them faster than most escorts. Fortunately for the Allies they do not enter service in numbers until too late in 1945.

For now the Germans must rely on the U-boats currently in service and building. Total numbers stay at around the 400 mark for the remainder of the war, in spite of a 40 boat per month construction programme, and various steps are taken to improve their offensive and defensive capability. Apart from extra AA armament, the Gnat acoustic torpedo is being introduced specifically to combat the convoy escorts. Its first test comes in September. Then in July the schnorkel, a Dutch development that allows batteries to be recharged at periscope depth, starts trials. It will not enter general service until mid-1944, but then will go quite some way to nullifying the radar of the air escorts and patrols. Even now the German Navy is unaware that the Allies are using short wavelength radar, but when they do, early in 1944, an effective detector is soon introduced.

EUROPE

JUNE

RAF bombers fly on to North Africa for the first time after attacking German targets. On their return they hit northern Italy.

Merchant Shipping War

Losses
- 1 ship of 150 tons.

MEDITERRANEAN

JUNE

2nd — Destroyers *Jervis* and Greek *Queen Olga* sink two merchantmen and the Italian torpedo boat *Castore* off Cape Spartivento, southwest Italy.

After heavy sea and air bombardments the Italian islands of Pantellaria and Lampedusa to the west of Malta surrender to the Allies on the 11th and 12th.

Merchant Shipping War
Losses
● 7 ships of 25,000 tons.

INDIAN & PACIFIC OCEANS

JUNE

New Georgia Islands, Central Solomons

Apart from the unopposed landings on islands to the north of Guadalcanal in February, only now are US forces under Adm Halsey ready to make their next move up the Solomons chain with the New Georgia group. On the 21st, US Marines land in the south of the main island of New Georgia and on the 30th Army troops on the nearby island of Rendova. New Georgia is not fully secured until the end of August, by which time other landings have been made. Like the Guadalcanal campaign, Japanese attempts to bring in reinforcements lead to a series of naval battles.

Merchant Shipping War
Losses
● Indian Ocean — 12 ships of 68,000 tons.
● Pacific — 1 ship of 1,200 tons.

The 'Porpoise' class, minelaying submarine *Porpoise* was lost in January 1945. Five of the class of six boats were lost. Completed 1933-39, they displaced 1,500/2,100 tons, could make 15/9kt, had a crew of 60 and were armed with six torpedo tubes and 50 mines and a 4in gun. *Real Photos (S355)*

355

ATLANTIC

Losses

- 7 ships of 30,000 tons.
- 16 German and 1 Italian U-boats including 4 by US and RAF aircraft off Iceland and the Strait of Gibraltar, and the Italian boat in the North Atlantic; 3 by the US Navy, one off the east coast of America and two to escort carrier *Bogue* off the Azores; 1 by French aircraft off Dakar.

JULY

15th — *U135* attacks UK/West Africa convoy OS51 off the Canary Islands, and is depth-charged by the escort including sloop *Rochester* and corvette *Balsam*, and finished off by corvette *Mignonette* by ramming.

After six months effort the bombing campaign against the U-boats claims its first success when on the 24th *U622* is badly damaged in a USAAF raid on Trondheim and paid off.

30th — The Bay of Biscay offensive by the RAF and Australian, Canadian and American aircraft reaches an intensity and by the 29th, 10 U-boats have been sunk and many others damaged. On the 30th, two 'milchcows', *U461* and *U462* escorted by *U504*, are located to the northwest of Cape Ortegal. In a running battle *U461* is finally sunk by Sunderland U/461 of RAF No 461 Squadron. *U462* also goes down in the fighting. Capt Walker's 2nd EG is called to the scene and accounts for *U504* with *Kite*, *Woodpecker*, *Wren* and *Wild Goose*.

Battle of the Atlantic

Losses

- 29 ships of 188,000 tons.
- 34 U-boats including 3 by RAF and US aircraft off Portugal; 7 by US escort carrier groups south and west of the Azores (6 of these by aircraft from *Core*, *Santee* or *Bogue*); 9 by US aircraft in the Caribbean and off Brazil.

EUROPE

JULY

Following the RAF's Battle of the Ruhr, heavy attacks on Hamburg in late July/early August start the first fire-storms. The Battle of Hamburg continues through until November.

Eastern Front

There is little activity in the north and Leningrad must wait until early 1944 for its siege to be fully lifted. But it is a different matter in the centre/south where the Battle of Kursk is fought. The Germans attack the 100-mile wide salient around the city from the Orel area in the north and from near Kharkov in the south. Total forces engaged on both sides include 6,000 tanks and 5,000 aircraft. Russian defences are well-prepared and in depth and the Germans make little progress. Within a week they have ground to a halt. Losses are heavy on both sides. Now the Russian armies launch the first of their numerous offensives in these sectors which by year's end will see them reaching Byelo-Russia and in possession of over half the Ukraine. They start in the northern part against the German's own Orel salient, and in early August it is the turn of Kharkov.

Merchant Shipping War

Losses

- Until November only two small ships are lost in UK waters.

HMS *Cleopatra*, a 'Dido' class AA cruiser. She took part in the Sicily invasion, and on Friday 16 July 1943, was damaged by a torpedo. *Real Photos (S2930)*

JULY

10th — Invasion of Sicily: Operation 'Husky' — The Americans still want to concentrate on the cross-Channel invasion of France, but at the Casablanca Conference somewhat reluctantly agree to go ahead with the Sicily landings. Amongst the benefits will be the opening of the Mediterranean to Allied shipping. The final plan is approved in mid-May and not much more than a month later the first US troop convoys are heading across the Atlantic for an operation even greater than the French North African landings the previous November.

Supreme Allied Commander
US Gen Dwight D. Eisenhower

Naval Commander-in-Chief
Adm Sir Andrew Cunningham

Landing areas:	Gulf of Gela, south coast	South of Syracuse, south east corner
Forces landing:	US Seventh Army (Gen Patton) 66,000 US troops	Eighth Army (Gen Montgomery) 115,000 British and Canadian troops
Departure from:	United States, Algeria and Tunisia	Egypt, Libya, Tunisia and Malta; Canadian division from Britain
Naval Task Forces and Commanders:	*Western* Vice-Adm H. K. Hewitt USN	*Eastern* Adm Sir Bertram Ramsey
Total naval forces:	*United States*	*British and Allied*
Battleships	—	6
Carriers	—	2
Cruisers	5	10
Destroyers	48	80
Submarines	—	26
Other warships	98	250
Troop and supply transports, LSIs, etc	94	237
Landing ships and craft (major only)	190	319
Totals	435	930
Grand total	1,365	

Plus 510 US and 715 RN minor landing craft.

The US and British warships are mostly allocated to their own landing sectors, but the RN totals include the covering force against any interference by the Italian fleet. The main group under Vice-Adm Sir A. U. Willis of Force H includes battleships *Nelson*, *Rodney*, *Warspite* and *Valiant* and fleet carriers *Formidable* and *Indomitable*. Seven RN submarines act as navigation markers off the invasion beaches.

Many of the troops coming from North Africa and Malta make the voyage in landing ships and craft. As they approach Sicily with the other transports late on the 9th in stormy weather, Allied airborne landings take place. Sadly, many of the British gliders crash into the sea, partly because of the weather. However, early next day, on the 10th, the troops go

JULY

New Guinea

On 30 June, Allied forces land south of Salamaua. By mid-July they link up with the Australians fighting through from Wau, and prepare to advance on Salamaua itself. The struggle against the usual fierce resistance continues right through July and August.

New Georgia Islands, Central Solomons

As the fighting for New Georgia Island continues, naval battles and other actions lead to losses on both sides:

Battle of Kula Gulf — On the night of the 5th/6th, three US cruisers and four destroyers are in a fight with 10 'Tokyo Express' destroyers off the north coast of New Georgia. The Japanese lose two destroyers in total, but another US cruiser goes down to Long Lance torpedoes.

13th — Battle of Kolombangara — Four destroyers covered by cruiser *Jintsu* and five more destroyers run supplies into Kula Gulf on the night of the 12th/13th. Opposing them are two American cruisers and the New Zealand *Leander* (Capt S. W. Roskill) with 10 US destroyers. The Japanese cruiser is shelled to pieces, but all three Allied cruisers are disabled by torpedo hits and a destroyer sunk. **Leander** is out of action for 25 months, the last of the two New Zealand cruisers serving with Adm Halsey.

20th — Task Force 74 with *Australia*, *Hobart* and US destroyers sails from the New Hebrides for the New Georgia area of operations. In the Coral Sea, **Hobart** is torpedoed and badly damaged by submarine *I11*

Merchant Shipping War
Losses
● Indian Ocean only — 17 ships of 97,000 tons.

The 'King George V' class battleship HMS *Howe*. The class of five (also *Anson, Duke of York, King George V* and *Prince of Wales*) were the only RN battleships built during the war. Completed 1940-42, they displaced 35,000 tons and could make 29kt. They carried 10 14in guns and c1,550 crew. *Real Photos (S2931)*

The six 'Illustrious' class fleet carriers were completed between 1940 and 1944 in the order *Illustrious, Formidable, Victorious, Indomitable, Indefatigable* and *Implacable*. Standard displacement was 23,000 tons, and they could make 31kt. However, they carried only about 36 aircraft, plus 1,400 crew. *IWM (A12788)*

ashore under an umbrella of aircraft. The new amphibious DUKWS developed by the Americans play an important part in getting the men and supplies across the beaches.

There is little resistance by the Italians and few Germans, and the counter-attacks that are mounted are soon driven off. Syracuse is captured that day and within three days the British Eighth Army has cleared the south east corner of Sicily. The Americans meanwhile push north and northwest and capture Palermo on the 22nd. By then, Eighth Army has been checked south of Catania. Nevertheless, at month's end the Allies hold all the island except the northeastern part.

As the capture of Sicily progresses, important political developments take place in Italy. On the 25th Mussolini is arrested and stripped of all his powers, and Marshal Badoglio forms a new government which immediately and in secret seeks ways to end the war. By August the surrender of Italy is being negotiated with the Allied powers.

16th — German and Italian aircraft sink and damage a number of warships and transports in the invasion area including a US destroyer on the 10th. On the 16th the carrier **Indomitable** is damaged by Italian torpedo aircraft.

Axis submarines have fewer successes, which include two RN cruisers damaged, but in return lose 12 of their number in and around Sicily over the next four weeks:

11th — *Flutto* off the south end of the Strait of Messina in a running battle with MTBs *640*, *651* and *670*.

12th — *U561* torpedoed in the Strait of Messina by *MTB81*; *Bronzo* captured off Syracuse by minesweepers *Boston*, *Cromarty*, *Poole* and *Seaham*; and *U409* sunk off Algeria by escorting destroyer *Inconstant* as she attacks a returning empty convoy.

13th — *Nereide* is lost off Augusta to destroyers *Echo* and *Ilex*; and north of the Strait of Messina *Acciaio* is torpedoed by patrolling submarine *Unruly*.

15th — Transport submarine *Remo* on passage through the Gulf of Taranto during the invasion is lost to submarine *United*.

16th — Cruiser **Cleopatra** is torpedoed and badly damaged off Sicily by submarine *Dandolo*.

18th — *Remo's* sister-boat *Romolo* is sunk off Augusta by the RAF.

23rd — Cruiser **Newfoundland** is damaged off Syracuse by a torpedo from *U407*, and as *Ascianghi* attacks a cruiser force off the south coast of Sicily she is sunk by destroyers *Eclipse* and *Laforey*.

29th — *Pietro Micca* is torpedoed by submarine *Trooper* in the Strait of Otranto.

30th — *U375* is lost off southern Sicily to an American sub-chaser.

3rd (August) — *Argento* is sunk off Pantellaria by US destroyer *Buck*.

Merchant Shipping War

Losses
● 14 ships of 80,000 tons.

The light cruiser *Philadelphia* was one of the US warships operating off the shores of Sicily during July 1943. *IWM (C5400)*

The escort carrier HMS *Audacity* (lost in December 1941) was the RN's first escort carrier, converted by June 1941 from the German prize *Hannover*. Of 11,000 tons deep load she could make 15kt and carried six aircraft. Five more escort carriers were later built in Britain on merchant ship hulls. *IWM (FL1203)*

ATLANTIC

AUGUST

Quebec Conference: 'Quadrant'

Prime Minister MacKenzie King of Canada hosts the next series of meetings in the middle of the month to discuss Allied strategy. Winston Churchill and Franklin Roosevelt agree the outline plans for 'Overlord' — the main invasion of Europe — to the use of 'Mulberry' harbours, and to the supreme commander being an American.

In the Far East, a South-East Asia Command is to be set up with Adm Mountbatten as supreme commander and a second Chindit operation mounted in Burma. Agreement is also reached on the sharing of nuclear research.

U647 on passage out may have been lost on the Iceland/Faeroes mine barrage around the 3rd of the month. If so she is the only casualty of this vast minefield throughout the war. RCAF aircraft sink U489 in the same area.

On the 11th U468 is sunk off Dakar by a RAF Liberator of No 200 Squadron. The final attack is carried out with the aircraft in flames and just before she crashes. ✠ The Liberator's commanding officer, Plt Off Lloyd Trigg RNZAF, is posthumously awarded the Victoria Cross, solely on the evidence of the U-boat's survivors.

25th — U523 attacks UK/Gibraltar convoy OG92 to the far west of Cape Finisterre and is sunk by destroyer *Wanderer* and corvette *Wallflower*.

27th — Bay of Biscay air patrols sink five U-boats in August and continue to co-operate with surface ships. As they do, on the 27th, German Do217s launch some of the first Hs293 glider bombs against ships of the 1st EG. To the south of Cape Finisterre, sloop **EGRET** is hit and blows up and Canadian destroyer **Athabaskan** is damaged.

30th — In attacks on Sierra Leone/UK convoy SL135 northeast of the Azores, U634 is sunk by sloop *Stork* and corvette *Stonecrop*.

Battle of the Atlantic

Losses
- 4 ships of 25,000 tons and 1 escort.
- 20 U-boats including 6 by aircraft of US escort carriers *Card* and *Core* off the Azores and in mid-Atlantic; 2 by US aircraft in the Caribbean area; 1 by RAF and French aircraft off Dakar; 1 by US forces in the South Atlantic.

SEPTEMBER

19th–22nd — Assault on the Escorts: Convoys ONS18 and ON202 — The wolf-packs return to the North Atlantic armed with Gnat acoustic torpedoes to home in on and disable the escorts so they can get in amongst the merchantmen. Adm Dönitz establishes a patrol line of 19 U-boats southwest of Iceland ready for UK-out convoys ONS18 (27 ships escorted by the British B3 group) and ON202 (42 ships and Canadian C2 group), which set out separately.

First blood goes to the RCAF on the 19th when U341 is sent to the bottom. Thereafter for the next three days six merchant ships are lost and the escorts suffer badly in the Gnat attacks. Two more U-boats are also sunk:

19th — Destroyer **Escapade** of B3 is badly damaged by a premature explosion of her Hedgehog.

EUROPE

AUGUST

On the 17th the USAAF loses 20% of its attacking aircraft in raids on ball-bearing production facilities at Schweinfurt and Regensburg — a major setback to its daylight bombing policy. That night the RAF inflicts damage on the German rocket research establishment at Peenemünde on the Baltic coast.

Disturbances in Denmark lead the German authorities to declare martial law throughout the country and to take over full control. As they do so most of the ships of the small Danish Navy are scuttled.

Eastern Front

From east of Smolensk south to the sea of Azov the Russians attack and push foward all along the line:

- In the centre towards Smolensk itself;

- In the centre/south Orel and then Kharkov are captured, after which they continue on towards Kiev, capital of the Ukraine;

- From the Rostov area in the south in the direction of Odessa and threatening to cut off the Germans in the Crimea.

SEPTEMBER

Eastern Front

The Russians continue to push forward in the centre and south and capture Smolensk on the 25th, but thereafter they make little progress in this area for the rest of the year.

MEDITERRANEAN

AUGUST

Sicily

As the Germans and Italians prepare to evacuate Sicily across the Strait of Messina, the Allies start their final push — the US Seventh Army along the north coast aided by three small amphibious hops and Eighth Army up the east side from Catania with one small landing. Gen Patton's men enter Messina just before Gen Montgomery's on the 17th. Sicily is now in Allied hands but 100,000 Axis troops manage to escape without any serious interference.

4th — Destroyer **ARROW** assists with unsuccessful fire-fighting alongside the burning merchantman *Fort La Montee* off Algiers harbour. She is badly damaged in the resulting explosion and never fully re-commissioned.

RN submarines continue to patrol the Mediterranean and sink numerous Axis ships including two Italian warships, but lose two of their number in August, the first for over three months:

9th — *Simoom* sinks destroyer *Gioberti* off Spezia, northwest Italy.

11th — **PARTHIAN** is overdue on this date. She left Malta on 22 July for the southern Adriatic and fails to return to Beirut.

14th — **SARACEN** on patrol off Bastia, Corsica is lost to Italian corvettes *Minerva* and *Euterpe*.

28th — *Ultor* torpedoes the torpedo boat *Lince* in the Gulf of Taranto.

22nd — Escort destroyers *Easton* and Greek *Pindos* sink *U458* southeast of Pantellaria.

Merchant Shipping War
Losses
● 11 ships of 43,000 tons.

SEPTEMBER

6th/12th — On passage to Oran, escort destroyer **PUCKER-IDGE** is sunk just east of Gibraltar by *U617*. Six days later the U-boat is damaged by a RAF Wellington of No 179 Squadron and beached on the coast of Spanish Morocco. There she is destroyed by gunfire from trawler *Haarlem*, supported by corvette *Hyacinth* and Australian minesweeper *Wollongong*.

7th — Submarine *Shakespeare* on patrol off the Gulf of Salerno sinks Italian submarine *Velella*.

Italy — Surrender and Invasion

The surrender is signed in Sicily on the 3rd, but not announced until the 8th to coincide with the main Allied landing at Salerno, and in the forlorn hope that the Germans can be prevented from taking over the country. Before long they are in control of

INDIAN & PACIFIC OCEANS

AUGUST

In Australia, John Curtin is re-elected Prime Minister and his Labour Party returned to power.

Pacific — Strategic and Maritime Situation

In May, Allied agreement was reached on an offensive towards the Marshall and Caroline Islands in the Central Pacific to parallel Gen MacArthur's advance along the north coast of New Guinea. Now, at the Quebec Conference, the Gilbert Islands are chosen as the first step in the island hopping campaign under the overall command of Adm Nimitz, C-in-C, Pacific Fleet.

New Georgia Islands, Central Solomons

As the fighting on New Georgia comes to an end, the Japanese evacuate their forces to Kolombangara, the next island in this group. Now the Americans start their policy of by-passing heavily defended areas whenever strategically possible, sealing them off and letting them 'wither on the vine'. On the 15th they start with landings on Vella Lavella to the north of Kolombangara. By early October, by which time New Zealand troops have joined the fighting for Vella Lavella, the Japanese have left both islands, and the Central Solomons are cleared. In early August another naval battle takes place:

Battle of Vella Gulf — This time the US Navy well and truly bests the Japanese 'Tokyo Expresses'. Six US destroyers on the night of the 6th/7th sink three out of four Japanese destroyers with torpedoes in the waters between Kolombangara and Vella Lavella.

19th — In the New Caledonia area, New Zealand trawler *Tui* and USN aircraft sink submarine *I17*.

Aleutians

In mid-month US and Canadian troops land on Kiska after heavy preliminary bombardments to find that the Japanese have quietly evacuated their forces. The Aleutians are now back in US hands.

Merchant Shipping War
As submarines continue to take a toll of Indian Ocean shipping, German *U197* is sunk by RAF aircraft off Madagascar on the 20th, the first of two lost in the Indian Ocean in 1943.
Losses
● Indian Ocean — 7 ships of 46,000 tons.
● Pacific — 2 ships of 4,000 tons.

SEPTEMBER

SOE Raid on Singapore — Working for Special Operations Executive, a small group of Australian and British servicemen are carried from Australia in an old fishing vessel, and on the night of the 24th/25th penetrate Singapore harbour in canoes. Several ships are sunk. In a similar raid in September 1944 the attackers are captured and executed.

New Guinea

As the Allies fight towards Salamaua, further north a three-pronged attack is launched on Lae by mainly Australian troops — from landings to the east, by men airlifted inland to the northwest, and from the direction of Wau. As the Japanese withdraw from both areas towards the north coast of the Huon Peninsular, Australians enter Salamaua on the 11th and Lae five days later. To prevent the Japanese holding on to the

20th — Frigate *Lagan* of C2 is damaged by *U270* or *U260*, but shortly afterwards *U338* is sunk by a VLR aircraft of RAF No 120 Squadron using the Allies' own acoustic torpedo — 'Fido'. **LAGAN** is towed home as a constructive total loss.

The convoys join together southeast of Greenland and the escort is reinforced by the Canadian 9th EG.

20th — Canadian destroyer **ST CROIX** (ex-US) of the 9th EG is lost to an attack by *U305* and corvette **POLYANTHUS** of C2 by a Gnat, probably from U952 or possibly U641.

22nd — Destroyer *Keppel* of B3 sinks *U229*, by which time the convoys are south of Cape Farewell. By now frigate **ITCHEN** of the 9th EG has on board most of the survivors of *St Croix* and *Polyanthus*, and around midnight she is hit, in all likelihood by *U666*. She goes down and takes all but three of the three ships' companies with her. (Note: *U952* or *U260* might also have been responsible for *Itchen's* loss.)

Fortunately the Allies have already anticipated the introduction of acoustic torpedoes and soon put into service the 'Foxer' noise-maker, which is towed astern to attract the Gnat away from the vessel. The U-boats do not repeat their successes.

22nd — Midget Submarine Attack on *Tirpitz*: Operation 'Source' — *Tirpitz* poses such a threat to the Russian convoys and holds down so much of Home Fleet's strength that almost any measures to immobilise her are justified. One gallant attempt was made in October 1942 when a small fishing vessel, the *Arthur*, penetrated to within a few miles of the battleship in Trondheimfiord with Chariot human torpedoes slung underneath. Just short of the target they broke away and all her efforts were in vain.

Now it is the turn of midget submarines — the X-craft each with their two 2-ton charges. Six of them leave for northern Norway towed by 'S' or 'T' class submarines. Two are lost on passage, but on the 20th, off Altenfiord, *X5*, *X6* and *X7* set out to attack *Tirpitz* and *X10* for the *Scharnhorst*. *X5* is lost and *X10* is unable to attack, but *X6* (Lt Cameron) and *X7* (Lt Place) penetrate all the defences to reach *Tirpitz* laying in Kaafiord at the far end of Altenfiord. Both drop their charges under or near the battleship before they sink and some of their crews escape. *Tirpitz* manages to shift her position slightly, but not enough to avoid damage when the charges go up. She is out of action for six months.

✠ Lt Donald Cameron RNR and Lt Basil Place RN are awarded the Victoria Cross.

Battle of the Atlantic

Losses
- 11 ships of 54,000 tons and 4 escorts.
- 6 U-boats including one each by RAF and RCAF Bay of Biscay patrols, and one by US aircraft off Brazil.

Top:
HMS *Mauritius*, the 'Fiji' class light cruiser which formed part of the gunfire support force for the 9 September 1943 landings at Salerno. Her sister-ship *Uganda* was damaged off the beaches on the 13th
Real Photos (S1784)

Above:
The 'Archer' class escort carrier HMS *Archer* was one of five ships built in US on merchant ship hulls and completed 1941-42 — 8,200 tons, 17kt, 15 aircraft, 550 crew. Of the five, *Avenger* and *Dasher* were both lost, and *Charger* was retained by US Navy as a training ship. *IWM (A14603)*

MEDITERRANEAN

north and central Italy, fighting a delaying action in the south, have occupied Rome, are regrouping their main forces near Naples, and have disarmed — often bloodily — Italian forces in the Dodecanese and Greece. On the 12th Mussolini is rescued from his Italian captors in the Abruzzi mountains by Otto Skorzeny and his paratroops, and flown to Germany. Later in the month he proclaims the establishment of the Italian Social Republic.

However, off the west coast of Italy, the Germans decide to evacuate their forces from Sardinia by way of Corsica starting on the 10th. French troops themselves land in Corsica in mid-month, but by early October the Germans have gone. Both islands are now in Allied hands.

Following the announcement of the Italian surrender, the bulk of the Italian fleet sails for Malta — three battleships, cruisers and destroyers from Spezia and Genoa, and three more battleships and other vessels from Taranto and the Adriatic. As the first group comes south, battleship *Roma* is sunk by a FX1400 radio-controlled bomb (unpropelled, unlike the Hs293 rocket-boosted, glider-bomb), but next day the remaining ships are escorted into Malta by *Warspite* and *Valiant*. Over 30 submarines head for Allied ports. On the 11th, and as it should be, Adm Cunningham has the honour of signalling to the Admiralty the arrival of the Italian battlefleet in Malta.

Meanwhile the invasion and occupation of southern Italy gets underway. A start is made on the 3rd when British and Canadian troops of Gen Montgomery's Eighth Army cross over the Strait of Messina from Sicily in 300 ships and landing craft (Operation 'Baytown'), and push up through Calabria, eventually to join up with the forces landed at Salerno. Early on the 9th, in conjunction with these landings, the Eighth Army's 1st Airborne Division is carried into Taranto by mainly RN warships (Operation 'Slapstick'). Shortly afterwards the ports of Brindisi and Bari are in Allied hands.

9th — Around midnight in Taranto harbour, cruiser-minelayer **ABDIEL**, loaded with 1st Airborne troops, detonates one of the magnetic mines dropped by E-boats *S54* and *S61* as they escape, and sinks with heavy loss of life.

9th — Salerno Landings: Operation 'Avalanche'

Landing area	Gulf of Salerno, south of Naples	
Forces landing:	US Fifth Army (US Gen Mark Clark) 55,000 British and US troops with 115,000 follow-up	
Departure from:	British 10th Corps Tunis and Libya	US Sixth Corps Algeria
Naval Attack Forces and Commanders:	*Western Naval Task Force Commander* Vice-Adm H. K. Hewitt USN	
	Northern Cdre G. N. Oliver	*Southern* Rear-Adm J. L. Hall USN
Naval assault and follow-up forces:	*British and Allied*	*United States*
Cruisers	4	4
Destroyers	18	18
Other warships	77	90
Troop and supply transports, LSIs, etc	29	13
Totals	128	125
Landing ships and craft (major only)	333	
Grand total	586	

INDIAN & PACIFIC OCEANS

Peninsular, Australian forces land north of Finschhafen on the 22nd as others push overland from Lae in the direction of Madang.

Merchant Shipping War

Losses
- Indian Ocean — 6 ships of 39,000 tons.
- Pacific — 1 ship of 10,000 tons.

The 'Attacker' class escort carrier HMS *Fencer*, one of a further eight escort ships built in the US. Completed 1942-43 and displacing 11,400 tons, these vessels could make 17kt and carry 18 aircraft and 650 crew. *Real Photos (S1555)*

MEDITERRANEAN

In addition to the Allied naval forces directly engaged in the landings, most of which are in their respective British or American sectors, Adm Cunningham as C-in-C provides a strong RN cover force and carrier support group. The cover force is again Force H under Adm Willis with battleships *Nelson*, *Rodney*, *Warspite* and *Valiant* and carriers *Formidable* and *Illustrious*. Rear-Adm Vian commands the support carriers with light carrier *Unicorn*, escort carriers *Attacker*, *Battler*, *Hunter* and *Stalker*, three cruisers and destroyers.

Most of the troops are carried to Salerno via Sicily in the landing ships and craft, and, early on the 9th and without any preliminary air or naval bombardment, landed in the face of strong German resistance. By the end of the day, with the support of the covering warships and carrier aircraft, both the British and Americans have established bridgeheads but with a gap between them. Over the next few days the Germans counter-attack and on the 13th and 14th come dangerously close to breaking through the Allied lines and reaching the beaches. They are held, and much of the credit for this goes to the supporting warships, especially *Warspite* and *Valiant* which arrive on the 15th. On the 16th, any threat of dislodgement is over.

13th/16th — All this time German Do127s using both kinds of guided bombs are attacking the Allied shipping laying off the beaches. On the 13th, cruiser **Uganda** is damaged as she provides supporting gunfire. And on the 16th, after **Warspite** has done her most valuable work, she is hit and near-missed by three or four of the bombs. Damaged, she has to be towed to Malta.

On the 16th the German troops start pulling back from Salerno towards the line of the Volturno River, north of Naples. That same day, units of Fifth and Eighth Armies make contact to the east of the landing area, and then slowly push north — Fifth Army up the west half of Italy and Eighth to the east. At the end of the month the Allies approach Naples.

British Aegean Campaign

With the surrender of Italy, Winston Churchill wants to seize the Italian Dodecanese Islands in the southern Aegean before the Germans can establish themselves. From here the Allies can threaten Greece and support Turkey, but the Americans and some British commanders are lukewarm on what they see as a side-issue compared with the battle for Italy. Insufficient forces, and especially aircraft, are made available, and the Germans soon take Rhodes, from where, together with other bases, they maintain air superiority throughout the coming campaign.

On the 15th and 16th, British troops occupy Kos, Leros, Samos and other smaller islands. The Royal Navy then has the task of supplying and reinforcing them, as well as attacking German supply routes. The potential parallels with Norway, Greece and Crete all those many months back are too obvious, if only in hindsight.

26th — After carrying troops to Leros, destroyers *Intrepid* and Greek **Queen Olga** are attacked by Ju88s while at anchor in the harbour. The Greek ship soon goes down and **INTREPID** follows her next day when she capsizes.

Merchant Shipping War
Losses
● 11 ships of 52,000 tons.

INDIAN & PACIFIC OCEANS

Top left:
The 'Ruler' class escort carrier HMS *Queen* at Port Said. She was one of a last group of 26 ships — 11,400 tons, 17kt, 24 aircraft, 650 crew — built in the US between 1943 and 1944, with both *Nabob* (RCN-manned) and *Thane* badly damaged and not repaired. *Real Photos*

Bottom left:
The 'Colossus' class light fleet carrier HMS *Colossus*. Six ships were completed between 1944 and the war's end, one as a repair ship. At 13,200 tons they could make 25kt and carried a useful complement of 40 aircraft, plus 1,300 crew. *Real Photos (S1652)*

The 'Dido' class AA cruiser HMS *Dido*. Of a total of 11 ships, *Bonaventure*, *Naiad*, *Hermione* and *Charybdis* were lost. Completed 1940-42 at 5,500 tons and with a speed of 33kt, they were armed with either 10 5.25in or eight 4.5 guns and carried c530 crew.
Real Photos (S2926)

ATLANTIC

OCTOBER

Covered by battleships *Anson* and *Duke of York* and other units of the Home Fleet, US carrier *Ranger* launches air attacks against shipping off Bodo, northern Norway on the 4th. Four ships are sunk and others damaged.

8th — In attacks on Halifax/UK convoy SC143, *U610* or *U378* sinks Polish destroyer **Orkan** (ex-*Myrmidon*) with an acoustic torpedo. Later in the day RAF and RCAF air escorts sink *U419*, *U643* and *U610*.

16th/17th — Six U-boats are lost in exchange for a single merchantman in attacks on UK-out convoys ON206 (B6 group) and ONS20 (4th EG). The 4th is mainly composed of the new US lease-lend 'Captain' class frigates.

The B7 group commanded by Cdr Gretton first of all reinforces ON206.

On the 16th, southeast of Greenland, RAF Liberators account for *U470*, *U844* and *U964*, and next day *U540*. Shortly after, as B7 group now transfers to ONS20, corvette *Sunflower* sinks *U631* with her Hedgehog. Still on the 17th, frigate *Byard* of the 4th EG and ONS20 sinks *U841*. B7 next moves to nearby ON207.

23rd-29th — Now to the south of Iceland, B7 reinforces ON207's already formidable escort consisting of the Canadian C1 group and Capt Walker's 2nd EG. On the 23rd a RAF Liberator of No 224 Squadron and B7 destroyers *Duncan* and *Vidette* share in the sinking of *U274*. Three days later the RCAF gets *U420*. Then on the 29th, by now with ON208, *Duncan*, *Vidette* and *Sunflower* sink *U282*.

31st — Northeast of the Azores, destroyer *Whitehall* and corvette *Geranium* of the B1 group escorting North and West Africa/UK convoys MKS28 and SL138 detect *U306* by HF/DF and send her to the bottom.

Battle of the Atlantic

After lengthy negotiations, in August Portugal granted the Allies the right to establish air and sea bases in the Azores as from October. This greatly extends the Allies' ability to cover the central Atlantic and the convoy routes between Britain and North and West Africa; also between North America and the Mediterranean.

Losses

● 13 ships of 61,000 tons and 1 destroyer.

● 23 U-boats including 4 by RAF and US aircraft in North Atlantic and off Portugal; 6 by US escort carriers *Card*, *Core* and *Block Island* off the Azores and in mid-Atlantic.

EUROPE

OCTOBER

Adm of the Fleet Sir Dudley Pound, First Sea Lord since 1939, suffered a stroke in August at the time of the Quebec conference. He has since resigned and dies on 21 October — Trafalgar Day. Adm Fraser is offered the post as Winston Churchill's first choice, but declines, and the Navy's most senior position is filled on the 15th by Adm Sir Andrew B. Cunningham.

23rd – Cruiser *Charybdis*, accompanied by two fleet and four 'Hunt' class destroyers, sails from Plymouth to intercept a German blockade runner off the coast of Brittany — Operation 'Tunnel'. Early in the morning the force is surprised by a group of torpedo boats. **CHARYBDIS** is hit twice by torpedoes fired by *T23* and *T27* and sinks with heavy loss of life. The 'Hunt' class vessel **LIMBOURNE** follows her after a hit from *T22*.

Eastern Front

In the centre and south the Russians make only limited progress in the face of fierce German resistance. However, further south still, the remaining German troops evacuate the Taman Peninsula and cross over to the Crimea.

The US carrier *Ranger* served with the British Home Fleet and on 4 October 1943 raided shipping off Norway. *IWM (A19601)*

MEDITERRANEAN

OCTOBER

Two RN submarines fail to return from patrol in the month. **USURPER** leaves Algiers on 24 September for the Gulf of Genoa, and fails to answer a signal on the 11th. She may have been mined or fallen victim to German A/S forces. **TROOPER** sets out from Beirut on 26 September for the Dodecanese and does not get back on the 17th. German records claim she was sunk by a Q-ship off Kos on the 14th.

Italy

British units of the US Fifth Army enter Naples on the 1st as the Germans fall back, ready to make the Allies fight long and hard for every gain over the next eight months. They are holding the line of the Volturno River in the west and the Biferno River in the east. Meanwhile, they prepare their main defences — the Gustav Line — along the Garigliano and Rapido rivers below Monte Cassino, and on to Ortona on the Adriatic coast.

On the West, Gen Mark Clark's Fifth Army manages to fight its way across the Volturno by mid-month and then comes up against the formidable defences in front of the main Gustav Line. To the east, Gen Montgomery's Eighth Army has to cross a number of well-defended rivers before reaching the Line. By the end of the month he is over the Biferno and starting to cross the Trigno.

While the struggle continues, Italy declares war on Germany on the 13th.

British Aegean Campaign

7th — On the 3rd, German troops land on Kos which falls next day. More forces head for the Island and on the 7th a convoy of seven small ships and one escort is annihilated by cruisers *Penelope* and *Sirius* and two destroyers. As they withdraw through the Scarpanto Strait, **Penelope** is damaged in attacks by Ju87s and Ju88s.

9th — Returning from a similar sweep west of Kos, cruiser *Carlisle* and destroyers are dive-bombed in the same area by Ju87 Stukas. **CARLISLE** is seriously damaged and never fully repaired and destroyer **PANTHER** sunk.

More sweeps and more supply trips lead to further losses, particularly amongst the 'Hunts', through to November:

17th — Cruiser **Sirius** is damaged by bombs south of Scarpanto Strait.

22nd — Greek 'Hunt' **Adrias** is badly damaged off Kos on mines laid by the German *Drache*; and as another 'Hunt' the **HURWORTH**, goes to her aid, she is also mined but in this case sinks with heavy casualties.

24th — Destroyer **ECLIPSE** falls victim to the same minefield.

30th — Cruiser **Aurora** is damaged in bombing attacks.

Adm Sir John H. D. Cunningham succeeds Adm Sir Andrew Cunningham as C-in-C, Mediterranean Fleet, in the middle of the month. (They are not related.)

30th — Submarine *Ultimatum* on patrol off Toulon sinks *U431*.

Five German U-boats set out for the Mediterranean, but one is sunk by the RAF while still in the Atlantic and two are disposed of by Gibraltar air and sea patrols:

31st — *U732* is sunk off Tangiers by destroyer *Douglas* and trawlers *Imperialist* and *Loch Oskaig*.

INDIAN & PACIFIC OCEANS

OCTOBER

New Guinea

Finschhafen is taken on the 2nd, but fighting continues in the area right through until December when the Australians start pushing slowly along the north coast towards Madang to parallel their inland drive.

North and Central Solomons

Battle of Vella Lavella — As nine Japanese destroyers complete the evacuation of the island on the night of the 6th/7th, they are intercepted by three US ships. A destroyer on each side is lost.

In preparation for the invasion of the northern island of Bougainville, New Zealand troops are landed on the Treasury Islands on the 27th.

The last operational German raider is sunk on the 17th. Heading for Japan, *Michel* is torpedoed off Yokohama by US submarine *Tarpon*. Since leaving Europe in March 1942 she has accounted for 18 ships of 127,000 tons.

Merchant Shipping War

RAF aircraft sink their second U-boat of 1943 in the Indian Ocean with *U533* on the 16th in the Gulf of Oman.

Losses
- Indian Ocean — 6 ships of 26,000 tons.
- Pacific — 1 ship of 7,000 tons.

HMS *Aurora*, an 'Arethusa' class light cruiser, was hit amidships by a single bomb on Saturday 30 October 1943, with almost 50 men being killed. *Real Photos (N1024)*

NOVEMBER

6th — Capt Walker's Escort Group with escort carrier *Tracker* patrols east of Newfoundland in support of convoy HX264. *U226* is sighted by *Tracker's* aircraft and destroyed by sloops *Starling*, *Kite* and *Woodcock*. Shortly afterwards, *Starling*, this time with *Wild Goose*, accounts for *U842*.

Combined UK-bound convoys MKS30 and SL139 are escorted by the 40th EG and joined in turn by the 7th, 5th and 4th Escort Groups to the far west and northwest of Portugal. One merchantman is lost to air attack, but three U-boats go down in the fighting:

19th — *U211* to a RAF Wellington.

20th — Frigate *Nene* and Canadian corvettes *Calgary* and *Snowberry* of the 5th EG sink *U536*.

21st — Frigate *Foley* and sloop *Crane* of the 40th account for *U538*.

Northwest of Cape Finisterre, Hs293 glider bombs sink the one merchant ship lost. The surviving U-boats are next deployed against other convoys in the area.

23rd/25th — As the U-boats approach southbound convoys KMS30/OS59 they run into the 4th EG, which has also been diverted. On the 23rd, frigates *Bazely*, *Blackwood* and *Drury* sink *U648*, and two days on the first two sink *U600*. Later, in the same area around the Azores, a RAF Wellington accounts for *U542*, and aircraft from US escort carrier *Bogue* the *U86*.

The first Russian convoys since March set out and arrive at the end of the month and in early December. Convoys JW54A and JW54B to Kola Inlet, and return RA54A and RA54B, pass through a total of 54 ships without loss.

Battle of the Atlantic

Losses
- 7 ships of 28,000 tons and 1 US destroyer off the Azores.
- 16 U-boats including 2 by RAF and US Bay of Biscay air patrols; 2 by RAF in North Atlantic and off the Azores; 3 by US forces in mid-Atlantic and off Ascension in the South Atlantic.

NOVEMBER

E-boats and mines are still capable of taking a toll of coastal shipping. In the night of the 4th/5th, Channel convoy CW221 loses three ships off Beachy Head to E-boat attack, and later in the month two more are mined off Harwich.

RAF Bomber Command launches the Battle of Berlin with heavy raids in the middle of the month, the first of 16 major attacks through to March 1944.

Eastern Front

In the centre/south, Kiev, capital of the Ukraine, is captured on the 6th and the Russians push on beyond. However, the Germans manage to mount a counter-attack and recapture some of the towns to the west of the city. A larger counter-offensive in the same area fades out by early December.

Further south the attacks towards Odessa finally cut off the Germans in the Crimea where they hold out until May.

Merchant Shipping War

Losses
- 7 ships of 13,000 tons.

HMS *Birmingham* was built as a 'Southampton' class light cruiser. At 12.22hrs on Sunday 28 November 1943, unescorted, she was torpedoed forward (with 29 men killed) at 33°05N, 21°43E. She was out of action for a year. *Real Photos (S1087)*

MEDITERRANEAN

1st (November) — *U340* by destroyers *Active* and *Witherington*, sloop *Fleetwood* and RAF aircraft of No 179 Squadron.

Merchant Shipping War
Losses
● 9 ships of 46,000 tons.

NOVEMBER

Italy

In the west, Fifth Army struggles to make progress towards the main Gustav Line but is still short of the Garigliano River and Cassino. To the east, Eighth Army is over the Trigno and preparing to attack new German positions behind the Sangro River. A major offensive is launched on the 28th led by British and New Zealand troops with the aim of breaking through the east end of the Gustav Line and taking Ortona.

It is in November that Luftwaffe Field Marshal Kesselring is given command of all German forces in Italy. Right through until the end of 1944 he is responsible for the stubborn and skilful defence of the country against strong Allied attacks.

British Aegean Campaign — Conclusion

German forces land on Leros on the 12th and capture the Island after four days of heavy fighting against the British and Italian defenders. The campaign comes to an end when Samos is evacuated on the 20th, but not before two more 'Hunts' fall victim, this time to Hs293s:

11th — *ROCKWOOD* is severely damaged off Kos following an attack with other destroyers on Kalymnos (Calino). She is not repaired and goes into reserve.

13th — *DULVERTON* is sunk off Kos as she withdraws from searching for German shiping making for Leros.

The cost of this abortive campaign to the Royal Navy can now be added up — four cruisers damaged with one never repaired, six destroyers lost or permanently out of action and others damaged. In addition the small Greek Navy has lost two destroyers.

Submarine **SIMOOM** sails from Port Said on the 2nd for the Aegean and fails to answer a signal on the 19th. She is presumed mined although German records claim she was torpedoed by *U565* off Kos on the 15th.

28th — On passage through the Mediterranean to join the Eastern Fleet, cruiser **Birmingham** is badly damaged northwest of Derna by *U407*.

Cairo and Teheran Conferences

On their way to Teheran to meet Marshal Stalin, Winston Churchill and President Roosevelt stop over at Cairo to discuss operations in Burma and China with the Chinese Generalissimo Chiang Kai-Shek. Arriving at Teheran on the 28th, they cover the Allied invasion of Normandy and southern France, and Russia's agreement to declare war on Japan once the Germans are defeated.

Merchant Shipping War
Losses
● 10 ships of 68,000 tons.

INDIAN & PACIFIC OCEANS

NOVEMBER

12th — On patrol off Penang in the Malacca Strait, submarine *Taurus* sinks the Japanese *I34* on passage out for a supply trip to Europe.

Bougainville, Northern Solomons

The large Japanese garrison on this island is mainly established in the south and so the US Marines are landed on the weakly defended western side near Empress Augusta Bay on the 1st. They soon have a large beachhead, and it is not until March that the Japanese mount a strong counter-attack. Two main naval battles result in November:

Battle of Empress Augusta Bay — Japanese force of four cruisers and six destroyers sails to attack the invasion shipping. On the night of the 1st/2nd in a confused night action with four US light cruisers and eight destroyers, the Japanese are driven off with the loss of a cruiser and destroyer.

Battle of Cape St George — Five Japanese 'Tokyo Express' destroyers head for the Bougainville area and early on the 25th are intercepted by five US destroyers off the southern tip of New Ireland. Three of the Japanese are sent to the bottom in the last of the numerous Solomon Islands actions that started only 15 months before with the Battle of Savo Island.

Gilbert Islands, Central Pacific

US forces now start their advance through the Central Pacific with the invasion of the British Gilbert Islands. Under the overall command of Adm Nimitz, C-in-C, Pacific Fleet, Adm Spruance's Fifth Fleet lands US Marines and Army troops on the atolls of Tarawa and Makin respectively on the 20th. Both are strongly defended but US losses on Tarawa are particularly heavy, although as usual few Japanese survive. Both atolls are secured by the 23rd. Next day, escort carrier Liscome Bay is sunk off Makin by a submarine. The next step will be to the Marshalls laying to the northwest.

Merchant Shipping War
Losses
● Indian Ocean — 4 ships of 29,000 tons.
● Pacific — 1 ship of 7,000 tons.

DECEMBER

24th — Destroyer **HURRICANE** of the 1st EG with UK/African convoys OS62 and KMS36 is torpedoed by *U305* or *U415* northeast of the Azores. Next day she has to be scuttled.

26th — The Battle of North Cape and Russian Convoy JW55B — Russian convoys are still sailing in two sections. JW55A leaves Loch Ewe on the 12th and arrives safely with all 19 merchant ships on the 20th. Adm Fraser with *Duke of York* goes right through to Russia for the first time before returning to Iceland.

Convoy JW55B, also with 19 ships, sails on the 20th. Three days later return convoy RA55A (22 ships) sets out. Cover for both convoys through the Barents Sea is to be provided by Vice-Adm R. L. Burnett with cruisers *Belfast*, *Norfolk* and *Sheffield* which leave Kola Inlet on the same day as RA55A. The Admiralty expects the 11in *Scharnhorst* to attack the convoys and Adm Fraser with *Duke of York* and cruiser *Jamaica* leaves Iceland and heads for the Bear Island area.

Scharnhorst (Rear-Adm Bey) and five destroyers sail from Altenfiord late on the 25th, Christmas Day. Early next morning JW55B is 50 miles south of Bear Island, the weather stormy, as the Germans head north to intercept. Meanwhile Adm Fraser is 200 miles away to the southwest and Adm Burnett's cruisers are approaching the convoy from the east. At 07.30 the German destroyers are detached to search for the convoy, fail to make contact and are later ordered home. They play no part in the battle.

First contact is just before 09.00 on the 26th when *Belfast* detects *Scharnhorst* by radar as she is heading south and only 30 miles to the east of the convoy. *Norfolk* engages and hits the battlecruiser which turns north and away to try to get around to JW55B. Adm Burnett anticipates this move and instead of shadowing, carries on towards the convoy.

Belfast regains contact at noon and all three cruisers open fire. In the next 20min *Scharnhorst* is hit and **Norfolk** badly damaged by 11in shells. The German ship now heads south away from the convoy as Adm Burnett shadows by radar. At this time, Adm Fraser is now to the south-southwest and in a position to cut off her retreat. He makes radar contact soon after 16.00 at a range of 22 miles and closes in.

Fifty minutes later, *Belfast* illuminates *Scharnhorst* with starshell and Adm Burnett's cruisers engage from one side and *Duke of York* and *Jamaica* from the other. Hard hit, especially by the battleship's 14in shells, the German ship's main armament is eventually silenced. Finally the cruisers and accompanying destroyers fire torpedoes, 10 or 11 of which strike home, and soon after 19.30 *Scharnhorst* goes down. Only 36 men can be rescued. Now only *Tirpitz* remains as a potential big ship threat to the Russian convoys.

On the 29th JW55B reaches Kola safely. Return convoy RA55A is well clear of Bear Island by the time the battle has started and makes Loch Ewe on 1 January. The second return half — RA55B of eight ships — leaves Russia on the last day of the year and gets in on 8 January.

Battle of the Atlantic

Losses

● 7 ships of 48,000 tons and 2 destroyers including one US in the North Atlantic.

● 1 battlecruiser and 5 U-boats including 1 by RAF Bay of Biscay patrol; 3 by US Navy in Azores and Madeira areas; 1 scuttled after storm damage in mid-Atlantic.

DECEMBER

28th – Eleven German destroyers and torpedo boats sortie into the Bay of Biscay to bring in the blockade runner *Alsterufer*. She is sunk by a Czech Liberator of RAF Coastal Command on the 27th, and next day as the German warships return to base they are intercepted by cruisers *Glasgow* and *Enterprise*. Although vastly outnumbered and out-gunned they sink destroyer *Z27* and torpedo boats *T25* and *T26*. This marks the virtual end of German attempts to bring in vital supplies from the Far East by surface ships. Since 1941, of 35 ships that have set out, only 16 have broken through Allied patrols.

In late December the commanders for the invasion of Europe are announced. US General Eisenhower will be Supreme Allied Commander with Air Marshal Tedder as his deputy. In charge of all naval operations under the code name 'Neptune' is Adm Sir Bertram Ramsey.

Eastern Front

Since October, five Russian attacks have been launched in the centre against the Germans west of Smolensk. The greatly out-numbered defenders have held on, but the Russians now have a foothold back in Byelo-Russia.

In the centre/south, all the Ukraine east of the Dnieper River together with deep bridgeheads across much of its length are now in Russian hands. They are ready to take the rest of the Ukraine, push into the Crimea and move on Poland and Roumania.

Merchant Shipping War

Losses

● 1 ships of 6,000 tons.

Right:
The 'Fiji' class light cruiser HMS *Bermuda*. The class of 11 ships completed 1940-43, 8,000 tons, 33kt, 12 6in guns, 730 crew — lost *Fiji* and *Trinidad*. From 1944, *Gambia* served with the RNZN and *Uganda* with the RCN as HMCS *Quebec*. *Real Photos*

Below:
HMS *Jamaica*, a 'Fiji' class light cruiser. She was one of the victors of the 26 December 1943 Battle of the North Cape. *Real Photos (S1659)*

MEDITERRANEAN

DECEMBER

Italy

Fifth Army continues its bloody struggle in the west of the country towards the Gustav Line, but has only just reached the Garigliano River and is still short of Cassino and the Rapido River. Meanwhile Eighth Army has breached the Line in the east and the Canadians have taken Ortona, where the Allies remain until June. Gen Montgomery now returns to England to prepare for his part in the Normandy invasion.

Gen Eisenhower also heads for England and Gen Sir Henry Maitland Wilson succeeds him as Supreme Allied Commander, Mediterranean. Later, in November, Field Marshal Alexander takes over this post.

With the surrender of the Italian fleet, the big ships of the RN are being released for the Eastern Fleet and in preparation for the landings in Normandy. The smaller vessels left behind continue to escort the convoys needed to supply the Allied forces in Italy, and to support both Fifth and Eighth armies on their seaward flanks. The RN also goes over to the offensive against Germany supply traffic down the west coast of Italy and also from the northeast through the Adriatic to Yugoslavia. From bases such as Corsica and Bari, light and coastal forces strike regularly at shipping, and also at land targets along the coast of Yugoslavia in support of Tito's partisan armies.

A major disaster mars these successes when on the 2nd an air raid on Bari blows up an ammunition ship with 16 more merchantmen lost in the resulting fires.

11th-16th — U-boats attack UK/North Africa convoy KMS34 with acoustic torpedoes off the Algerian coast. On the 11th *U223* damages frigate **Cuckmere**. Next day, northeast of Bougie, *U593* sinks 'Hunt' escort destroyer **TYNEDALE**. A long hunt ensues by escort destroyers *Calpe* and *Holcombe* and US destroyers *Benson*, *Niblack* and *Wainwright*, in the course of which the U-boat manages to sink **HOLCOMBE**. After more than 30 hours the escorts finally send *U593* to the bottom on the 13th.

Other US destroyers including *Niblack* sink *U73* on the 16th. This is the 23rd U-boat lost in the Mediterranean in 1943.

Merchant Shipping War

Losses
● 18 ships of 83,000 tons.

INDIAN & PACIFIC OCEANS

DECEMBER

Burma

Under Adm Mountbatten, Supreme Allied Commander, South East Asia, Gen Slim's 14th Army prepares for a major offensive into northern Burma from the area of Kohima and Imphal in India. Preceeding this will be a second Arakan campaign to the south, and in the far north a parallel Chindit and American/Chinese operation in part to open up a new route to the Burma Road from Ledo in India. The Arakan push starts late in December. Throughout the rest of the war, Adm Mountbatten's plans to prosecute the campaign even more vigorously in South East Asia are continually frustrated by his lack of amphibious capability.

New Britain, Bismarck Archipelago

Gen MacArthur prepares to complete his part in the isolation of Rabaul by preliminary landings on the southwest coast of New Britain, followed by a major assault at the western tip of Cape Gloucester on the 26th. Cover is partly provided by Rear-Adm Crutchley with cruisers *Australia* and *Shropshire*. Fighting continues until March when, assisted by further landings, the western third of the island is secured. By November 1944, when Australian troops relieve the US forces, still considerable numbers of Japanese are penned in around Rabaul where they stay until the war's end.

Merchant Shipping War

Losses
● Indian Ocean only — 5 ships of 31,000 tons.

The 'Abdiel' class cruiser-minelayer HMS *Apollo*. The class of six ships lost *Latona*, *Welshman* and *Abdiel* in the Mediterranean. Completed 1941-44 at 2,600 tons, they could make a fast 40kt, and carry six 4in guns, 150 mines and 240 crew. *Real Photos*

ATLANTIC

JANUARY

7th — As the 5th EG sweeps to the west of Cape Finisterre, frigate **TWEED** is torpedoed and sunk by *U305*. Intense A/S activity further north will see *U305* lost well before the month is out.

U-boats concentrate against UK/West and North African convoys, mainly to the west and southwest of Ireland, and eight are lost from all causes:

8th — *U757* to frigate *Bayntun* and Canadian corvette *Camrose* of the 4th and 5th EGs escorting OS64/KMS38.

13th — Northeast of the Azores *U231* is lost to a RAF Leigh light Wellington.

15th — Off the Azores *U377* is sunk by one of her own torpedoes.

17th — Back to the waters west of Ireland, and *U305* is now sunk by destroyer *Wanderer* as she returns from a search for blockade runners.

19th — *U641* attacks OS65 and KMS39 and goes down to corvette *Violet* of the British B3 group.

28th — Operations against OS66/KMS40 lead to the loss of *U271* to a US Navy Liberator and *U571* to a RAAF Sunderland.

To the west of Ireland *U972* suffers a similar fate to *U377*.

30th — Escorting Russian convoy JW56B, destroyer **HARDY (2)** is torpedoed by *U278* to the south of Bear Island and has to be scuttled. On the same day *U314* is sunk by destroyers *Whitehall* and *Meteor* of the escort. All 16 of JW56B's ships reach Kola Inlet. JW56A earlier in the month has not been so fortunate — of the 20 merchantmen, five return due to the weather, and three are lost to U-boats.

31st — Capt Walker with sloops *Starling, Kite, Magpie, Wild Goose* and *Woodpecker* accompanied by escort carriers *Activity* and *Nairana* arrives in the waters to the southwest of Ireland. Over the next three weeks the five sloops share in the sinking of six U-boats operating against the convoys passing through the area. They start on the 31st when *Starling, Magpie* and *Wild Goose* depth-charge *U592* to destruction.

Battle of the Atlantic

Over the next five months U-boat losses are so heavy that, by May, North Atlantic operations are virtually stopped. In this period only 25 merchant ships are lost in the North and South Atlantic at a cost of 77 U-boats from all causes. At the same time the Allies are not so successful against them as they pass through the Bay of Biscay and the northern transit area. Now equipped with 10cm radar detectors they only lose five of their number in the Bay, but in mid-May are badly hit by Coastal Command off Norway. By then the whole complexion of the U-boat war near the shores of Europe is about to change with the invasion of Normandy.

Losses
- 5 ships of 36,000 tons, 2 destroyers incuding one US off New York, and 1 frigate.
- 14 U-boats including 2 by RAF and RAAF Bay of Biscay patrols; 1 by RAF-laid mine in Bay of Biscay; 1 by US escort carrier *Guadalcanal* off the Azores.

EUROPE

JANUARY

RAF and USAAF operations against Germany and occupied Europe increase in intensity. Much of the RAF's efforts are still directed by night at Berlin, but both air forces are now attacking the V-1 buzz-bomb launch sites in northern France. The recently introduced long-range P-51 Mustang fighter allows the Americans to continue daylight bombing, but losses remain heavy. Italy also stays high on the list of Allied targets. In February the Luftwaffe carries out a number of raids on London in the 'Little Blitz'.

Eastern Front

Now it is the turn of the German invaders in the north to feel the weight of Russian attacks. Here a series of offensives drive them back from the gates of Leningrad by the end of the month. By early March the Russian armies have regained a large chunk of their territory that takes them just over the border of northern Estonia and close to Latvia. Here they stay until July.

Meanwhile, the massive assaults continue in the centre/south from north of Kiev to the Black Sea, and the lost ground to the west of that city is soon regained. The Russians push on and early in the month cross into the southeast corner of prewar Poland.

Merchant Shipping War
Losses
- 8 ships of 7,000 tons in UK waters.

HMS *Vesper*, a 'V' & 'W' class destroyer. Early in 1944 she was still in service escorting convoys in the North Atlantic. *Real Photos (S545)*

MEDITERRANEAN

JANUARY

Italy

Four months after the Salerno landings the Allies have only moved on a further 70 miles and are still well short of Rome. Both Fifth and Eighth Armies have suffered badly and, in an attempt to break the deadlock, the decision is made to go ahead with landings at Anzio to coincide with fresh attacks on the Gustav Line and Monte Cassino. As the landings get underway, British units of Fifth Army manage to get across parts of the Garigliano River and the French over the Rapido, but in the centre, in the First Battle of Cassino, the US troops are badly mauled. All attacks are held by the Germans.

22nd — Anzio Landings: Operation 'Shingle'

Landing area:	North and south of the town of Anzio	
Forces landing:	US Sixth Corps (US Gen Lucas) 50,000 British and US troops	
	British 1st Division	US 3rd Division
Departure from:	Naples	

	Naval Commander Rear-Adm F. J. Lowry USN	
Naval Assault Forces and Commanders:	*Northern* Rear-Adm T. Troubridge	*Southern* Rear-Adm Lowry USN
Naval assault forces:	*British and Allied*	*United States*
Cruisers	3	1
Destroyers	14	10
Other warships	30	59
LSIs, landing craft and ships (major only)	168	84
Totals	215	154
Grand total	369	

The British and US warships are not strictly allocated to their own sectors and two RN submarines provide the usual navigational markers.

Landings take place early on the 22nd and are virtually unopposed. By next day the beachheads are secured, but by the time Sixth Corps is ready to move out on the 30th, powerful German reinforcements are ready to stop it in its tracks. For over a month until early March the Allies are hard pushed to hold on to their gains.

23rd/29th — The supporting warships are heavily attacked from the air. On patrol off the beaches on the 23rd, destroyer **JANUS** is torpedoed and sunk by a He111 bomber. Six days later, cruiser **SPARTAN** is hit by a Hs293 glider bomb and capsizes with many casualties.

Merchant Shipping War
Losses
● 5 ships of 31,000 tons.

INDIAN & PACIFIC OCEANS

JANUARY

11th/26th — Late in the month the British Eastern Fleet is considerably strengthened by the arrival of capital ships *Queen Elizabeth*, *Valiant*, *Renown* and carriers *Illustrious* and *Unicorn*, cruisers and destroyers. To date only the Ceylon-based submarines have been available to carry out offensive operations in the Indian Ocean, and in January they have two successes against Japanese light cruisers of the 'Kuma' class, both off Penang in the Malacca Strait. On the 11th *Tally Ho* (Lt-Cdr L. W. A. Bennington) sinks the *Kuma* herself. Two weeks later *Templar* damages *Kitakami*.

New Guinea

US Army troops land at Saidor on the 2nd covered by Rear-Adm Crutchley's mixed force of Australian and American warships. Saidor is soon taken as the Australian forces continue to push along the north coast and overland from Lae. They link up with the Americans near Saidor on the 10th February, and the Huon Peninsula is now almost entirely in Allied hands.

Merchant Shipping War
Losses
● Indian Ocean only — 8 ships of 56,000 tons.

HMS *Kenya*, steaming through heavy seas in the Arctic. By 1944 she was one of the cruisers serving with the British Eastern Fleet in the Indian Ocean. *Real Photos (S1774)*

ATLANTIC

FEBRUARY

U-boat concentrations again suffer badly to the west and southwest of Ireland, and 10 boats are lost, all to the RN in exchange for a sloop and one straggler. Capt Walker's 2nd EG accounts for five of them, which added to the one on 31 January gives a record for U-boat sinkings in one patrol only equalled by the US destroyer escort *England* in the South West Pacific in May 1944.

8th/9th — In support of convoys SL147/MKS38, Capt Walker in *Starling* together with *Kite*, *Magpie*, *Wild Goose* and *Woodpecker* share in the sinking of *U762* on the 8th, and *U734* and *U238* next day.

10th — West of Ireland, *U666* is sunk by Swordfish of 842 Squadron from escort carrier *Fencer* in support of trans-Atlantic convoy ON223.

11th — Back to the southwest of Ireland, *Wild Goose* and *Woodpecker* hunt down *U424* and destroy her with depth charges.

18th — Frigate *Spey* of the 10th EG with ONS29 sinks *U406*.

19th — The 2nd EG now supporting ON224 is attacked by *U264*. Brought to the surface by *Starling* and *Woodpecker*, she is scuttled, the first of the schnorkel-equipped boats to be lost. As the 10th EG transfers to this convoy, *Spey* claims another success with the sinking of *U386*.

19th/27th — Capt Walker's Group is now looking for its seventh victim when **WOODPECKER** loses her stern to an acoustic torpedo from *U764*. Slowly towed home, she eventually sinks on the 27th off the Scilly Islands.

24th — West of Ireland, *U257* is sunk by Canadian frigate *Waskesiu* of the 6th EG with Halifax/UK convoy SC153.

25th — Further south *U91* is lost to frigates *Affleck, Gore* and *Gould* of the 1st EG carrying out an A/S patrol in support of the convoys in the vicinity.

24th/25th — The 42 merchantmen of Russian convoy JW57 all reach Kola on the 28th, but one of the escort and two U-boats are sunk in the battles that surround them. On the 24th, to the northwest of Norway, *U713* is put down by destroyer *Keppel* of the escort. Next day destroyer **MAHRATTA** is lost to an acoustic torpedo from *U956* or *U990* and sinks with heavy loss of life. A RAF Catalina of No 210 Squadron flying at extreme range manages to sink *U601*. Return convoy RA56 earlier in the month makes Loch Ewe with its 37 ships.

Battle of the Atlantic

Losses
- 2 ships of 12,000 tons, 1 destroyer and 1 sloop.
- 15 U-boats including 2 by RAF to the west of Scotland; 1 by US Navy aircraft off Ascension.

EUROPE

FEBRUARY

5th – Escort carrier **Slinger** is mined and damaged in the Thames Estuary off Sheerness.

20th – On patrol off Trevose Head, southwest England, for a reported U-boat, destroyer **WARWICK** is torpedoed and sunk by *U413*. This is the first enemy submarine effectively to penetrate British coastal waters since 1940.

Norwegian resistance fighters sink a cargo of heavy water bound for Germany for nuclear research.

Eastern Front

In the centre the Russians move further into Poland. All this time the German commanders are severely restricted by Hitler's refusal to allow them to fall back on more defensible positions. Large formations find themselves encircled by the Russians and the Germans' by now limited resources have to be expended in getting them out.

Merchant Shipping War

Losses
- 3 ships of 4,000 tons.

MEDITERRANEAN

FEBRUARY

Italy

Before the Second Battle of Cassino, the decision is taken to bomb the monastery of Monte Cassino on the 15th, but the only result is to provide the Germans with even better defensive positions. This time it is the attacking Indian and New Zealand troops who take the losses for no gains.

Throughout the month the Germans launch more attacks at Anzio to prevent the Allies breaking out of the beachhead. By early March they have exhausted themselves and move over to the defensive.

18th/25th — RN ships continue to suffer casualties during the Battle for Anzio. As she returns to Naples on the 18th, the seemingly indestructible cruiser **PENELOPE** is torpedoed and sunk by *U410*. One week later destroyer **INGLEFIELD** is hit off the beaches by another Hs293 and goes down.

24th — In the Strait of Gibraltar, USN Catalinas equipped with the new Magnetic Anomaly Detector (MAD) locate *U761* trying to break in to the Mediterranean. Destroyers *Anthony* and *Wishart* of the Gibraltar patrol sink her.

Merchant Shipping War
Losses
- 8 ships of 36,000 tons.

INDIAN & PACIFIC OCEANS

FEBRUARY

As German and Japanese submarines continue to attack Allied shipping in the Indian Ocean, two Japanese are sunk, but in the second case only after the loss of many lives:

11th — *RO110* attacks a Calcutta/Colombo convoy in the Bay of Bengal and is sunk by the escorts — Indian sloop *Jumna* and Australian minesweepers *Ipswich* and *Launceston*.

12th — Off Addu Atoll *I27* attacks a five-ship troop convoy bound for Colombo from Kilindini in East Africa, and escorted by the old cruiser *Hawkins* and destroyers *Paladin* and *Petard*. The *Khedive Ismail* goes down with over 1,000 men, but *I27* is eventually sunk in return by the two destroyers.

14th — On patrol in the Malacca Strait, submarine *Tally Ho* has another success when she sinks the German submarine *Ult23* (ex-Italian) bound for Europe with cargo from the Far East.

Burma

The Arakan offensive to the south is slowly progressing when early in the month the Japanese start their own attack, and manage to outflank and surround the British and Indian troops. Supplied by air they hold out and by June have established themselves on a line north of Akyab, where they stay through the monsoon until December.

Marshall Islands, Central Pacific

After taking the southeastern and undefended atoll of Majuro on 31 January, Adm Spruance's Fifth Fleet lands US forces half way up the Marshall's group on the huge atoll of Kwajalein the same day. The Japanese defenders resist stubbornly, but with their wild Banzai charges are soon wiped out. At the western end of the Marshalls, Eniwetok atoll is similarly taken starting on the 17th.

The Truk Raid — With the Japanese major fleet base of Truk only 700 miles away in the Carolines, the ships and aircraft of Fifth Fleet attack, and together with patrolling submarines sink three cruisers, four destroyers and much shipping in mid-month.

Merchant Shipping War
Losses
- Indian Ocean only — 10 ships of 64,000 tons.

HMS *Penelope* entering Malta's Grand Harbour in December 1941. Two years later, at 07.30hrs on Friday 18 February 1944, she was hit by two torpedoes at 40°55N, 13°25E, and sank 10min later with only 250 survivors. The greater part of her ship's company were lost. *IWM (A9330)*

MARCH

1st — The 1st EG is now to the far southwest of Ireland, north of the Azores, and frigates *Affleck, Gould, Garlies* and *Gore* have already hunted a contact for 30hr when the last two have to leave for Gibraltar. Then late on the 1st the tables are turned and **GOULD** is hit by a Gnat acoustic torpedo and sinks. *Affleck* is left alone to locate *U358* and send her to the bottom with depth charges and gunfire. At 38hr this is probably the longest continuous U-boat hunt of the war.

4th-6th — The next return convoy from Russia, RA57, sails with the escort of the February JW57 including escort carrier *Chaser* and her rocket-firing Swordfish of 816 Squadron. On the 4th, to the north west of Norway, they damage *U472* which is finished off by destroyer *Onslaught*, and in the next two days, in spite of foul weather, destroy *U366* and *U973*.

6th — In another long hunt, lasting 30hr, the Canadian C2 group escorting Halifax/UK convoy HX280 sink *U744* in mid-Atlantic. Canadian destroyers *Chaudière* and *Gatineau*, frigate *St Catherines*, corvettes *Chilliwack* and *Fennel* and RN destroyer *Icarus* are joined by corvette *Kenilworth Castle* before the action is over.

9th — Corvette **ASPHODEL** with West and North Africa/UK convoys SL150/MKS41 is torpedoed and sunk by *U575* to the west of the Bay of Biscay. The U-boat herself is lost four days later.

10th — In an attack on Halifax/UK convoy SC154, *U845* is lost in mid-Atlantic to the Canadian C1 group including destroyer *St Laurent*, frigates *Owen Sound* and *Swansea* and RN destroyer *Forester*.

13th — RAF Wellingtons flying from the Azores attack *U575* well to the north. She is finally sent to the bottom by the aircraft and ships of the USS *Bogue* task group and Canadian frigate *Prince Rupert* from nearby convoy ON227.

15th — In mid-Atlantic, Swordfish of 825 Squadron from escort carrier *Vindex* working with *Starling* and *Wild Goose* sink *U653* — Capt Walker's 13th kill.

25th — 'Tsetse' Mosquitos of RAF Coastal Command on Bay of Biscay patrol sink *U976* with the new 6pdr guns — their first success.

29th — The 2nd EG is now with Russian convoy JW58. Two days after leaving Loch Ewe and by now off Iceland, *U961* is sunk by *Starling*. More U-boats are lost before the convoy reaches Russia early in April.

Battle of the Atlantic

To make more efficient use of available tonnage, trans-Atlantic convoys are now designated Fast, Medium or Slow. All this time great numbers of US servicemen are being carried across to Britain in preparation for the invasion of Europe, many by the fast, unescorted liners *Queen Elizabeth* and *Queen Mary* carrying 15,000 men on each trip.

Losses

● 8 ships of 41,000 tons, 2 escorts and 1 US destroyer off Iceland.
● 17 U-boats including 1 by RCAF off Ireland; 4 by the aircraft and ships of USS *Block Island* off the Azores and Cape Verde Islands; 1 by unkown causes in the North Atlantic; 1 by SAAF off South Africa.

MARCH

20th/28th – Two RN submarines, one of them ex-German, are lost. On the 20th **GRAPH** (ex-*U570*) breaks her tow and runs aground on Islay Island off the west coast of Scotland. After sinking a small ship off Bodo, Norway, a few days before, **SYRTIS** is sunk on the 28th in the minefields flanking the port.

Eastern Front

By now nearly all of the Ukraine is back in Russian hands and in the south the advance towards the southwest brings the Russians to the foothills of the Carpathian mountains, just inside prewar Roumania. Thoroughly concerned about the potential collapse of the Balkans, Hitler orders his troops into Hungary to prevent the country leaving the Axis. As this happens the Finnish Government is trying to negotiate an armistice with Russia.

Merchant Shipping War

Losses

● Between now and the invasion of Normandy only one small ship is lost in UK waters.

MEDITERRANEAN

MARCH

Italy

In the middle of the month the Third Battle of Cassino is fought again by the Indians and New Zealanders of Fifth Army. Once more they lose badly. The Germans still hold stubbornly on to Monte Cassino. Now there is a lull as Eighth Army is brought across from the east to add its weight to the struggle.

10th/30th — In operations against Allied shipping bound for Italy, three U-boats are lost together with one RN destroyer. On the 10th off Anzio, *U450* is sunk by 'Hunts' *Blankney, Blencathra, Brecon* and *Exmoor* and US destroyer *Madison.* That same day south of Sardinia, A/S trawler *Mull* sinks *U343.*

At the end of the month, destroyers *Laforey* and *Tumult* and 'Hunts' *Blencathra* and *Hambledon* locate *U223* north of Sicily. As the search proceeds, **LAFOREY** is torpedoed and sunk, but the remaining ships later find and finish off the U-boat.

16th — US Navy Catalinas use MAD to locate another U-boat in the Strait of Gibraltar on passage into the Mediterranean. Destroyer *Vanoc* and frigate *Affleck* are called up and account for *U392.*

Merchant Shipping War
Losses
● 5 ships of 41,000 tons.

The 'Bellona' class AA cruiser HMS *Diadem* was one of five ships; *Spartan* was sunk in January 1944. Completed 1943-44, they displaced 5,800 tons, carried eight 5.25in guns and 530 crew, and had a maximum speed of 33kt. *Real Photos (S2927)*

INDIAN & PACIFIC OCEANS

MARCH

Submarine **STONEHENGE** sails from Ceylon for patrol in the area between Sumatra and the Nicobar Islands. She is overdue on the 20th, cause of loss unknown.

Burma

In the north, as one Chindit group marches from Ledo into Burma, a second one is airlifted to a position northeast of Indaw on the 5th. At this time US Gen 'Vinegar Joe' Stillwell and his Chinese forces also leave from near Ledo and start their own march into Burma heading for Myitkyina. Behind them the new Burma Road is constructed through the mountainous country, but will not link up with the old road until January 1945. Major Gen Orde Wingate is killed in an air crash on the 24th, and shortly afterwards the Chindits are used to support Gen Stillwell's campaign.

Further to the south and west the Japanese choose this time to start their own major offensive into India to pre-empt 14th Army's planned attack. By the end of the month they are over the Assam border and approaching the British and Indian defenses at Kohima and Imphal.

Admiralty Islands, Bismarck Archipelago

To complete Allied strategic control of the Bismarcks, Gen MacArthur's US forces land on the Admiralty Islands on the last day of February. Further landings are made during March, but by the end of the month, in spite of fierce resistance, they are secured. Some fighting continues through until May. The main island of Manus becomes one of the major Allied bases for the rest of the war.

Bougainville, Northern Solomons

Only now do the Japanese launch their main attack on the US beachhead, but they are soon beaten back. The survivors are left to themselves in the south of the Island. In November, Australian forces relieve the Americans and early in 1945 start a long and tedious campaign to clear them out.

Merchant Shipping War
Losses
● Indian Ocean only — 12 ships of 75,000 tons.

APRIL

1st-3rd — U-boats are now attacking JW58 to the northwest of Norway and lose three of their number. On the 1st an Avenger of 846 Squadron from *Tracker* damages *U355* with rockets, and destroyer *Beagle* completes the job. Next day destroyer *Keppel* sinks *U360* with her Hedgehog, and on the 3rd it is the turn of *U288*. A Swordfish, Wildcat and Avenger from *Tracker's* 846 Squadron and *Activity's* 819 send her to the bottom. Apart from one merchantman returning, all of JW58's remaining 48 ships arrive at Kola on the 5th.

Return convoy RA58 passes through 36 merchantmen by mid-month without loss.

3rd — Fleet Air Arm Attack on *Tirpitz*: Operation 'Tungsten' — The damage inflicted by midget submarines in September is nearly repaired and the Admiralty decides to launch a FAA attack on *Tirpitz*. On the 30th, Adm Fraser leaves Scapa Flow with battleships *Duke of York* and *Anson*, fleet carriers *Victorious* and the old *Furious*, escort carriers *Emperor*, *Fencer*, *Pursuer* and *Searcher*, cruisers and destroyers, split into two forces, and heads north, partly to cover JW58.

By the 2nd the two forces have joined up 120 miles off Altenfiord and, early next morning, two waves each of 20 Barracuda bombers with fighter cover surprise *Tirpitz* at anchor. A total of 14 hits are made, but the damage is not serious. However, the battleship is out of action for another three months. Home Fleet is back in Scapa on the 6th.

A similar operation is attempted later in the month, but bad weather prevents any attacks on *Tirpitz*. Instead a German convoy is found in the area and three ships sunk. The weather again saves *Tirpitz* from two sorties in May, but the fleet and escort carrier aircraft do manage to sink several more merchant ships at these and other times during the month.

6th — *U302* sinks two ships from Halifax/UK convoy SC156 to the northwest of the Azores before being destroyed by frigate *Swale* of the British B5 group.

8th — To the northwest of Cape Finisterre, sloops *Crane* and *Cygnet* of the 7th EG account for *U962*.

14th — North of the Azores *U448* attacks escort carrier *Biter* but is detected by Canadian frigate *Swansea* of the 9th EG and sunk by her and sloop *Pelican* of the 7th.

19th — Norwegian submarine *Ula* working with the Home Fleet flotillas and on patrol off Stavanger sinks *U974*.

Battle of the Atlantic
Losses
- 7 ships of 48,000 tons.
- 16 U-boats including 2 by RAF in North Atlantic; 1 by RAF Bay of Biscay patrol; 6 by US Navy forces off America, Madeira, Cape Verde and in North Atlantic.

MAY

1st/2nd — Return Russian convoy RA59 (45 ships) is attacked by U-boats to the northwest of Norway. One ship is lost, but in return the Swordfish of 842 Squadron from *Fencer* sink three with depth charges — on the 1st, *U277*, and next day *U674* and *U959*. The convoy arrives at Loch Ewe with the rest of its 44 ships on 6 May.

5th/6th — The 2nd and 5th EGs in the North Atlantic detect U-boats by HF/DF after the torpedoing of a US destroyer. *U473* is found by 2nd EG (Capt Walker) and sunk on the 5th by

APRIL

Two surface actions take place in the English Channel off the coast of Brittany, both involving Canadian destroyers:

26th – Cruiser *Black Prince* with four destroyers — three of them RCN — is on Western Channel patrol out of Plymouth. Early that morning they run into German torpedo boats *T24*, *T27* and *T29* on a minelaying mission. *T27* is damaged and *T29* sunk by the Canadian *Haida*.

29th – This time *Haida* and sister ship *Athabaskan* are covering Allied minelaying, when they are surprised by the surviving *T24* and *T27*. **ATHABASKAN** is hit by a torpedo from *T24* and blows up, but *Haida* manages to drive *T27* ashore where she is later destroyed. The remaining *T24* hits a mine but gets into port.

These operations are only one part of the Allied air and sea offensive against German shipping off the coasts of occupied Europe, which is mounted by strike aircraft of Coastal Command, the MTBs and MGBs of coastal forces, and submarines patrolling off the Biscay bases. RAF Bomber Command also continues to lay mines in the Baltic.

Eastern Front

In the south the Russians start the task of clearing the Crimea; and, further west, on the 10th, capture the major Black Sea port of Odessa.

MAY

The Allied air forces are now concentrating their considerable energies against targets, mainly in France, in preparation for the D-day landings. In another facet of the air war, a V-2 rocket crashes near Warsaw and resistance groups manage to arrange for the parts to be successfully air-lifted to Britain.

Eastern Front

Against fierce resistance the Russians have now re-captured all of the Ukraine including the Crimea and are over the border into prewar Poland and Roumania.

MEDITERRANEAN

APRIL

Merchant Shipping War

Losses
- 5 ships of 34,000 tons.

INDIAN & PACIFIC OCEANS

APRIL

On the 14th the freighter *Fort Stikine* loaded with ammunition and cotton catches fire and blows up in Bombay harbour. Damage is widespread to both shipping and installations.

Burma

By the 6th, both Kohima and Imphal have been surrounded. Although the ring around Kohima is partly broken on the 18th, the defenders have to hold out in the two areas in often desperate conditions, supplied by air, throughout April and May.

19th — Carrier Attack on Sabang, Sumatra — Adm Somerville's Eastern Fleet almost has enough strength to start offensive operations although the loan of US carrier *Saratoga* is necessary for this first attack on the oil installations at Sabang, together with shipping and airfields. Sailing from Ceylon with *Saratoga* and *Illustrious* are battleships *Queen Elizabeth*, *Valiant* and the French *Richelieu*, cruisers and destroyers. From a position to the southwest of the target, bombers and fighters fly off from the two fleet carriers for a successful strike on the 19th, before returning to Ceylon.

New Guinea

As Australian forces approach Madang, which they enter on the 24th, the Japanese are concentrating their weakened divisions around Wewak. Now Gen MacArthur is ready to occupy most of the north coast with a series of leap-frog landings with US troops beyond the Japanese fall-back positions. He starts on the 22nd with Aitape and across the border in the Dutch half of the Island around Hollandia, which is soon secured. Aitape takes longer.

Merchant Shipping War

Losses
- There are no merchant shipping losses in either the Indian or Pacific Oceans in April and May.

Left:
HMS *Pursuer* seen from *Fencer* — both of them 'Attacker' class escort carriers — entering Scapa Flow after the 3 April 1944 raid on the *Tirpitz*. *Real Photos (S1557)*

MAY

Italy

At last, with the help of Eighth Army, the Allies pierce the Gustav Line with an offensive starting on the 11th. The British, Indian and Polish troops of Eighth Army go in around the Cassino area, followed up by the Canadians. Nearer the sea, US and French divisions of US Fifth Army attack. It is the French in the centre who make the first decisive push, but it falls to the Poles to finally take the heights of Monte Cassino on the 18th.

MAY

On the 17th the Eastern Fleet carries out another raid, this time on the oil facilities at Surabaya, Java, and with the same ships as for the Sabang strike. Afterwards *Saratoga* returns to the US.

New Guinea

US forces make their next landings on Wadke Island on the 16th, and further west still on Biak Island on the 27th. The Japanese are not yet finished and fight hard against US attempts to break out from their positions around Aitape, the

Starling, Wren and *Wild Goose.* Next day it is the 5th EG's turn (Cdr MacIntyre). Aircraft of 825 Squadron from escort carrier *Vindex* locate *U765* and frigates *Aylmer, Bickerton* and *Bligh* share in her destruction.

US escort carrier **Block Island** and her task group are again on patrol in the Atlantic off the Canaries and being directed to U-boats by the work of 'Ultra' and the Admiralty Tracking Room. On the 6th her aircraft and accompanying destroyer escorts sink *U66.* Then, towards the end of the month, on the 29th, the carrier is torpedoed and sunk by *U549*, but the escorts soon avenge the loss of their leader.

7th — Canadian frigate **VALLEYFIELD**, with a Canadian group escorting UK/North America convoy ONM234, is sunk off Cape Race, Newfoundland by *U548.*

RAF Coastal Command and one of its Norwegian squadrons are particularly successful between the 16th and 27th against the U-boats passing through the northern transit area off south and west Norway. In the space of 12 days, *U240, U241, U476, U675, U990* and *U292* are sunk.

30th — Destroyer *Milne* sinks *U289* to the southwest of Bear Island.

Battle of the Atlantic

Losses

● 3 ships of 17,000 tons, 1 frigate and 1 US escort carrier.
● 15 U-boats including 1 by RCAF Bay of Biscay patrol.

The 'Swiftsure' class light cruiser HMS *Superb.* Only *Swiftsure* and HMCS *Ontario* of the class were completed by war's end. Their major statistics: 8,800 tons, 32kt, nine 6in guns, 730 crew.
Real Photos (S2923)

JUNE

Off West Africa on the 4th, *U505* is captured by the USS *Guadalcanal* and her task group. Later in the month, tanker *U490* is sunk in mid-Atlantic by the ships and aircraft of the *Croatan* group and *U860* in the South Atlantic by aircraft from *Solomons.*

15th — Submarine *Satyr* on Arctic patrol torpedoes and sinks *U987* to the west of Narvik.

U-boats passing through the Bay of Biscay are the target for aircraft covering the Normandy invasion, and also continue to

JUNE

6th — Normandy Invasion: Operation 'Overlord' – *Following approval of the outline plans for the Allied landings in France at the August 1943 Quebec Conference, detailed preparation was put in hand for putting ashore three divisions on the Normandy coast between the Rivers Vire and Orne. Supplies are to be carried in initially through two 'Mulberry' artificial harbours. When Eisenhower and Montgomery arrive on the scene they insist on a five-division assault, including one on the Cotentin Peninsula to speed up the capture of Cherbourg. The extra shipping and landing craft needed has meant pushing the date from May to 5 June. Unseasonably bad*

MEDITERRANEAN

US Sixth Corps starts its break-out from the Anzio bridgehead on the 23rd and meets up with the advancing Fifth Army two days later. The Germans retreat to a line south of Rome, but as the Allies head towards the city, they fall back to the north of Italy's capital.

3rd/4th — *U371* attacks North Africa/US convoy GUS38 off Algeria on the 3rd and is detected but damages one of the escorting US destroyers. Throughout the night she is hunted by a mixed group of British, US and French warships including the 'Hunt' *Blankney*, and this time manages to torpedo a French destroyer. Later that day *U371* is sunk northeast of Bougie.

15th — *U731* on passage through the Strait of Gibraltar is detected by USN Catalinas and lost to attacks by patrol sloop *Kilmarnock* and trawler *Blackfly* of the Gibraltar patrol. No more U-boats make the attempt to get into the Mediterranean.

21st — U-boats gain their last success of the war in the Mediterranean. East of Sicily *U453* attacks Taranto/Augusta convoy HA43 and its Italian escort and sinks one ship. Destroyers *Termagant*, *Tenacious* and the 'Hunt' *Liddlesdale* are brought up and send her to the bottom on the 21st. U-boats have only managed to sink 10 merchantmen in the Mediterranean in the first five months of 1944. In return 15 of them have been lost, including three breaking through the Strait of Gibraltar and four in USAAF raids on Toulon and Pola.

Merchant Shipping War
Losses
- 2 ships of 10,000 tons.

INDIAN & PACIFIC OCEANS

mainland near Wadke Island, and on Biak, in some cases right through until August. All this time the Australians are pushing west along the north coast from Madang.

Rear-Adm Crutchley's TF74 and other units of Seventh Fleet are landing Gen MacArthur's troops and supporting and supplying them. In June they drive off a determined Japanese operation to reinforce Biak Island by sea.

Merchant Shipping War
Losses
- Although no Allied merchant ships have been lost in April and May, throughout the Indian Ocean 29 were sunk in the first three months of the year, and by never more than six German and four Japanese submarines. In return only four, including one transport boat, have been sunk, the last being *U852* off the Gulf of Aden to RAF aircraft on 3 May.

DEFENCE OF TRADE — JUNE 1943 TO MAY 1944

Summary of Losses

North Atlantic	UK waters	Mediterranean	Indian Ocean		Submarines	216 ships of 1,219,000 tons.
76 ships of 443,000 tons.	23 ships of 31,000 tons.	105 ships of 550,000 tons.	87 ships of 532,000 tons.		Aircraft	64 ships of 378,000 tons.
					Mines	19 ships of 55,000 tons.
South Atlantic			Pacific Ocean		Raiders	4 ships of 35,000 tons.
27 ships of 147,000 tons.			6 ships of 30,000 tons.		Other causes	9 ships of 20,000 tons.
					Coastal forces	11 ships of 18,000 tons.
= 324 British, Allied and neutral ships of 1,733,000 tons: ie 144,000 tons per month.					Warships	1 ship of 8,000 tons.

MEDITERRANEAN

JUNE

Italy

On the 4th, units of Gen Mark Clark's US Fifth Army enter Rome. The Germans now withdraw, fighting as they go, to the Gothic Line running north of Florence and across the Apennine mountains to the Adriatic, and with its forward defences along the River Arno in the west. They reach there by mid-July as the Allies come up and prepare for their main attack at the end of August. On 17 June, RN and US warships land French troops on Elba.

INDIAN & PACIFIC OCEANS

JUNE

Burma

By early June, units of 14th Army are advancing from Kohima to Imphal, which is completely relieved on the 22nd after some of the bitterest fighting of the campaign. By July the Japanese are retreating back across the Burmese border. Fourteenth Army now prepares for its main offensive into Burma later in the year.

ATLANTIC

suffer badly at the hands of the aircraft of the northern transit area patrol. Throughout the month, seven are sunk and one severely damaged by RAF and RCAF and Norwegian aircraft. In the case of *U1225* on the 24th, to the northwest of Bergen, the attacking Canadian Canso (or Catalina) is badly hit and crashes but not before sinking her. ✠ Flt Lt David Hornell RCAF, pilot of the Canso of No 162 Squadron, Coastal Command, is posthumously awarded the Victoria Cross.

26th — Destroyer *Bulldog* on patrol off the northwest coast of Ireland sinks *U719*.

Battle of the Atlantic
Losses
- 3 ships of 7,000 tons.
- 13 U-boats excluding those sunk in Bay of Biscay.

HMS *Boadicea*, a 'B' class destroyer. She was sunk on Tuesday 13 June 1944 by two torpedoes dropped by Ju88s off Portland Bill, in the English Channel. *IWM (A15522)*

EUROPE

weather postpones the actual landings to the 6th.

After gaining bridgeheads in Normandy, Eisenhower's aims are to build up enough strength for a decisive battle in the area, before breaking out to take the Channel ports and reach the German border on a broad front. Meanwhile, the right flank will link up with Allied forces coming from southern France. A further increase in strength will be used to destroy the German forces west of the Rhine before crossing this major barrier and encircling the important Ruhr industrial centre. The final advance through Germany can then follow. Vital to all these steps are the opening of enough ports to bring in the reinforcements and vast amount of supplies needed.

Supreme Commander, Allied Expeditionary Force
Gen Dwight D. Eisenhower

Deputy Commander
ACM Sir Arthur Tedder

Allied Naval Expeditionary Force Adm Sir Bertram Ramsey	*21st Army Group* Gen Sir Bernard Montgomery	*Allied Expeditionary Air Force* ACM Sir Trafford Leigh-Mallory

Gen Montgomery will remain in command of ground forces until September when Gen Eisenhower assumes direct control. For the purposes of 'Overlord', RAF Bomber Command and the Eighth US Air Force are placed under the operational direction of the Supreme Commander to add to the aircraft of the Allied Tactical Air Forces.

From his headquarters outside Portsmouth, on 1 June, Adm Ramsey takes command of the immense armada of ships collected together for Operation 'Neptune', the naval part of 'Overlord'.

Landing areas:	Normandy coast on the southeast edge of the Cotentin Peninsular ('Utah' beach) and between the Rivers Vire and Orne	
Forces landing:	21st Army Group (Gen Montgomery) Five US, British and Canadian infantry divisions with immediate follow-up of one US infantry and one British armoured division: = 130,000 Allied troops	
	US beaches	*British and Canadian beaches*
	US First Army (Gen Bradley)	British Second Army (Gen Dempsey)
	'Utah' — US Seventh Corps from Dartmouth area	'Gold' — British 30th Corps from Southampton area
	'Omaha' — US Fifth Corps from Portland area	'Juno' — Canadian forces of British First Corps from Portsmouth area
		'Sword' — British First Corps from Newhaven area
Immediate follow-up and area of departure:	US infantry division for 'Omaha' from Plymouth	British armoured division from the Thames
Naval Task Forces and Commanders:	*Western* Rear-Adm A. G. Kirk, USN	*Eastern* Rear-Adm Sir Philip Vian
	(Royal and Dominion Navies unless otherwise stated)	
Assault Phase warships:		
Battleships	3 US	3
Cruisers	10 (3 US, 2 French)	13 (1 Allied)
Destroyers and escorts	51 (36 US, 4 French)	84 (3 French, 7 Allied)

MEDITERRANEAN

Submarine **SICKLE** on patrol in the Aegean fails to return to Malta when recalled on the 14th, and is presumed lost on mines.

18th — Destroyer **QUAIL**, damaged by a mine in the southern Adriatic the previous November, founders on tow from Bari around to Taranto.

Merchant Shipping War

Losses
● 1 ship of 2,000 tons.

The 'Hunt' class escort destroyer HMS *Bleasdale*. Of a total of 86 ships, 19 were lost, including the Free French *La Combattante*, Norwegian *Eskdale* and Polish *Kujawiak*, and six more were not repaired, including the Greek *Adrias*. Completed 1940-43, they displaced 1,000 to 1,175 tons, could make 26kt to 29kt, carried four to six 4in guns and two to three torpedo tubes; and 145 to 170 crew. *Real Photos (S1657)*

INDIAN & PACIFIC OCEANS

Saipan, Mariana Islands

With the Solomons campaign virtually over, Adm Halsey transfers from the South to the Central Pacific theatre to share in the command of the vast and ever-growing Pacific Fleet. He and Adm Spruance will take turns planning and executing the assaults to come, and the Fleet will be renumbered accordingly — Third for Halsey and Fifth for Spruance. Gen MacArthur's much smaller fleet in the South West Pacific remains the Seventh under Adm Kinkaid.

It is Fifth Fleet that carries out the Marianas landings. From here US airpower can strike at the Philippines and Formosa, but most importantly initiate the strategic bombing campaign of Japan using the new B-29 Superfortresses. Over the next year these will devastate Japanese cities and, in conjunction with the highly successful submarine offensive against Japan's merchant marine, nearly cripple the country's war production.

The island of Saipan is the first target, and after heavy air and sea bombardments, US Marines land on the 15th. Effective resistance is over by early July, by which time one of the most crucial naval battles of the Pacific war has been fought. At the finish, Japanese naval airpower will have received a beating from which it never recovers.

Battle of the Philippine Sea — The Japanese have prepared for these landings and from the direction of the Philippines despatch a strong naval force that includes nine carriers and five battleships including the 18.1in *Musashi* and *Yamato*. Their carrier aircraft are knocked out of the sky by their better equipped and trained US counterparts in the 'Great Marianas Turkey Shoot'. On the 19th, US submarines sink carriers *Shokaku* and *Taiho*, and next day carrier aircraft destroy the *Hiyo*. Just the loss in pilots is a major defeat for the Japanese, and the Americans are left free to complete the capture of the Marianas. The Philippine's inner shield will then be broken.

Merchant Shipping War

Losses
● Indian Ocean only — 3 ships of 19,000 tons.

Other warships, including minesweepers and coastal forces	260 (124 US, 1 Allied)	248 (30 US, 1 Allied)
Total warships	324 (166 US, 6 French, 1 Allied)	348 (30 US, 3 French, 9 Allied)
Assault Phase LSIs, landing ships and craft (major only)	644 (497 US)	955 (62 US)
Ferry service vessels and landing craft (major only)	(British and US) 220	316
Total warships and major landing ships and craft	1,188	1,619
Grand total	2,807	
Plus minor landing craft	836	1,155

The two Naval Task Forces total 672 warships for assault convoy escort, minesweeping, shore bombardment, local defence, etc, and 4,126 major and minor landing ships and craft for initial assault and ferry purposes: a grand total of 4,798. To this can be added the following (Royal and Dominion Navies unless otherwise stated):

1. *Home Command for follow-up escort and Channel patrols, plus reserves:*
- 1 battleship;
- 118 destroyers and escorts (of which 4 US, 1 French and 5 Allied);
- 364 other warships including coastal forces (of which 8 French and 16 Allied).

2. *Western Channel Approaches A/S Escort Groups and reserves:*
- 3 escort carriers;
- 55 destroyers and escort vessels.

3. *Merchant ships in their hundreds — mainly British liners, tankers, tugs, etc to supply and support the invasion and naval forces.*

4. *For the 'Mulberry' harbour project of two artificial harbours and five 'Gooseberry' breakwaters:*
- 400 'Mulberry' units totalling 1½ million tons and including up to 6,000-ton 'Phoenix' concrete breakwaters;
- 160 tugs for towing;
- 59 old merchantmen and warships to be sunk as blockships for the 'Gooseberries'. All are in place by the 10th June.

5. *Specially equipped vessels for laying PLUTO — Pipeline Under The Ocean — across the Channel from the Isle of Wight to carry petroleum fuel.*

The assault forces sail from their ports of departure on the 5th to a position off the Isle of Wight, and head south through swept channels down 'The Spout' towards Normandy. Two midget submarines are already on station off the British sector, ready to guide in the landing craft. Partly because of elaborate deception plans, partly because of the poor weather, both strategic and tactical surprise is achieved.

Soon after midnight on the morning of the 6th, the invasion gets underway when the US 82nd and 101st Airborne Divisions drop behind 'Utah' beach, and the British 6th Airborne between 'Sword' beach and Caen. At dawn, after heavy preliminary air

and sea bombardments, and with complete Allied air supremacy, the landings go ahead. Royal Marine Commandos Nos 47, 48 and 41 take part in the assaults on the British and Canadian beaches. Against varying degrees of resistance, the toughest being on 'Omaha', all five beachheads are established by the end of the day and 150,000 Allied troops are on French soil. 'Omaha' links up with the British and Canadian beaches by the 8th, and two days later 'Utah' makes contact with 'Omaha'. On the 12th, a third of a million men and 50,000 vehicles are ashore.

Now, as the US Seventh Corps fights its way across Cotentin, the rest of US First Army thrusts forward around St Lô. Further east the British and Canadian Corps of British Second Army battle their way around Caen against fierce German counter-attacks. By the 18th the Americans have reached the western side of Cotentin and Seventh Corps heads north for the port of Cherbourg.

Between the 19th and 22nd, violent Channel gales wreck the US 'Mulberry' harbour off 'Omaha' and seriously damage the British one off 'Gold' beach. Many landing craft and DUKWS are lost and a total of 800 are driven ashore. Only the British harbour is repaired and the need for Cherbourg becomes that much more important. By the 27th, with strong gunfire support from Allied warships, the port is in US hands. Although the installations are wrecked and the waters heavily mined, the first supply ships are discharging their cargoes by mid-July.

As Cherbourg falls so British troops of Second Army start a major attack to the west of Caen (Operation 'Epsom') but are soon held by the Germans.

By the end of June nearly two-thirds of a million men have landed in France. Although the Allies are well established on the coast and have all of the Cotentin Peninsular, the Americans have still not taken St Lô, nor the British and Canadians the town of Caen, originally a target for D-day. German resistance, particularly around Caen, is ferocious, but the end result will be similar to that of the Tunisian campaign. More and more German troops will be thrown into the battle, so that when the Allies do break out of Normandy the defenders will lose heavily and lack the men to stop the Allied forces from almost reaching the borders of Germany.

In spite of the vast number of warships laying off the Normandy beaches and escorting the follow-up convoys, losses are comparatively few, although mines, especially of the pressure-operated variety are troublesome:

6th – Destroyer **WRESTLER**, escorting a Canadian assault group to 'Juno', is badly damaged by a mine and not repaired.

8th – Frigate **LAWFORD** on patrol in Seine Bay, also after escorting an assault group to 'Juno', is bombed and sunk.

9th – Old light cruiser **DURBAN** is expended as one of the 'Gooseberry' breakwaters (off Ouistreham). A sister ship, the Polish-manned **Dragon**, is damaged in early July and joins her in this final but important role.

12th – By now the battleship **Warspite**, the ship that ends the war with the greatest number of RN battle honours, has had to leave her support duties for replacement guns. On passage to Rosyth she is damaged by a mine of Harwich and is out of action until August. Then she is to be found bombarding Brest.

13th – Escorting a follow-up convoy to the beaches, destroyer **BOADICEA** is sunk off Portland Bill by torpedo bombers.

18th – Battleship **Nelson** is slightly damaged by a mine as she fires her guns off the beaches.

21st – Destroyer **FURY** is mined and driven ashore in the gales. She is refloated but not repaired.

23rd – Adm Vian's flagship, the AA cruiser **Scylla**, is also mined in Seine Bay. Seriously damaged, she is out of action until after the war and then never fully re-commissioned.

24th – Mines claim yet another victim: destroyer **SWIFT's** back is broken and she goes down some five miles off the British beaches.

25th – As cruiser **Glasgow**, in company with US warships, bombards Cherbourg, she receives several hits from shore batteries and plays no more part in the war. Nine days after carrying King George VI on a visit to Normandy, cruiser **Arethusa** is slightly damaged by a mine or bomb while at anchor off the beaches.

Three US destroyers and a destroyer escort are also lost off Normandy in June.

8th/9th – Attempts by German light forces to interfere with invasion shipping have little effect and they suffer heavy losses. However, on D-day, torpedo boats sink the Norwegian destroyer *Svenner*. Then on the night of the 8th/9th another force of destroyers and torpedo boats tries to break through from Brest but is intercepted by the 10th Destroyer Flotilla off Ushant. Destroyer *ZH1* (ex-Dutch) is damaged by *Tartar* and torpedoed and sunk by *Ashanti*, and *Z32* is driven ashore by the Canadian *Haida* and *Huron* and later blown up.

Aircraft of Coastal Command and the Escort Groups of the RN and RCN on patrol at the west end of the Channel and its approaches are ready for any attempt by U-boats to reach the 'Neptune' ships. Only schnorkel-equipped boats dare try, and the few that do have little success. In June they lose 12 of their number: off the Channel, aircraft sink five including *U629* and *U373* to one RAF Liberator of No 224 Squadron (Flg Off K. Moore) on the 8th. Two more go down in the Bay of Biscay as they return from Atlantic patrol. Warships account for the remaining five, but two frigates are sunk and other escorts severely damaged.

15th – Frigate **BLACKWOOD** is torpedoed off Brittany by *U764* and sinks in tow off Portland Bill.

15th/18th – Frigate **MOURNE** is sunk by *U767* off Land's End. Three days later the U-boat is caught off the Channel Islands by destroyers *Fame*, *Havelock* and *Inconstant* of 14th EG and sent to the bottom.

24th – Destroyers *Eskimo* and Canadian *Haida* of 10th Flotilla, together with a Czech Wellington of No 311 Squadron, sink *U971* off Ushant.

25th – Two U-boats are lost off Start Point in the English Channel — *U1191* to frigates *Affleck* and *Balfour* of the 1st EG, and *U269* to *Bickerton* (Capt MacIntyre) of the 5th EG.

27th/29th – Two days after badly damaging corvette **PINK** (constructive total loss) on the 27th and sinking two merchantmen, *U988* is caught off the Channel Islands by frigates *Cooke*, *Domett*, *Duckworth* and *Essington* of 3rd EG and a RAF Liberator of No 224 Squadron.

On the 13th the first V-1 flying bomb lands on London at the start of a three-month campaign against southeast England. Amongst the weapons soon to be used against them is Britain's

first jet fighter, the Gloster Meteor. By then Germany's Me262 jet has been in action against Allied bombers.

Adm Sir Henry Moore is appointed C-in-C, Home Fleet, in succession to Adm Fraser, who is to command the British Pacific Fleet.

Eastern Front

Russia attacks into southern Finland on the 10th to force the government to the negotiation table. Fighting carries on into July, but by early September a cease-fire is in effect.

In the centre of the main front, the Russians start the first of their major summer offensives on the 23rd from around Smolensk. Their aim is to clear the Germans out of Byelo-Russia and head on for Warsaw, East Prussia and the Baltic through Lithuania.

Merchant Shipping War
Until the closing days of the war, the schnorkel U-boats operating in UK waters are especially worrying. When submerged, as invariably they are, detection from the air is difficult, even with the 10cm wavelength radar, and location usually has to wait until after they have carried out an attack. Then they lose heavily, in the main to the surface escorts.
Losses
● 19 ships of 75,000 tons.

HMS *Fury*, the 'F' class destroyer which became a constructive total loss off the Normandy beaches on Wednesday 21 June 1944.
Real Photos (S1013)

ATLANTIC

JULY

Barracuda torpedo bombers from Home Fleet carriers *Formidable*, *Indefatigable* and *Furious* attempt to hit *Tirpitz* in Altenfiord on the 17th, but fail, partly because of defensive smokescreens. U-boats are sent to attack the carrier force, but over a period of four days, RAF Coastal Command sinks three of them in the northern transit area and wins another Victoria Cross. On the 17th, west of Narvik, *U347* is lost to a RAF Catalina of No 210 Squadron. ✠ Flg Off John Cruickshank RAFVR, pilot of the Catalina, continues to attack in spite of his wounds from the return fire, and is awarded the Victoria Cross.

The RAF also sinks a fourth U-boat off southwest Norway.

Two major international conferences are held in the United States, starting in July with monetary and financial affairs at Bretton Woods, New Hampshire, which leads to the setting up of the International Monetary Fund and the International Bank for Reconstruction & Development. In August, talks start at Dumbarton Oaks, just outside Washington DC, on the establishment of the United Nations.

Battle of the Atlantic

Losses
- 4 ships of 29,000 tons.
- 7 U-boats including one each by task groups of US escort carriers *Wake Island*, *Croatan* and *Card* off the Canaries, Madeira and Nova Scotia respectively.

The US battleship *Texas* which was part of the US gunfire support force off the Normandy invasion beaches in June 1944. *IWM (A8058)*

EUROPE

JULY

Western Front

At the beginning of the month, the Americans are still struggling to take St Lô and the British and Canadians to capture Caen. As they do so, other units of US First Army start to push slowly south out of the Cotentin Peninsula. Much of Caen is eventually taken on the 9th and St Lô on the 18th. On this latter day, in Operation 'Goodwood', the British and Canadians mount a major offensive to the east and south of Caen. The attack makes slow progress against fierce German resistance as Caen becomes the pivot for the American drive to the west.

Now the Canadian First Army under Gen Crerar becomes operational.

On the 25th, in Operation 'Cobra', the US First Army attacks from west of St Lô towards Avranches. As in all the battles great use is made of Allied air power; and on the 30th, Avranches is in American hands. The Allies now prepare to trap the Germans in the Falaise area and then break out across France.

The heavy ships of the RN are still providing gunfire support off both the British and American sectors, and supplies and reinforcements continue to pour in through the British 'Mulberry' harbour as Cherbourg starts to become operational.

Those U-boats that do get through the Channel defences sink and damage a number of ships, but six are lost to warship patrols:

5th – After attacking a convoy off Normandy, *U390* is sunk by destroyer *Wanderer* and frigate *Tavy*.

6th – In a convoy attack off Beachy Head, *U678* is lost to Canadian destroyers *Ottawa* and *Kootenay* and Royal Navy corvette *Statice*.

18th – Frigate *Balfour* on patrol southeast of Start Point sinks *U672*.

21st – Escorting frigates *Curzon* and *Ekins* sink *U212* off Beachy Head.

26th – As *U214* tries to lay mines off Start Point, she is sunk by frigate *Cooke* of the 3rd EG.

31st – *U333* is destroyed to the west of the Scilly Islands by sloop *Starling* and frigate *Loch Killin* of the 2nd EG using the new Squid. This marks the first success with this ahead-throwing A/S weapon with its three large mortar bombs.

Three more U-boats are sunk in the Bay of Biscay; one each to RAF and RAAF aircraft and the third on a mine off Brest. Allied air raids on Germany are also becoming more effective and four more are destroyed at Kiel and Bremen.

20th/24th – Attacks on the beachhead shipping by E-boats and such small battle units as the newly introduced Neger and Marder human torpedoes have limited successes, and the most damage is still caused by mines. On the 20th, destroyer **ISIS** is sunk by a mine or possibly a Neger off the beaches. Four days later, escort destroyer **GOATHLAND** is badly damaged on a mine and, although saved, is not repaired.

In the 20 July bomb plot against Hitler, a device left in his East Prussia headquarters by Col von Stauffenberg only slightly

MEDITERRANEAN

JULY

Merchant Shipping War

Losses

● No Allied merchant ships are lost.

INDIAN & PACIFIC OCEANS

JULY

On the 25th, aircraft from *Illustrious* and *Victorious* attack Sabang, after which three battleships, cruisers and destroyers bombard the area. This is the last Eastern Fleet operation under the command of Adm Somerville. He moves on to Washington DC as Adm Fraser takes over as C-in-C in August. Similar raids are carried out on Sumatra in August and September.

17th — As the Ceylon-based submarines continue to cut Japanese supply lines to their armies in Burma, *Telemachus* on patrol in the Malacca Strait sinks Japanese submarine *I166* outward bound for Indian Ocean operations.

Guam and Tinian, Mariana Islands

With Saipan secure and the Japanese fleet in disarray, the Americans go ahead with their landings on the US island of Guam on the 21st and Japanese island of Tinian three days later. Against the usual suicidal resistance, both islands are won by early August, although the last Japanese soldier hides out on Guam until 1972. The Marianas are now in US hands, and their fall has a political consequence. Gen Tojo's government resigns, but a cabinet apparently just as committed to continuing the war comes to power.

Merchant Shipping War

Losses

● Indian Ocean only — 5 ships of 30,000 tons.

The 'J' class destroyer HMS *Jackal* was lost in May 1942. The 16 'J' and 'K' class ships — completed 1939, 1,690 tons, 36kt, six 4.7in guns/10 torpedo tubes, 185 crew — suffered 12 losses, all but *Khartoum* and *Jupiter* in the Mediterranean.   *Real Photos (N1045)*

hurts him. In revenge, many die and Field Marshal Rommel, implicated in this attempt on Hitler's life, is forced to commit suicide in October.

Eastern Front

The attacks in the centre push on; Minsk, capital of Byelo-Russia is taken by the 4th; and by mid-month all of the Russian republic has been liberated. Vilna, disputed capital of Lithuania, is captured on the 13th, and by the end of July the Russians are approaching the outskirts of Warsaw.

By now to the north, the second main phase of the summer offensive has got underway, with the aim of ejecting the Germans from the Baltic states. Then in the middle of the month the third phase starts in the centre/south from the Ukraine into southern Poland. Lvov is taken on the 27th.

Merchant Shipping War
Losses
● 8 ships of 19,000 tons.

AUGUST

Attacks on *Tirpitz* and Russian Convoy JW59 — Russian convoy JW59 (33 ships) leaves Loch Ewe on the 15th with a heavy escort including escort carriers *Striker* and *Vindex* and the 20th and 22nd EGs. Home Fleet, under the command of Adm Moore, sails in two groups, partly to cover the convoy but mainly to launch further FAA attacks on *Tirpitz* in Altenfiord. One group includes *Formidable*, *Indefatigable* and *Furious* and battleship *Duke of York*; the other escort carriers *Trumpeter* and the Canadian-manned *Nabob* together with the 5th EG (Cdr MacIntyre). Between the 22nd and 29th, three strikes are made, but in two of them the German ship is obscured by smoke; and although a hit is obtained on the 24th, the bomb fails to explode. In the course of these manoeuvres the escort carrier group suffers two casualties:

22nd — *U354* encounters them to the northwest of North Cape and attacks. Frigate **BICKERTON** of the 5th EG is sunk and escort carrier **NABOB** so badly damaged she is not repaired. The U-boat will soon be sunk herself.

The convoy (JW59) is also subjected to U-boat attack and losses are sustained by both sides:

21st — Sloop **KITE** of the 22nd EG is torpedoed by *U344* to the northwest of Norway in the Greenland Sea and goes down. There are few survivors, but the attacker will go the same way as *U354*.

24th — As *U344* tries to approach the convoy to the north of North Cape, she is sunk by destroyer *Keppel*, frigate *Loch Dunvegan* and sloops *Mermaid* and *Peacock* of the 20th EG.

25th — *U354* now prepares for the arrival of return convoy RA59A in the Bear Island area and is destroyed by a rocket-firing Swordfish of 825 Squadron from *Vindex*. (Note: Some sources reverse the cause of loss of *U344* and *U354* and with *U344* going down on the 22nd and *U354* on the 24th.)

JW59 arrives at Kola Inlet on the 25th with all 33 merchant ships.

AUGUST

Western Front

On the 1st, US General Patton's Third Army becomes operational. Still under Gen Montgomery, the Allied land forces are organised from west to east as follows:

US 12th Army Group (Gen Bradley)		British 21st Army Group (Gen Montgomery)	
US Third Army (Patton)	US First Army (Hodges)	British Second Army (Dempsey)	Canadian First Army (Crerar)

As part of the plan to trap the Germans at Falaise and then liberate the rest of France, US Third Army's roles are to overrun Brittany, wheel east from Avranches towards Le Mans and Orléans and head to the south of Paris, and to help close the Falaise net. US First Army is to attack east from Avranches through Mortain towards Falaise. Meanwhile the British 21st Army Group moves on Falaise from Caen, the Canadians on the left and British on the right.

US Third Army has taken most of Brittany by early month and sealed off Brest, Lorient and St Nazaire. Brest falls in mid-September, but the other two naval bases hold out for the rest of the war, as do the Channel Islands garrisons. US First Army's push east is stopped on the 7th when the Germans counter-attack strongly through Mortain towards the American bottleneck at Avranches. The assault is held, assisted by the aircraft of the Tactical Air Forces, especially the tank-busting Typhoons. By the 11th the danger is over.

In the struggle south by British 21st Group, the Canadians take Falaise on the 17th, and three days later the pocket is completely sealed and the remaining Germans trapped. By then the Allied spearheads are rushing eastward. The Americans cross the Seine on the 20th and shortly after a French armoured division is brought forward to complete the liberation of Paris on the 25th.

Now the Canadian First Army heads along the coast to capture the Channel ports and nearby V-1 launch sites, British Second Army moves up on its right towards Brussels, and the Americans race across France for the Belgian border, Luxembourg and eastern France. Lack of supplies, particularly fuel, starts to become a major problem, and capturing Antwerp is a matter of the highest priority.

The assault on Brest which begins later in the month is assisted by naval gunfire including *Warspite's* 15in guns. Now as the

AUGUST

15th — South of France Landings: Operation 'Dragoon'
— Originally code-named 'Anvil', the South of France invasion was planned to coincide with the Normandy landings. Since that decision was made, Britain has pushed for the Allies to concentrate on the Italian campaign, but under US pressure agrees to go ahead with the now re-named Operation 'Dragoon' using forces withdrawn from US Fifth Army in Italy. No major British units are involved and for the first time in the Mediterranean the RN is in the minority in both numbers of ships and commanders. However, Adm Sir John Cunningham remains Naval C-in-C.

Landing areas:	Three attack forces landing on the mainland between Toulon and Cannes, and a fourth force on offshore islands		
Forces landing:	US Seventh Army (Gen Patch) US Sixth Corps followed-up by French Second Corps		
Departure from:	Italy and Algeria		
	Naval Control Force Commander Vice-Adm H. K. Hewitt USN		
Naval Attack Force Commanders:	US Rear-Adms Davidson, Lewis, Lowry and Rodgers		
Naval Control, Attack and Convoy Escort Forces:	British and Allied	French	United States
Battleships	1	1	3
Cruisers	7	5	8
Destroyers and escorts	27	19	52
Other warships	69	6	157
Attack transports and LSIs	9	—	23
Landing ships and craft (major only)	141	—	369
Totals	254	31	612
Grand total	897		

The warships are allocated across the four attack forces and, in addition, over 1,300 mainly assault landing craft take part in the landings. Air cover and support is provided by Rear-Adm Troubridge with seven RN and two US escort carriers. After intensive air and sea bombardments, the landings take place against light resistance and accompanied by US airborne drops inland. Both the US and French Corps soon spread out and head north after the retreating Germans. Before the month is

AUGUST

8th — Battleship **Valiant** is seriously damaged at Trincomalee when the floating dock she is in collapses.

12th — An escort carrier task group is formed to hunt for German and Japanese submarines operating in the Indian Ocean off the coast of Africa. *U198* is located and, two days later, on the 12th, sunk off the Seychelles by frigate *Findhorn* and Indian sloop *Godavari*.

New Guinea — Conclusion

On 30 July, US troops are landed near Cape Sansapor at the extreme west end of New Guinea, and the Allies are now firmly established along the whole length of this huge island. Gen MacArthur is ready to return to the Philippines. However, it is only now, in August, that the fighting finally dies down around Aitape and on Biak Island, and the Australian forces still have the task of finishing off the remnants of by-passed Japanese divisions, in some areas until August 1945. But strategically the New Guinea campaign is over.

Merchant Shipping War
Losses
● Indian Ocean only — 9 ships of 58,000 tons.

Above:
The 'M' class destroyer HMS *Martin* was lost in November 1942. Of a total of 16 ships, eight were lost, including *Gurkha* (2) and the Polish *Orkan*, and two were not repaired. Completed 1940-42, the 'L' and 'M' classes displaced 1,930 tons, could make 36kt, were armed with six 4.7in guns and eight torpedo tubes, and had a crew of c190.
Real Photos (S1601)

Battle of the Atlantic

Losses

- 1 ship of 6,000 tons, 1 escort carrier, 2 escorts and 1 US destroyer escort off the Azores.
- 3 U-boats including 1 by aircraft of escort carrier *Bogue* off Newfoundland.

The heavy cruiser *Tuscaloosa* was another of the US warships that provided gunfire support off Normandy during June 1944. *IWM (A19976)*

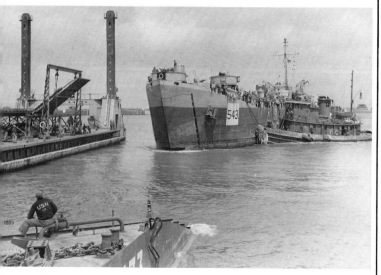

A US Navy LST moves in to secure to the 'Omaha' Mulberry. *Real Photos*

German Biscay bases become untenable, the South Western Approaches to the British Isles are opened to Allied convoys for the first time in four years. West and North Africa/UK convoys SL167 and MKS58 are the first to benefit from the shortened journey.

3rd/9th – German coastal forces and the small units continue to attack shipping off the invasion beaches, sinking and damaging a number of vessels in return for heavy casualties. On the 3rd the 'Hunt' class escort destroyer **QUORN** on patrol off the British sector is sunk, probably by a Linsen explosive motor boat. On the 9th the old cruiser *Frobisher*, acting as a depot ship for the British 'Mulberry', is badly damaged by a Dackel long range torpedo fired by E-boats.

U-boats passing through the Bay of Biscay and operating in the Channel and its approaches suffer badly at the hands of the air and sea patrols and escorts. However, the RCN loses two corvettes:

4th – Escort destroyer *Wensleydale* and frigate *Stayner* on patrol off Beachy Head, sink *U671* shortly after she sails from Boulogne.

6th-11th – The 2nd EG has a hand in three sinkings in the Bay of Biscay. On the 6th, to the west of St Nazaire, frigate *Loch Killin* and sloop *Starling* use the new Squid A/S mortar again to account for *U736*. The other two attacks are carried out off La Rochelle. On the 10th, *U608* is lost to sloop *Wren* and aircraft of No 53 Squadron, and next day *U385* to *Starling* working with RAAF aircraft of No 461 Squadron.

8th – Canadian corvette **REGINA** is sunk off Trevose Head by *U667* as she escorts Bristol Channel convoy EBC66. The U-boat is lost on mines off La Pallice later in the month.

14th – West of St Nazaire, *U618* is accounted for by RAF aircraft of No 53 Squadron, this time with frigates *Duckworth* and *Essington* of 3rd EG.

15th – Attacking a convoy to the south of the Isle of Wight, *U741* is sent to the bottom by corvette *Orchis*.

18th/20th — Canadian destroyers *Chaudière*, *Kootenay* and *Ottawa* of the 11th EG sink *U621* on the 18th off La Rochelle and *U984* two days later to the west of Brest.

20th – After sinking one merchantman from a convoy off Beachy Head, *U413* is counter-attacked and lost to destroyers *Forester*, *Vidette* and escort destroyer *Wensleydale*.

21st/22nd – Off the Isle of Wight, *U480* sinks Canadian corvette **ALBERNI** on the 21st and RN fleet minesweeper **LOYALTY** next day.

24th – As most of the U-boats leave their Biscay bases for Norway, frigate *Louis* on patrol off St Nazaire sinks *U445*.

Throughout the month a total of 21 U-boats are lost in and around French waters. Apart from *U667*, one other is mined in the Bay of Biscay, three are lost to RAF and RAAF Bay patrols, and six more are scuttled or paid off in their Biscay bases.

27th – In a tragic mistake off Le Havre, RAF Typhoons attack and sink fleet minesweepers **BRITOMART** and **HUSSAR** and severely damage **SALAMANDER** (constructive total loss).

MEDITERRANEAN

out, Cannes, Toulon and Marseilles have fallen into Allied hands.

Italy

On the Adriatic side the Allies launch the first part of their offensive against the Gothic Line on the 25th, when Eighth Army attacks towards Rimini. By the end of the month they are breaking through the Line, while to the west, US Fifth Army is crossing the Arno.

Merchant Shipping War
Losses
● 1 small ship is lost.

INDIAN & PACIFIC OCEANS

The 'N' class destroyer HMAS *Nestor* (the only class loss) was sunk in June 1942. The class of eight ships saw five serving in the RAN, plus two in the Dutch and one in the Polish navies. Completed in 1940-42, they were otherwise similar to 'J' and 'K' classes. *IWM (A4690)*

ATLANTIC

EUROPE

Eastern Front

By now nearly all of prewar Russia has been liberated. In Poland on the 1st, the Polish Home Army in Warsaw rises up against the German oppressors. With little help from outside, least of all from the Russians, the fight goes on through August and September until the Poles are finally crushed with great brutality. Some 200,000 have died by the time the survivors surrender on 2 October. Further south the Russians gain a bridgehead over the River Vistula and are up against much of the length of the Carpathian mountains by month's end. But now they are running short of supplies and facing increasing German resistance. This part of the front stabilises until January.

As this happens, the fourth phase of the summer offensive starts in the far south, aimed at clearing the Balkans. The Russian armies attack on the 20th from the Ukraine south and west into Roumania. Events move rapidly. Three days later the country accepts the Russian armistice terms, on the 25th declares war on Germany, and by the 31st the Russians are entering Bucharest. Now Bulgaria tries to declare its neutrality and withdraw from the war, just as the Russian forces are swinging west and north towards Hungary and on to Yugoslavia threatening to cut off the Germans in Greece.

Merchant Shipping War
Losses
- 12 ships of 55,000 tons.

SEPTEMBER

2nd — Return Russian convoy RA59A (nine ships) is now off northwest Norway when *U394* is damaged by Swordfish of 825 Squadron again and sunk by destroyers *Keppel* and *Whitehall* and sloops *Mermaid* and *Peacock*. The convoy arrives safely at Loch Ewe on the 6th, and nine days later the next Russian-bound convoy, JW60, sets out with 30 merchantmen. They too arrive at their destination without loss before the month is out.

30th — The next convoy returning from Russia, RA60, leaves Kola on the 28th with 30 ships, but by the time it arrives at Loch Ewe in early October has lost two to U-boat attack. While still to the northwest of Norway on the 30th, Swordfish of 813 Squadron from escort carrier *Campania* sink *U921*.

At the second Quebec Conference, Prime Minister Churchill and President Roosevelt review the progress of the war, during which it is agreed that the British Pacific Fleet will serve under American Command.

Far across North America to the southwest, the massive atomic bomb programme approaches its climax at Los Alamos, New Mexico. Although intelligence reports suggest that Germany has made little progress with its nuclear research, the by now mainly American work continues and a B-29 bomber unit is formed to train for the task of dropping this awesome and untried weapon when it is ready.

Battle of the Atlantic
Losses
- 3 ships of 17,000 tons and 1 US destroyer in a hurricane off Bahamas.
- 7 U-boats including 1 cause unknown and 1 mined off Iceland; 1 by RAF off the Azores; 1 by US Navy off Cape Verde Islands; 1 by US aircraft in South Atlantic.

Note: With the start of the U-boat campaign around the British Isles, U-boats sunk off Norway and in the Western Approaches as well as in the Bay of Biscay are included in the European theatre. The same applies to the RN and German surface warships lost.

SEPTEMBER

Western Front

On the 1st, Gen Eisenhower assumes direct command of all Allied ground forces and by mid-month has taken under his control the US and French forces advancing from the south of France. From north to south his Armies and their areas of operation are structured thus:

British 21st Army Group (Gen Montgomery)	
Canadian First Army	Channel coast of France and into Belgium and southern Holland.
British Second Army	Through central Belgium and into southern Holland and the German border opposite the Ruhr.
US 12th Army Group (Gen Bradley)	
US First Army	Through southern Belgium and Luxembourg towards Germany south of the Ruhr.
US Third Army	Through central and eastern France towards the German border opposite the Saar.
US Sixth Army Group (Gen Devers)	
US Seventh Army French First Army	From central France towards the east and the German border south of the Saar.

On the Channel coast, the Canadians capture Dieppe on the 1st, Boulogne on the 22nd and Calais on the 30th. By the 12th,

SEPTEMBER

South of France — Conclusion

The Allies reach Lyons on the 3rd and, by the 12th, French troops advancing from the south have met French units of Gen Patton's US Third Army near Dijon. All the French and US forces who landed on the Riviera only a month before are placed under Gen Eisenhower's command.

Italy

Eighth Army is over the Gothic Line but coming up against increasing German resistance south of Rimini, which is eventually captured by the Canadians on the 21st. However, they still have to cross a whole series of rivers before reaching the River Po, after which the Allies can spread out across northern Italy. To the west, Fifth Army is across the River Arno and has broken through its end of the Gothic Line, but is stopped from reaching Bologna by the German defences.

Greece

As the Russians attack through Roumania and Bulgaria towards Yugoslavia, a start is made on evacuating German troops from Crete, southern Greece and the islands of the Aegean. However, right up until May, garrisons hold out on Rhodes, western Crete and some of the Greek Islands.

19th — Germany loses its last U-boats in the Mediterranean to attack by sea and by air. On the 19th the schnorkel-equipped *U407* is sunk north of Crete by destroyers *Terpischore*, *Troubridge* and the Polish *Garland* of Adm Troubridge's escort carrier and cruiser force. Five days later in raids on Salamis near Athens, USAAF aircraft sink *U596* and the damaged *U565*. Since June the other eight surviving U-boats have all been lost at Toulon, either by USAAF raids or through scuttling.

In three years the comparatively few U-boats in the

SEPTEMBER

23rd — Submarine *Trenchant* on patrol off Penang in the Malacca Strait sinks *U859* as she arrives from operations in the Indian Ocean. At this time one flotilla of RN submarines moves from Ceylon to Western Australia to work in East Indies waters under American Seventh Fleet command.

Halmaheras, Palau Islands and Ulithi, Western Pacific

Gen MacArthur's South West Pacific campaign and the Central Pacific advance of Adm Nimitz' forces are about to meet for the invasion of the Philippines. Before they do, three more landings take place in the month, two on the 15th, and all to secure bases for the coming assaults.

To the northwest of New Guinea, Gen MacArthur's men are landed on Morotai in the Halmaheras by Seventh Fleet, which includes cruisers *Australia* and *Shropshire* of the Royal Australian Navy. Air bases are soon under construction. On the same day, Third Fleet under Adm Halsey sets US Marines ashore on the Palau Islands. Although vicious fighting continues for some weeks, the issue is in no doubt as the Japanese are wiped out, pocket by pocket, in the limestone caves. Then, on the 23rd, the unoccupied atoll of Ulithi in the western Carolines is taken as a major fleet anchorage.

Merchant Shipping War
Losses
- Indian Ocean only — 1 ship of 5,600 tons.

Above:
The 'O' class destroyer HMS *Obdurate*. Completed in 1941-42 — 1,540 tons, 37kt, four 4in or 4.7in guns, eight torpedo tubes — the class of 16 ships lost *Partridge*, *Pakenham* and *Panther*, all sunk in the Mediterranean, and two more not repaired. *Real Photos (S9955)*

British units of Canadian First Army have taken Le Havre, but Dunkirk holds out until the end of the war.

Further east, British Second Army crosses the Belgian border on the 2nd, liberates Brussels next day and Antwerp the day after that. Unfortunately this vital port can not be used until the Germans are cleared from the Scheldt approaches. The Dutch border is reached on the 11th and, shortly after, Operation 'Market Garden' is launched, aimed at getting across the Rhine in Holland and around the northern end of the Siegfried Line. On the 17th, US 101st Airborne Division lands around Eindhoven, the US 82nd near Nijmegen to take the bridges over the Rivers Maas/Meuse and Waal/Rhine, and the British 1st at Arnhem to capture the Lower Rhine bridge. As the drops take place, British Second Army thrusts forward. The entire operation almost succeeds, but the British paratroops, in spite of great gallantry, are not able to capture the bridge, nor Second Army to reach them. The survivors are evacuated across the Lower Rhine on the night of the 25th/26th.

On the rest of the Allied front, the US Army Groups to the south push on and, by mid-month, units of First Army have entered Luxembourg and crossed the German border near Aachen.

Allied supplies are now passing through the captured Channel ports in sufficient quantities to dispense with over-the-beach delivery. 'Juno' is the last to close on the 7th. 'Mulberry' carries on until December.

HM submarine *Sea Scout*, an 'S' class submarine, seen postwar with her deck-gun removed and a schnorkel fitted. She was sister ship to *Sickle*, the last RN submarine lost in the Mediterranean, and *Stratagem*, sunk in the Far East in 1944. *Real Photos (S2039)*

1st – On passage into the Bristol Channel as part of the U-boats' inshore campaign, *U247* is sunk just off Lands End by patrolling Canadian frigates *St John* and *Swansea* of the 9th EG.

1st/9th — Two U-boats are sunk in the North Western Approaches in attacks on Atlantic convoys in exchange for a corvette and several merchantmen. On the 1st, off the northwest Irish coast, *U482* attacks Caribbean/UK tanker convoy CU36 and sinks **HURST CASTLE** of the British B1 group with an acoustic torpedo. Just over a week later the two U-boats are lost. Northwest of Ireland, *U743* is sunk near UK/North America convoy ONF252 by escorting frigate *Helmsdale* and corvette *Portchester Castle*. Off the south Hebrides *U484* goes down to attacks by Canadian frigate *Dunver* and corvette *Hespeler* of C5 group. Later in the month, RAF aircraft sink two more in the northern transit area.

Although Allied bombers continue to strike at V-1 sites along the Channel coast of France, it is only when Canadian First Army overruns them that London and the southeast of England see the last one land. By then nearly 10,000 launchings have caused civilian casualties of 25,000 dead and wounded. And then on the 8th the first V-2 rocket hits London in a deadly campaign that lasts for over six months, and for which there is no defence. In October, with the Allied capture of Antwerp, the Germans start an equally heavy series of attacks with both V-1s and V-2s against the port, right through until April.

HMS *Anson*, a 'King George V' class battleship, on trials in 1942. In 1944 she was undergoing a lengthy refit at Plymouth before sailing in April 1945 for the Far East. *Real Photos (S1778)*

Now it is the turn of RAF Bomber Command to hit at *Tirpitz* in Altenfiord in the far north of Norway. Flying in difficult conditions from Russian bases near Archangel, the Lancasters manage to get one hit on the 15th in spite of the usual smokescreens. Partly because of the damage, the battleship is moved south to Trömso.

27th – Ex-US destroyer **ROCKINGHAM** is the last of her class to be lost while flying the White Ensign, when she hits a mine off Aberdeen and goes down in the North Sea. At the time she is acting as a target ship for aircraft training.

Mediterranean have inflicted heavy losses on the RN including one battleship, two carriers, four cruisers, a cruiser-minelayer and 12 destroyers. In return 68 German boats have been lost from all causes.

With so few German targets left, the famous 10th Submarine Flotilla is disbanded although some of the boats continue to work out of Malta in the Aegean. The last submarine to be lost was *Sickle* in June, the 45th RN one to go down in the Mediterranean. From June 1940 to the end of 1944 the RN flotillas have accounted for a million tons of Axis shipping in the Mediterranean theatre, three cruisers and over 30 destroyers, torpedo boats and German and Italian submarines. To these can be added the uncompleted light cruiser *Ulpio Traiano* sunk at Palermo in January 1943 by submarine-launched Chariot human torpedoes.

Merchant Shipping War

Losses
● 1 ship of 1,400 tons.

Below:
The 'R' class destroyer HMS *Roebuck*. The further wartime classes 'Q' and 'R' of 16 ships lost *Quail* and *Quentin* in the Mediterranean. Completed 1942-43 at 1,700 tons, with a maxium speed of 37kt, four 4.7in guns and eight torpedo tubes, they had a crew of 175. *Quiberon* and *Quickmatch* served in the RAN from 1942, and three more 'Qs' joined them from 1945. *Real Photos (S2933)*

Bottom:
The Japanese heavy cruiser *Takao* was damaged by US submarines while on passage for the October 1944 Battles of Leyte Gulf, and finally sent to the bottom off Singpore in July 1945 by RN midget submarine attack. *Real Photos*

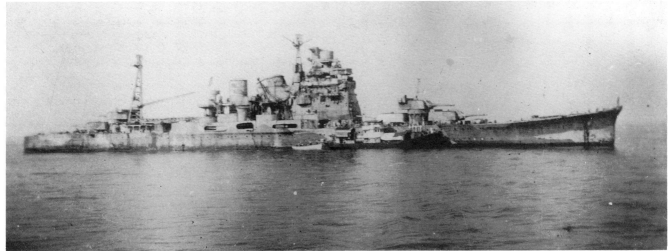

ATLANTIC

EUROPE

Eastern Front

In the far north Finland agrees to a cease-fire on the 4th and six days later in Moscow signs an armistice with Russia, followed by one with the Allies. By mid-month the Finns are effectively at war with Germany although the formal declaration is not made until March.

On the Baltic front, major attacks continue into Estonia and Latvia, and the Estonian capital of Tallinn is captured on the 22nd.

In the Balkans, Roumania signs an Allied armistice in Moscow on the 12th, by which time its troops are in battle alongside the Russians. The country is almost free of the Germans by the end of the month. From Roumania, the Russians reach the eastern border of Yugoslavia by the 6th and have crossed into southern Hungary before September is out. Russia declares war on Bulgaria on the 5th which in turn declares war against Germany three days later as Russian forces cross into the country near the Black Sea. They enter Sofia on the 16th and at the end of October an armistice is signed with the Allied powers. By then Bulgarian troops are attacking into Yugoslavia with the Russians.

Merchant Shipping War

Losses
- 3 ships of 21,000 tons.

OCTOBER

25th — Canadian destroyer **SKEENA** of the 11th EG is driven ashore in a gale at Reykjavik, Iceland and wrecked.

Russian convoy JW61 arrives at Kola by the end of the month with all 29 ships. On the last day of October, JW61A of just two liners carrying Russian POWs for repatriation, leaves Liverpool and gets to Kola Inlet by 6 November.

Battle of the Atlantic

Losses
- *In October for the first time since September 1939 no merchant ships are lost throughout the length and breadth of the North and South Atlantic.*
- *1 U-boat in the North Atlantic due to schnorkel defect.*

OCTOBER

Western Front

Canadian First Army attacks north into Holland and British Second east from the Nijmegen area towards the German border. Along the rest of the front, the US Army Groups also head for the border. At this time US Ninth Army becomes operational and in position between the British Second and US First Armies. In all sectors the Germans are tough opponents to budge, but by the 21st they have lost their first city when US First Army captures Aachen and breaches the Siegfried Line.

At this time the Canadians' task is the most crucial — to capture the banks of the Scheldt and allow vitally needed supplies to reach Allied forces through Antwerp. By the end of the month they have almost cleared the north and south sides ready for the final assault on Walcheren Island.

16th — Outward bound from Norway, U1006 is located by the patrolling 6th EG south of the Faeroes and sunk by Canadian frigate *Annan*.

27th — During Home Fleet operations against German shipping off Norway, aircraft of 1771 Squadron from fleet carrier *Implacable* drive *U1060* ashore near Namsos. She is finished off two days later by aircraft of Nos 311 (Czech) and 502 Squadrons RAF. Earlier in the month four more U-boats are lost in RAF raids on Bergen and another three by accident in Norwegian waters.

Eastern Front

In the Arctic the Russians start a series of attacks and amphibious hops which by the end of the month have driven the Germans back from the Murmansk area just over the border into Norway. There the Russians, now joined by Norwegian troops, stop.

Further south in the Baltic States, Riga, capital of Latvia, is captured by the 15th. By then the Russians have reached the Baltic north of Memel, which eventually falls in January. German troops fall back in to the Courland peninsula of Latvia

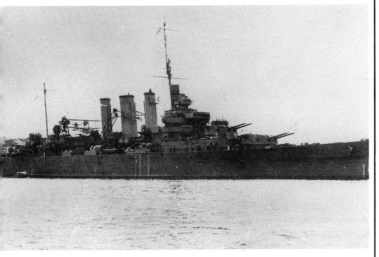

HMAS *Australia*, a 'County' class heavy cruiser, seen in Sydney Harbour in late 1943. She was damaged off the Leyte invasion beaches by kamikaze attack on Saturday 21 October 1944. *Real Photos (S1495)*

OCTOBER

Italy

Fifth Army's attack towards Bologna grinds to a halt in the wintry mountains, but over the next three months Eighth Army continues to push its way slowly and painfully to the southern edge of Lake Comacchio. Although fighting carries on right through until March the Allies will not start their main and final offensive of the Italian campaign until the better weather in April.

12th — Returning from bombarding shore targets on the northeast coast of Italy, destroyer **LOYAL** is mined in the Adriatic and not repaired.

Greece

The Germans are now coming to the end of their evacuation of the Aegean and northern Greece as British, Greek and Allied troops land in the south and on many of the islands. On the 12th Allied paratroops land near Athens.

7th/19th — Adm Troubridge's force continues to sweep the Aegean for German evacuation shipping as RN submarines also take a toll. On the 7th, destroyers *Termagant* and *Tuscan* sink torpedo boat *TA37* in the Gulf of Salonika. Further to the south it is the turn of *TA18*, lost to the same destroyers on the 19th. Both are ex-Italian vessels.

Merchant Shipping War
Losses
● 1 ship of 3,000 tons.

OCTOBER

Burma

Following the repulse of the Japanese around Kohima and Imphal in the spring, 14th Army, now including East African troops, has prepared for its main offensive towards Mandalay with all the attendant problems of movement and supply in mountainous and monsoon country, and over the major rivers of Burma. Gen Slim starts his advance in mid-month and by the middle of November is over the Chindwin and heading for central Burma and Mandalay, which is taken in March.

Between the 17th and 19th the ships and carrier aircraft of Eastern Fleet attack the Nicobar Islands, partly in an attempt to divert Japanese attention away from the Leyte landings.

Leyte, Central Philippines

Because of their faster-than-planned progress, the Americans decide to by-pass the southern island of Mindanao and go straight for Leyte, where, on the 20th, Gen MacArthur returns to the Philippines with four Army divisions.

In preparation for these landings, Task Force 38 (Adm Mitscher) of Adm Halsey's Third Fleet with a total of 17 fleet and light carriers has roamed the Philippine Sea, hitting the Ryukyu Islands, Formosa and the Philippines themselves. Now, with six modern battleships, they are off Leyte to cover the landings, throughout which Adm Halsey reports direct to Adm Nimitz in Pearl Harbor, a separation of command which contains the seeds of potential disaster in the coming Battles of Leyte Gulf.

Directly under Gen MacArthur, it is Vice-Adm Kinkaid's Seventh Fleet which carries out the invasion and provides close support. Including ships loaned from Third Fleet, he has 18 escort carriers and six old battleships. Australian cruisers *Australia* and *Shropshire* with two destroyers are again present, and the RN is represented by fast cruiser-minelayer *Ariadne* operating as an assault troop carrier. The US fleets total well over 800 ships.

21st — In one of the first kamikaze ('heavenly wind') suicide attacks on Allied shipping off the beaches, **Australia** is hit on the bridge and badly damaged.

Battles of Leyte Gulf

The Japanese have prepared their response to these landings. A Northern Decoy Force with four carriers and two converted battleship/carriers sails south from Japan to lure away Adm Halsey's fast carriers. Then from west of the Philippines, a Centre Strike Force of five battleships and 12 cruisers will approach Leyte Gulf from the northwest through the San Bernadino Strait. From the southwest via the Surigao Strait, a smaller Southern Strike Force in two parts with a total of two battleships and four cruisers will also head for Leyte Gulf. The resulting pincer movement should be powerful enough to destroy Gen MacArthur's transports and savage the Seventh Fleet now without Third Fleet's cover. In fact the Japanese are about to lose three battleships, four carriers (admittedly with few aircraft on board), 10 cruisers and nine destroyers in the battles and actions known collectively as the Battle of Leyte Gulf. The American transports will be saved, but warship losses

ATLANTIC

EUROPE

and hold out there until May, but by the end of October most of Estonia, Latvia and Lithuania are free of them.

Following an abortive uprising in eastern Czechoslovakia in late August, the Russians are now able to attack over the Carpathian mountains from southern Poland and cross the border in mid-month.

In the Balkans, the struggle up through Hungary continues, but the Russians can only reach the outskirts of Budapest in early November. Meanwhile the Eastern Allies are advancing into Yugoslavia and join up with units of Marshall Tito's partisan armies on the 4th. Belgrade falls to them on the 20th.

The battleships HMS *Resolution* and HMS *Warspite*. In November 1944 *Warspite* was in action for the last time off Walcheren. Her battle honours included Atlantic, Narvik, Norway, Calabria, Matapan, Crete, Malta convoys, Sicily, Salerno and Normandy — almost a summary of the Royal Navy's war at sea. *IWM (A9702)*

Merchant Shipping War

Losses

● 2 ships of 1,700 tons.

NOVEMBER

UK-bound convoys RA61 and RA61A leave Kola and pass through a total of 35 ships in the month without loss. Russian-bound JW62 sets out at the end of the month and reaches Kola in early December with all 30 merchant ships.

Franklin D. Roosevelt is re-elected for the fourth time as President of the United States. Harry Truman joins him as Vice President.

25th — Canadian corvette ***SHAWINIGAN*** on passage alone off the southwest corner of Newfoundland is torpedoed and

NOVEMBER

Western Front

Throughout the month Allied forces fight their way slowly towards the German border and the Siegfried Line. On the 28th the first deep sea merchant ships sail up the Scheldt and into Antwerp, and from then on the Allied supply position is totally changed for the better. To reach this situation, the assault and battle for Walcheren has to be fought.

1st — Assault on Walcheren: Operation 'Infatuate' — The island of Walcheren is heavily defended and largely flooded

The 'U' class destroyer HMS *Ulysses*. The five 'S', 'T', 'U', 'V' & 'W' classes totalled 40 ships, with *Hardy* (2), *Swift* and the Norwegian *Svenner* lost. Completed 1943-44, they were otherwise similar to the 'Q' and 'R' classes. The 'V' class *Algonquin* and *Sioux* served with the RCN. *Real Photos (S9985)*

will amount to one light and two escort carriers, three destroyer types and one submarine with other vessels damaged. The Americans could have lost far more.

On the 23rd, still to the north of Borneo, Centre Force loses two heavy cruisers and the *Takao* damaged to US submarines, one of which runs aground and has to be destroyed.

Battle of Sibuyan Sea — Next day, the same Centre Force is heavily attacked by Third Fleet aircraft as it nears the San Bernadino Strait. The giant battleship *Musashi* is sunk and the surviving ships appear to turn back.

While this is happening, US carrier *Princeton* off Luzon in the Philippine Sea is lost to land-based aircraft attack. Now the Northern Decoy Force does its job and Adm Halsey hurries north, leaving the San Bernadino Strait unguarded. Adm Kinkaid's Seventh Fleet is left with its escort carriers and old battleships to protect Leyte Gulf.

Battle of Surigao Strait — As the Southern Strike Force tries to pass through from the southwest on the night of the 24th/25th, it is ambushed by Adm Oldendorf with the six old battleships, cruisers and destroyers, including the Australian *Shropshire* and destroyer *Arunta*. In the last battleship action ever fought, the Japanese battleships *Fuso* and *Yamashiro* and a heavy cruiser are sunk.

Battle of Samar — Back to the north, early on the 25th, the threat is still great as the main Centre Strike Force with its surviving four battleships and eight cruisers sails through the San Bernadino Strait to attack the escort carriers and their accompanying destroyers. The escort ships and carrier aircraft fight back bravely, but escort carrier *Gambier Bay* and three destroyers are sunk by the heavy ships. Kamikaze aircraft also sink the escort carrier *St Lo* and damage others. In return, three of the Japanese cruisers are lost to escort carrier aircraft attack. Then, just when Centre Force could have got in among the transports, it retreats back the way it came.

Battle of Cape Engaño — While the US escort carriers are struggling to survive, Adm Halsey's Third Fleet aircraft sink all four carriers of the Northern Decoy Force — *Chitose*, *Chiyoda*, *Zuiho* and *Zuikaku* — although by this time their sacrifice has been in vain as Centre Force fails to press home its advantage. As the latter retreats, the returning Adm Halsey is too late to stop it getting through the San Bernadino Strait.

By any measure the USN and its carrier aircraft have struck the Japanese Navy a resounding blow from which it will never recover.

Merchant Shipping War

Losses

● Pacific only — 1 ship of 7,200 tons.

NOVEMBER

1st — Off Zara in the northern Adriatic, escort destroyers *Avon Vale* and *Wheatland* sink the torpedo boat *TA20* and two corvettes — all ex-Italian.

Greece and Albania

By mid-month Greece is free of those Germans that can escape and British troops have landed in the north. They also have the job of disarming the various resistance movements. In Albania the Germans are pulling out and on the 21st the capital of Tirana is occupied by Albanian partisans.

NOVEMBER

22nd — Three days after sinking a ship in the shallow Malacca Strait, submarine **STRATAGEM** is located and sunk by a Japanese destroyer on the 22nd.

Leyte, Central Philippines

Although the Japanese manage to reinforce Leyte, and fight back with a fierceness that comes as no surprise, they are too late to stop the US forces from pushing forward throughout the island. A second landing at Ormoc Bay on the west coast takes place in early December, and by the end of that month

sunk by *U1228*. Schnorkel-equipped boats are still capable of disrupting Allied shipping in distant waters.

Battle of the Atlantic
Losses
- 3 ships of 8,000 tons and 1 corvette.

HMS *Erebus* was a 15in gunned monitor, sister-ship to the *Terror* (lost off Derna in February 1941). She gave gunfire support off Walcheren with the more modern *Roberts*.   *Real Photos (S1095)*

DECEMBER

9th/13th — Return Russian convoy RA62 (28 ships) prepares to leave Kola Inlet on the 10th with the escort of JW62 and, beforehand, RN and Russian warships drive off the waiting U-boats. On the 9th, corvette *Bamborough Castle*, one of the vessels with the 8th and 20th EGs sinks *U387*. As the convoy later passes Jan Mayen Island on the 13th, *U365* is sent to the bottom by Swordfish of 813 Squadron from *Campania*. All merchantmen reach Loch Ewe on the 19th.

27th — *U877* encounters Halifax/UK convoy HX327 to the northwest of the Azores and is sunk by Canadian corvette *St Thomas* of the C3 group.

Battle of the Atlantic
Losses
- 1 ship of 5,000 tons.
- 3 U-boats.

when the battle takes place. On the 1st, Army units are carried across the Scheldt to land on the south side, while Royal Marines are put ashore to the west (at Westkapelle) against tough resistance. Under the command of Brig B. W. Leicester, the 4th Royal Marine Special Service Brigade consisting of Nos 41, 47 and 48 Commandos is carried from Ostend in 180 landing craft. Capt A. F. Pugsley commands the naval forces and heavy gunfire support is provided by *Warspite* in her last action of the war and the two monitors *Erebus* and *Roberts*.

Many landing craft are lost in the assault and by the time the Germans surrender on the 8th, Allied casualties total 8,000. By then the Canadians have crossed over to the eastern side from the mainland, and 10 flotillas of minesweepers have begun the job of clearing 80 miles of the Scheldt.

11th — On Arctic patrol off the Lofoten Islands, submarine *Venturer* sinks *U771* as she heads home for Narvik from operations in northern waters.

11th — South of Ireland *U1200* is sunk by patrolling corvettes *Kenilworth Castle*, *Launceston Castle*, *Pevensey Castle* and *Portchester Castle*, then supporting Halifax/UK convoy HX317.

Tirpitz is finally destroyed on the 12th as she lays at anchor, damaged, off Trömso. It is the Lancasters of Nos 9 and 617 (Dambuster) Squadrons RAF Bomber Command using 12,000lb bombs that put paid to the ship that for so long has tied down the Home Fleet. After several hits and near misses, she turns turtle, trapping nearly 1,000 of her crew inside.

21st — Escort destroyer **WENSLEYDALE** is badly damaged in collision with an LST in the Thames Estuary and placed in reserve.

25th — On passage out to the North Atlantic, *U322* is sunk west of the Shetlands by a Norwegian Sunderland of No 330 Squadron and patrolling frigate *Ascension*.

Eastern Front

The main activity is in Hungary where the Russians still battle towards Budapest, and in the Balkans as southern Yugoslavia is cleared by the Eastern Allies.

Merchant Shipping War
Losses
- 3 ships of 9,000 tons.

DECEMBER

Western Front

As the Allies push forward towards the Siegfried Line, the Battle of the Bulge starts in the Ardennes. Three German armies make a last desperate attempt to drive a wedge through the junction of US First and Third Armies, cross the Meuse and head for Antwerp. Starting on the 16th along a 60-mile front, the attackers soon surround American units at Bastogne where they hold out right through the battle. By Christmas the Germans have been stopped short of the Meuse. Now US First Army from the north and US Third from the south aided by part of the British Second Army pushing from the west begin to squeeze them back.

The inshore campaign of the U-boats around the British Isles gains some successes including two frigates, but four of them are lost:

MEDITERRANEAN

Merchant Shipping War — Conclusion

Losses
- Only one small Allied merchant ship is lost through to the end of the war in the Mediterranean.

The 'Z' class destroyer HMS *Zephyr*. The 'Z' and 'Ca' classes of 16 ships were completed 1944-45 and armed with four 4.5in guns, but were otherwise similar to the 'S' to 'W' classes. HMS *Cavalier* is still preserved in British waters. *Real Photos (S9993)*

INDIAN & PACIFIC OCEANS

organised resistance is over. All this time the USN suffers increasing damage in Philippine waters from kamikaze attack.

By the end of the war, Japan's merchant marine almost ceases to exist, a significant factor in its eventual defeat. US submarines account for 60% of sinkings as well as a third of warships. In November alone they sink battleship *Kongo* off Formosa, giant carrier *Shinano* (built on a 'Yamato' hull) off Tokyo only days after her completion, and the small carrier *Shinyo* off Shanghai.

Merchant Shipping War

Losses
- Indian Ocean — 2 ships of 14,000 tons.
- Pacific — 1 ship of 7,000 tons.

DECEMBER

14th — 'Hunt' escort destroyer **ALDENHAM** is the 67th and last RN destroyer to be lost in the Mediterranean. Returning from bombarding a German-held island off Fiume in the northern Adriatic, she is mined and sinks to the northwest of Zara.

By now all of the Mediterranean except the Ligurian Sea, the northern part of the Adriatic and some of the Greek islands are under Allied maritime control.

Greece

Disagreements with the Greek communist movement EAM/ELAS over the future government of the country leads to fighting and the declaration of martial law. British troops, supported by RN ships, have the unenviable task of warring with their estwhile allies. By month's end the fighting starts to die down as proposals for the setting-up of a regency are announced. The troubles are not over until February, and trouble flares again with the outbreak of civil war in 1946.

DECEMBER

Burma

As the central campaign aimed at Mandalay continues, the third and final Arakan offensive starts towards Akyab on the 11th with British, Indian and West African troops.

Formation of British Pacific Fleet

The RN now prepares to return to the Pacific in force, but even then as a junior partner to the vast US fleets. At the end of November, Vice-Adm Sir Arthur Power with the title of C-in-C, East Indies Fleet, takes over some of the ships of Eastern Fleet from Adm Fraser. These include capital ships *Queen Elizabeth* and *Renown*, four escort carriers and nine cruisers. Now, as the last U-boats that can head back for Europe, he has adequate convoy escort strength for the Indian Ocean.

Adm Fraser becomes C-in-C, British Pacific Fleet (BPF), and early in the month flies to Sydney, his planned main base, and then on to Pearl Harbor to discuss with Adm Nimitz how his

EUROPE

6th — Frigate **BULLEN** of the 19th EG is sunk off the north coast of Scotland by an acoustic torpedo from *U775*. On the same day and in the same area frigates *Goodall* and *Loch Insh*, also of the 19th EG, account for *U297*.

17th/18th — Attacking a convoy off the south coast of Ireland on the 17th, *U400* is sunk by escorting frigate *Nyasaland*. Next day *U1209* runs aground near Lands End and is wrecked.

26th — Frigate **CAPEL** of the 1st EG on patrol off Cherbourg is lost to *U486*.

30th — In one of the by now comparatively few successful attacks by aircraft on the schnorkel boats, *U772* is lost off Portland Bill to an RCAF Leigh light Wellington of No 407 Squadron.

In Norwegian waters one U-boat is lost in an RAF raid and another in collision off the Lofoten Islands.

Eastern Front

In Hungary the Russians attack towards Budapest, reaching Lake Balaton early in the month and encircling the city at Christmas. Following the setting up of a provisional Hungarian Government in the Russian-held area, war is declared on Germany on the 31st and an armistice signed with the Allies in late January.

Merchant Shipping War

Losses
● 18 ships of 86,000 tons.

INDIAN & PACIFIC OCEANS

Fleet will be employed. By the end of the year, fleet carriers *Illustrious, Indefatigable, Indomitable* and *Victorious*, battleships *Howe* and *King George V*, and seven cruisers including the New Zealand *Achilles* and *Gambia* have been allocated to BPF. Adm Fraser's greatest challenges are to equip and train his aircrews to US Navy standards of operation, and to assemble a balanced fleet train. This will enable him to supply and support his fleet so he can operate alongside the Americans in the vast stretches of the Pacific without being dependent on them. Even at the end he will lack many of the ships needed, especially fast tankers.

Meanwhile, Rear-Adm Sir Philip Vian takes command of the carriers and leads *Indomitable* and *Illustrious* on an attack against Belawan Deli, northern Sumatra, in mid-month. More raids take place on Sumatra in January.

Leyte and Mindoro, Central Philippines

As the Leyte fighting starts to draw to an organised close, Gen MacArthur's troops land on Mindoro on the 15th. They are soon in possession of the air bases needed for the invasion of the main Philippines island of Luzon to the north.

Merchant Shipping War

Losses
● Pacific only — 6 ships of 43,000 tons.

JANUARY

Russian convoy JW63 and return RA63 pass through a total of 65 ships in the month without loss.

Battle of the Atlantic

Losses
- 5 Allied ships of 29,000 tons.
- 1 U-boat by USN in mid-Atlantic.

HMS *Rodney* in the Atlantic in early 1945, whilst flagship, Home Fleet and based at Scapa Flow. *Real Photos (S1561)*

JANUARY

Adm Sir Bertram Ramsey, Allied Naval Commander, Expeditionary Force, whose accomplishments included the Dunkirk evacuation and major responsibility for the North African and Sicily landings as well as command of Operation 'Neptune', is killed in an air crash in France on the 2nd. He is succeeded by Vice-Adm Sir Harold Burrough.

Western Front

As fighting continues all along the front on the borders of Germany, the Battle of the Bulge finishes. By month's end the Germans have been pushed back to their start positions.

6th — Destroyer **WALPOLE** is the last of the 18 old 'V' and 'W' class vessels that are lost or not repaired in the war. Mined off the Scheldt Estuary while on North Sea patrol, she is saved but soon goes to the breakers.

As the U-boat campaign off the UK continues, losses are sustained by both sides:

15th/16th — Off the Clyde *U482* torpedoes a merchantman and badly damages escort carrier **THANE** (not repaired and laid up) as she ferries aircraft from Northern Ireland. After a long hunt the U-boat is sunk next day by frigate *Loch Craggie* and sloops *Amethyst, Hart, Peacock* and *Starling* of the 22nd EG.

21st — After torpedoing a merchant ship from a Thames/Bristol Channel convoy, *U1199* is sunk just off Lands End by escorting destroyer *Icarus* and corvette *Mignonette*.

26th — *U1172* severely damages frigate **MANNERS** (constructive total loss) off the Isle of Man and is then sunk in the counter-attack by sister ships *Aylmer, Bentinck* and *Calder* of the 4th and 5th EGs.

27th — Further to the south, in St George's Channel, and after attacking Halifax/UK convoy HX322, *U1051* is sunk by frigates *Bligh, Keats* and *Tyler* of the 5th EG.

Also one U-boat is lost in UK waters, possibly mined off the Moray Firth, and others are destroyed and damaged in air-raids on Germany.

Eastern Front

All along the Vistula front in Poland the Russians start a major offensive through Warsaw directed towards Berlin. Devastated Warsaw falls to them on the 17th and by the end of the month they have gained a huge wedge of territory that takes them over the border of Germany and to the River Oder only 60 miles from the German capital. The Germans are now cut off in East Prussia and some 1½ million servicemen and civilians are evacuated by the end of the war.

To the south, the Eastern Allies continue to fight their way through Czechoslovakia, as the Russians struggle to capture Budapest in Hungary.

Merchant Shipping War

E-boats and small battle units are operating out of Holland against Allied shipping in the North Sea and English Channel. Now the Seehunde midget submarines are added to their armoury. The new craft enjoy some successes, but the greatest problem is still due to the mines. Allied air and sea patrols and minesweeping keep all these dangers under control.

Losses
- 12 Allied ships of 47,000 tons in UK waters.

MEDITERRANEAN

JANUARY

Italy

Eighth Army continues to push slowly forward near Lake Comacchio in preparation for the spring offensive.

The 'Battle' class destroyer HMS *Barfleur*. The 'Battles' were larger ships intended for Pacific operations, with five completed between 1944 and the war's end. They displaced 2,310 tons and could make 36kt. They mounted four 4.5in guns and eight torpedo tubes, and had a crew of 250. *Real Photos (S9912)*

INDIAN & PACIFIC OCEANS

JANUARY

The RN loses its last submarine to enemy action with another badly damaged:

3rd — On patrol to the north of Sumatra, **SHAKESPEARE** surfaces to engage a merchant ship. Hit by return gunfire and later aircraft attack, she reaches Ceylon, but is not fully repaired.

16th — On or around the 16th, while on patrol in the Malacca Strait and minelaying off Penang, **PORPOISE** is probably sunk by Japanese aircraft. (Note: Some sources suggest the 19th.)

Burma

Only now do the mainly Chinese forces in the far north, pushing on from Myitkyina, reach the old Burma Road so allowing the Ledo Road link-up to be made. In the centre, 14th Army fights on towards Mandalay throughout January and February. And in the south the Arakan offensive moves on by a series of amphibious hops aimed at occupying suitable sites for air bases to support the central Burma campaign.

Early on the 3rd, British and Indian forces land on Akyab from destroyers and smaller vessels of the Royal, Australian and Indian Navies, to find that the Japanese have evacuated their troops. Then, on the 21st, more British and Indians are landed on Ramree Island with support and cover partly provided by battleship *Queen Elizabeth* and escort carrier *Ameer*. The few Japanese resist in their usual manner into February.

24th/29th — Fleet Air Arm Attack on Palembang — As the British Pacific Fleet transfers from Ceylon to Fremantle and then Sydney, Australia, successful strikes are made by aircraft from carriers *Indomitable, Illustrious, Indefatigable* and *Victorious* on oil installations around Palembang, southern Sumatra on the 24th and 29th. Adm Vian is in command.

Luzon, Northern Philippines

Three years after the Japanese themselves landed at Lingayen Gulf on the northwest coast of Luzon, Gen MacArthur's troops of Sixth Army go ashore early on the 9th, with the usual support of Seventh Fleet. As the US forces spread out and head south towards Manila, a secondary landing is made at the end of the month on Bataan Peninsula to stop the Japanese from falling back there as Gen MacArthur had done in 1942.

Kamikaze attacks continue to inflict heavy losses throughout the region, mainly in ships damaged, but on the 4th escort carrier *Ommaney Bay* on passage to Lingayen is sunk off Mindoro.

5th-9th — Off Lingayen, Australian heavy cruiser **Australia** is hit by kamikazes on the 5th, 6th, 8th and 9th and finally has to be withdrawn.

Merchant Shipping War
Losses
● Very few Allied merchant ships are lost in the Indian and Pacific Oceans for the rest of the war.

FEBRUARY

13th/17th — There is still no let up for the Russian convoys. JW64 arrives safely off Kola Inlet on the 13th with all 26 merchantmen, when corvette **DENBIGH CASTLE** is torpedoed by U992 and becomes a total loss. Four days later on the 17th, return RA64 is ready to set out. Just off the Inlet, U425 is sunk by sloop Lark and corvette Alnwick Castle, but later that day **LARK** is damaged by U968 and also becomes a total loss. Corvette **BLUEBELL** is then torpedoed by U711 and blows up with only one man surviving. Of the 34 ships with this convoy, one returns, one goes down to U-boats and, on the 23rd, the straggler Henry Bacon is sunk by Ju88 torpedo bombers, the last success by German aircraft of the war. The rest of the convoy arrives at Loch Ewe on the 28th after a voyage made even more difficult by violent storms of the type so often found in these northern waters.

22nd — In operations against convoys south of Portugal, U300, one of a small number of U-boats scattered across the North Atlantic, is sunk by escorting minesweepers Recruit and Pincher.

Battle of the Atlantic

Losses

- 6 ships of 39,000 tons and 3 escorts.
- 3 U-boats including 1 by US and French escorts off Morocco.

The oiler Dingledale, seen here with the cruiser Argonaut going alongside, was one of the fleet train so essential to the Royal Navy's operations, especially in the Pacific in 1945. *IWM (A12800)*

FEBRUARY

Yalta Conference

For a week early in the month, Prime Minister Churchill, President Roosevelt and Generalissimo Stalin meet at Yalta in the Crimea. With the Russians advancing through Eastern Europe and agreement on the future frontiers of Poland and the division of Germany into four occupation zones, the shape of much of postwar Europe is determined. Stalin agrees to declare war on Japan once the war in the west is over.

Western Front

Starting from the north, the Allies begin a series of offensives aimed at breaking through the Siegfried Line and destroying the German armies west of the Rhine. British 21st Army Group, which in addition to the British and Canadian Armies has the US Ninth temporarily attached, begins its moves on the 8th. The attacks towards the Rhine go in from south of Nijmegen along the River Maass to Aachen. The 12th Army Group is the next to go, on the 23rd, with US First and Third Armies aiming for the Rhine between Cologne and Koblenz.

U-boats still take a steady toll of shipping in their inshore campaign and sink two corvettes, but a number are lost, mainly to the RN:

3rd-17th — Frigates Bayntun, Braithwaite, Loch Dunvegan and Loch Eck of the 10th EG patrolling north of the Shetlands share in the sinking of three — U1279 on the 3rd, U989 on the 14th and U1278 three days later.

4th — Off the north coast of Ireland U1014 is accounted for by 23rd EG frigates Loch Scavaig, Loch Shin, Nyasaland and Papua.

9th — Submarine Venturer on patrol off Bergen sinks another U-boat when she torpedoes U864.

16th — In an attack on Scottish coastal convoy WN74 off the Moray Firth, U309 is lost to Canadian frigate St John of 9th EG.

20th — U1208 attacks convoy HX337 in St George's Channel and sinks escorting corvette **VERVAIN**. The U-boat is then hunted down and destroyed by sloop Amethyst of 22nd EG.

22nd — Off Falmouth, Bristol Channel/Thames convoy BTC76 is attacked by U1004 and the Canadian corvette **TRENTONIAN** is sent to the bottom.

24th — U927 is lost in the western Channel area to an RAF Wellington of No 179 Squadron.

24th/27th — During the inshore campaign, 10 U-boats are sunk in the Lands End area, three of them in February. On the 24th U480 sinks a merchant ship from coastal convoy BTC78 and is then hunted down and finished off by frigates Duckworth and Rowley of the 3rd EG. Three days later U1018 attacks BTC81 to be sunk by frigate Loch Fada of the 2nd EG. On the same day U327 is detected by a USN Liberator and sunk by Loch Fada again, working with Labuan and Wild Goose.

Two more U-boats are lost off Norway, one by accident and the other mined.

As the Allied strategic bombing campaign against Germany grows to its greatest intensity, the RAF by day and the USAAF by night strike at Dresden in mid-month. The controversial

MEDITERRANEAN

FEBRUARY

12th — German attacks with explosive motorboats on shipping in Split harbour, Yugoslavia, hit a landing craft, flak and slightly damage cruiser **Delhi** laying alongside.

Italian battleship *Conte di Cavour*, sunk in the FAA Taranto attack of 1940 and salvaged but not recommissioned, is finally destroyed by RAF raids on Trieste.

The 'S' class submarine *Spearfish*, which was lost in August 1940, was one of a prewar programme of 12 boats. Eight were lost off Western Europe (all but *Snapper* were lost in 1940), and in addition the Russian-manned *V.1* was lost in 1944. Completed 1932-38, they displaced 670/960 tons and could make 14/10kt. Their armament consisted of eight torpedo tubes and a 3in gun, and they were crewed by 40. Between 1942 and 1945 a further 48 slightly larger boats were completed, with nine lost and one not repaired. *Real Photos (N1050)*

INDIAN & PACIFIC OCEANS

FEBRUARY

11th — Supporting operations on Ramree Island, destroyer **PATHFINDER** is hit by Japanese bombers and goes to reserve, the 153rd and last destroyer or escort destroyer casualty of the Royal Navies.

Early in the month, the British Pacific Fleet arrives at Sydney for replenishment. Adm Fraser stays ashore as C-in-C and the Fleet is commanded by his number two, Vice-Adm Sir Bernard Rawlings in battleship *King George V*. Rear-Adm Vian is Flag Officer, First Aircraft Carrier Squadron. By this time nearly 60 ships of a diversity of types and flags are ready for the Fleet Train under Rear-Adm D. B. Fisher. BPF has been allocated Manus in the Admiralty Islands for its intermediate base, which Adm Rawlings has reached by mid-March.

Philippines — Conclusion

In Luzon, Bataan and Corregidor are taken, but the Japanese hold out in Manila until early March in a struggle that wrecks the city. By now all of the Philippines are under American strategic control, but to meet his promise to free all the islands, Gen MacArthur's men make amphibious landings on many through until April. On some of them, especially Luzon, fighting does not end until the Japanese surrender in August.

Iwo Jima, Volcano Islands

With Adm Spruance now back in command of Fifth Fleet, the next assault is on Iwo Jima, south of Japan, needed as an air base to support the USAAF strategic bombing campaign. Landings take place on the 19th, but before this eight square mile volcanic island is secured in mid-March, 6,000 US Marines and most of the 21,000 defenders are dead.

On the 21st February, escort carrier *Bismarck Sea* is sunk by kamikaze attack off the island.

attacks cause massive firestorms that kill in the region of 100,000 people, although even now there is little agreement on the actual numbers.

Eastern Front

Having penetrated into Germany the Russians now push out north towards the Baltic coast and southwest, so that by the beginning of March they are establishing themselves along the Oder-Niesse line of rivers.

In Hungary, Budapest finally falls on the 13th.

Merchant Shipping War
Losses
● 19 ships of 49,000 tons.

MARCH

20th — As Russian convoy JW65 approaches Kola Inlet with 24 merchant ships, two are sunk by waiting U-boats, and sloop **LAPWING** of the escort is lost to *U716*. Return RA65 sets out on the 23rd and all 25 ships get through to the Orkneys this time, on the last day of the month.

Battle of the Atlantic
Losses
● 4 ships of 27,000 tons and 1 sloop.
● 1 U-boat by USN off Nova Scotia.

MARCH

Western Front

In March the Allies not only reach the River Rhine all along its length, but by the end are across in great strength. At the beginning, the British 21st and US 12th Army Groups are still fighting towards the west bank and by the 10th stand along most of it from Nijmegen down to Koblenz. By then, and in a stroke of great good fortune, the bridge at Remagen is found standing on the 7th and units of US First Army rush over. Further south the rest of US Third Army on the 14th, followed by the US Seventh, starts to clear the west side of the river from Koblenz down to Karlsruhe, surrounding and taking the Saar region in the process. This is achieved in less than two weeks.

Between the 22nd and 31st, from north to south the Allied armies cross the Rhine and move further into the Reich. British 21st Army Group aided by paratroop drops goes over around Wesel; US First Army pushes out from its Remagen salient; US Third crosses around Mainz; US Seventh near Mannheim; and the French First Army north of Karlsruhe. The Germans are also about to lose the Ruhr industrial centre as US Ninth Army circles to the north and US First to the south.

The inshore campaign continues:

7th — *U1302* successfully attacks Halifax/UK convoy SC167 in St George's Channel, but after a long search off the coast of western Wales is sunk by Canadian frigates *La Hulloise*, *Strathadam* and *Thetford Mines* of the 25th EG.

10th/12th — Deep minefields laid by the RN to protect UK inshore waters from the U-boats claim two victims. On the 10th, *U275* is lost in the Channel off Beachy Head, and two days later *U260* is mined off Fastnet Rock, southern Ireland, and then scuttled.

12th-29th — Three more go down close to Lands End, starting with *U683* to frigate *Loch Ruthven* and sloop *Wild Goose* of the 2nd EG. On the 26th and 29th, *U399* and *U246* respectively are sunk by frigate *Duckworth* and other ships of 3rd EG. Before being hunted down, the latter U-boat has torpedoed and badly damaged Canadian frigate **TEME** (constructive total loss).

14th — South African frigate *Natal* on passage off the Firth of Forth sinks *U714*.

21st/22nd — Two U-boats are lost off the north coast of Ireland. *U1003* is damaged by Canadian frigate *New Glasgow* of the 26th EG and later scuttled. On the 22nd, RAF aircraft of No 120 Squadron account for *U296*.

The German 5.9in-gunned destroyer *Z28* at Kiel in 1943. As an increasing number of major warships were lost by Allied air attack, *Z28* went down on 6 March 1945 off the German Baltic coast. *Real Photos (S1863)*

MARCH

18th — Two ex-Italian torpedo boats and a destroyer minelaying off the Gulf of Genoa are engaged by destroyers *Meteor* and *Lookout*. In the last RN destroyer action of the Mediterranean, torpedo boats *TA24* and *TA29* are sent to the bottom.

Above:
The 'T' class submarine *Talent*. The wartime programme of 34 boats — 1,090/1,580 tons, 15/9kt, 11 torpedo tubes, one 4in gun, 60 crew — was completed by war's end, with six lost and one not repaired. The prewar 'T' programme, completed 1938-41, consisted of 15 boats of which nine were lost. *Real Photos (S1687)*

Below:
HMS *Illustrious* postwar. In March 1945 she was one of the four 'Illustrious' class fleet carriers starting operations with the British Pacific Fleet. *Real Photos (S9937)*

MARCH

Burma

On the central front the attacking British and Indian divisions take Mandalay on the 20th after a fierce struggle. As the Japanese start to retreat, 14th Army pushes on south towards Rangoon until early May.

British Pacific Fleet Starts Operations

On the 15th, Adm Rawlings signals from Manus to Adm Nimitz that the British Pacific Fleet is ready to join Adm Spruance's Fifth Fleet. Now known as Task Force 57, battleships *King George V* and *Howe*, carriers *Illustrious, Indefatigable, Indomitable* and *Victorious*, five cruisers including the New Zealand *Gambia* and 11 destroyers, two of them Australian, sail for Ulithi to refuel. On the 26th they are on station off the Sakishima Islands of the Ryukyu group, ready to stop them being used as staging posts for reinforcements flying from Formosa to Okinawa. BPF's main weapon is of course not the battleships, but the Seafires and American-made Avengers, Hellcats and Corsairs of the carriers' strike squadrons, which start their attacks that day.

The German pre-Dreadnought *Schleswig-Holstein* going into dry dock at Kiel in 1941. She fired the first shots of the war at sea off Poland on 1 September 1939, but became another casualty of the 1945 Allied air raids. *Real Photos (S1853)*

APRIL

On the 12th, Franklin Roosevelt dies in America and Vice President Truman assumes the Presidency of the United States. Britain and especially Winston Churchill lose a great friend who did so much to bolster the country at a time when the British Empire stood alone and many of the American peoples were staunchly isolationist. Harry Truman is soon faced with the decision whether or not to use the A-bomb.

Starting towards the end of the month, San Francisco hosts an international conference to draw up the constitution of the United Nations Organisation. The UN Charter is signed by 50 countries on 26 June.

29th — Last Convoy Battle of the war: Russia/UK Convoy RA66 — On the 25th, Kola Inlet bound convoy JW66 (22 ships) arrives safely, escorted by escort carriers *Premier* and *Vindex*, cruiser *Diadem*, Home Fleet destroyers and the 8th and 19th EGs all under the command of Rear-Adm A. E. Cunninghame-Graham. Return convoy RA66 (24 ships) sets out on the 29th with JW66s escort, some of which go ahead to clear the 14 U-boats waiting off the Inlet. That same day frigates *Anguilla*, *Cotton*, *Loch Insh* and *Loch Shin* of the 19th EG account for *U307* and then *U286*, the last U-boats sunk by RN warships. In the process **GOODALL**, also of the 19th EG, is torpedoed by *U968* and goes down with heavy loss of life. She too is the last

27th/30th — The frigates of 21st EG, split into two divisions, sink three U-boats in the Hebrides area. On the 27th, *U965* is sunk by Hedgehog off the northern end of the islands by *Conn*, accompanied by *Deane* and *Rupert*. That same day to the south, *U722* goes down to *Byron*, *Fitzroy* and *Redmill*. Three days later and the first division, still to the north, sinks *U1021*.

One more is lost to US aircraft in southern UK waters and two to the RAF on northern transit area patrols, but now the Allied air-raids are really starting to bite. In Germany some 12 boats, completed or in service, are destroyed in the month, mainly by the USAAF on the night of the 30th.

The end of the remaining German big ships is in sight. Battlecruiser *Gneisenau*, out of service since 1942 and now hulked, is sunk as a blockship in Gdynia (Gotenhafen) on the 27th. Light cruiser *Köln* is also sunk at Wilhelmshaven by Allied bombing. Only two pocket battleships, two heavy and three light cruisers remain, and most of these will only survive a few more weeks.

As the V-weapon attack on Antwerp continues, the last V-2 lands on London on the 27th, by which time 1,000 of them have killed and wounded nearly 10,000 people in southeast England.

Eastern Front

By the end of March the Russians have taken most of the Baltic coast of Germany and Poland east of the River Oder and captured Gdynia and Danzig. They are now poised along the Oder-Niesse Line ready for the final attack towards Berlin.

To the south, the Eastern Allies continue to progress into Czechoslovakia. In Hungary the Germans make their last important counter-offensive of the war around the Lake Balaton area. By mid-month they have been stopped and the Russians drive on towards eastern Austria.

Merchant Shipping War

E-boat laid mines continue to cause a high proportion of merchantmen sinkings.

Losses
● 23 ships of 84,000 tons.

APRIL

Western Front

American forces complete the encirclement of the Ruhr on the 1st when they meet at Lippstadt, trapping a third of a million German troops. The vital industrial area is slowly reduced and on the 18th they surrender. Meanwhile the Allies break out through Germany, eventually to meet up with the Russians:

● *British 21st Army Group heads into northern Holland and Germany, the Canadians taking Arnhem on the 15th and moving on Emden, as the British capture Bremen on the 26th and make for Hamburg and the Baltic coast at Lübeck.*

● *US 12th Army Group pushes into central Germany. Ninth Army passes to the north of the Ruhr and reaches the River Elbe opposite Berlin by the 12th where it stops. The First Army gets to the Elbe at Torgau south of Berlin on the 25th and is the first to meet the advancing Russians. Germany is now cut in half. Meanwhile General Patton's Third Army swings south and races on to western Czechoslovakia and northern Austria.*

● *US Sixth Army Group, including the French First Army, occupy southern Germany and heads for the north Swiss border and western tip of Austria.*

The 'U' class submarine *Usurper* was lost around October 1943. Of a wartime programme of 68 boats completed between 1940 and the war's end, 18 were lost, including the Norwegian *Uredd*. These boats displaced 540/740 tons, could make 11/10kt, were armed with four torpedo tubes and a 12pdr or 3in gun, and had a crew of 30. The prewar programme of three 'U' boats, of which *Undine* and *Unity* were lost, was completed in 1938. *Real Photos (S1665)*

APRIL

Italy

The last and decisive Allied offensive aimed at clearing the Germans from Italy gets underway with commando assaults near Lake Comacchio on the 1st. ✛ It is in these operations that the Royal Marines win their only VC of the war, when Cpl Thomas Hunter, 43 Commando, is posthumously awarded the Victoria Cross for gallantry in action against German forces on the 2nd.

Eighth Army starts towards the Argenta gap on the 9th, and by the 18th is through. US Fifth Army moves on Bologna on the 14th and a week later has captured the city. After that the British, Brazilian, Indian, New Zealand, Polish, South African and US divisions of Fifth and Eighth Armies reach the River Po and race across the north of Italy. By the end of the month, Spezia, Genoa and Venice have been liberated.

Throughout the campaign Italian partisans have waged a bloody war behind German lines. On the 28th, near Lake Como, they capture and execute Benito Mussolini and his mistress. Since February senior German officers have secretly negotiated with the Allies to end the war in Italy. On the 29th, and without reference to Berlin, a document of unconditional surrender is signed to take effect from 2 May.

APRIL

Okinawa, Ryukyu Islands

Okinawa, the main island in the Ryukyu group and half way between Formosa and Kyushu, is needed as a major base for the coming, bloodiest invasion of all — that of mainland Japan. The Japanese are therefore committed to defending Okinawa for as long as possible and with the maximum use of kamikaze attack. Under Adm Spruance and Fifth Fleet, the greatest amphibious operation of the Pacific war starts on the 1st when US Tenth Army of Marines and Army forces lands on the west side of the island. There is little opposition at first, but by the time the Americans have taken the northern five-sixths of the island on the 13th, bitter fighting is raging in the south, and continues through April, May and into June. Air and sea kamikaze missions lead to losses on both sides:

1st — As the British Pacific Fleet operates off the Sakishimas, **Indefatigable** is hit by a suicide aircraft, but saved from serious damage by her armoured flightdeck.

6th — The Japanese launch the first of 10 'kikusui' (floating chrysanthemum) mass kamikaze attacks which carry on through until June. US losses in men and ships sunk and damaged are severe. On the 6th, carrier **Illustrious** is hit.

major warship of the Royal and Dominion Navies lost in the war against Germany. RA66 arrives safely in the Clyde on 8 May.

Battle of the Atlantic

Losses

- 5 ships of 32,000 tons, 1 frigate and 1 US destroyer off the Azores.
- 9 U-boats including 7 by USN off east coast of USA, off the Azores and in mid-Atlantic.

HMS *Devonshire*, a 'County' class heavy cruiser, photographed in 1937. In June 1940 *Devonshire* carried the Norwegian King Haakon into exile; and from April 1945 took part in the liberation of Norway.
Real Photos (S1092)

In their advance, the Allies over-run Belsen, Buchenwald and Dachau to reveal to the world the full horror of the Nazi regime. By now the Russians have captured similar camps in the east.

Throughout the month over 40 U-boats are lost in and around the waters of northwest Europe, 12 of them involving the RN.

5th — One is lost in another deep-laid minefield near the UK: *U1169* goes down in the St George's Channel off the southeast coast of Ireland.

6th/15th — Two are sunk in Channel operations. After sinking a ship from a convoy off the Isle of Wight, *U1195* is lost to the old escorting destroyer *Watchman*. A week or so later on the 15th, *U1063* attacks another convoy off Start Point, only to be sent to the bottom off Land's End by frigate *Loch Killin* of 17th EG.

8th-15th — Four more go down to the south and southwest of Ireland. On the 8th, frigates *Byron* and *Fitzroy* of 21st EG sink *U1001*, and *Bentinck* and *Calder* of 4th EG account for *U774*. Two days later *U878* sailing from still uncaptured St Nazaire attacks a UK-out convoy and falls victim to destroyer *Vanquisher* and corvette *Tintagel Castle* of the escort. Then on the 15th *U285* is sunk by frigates *Grindall* and *Keats* of the 5th EG.

12th — Home Fleet submarines gain another success when *Tapir* sinks outward-bound *U486* off Bergen.

12th/30th — Two more are lost in the Irish Sea to the northwest of Anglesey. On the 12th *U1024* is disabled by the Squid of frigate *Loch Glendhu* of 8th EG. Boarded from *Loch More*, she is taken in tow but founders. On the last day of the month *U242* is detected by a RAF Sunderland of No 201 Squadron and sunk by destroyers *Havelock* and *Hesperus* of the 14th EG.

16th — *U1274* attacks Forth/Thames convoy FS1784 off St Abbs Head, sinking one ship, but is then lost to destroyer *Viceroy* of the escort.

21st — Frigates of the 4th EG are now to the northwest of Ireland, and *Bazely*, *Bentinck* and *Drury* sink *U636*.

The other U-boats are lost as follows:

- 6 by RAF and US aircraft in and around the British Isles;
- 1 by accident and 2 more missing, cause of loss unknown, during the inshore campaign;
- 5 in the Skagerrak and Kattegat, 3 of these by rocket-firing Mosquitos of RAF Coastal Command;
- Some 17 completed boats in air-raids on Germany.

End of the German Surface Fleet

April sees the end of the German Navy's remaining big ships. In RAF raids on Kiel early in the month, pocket battleship *Admiral Scheer* capsizes and heavy cruiser *Admiral Hipper* and the light *Emden* are badly damaged. A few days later pocket battleship *Lützow* is also put out of action at Swinemünde. All three damaged ships are scuttled in the first week of May.

When Germany surrenders, three cruisers survive. *Prinz Eugen* will be used in A-bomb trials in the Pacific; *Leipzig* scuttled in the North Sea in 1946 loaded with poison gas

MEDITERRANEAN

13th — Torpedo boat *TA45* is sunk by RN coastal forces off Fiume in the northern Adriatic, the last major enemy warship to fall to the Service in the Mediterranean.

HM Submarine *Astute*, one of two 'A' boats completed by the end of the war. Mainly intended for Pacific operations, these craft displaced 1,120/1,620 tons and could make 18/8kt. They were armed with 10 torpedo tubes and a 4in gun, and had a crew of 60. *Real Photos (S1598)*

INDIAN & PACIFIC OCEANS

Damage is slight and she carries on, but this much battered ship is shortly relieved by *Formidable*.

Battle of the East China Sea — the giant battleship *Yamato* with one cruiser and destroyers sails on a one-way mission for Okinawa. Overwhelmed by aircraft of Fifth Fleet on the 7th, *Yamato*, the cruiser and four destroyers are sent to the bottom to the southwest of Nagasaki.

BPF continues its attacks on the Sakishima Islands and also against airfields of northern Formosa, with short breaks for refuelling. It sails for Leyte on the 20th to replenish.

Merchant Shipping War

Losses

● Pacific only — 3 ships of 23,000 tons.

munitions; and *Nürnberg* ceded to Russia. A dozen or so of the big destroyers will also stay afloat.

Eastern Front

As the Eastern Allies fight on through Czechoslovakia towards Prague, Hungary is finally freed of the Germans, and the Russians push into Austria, capturing Vienna on the 13th.

To the north, as the Western Allies come to a halt along the line of the River Elbe, the Russians start their final and massive drive into eastern Germany from the Oder-Neisse Line. They have surrounded the German capital by the 25th and the Battle for Berlin gets underway.

Germany — The End of Adolf Hitler

As the month draws to a close and the Allies start to complete the destruction of the German Reich, Himmler, through Swedish intermediaries, tries to surrender to Britain and the United States, but anything short of unconditional surrender is refused. Then on the 29th in his Berlin bunker, Hitler marries Eva Braun and nominates Grand-Adm Dönitz as his successor. Next day Hitler and his wife commit suicide and Dönitz assumes the position of Führer on 1 May.

Merchant Shipping War
Losses
● 14 ships of 50,000 tons.

MAY

Last Russian Convoys

One last convoy sails each way soon after the German surrender. JW67 leaves the Clyde on the 12th with 23 merchantmen and reaches Kola on the 20th. Three days later return RA67, again with 23 ships, sets out and on the last day of the month sails up the Clyde.

Since August 1941, 78 convoys have sailed in both directions and passed through nearly 1,400 merchant ships for the loss of 85. In doing so, millions of tons of vital cargo and thousands of tanks and aircraft have been delivered to the Russians, but the cost to the RN has included one escort carrier severely damaged and two cruisers, six destroyers and eight other escorts sunk in the cold and often stormy waters of the Arctic. At the same time, the Germans have seen the destruction of *Scharnhorst* and indirectly the *Tirpitz*, three of their big destroyers, and well over 30 U-boats.

Battle of the Atlantic — conclusion

Just 68 months before, to the northwest of the British Isles, the liner *Athenia* was torpedoed by *U30* and 11 days later *U39* sunk by RN destroyers. Since then, tens of thousands of lives, thousands of ships and hundreds of U-boats have been lost in the battle to sustain Britain as the base without which the liberation of Europe would have been impossible. As the United States takes over from Britain the mantle of the world's most powerful navy, so the last merchantmen and U-boats of the Battle of the Atlantic go to the bottom in American waters and involving American ships. On the 6th, *U881* is sunk by the USN south of Newfoundland. That same day, after she has torpedoed the freighter *Black Point* off New York, *U853* is hunted down and sunk by US destroyer escort *Atherton* and frigate *Moberley*.

Understandably the cost of the Battle is usually measured in terms of the 2,400 merchantmen sunk in the North and South Atlantic. To this must be added the battlecruiser, three fleet and

MAY

End of the U-boats

Right to the end of the war there is no let-up in the struggle against the U-boats, especially with the potential threat from the new and dangerous Types XXI and XXIII. Between the 2nd and 6th, 23 U-boats of all types are destroyed by the Typhoons, Beaufighters, Mosquitos and Liberators of the RAF and Allied Tactical Air Forces. As the German fighter defences crumble, the Allied aircraft roam the Kattegat and nearby waters catching many of the U-boats in the Baltic or sailing for Norway. One more is lost by unknown causes off Scotland. Two others represent the last U-boat destroyed by the RN and the final sinking of the European war, respectively. While much of this is happening, steps are taken to arrange for the surrender of Germany's still formidable submarine fleet.

4th — As a RN task force consisting of escort carriers *Queen*, *Searcher* and *Trumpeter* with cruisers and destroyers and under the command of Vice-Adm R. R. McGrigor returns from Murmansk, strikes are launched against shipping off Norway. During these *U711* is sunk near Narvik. That same day Adm Dönitz orders his U-boats to stop operations and return to base. Many crews prefer to scuttle their boats.

7th — The U-boats gain their last success when Type XXIII coastal boat *U2336* sinks merchantmen *Avondale Park* and *Sneland* off the Firth of Forth. Further north to the west of Bergen, a RAF Catalina of No 210 Squadron on northern transit area patrol destroys *U320*, the very last U-boat loss.

8th — Operational U-boats are ordered to surface and sail for Allied ports flying a black flag of surrender. Most make for the UK, although a few reach the US.

9th — The first of over 150 surrendered boats start to arrive, but more than 200 are scuttled. Of those that surrender, a

MAY

Italy — Conclusion

As agreed, the cease-fire takes place on the 2nd just as the Allies reach Trieste near the Yugoslavian border. On the 6th they arrive at the Brenner Pass into Austria in time to meet units of the US Seventh Army coming from the north through Germany.

Mediterranean — Final Victory

The entire Mediterranean basin, the Middle East, and North and East Africa are now completely free from threat of German and Italian military domination. In five short years the RN has moved from having to fight hard to maintain a presence in the Mediterranean, to where it has been largely responsible for landing large Allied armies on enemy shores and supplying and supporting them. The cost has been high — over 40% of total major warship losses of the RN worldwide — one battleship, two fleet carriers, 20 cruisers and cruiser-minelayers, 67 destroyers and escort destroyers, 45 submarines and thousands of its officers and men.

Above:
The Japanese heavy cruiser *Haguro*, which was sunk by the 26th Destroyer Flotilla on 16 May 1945. *Real Photos*

MAY

Burma — Conclusion

2nd — Landings Near Rangoon: Operation 'Dracula' — Concerned that 14th Army coming from the north will not reach Rangoon before the monsoon breaks, the go-ahead is given for airborne and amphibious landings. On the 1st, Gurkha paratroops land near the coast. Early next morning the main landings take place.

Under the naval command of Rear-Adm B. C. S. Martin, an Indian division is carried from Ramree in landing ships and craft and put ashore, covered by Cdre G. N. Oliver and his escort carriers, cruisers and destroyers. As this takes place, diversionary attacks are made on the Andaman and Nicobar Islands by Vice-Adm H. T. C. Walker with battleships *Queen Elizabeth* and *Richelieu* and aircraft from two escort carriers.

Rangoon is entered on the 3rd by the landing forces to find the Japanese have gone, and on the 6th they meet the 14th Army units just a few miles north of the capital and major port of Burma. The rest of the war is spent mopping up those Japanese unable to escape to Thailand.

16th — Sinking of the *Haguro*: The Last Major Surface Warship Action of the War — As Japanese heavy cruiser *Haguro* sails for the Andamans to evacuate the garrison, she is reported by East Indies Fleet submarines in the Malacca Strait. Adm Walker sets out with his escort carriers to catch her, but on the 11th they are sighted and *Haguro* turns back. She tries again a few days later. This time the 26th Destroyer Flotilla (Capt M. L. Power) of *Saumarez*, *Venus*, *Verulam*, *Vigilant* and *Virago* are ready for her off Penang. In a classic night destroyer torpedo action they attack from all sides and send her to the bottom early on the 16th.

19th — On patrol in the Java Sea, submarine **TERRAPIN**

ATLANTIC	EUROPE

ATLANTIC

escort carriers, two cruisers and 47 destroyers and escorts of the Royal and Canadian Navies lost in the Atlantic, excluding the convoy routes to Russia.
Losses
- 1 ship of 5,000 tons.
- 2 U-boats.

HMS *Swiftsure*, a 'Superb' class light cruiser, was present at one of the last events of the war, the surrender of Kong Kong on 16 September 1945 *Real Photos (S9974)*

EUROPE

quarter are taken over by the Allied powers, and the rest are sunk in the Atlantic off Northern Ireland by the RN in Operation 'Deadlight' which lasts until January 1946.

Germany — Final Defeat and Surrender

Western Front
In the last week of the war in Europe, US First and Ninth Armies stand along the west bank of the River Elbe. To their north, British Second Army reaches the Baltic on the 2nd and next day takes Hamburg. In the south, US Third Army pushes into Czechoslovakia as far as Pilsen and Austria around Linz, and Seventh Army into Austria and through Innsbruck before crossing the Brenner Pass into Italy. There the Western Allies stop.

On the 4th outside Hamburg, German envoys surrender their forces in Holland, Denmark and northwest Germany to Field Marshal Montgomery.

Eastern Front
Berlin falls to the Russian Army on the 2nd. Fighting continues in Czechoslovakia and Austria and, on the 5th, resistance forces rise to take over Prague. A few days later the last major German units surrender to the Russians to the east of the Czech capital.

Surrender and Occupation
At Gen Eisenhower's HQ at Rheims in France on the 7th, the unconditional surrender of Germany is signed to take effect from midnight on the 8th — VE day. On the 9th it is ratified in Berlin and signed for the Allies by ACM Tedder (as Gen Eisenhower's Deputy) and Russian Marshal Zhukov.

As the last remaining German forces surrender in France, Germany, Norway and elsewhere, and the Allies complete the liberation of all Europe from their hold, the four major powers move into their zones of occupation in Germany and Austria. The war in Europe is over.

Merchant Shipping War
Losses
- 2 ships of 4,700 tons.

DEFENCE OF TRADE — JUNE 1944 TO MAY 1945

Summary of Losses

North Atlantic 31 ships of 177,000 tons.	*UK waters* 135 ships of 500,000 tons.	*Mediterranean* 5 ships of 7,000 tons.	*Indian Ocean* 21 ships of 134,000 tons.	Submarines	120 ships of 629,000 tons.
				Mines	50 ships of 162,000 tons.
				Aircraft	14 ships of 96,000 tons.
South Atlantic 5 ships of 28,000 tons.			*Pacific Ocean* 13 ships of 96,000 tons.	Other causes	15 ships of 28,000 tons.
				Coastal forces	11 ships of 27,000 tons.

= 210 British, Allied and neutral ships of 942,000 tons: ie 78,000 tons per month.

attacks an escorted tanker and is badly damaged by depth charges in the counter-attack. She is not repaired, the last RN submarine casualty of the war.

Borneo

Australian forces under Gen MacArthur start landing operations on Borneo, in part to recover the oil fields. On the 1st they go ashore at Tarakan on the east coast of Dutch Borneo, covered by ships of Seventh Fleet including the Australian cruiser Hobart. Similar assaults take place at Brunei Bay on the British north coast on 10 June, after which the Australians advance south down the coast of Sarawak.

Finally, on 1 July, in the last major amphibious operation of the war, they land at Balikpapan, south of Tarakan on the east coast, which they secure after some tough fighting.

Okinawa, Ryukyu Islands

As the struggle for Okinawa continues, the US Fifth Fleet is hit by four 'kikusui' attacks in May. By the 4th, BPF is back off the Sakishimas and also under fire:

4th — **Formidable** and **Indomitable** are hit by one aircraft each.

9th — **Formidable** is hit again and **Victorious** also damaged by a suicide aircraft.

In all cases the carriers' armoured deck allows them to resume flight operations in a remarkably fast time. On the 25th the RN ships head first for Manus to prepare for the next stage of the attack on Japan. In two months the aircraft of BPF have flown over 5,000 sorties.

Finale! HMS *Wolverine*, a World War 1 'V' & 'W' class destroyer, which in 1941 sank Cdr Prien's *U47* and then *U76*. She is shown here in September 1945 at Barrow in northwest England. She was scrapped a year later. *Real Photos (S1537)*

JUNE

8th — As Japanese heavy cruiser *Ashigara* (sister-ship to *Haguro*) carries troops from Batavia to Singapore, she is torpedoed five times by submarine *Trenchant* and sinks in the Banka Strait off southeast Sumatra.

The main body of the British Pacific Fleet prepares to leave Sydney to join the US fleet, now the Third under Adm Halsey. While they do so, the newly arrived fleet carrier *Implacable*, with an escort carrier and cruisers in support, launches raids on the by-passed island of Truk in the Carolines on the 14th and 15th.

Okinawa, Ryukyu Islands

The fighting finally comes to an end on the 22nd after one of the bitterest of campaigns. Over 7,000 members of the US land forces have been killed — and nearly 5,000 Navy men, mainly from kamikaze attacks — to add to the Japanese killed of well over 100,000. USN losses in ships include five carriers badly damaged and 32 destroyer types, many on radar picket duty, sunk or never repaired. Over 7,000 Japanese aircraft crash in one way or another.

TOTAL MERCHANT SHIP LOSSES —
SEPTEMBER 1939 TO AUGUST 1945

Although the war in the Pacific is far from over only one more merchant ship is sunk in that theatre (in June), and just seven others will be lost elsewhere, mainly on mines. It is convenient therefore to summarise here, and in all their immensity, the losses in ships suffered by Britain, its Allies and neutral countries throughout the war. Of the grand totals that follow, Britain's losses amounted to around 50% of tonnage, with a similar percentage applying to sinkings in the North and South Atlantic, both pointing to the critical importance of the Battle of the Atlantic and to the price Britain paid for keeping open the sea lanes. In concentrating on losses, it should not be overlooked that taking the war as a whole, well over 99% of merchantmen reached their destination safely. On the other side of the balance sheet, more than 30,000 officers and men of the British Merchant Navy did not.

North Atlantic	UK waters	Mediterranean	Indian Ocean
2,232 ships of 11,900,000 tons.	1,431 ships of 3,768,000 tons.	413 ships of 1,740,000 tons.	385 ships of 1,790,000 tons.

South Atlantic			Pacific Ocean
174 ships of 1,024,000 tons.			515 ships of 1,348,000 tons.

= 5,150 British, Allied and neutral ships of 21,570,000 tons: ie 300,000 tons per month.

Submarines	2,828 ships of 14,686,000 tons.
Aircraft	820 ships of 2,890,000 tons.
Mines	534 ships of 1,406,000 tons.
Other causes	632 ships of 1,030,000 tons.
Raiders	133 ships of 830,000 tons.
Warships	104 ships of 498,000 tons.
Coastal forces	99 ships of 230,000 tons.

JULY

The world's first atomic bomb is successfully exploded at Alamagordo, New Mexico on the 16th, in Operation 'Trinity'.

Potsdam Conference

In the second half of the month, the heads of the three great powers meet at Potsdam outside Berlin to discuss further the future of Europe and the defeat of Japan. By the end of the conference only Stalin will remain of the original three that have met in the past. At the start, President Truman is there for the first time, representing the United States. On the 26th the Potsdam Declaration, demanding the unconditional surrender of Japan, is broadcast.

That same day the results of the British general election held earlier in the month are announced. Winston Churchill's Conservative Party is swept from power and the Labour Party under Clement Attlee takes over the reins of the wartime Coalition Government. He travels to Potsdam for the rest of the conference.

JULY

In Australia, Prime Minister John Curtin fails to see the end of the war when he dies on the 5th after an illness. His then acting PM, Joseph Chiffley, succeeds him.

Last Major Warship Casualties of the RN in the War

24th/26th — In East Indies Fleet operations against the Phuket Island area off the west coast of southern Thailand, including mine clearance, fleet minesweeper **SQUIRREL** is herself mined on the 24th and sinks. Two days later in the same area, kamikaze aircraft attack for the first and last time in the Indian Ocean theatre. Fleet minesweeper **VESTAL** is hit and has to be scuttled, and cruiser **Sussex** very slightly damaged by a near miss.

31st — Sinking of the *Takao* — The Japanese heavy cruiser *Takao*, previously damaged by US submarines on passage to the Battle of Leyte Gulf, is now laying off Singapore. On the night of the 30th/31st, midget submarines XE1 (Lt Smart) and XE3 (Lt Fraser), after being released from towing submarines *Spark* and *Stygian*, manage to reach the cruiser and drop their charges. As they do, XE3 is almost trapped beneath the hull. *Takao* is badly damaged in the resulting explosions and sinks to the bottom. Around this time other XE craft cut the undersea telephone cables off Saigon and Hong Kong.

✠ Lt Ian Fraser RNR and his diver, Leading Seaman James Magennis, are awarded the Victoria Cross.

Adm Rawlings, now with *King George V*, *Formidable*, *Implacable*, *Victorious* and six cruisers including the RCN *Uganda* and RNZN *Achilles* and *Gambia* joins Third Fleet in mid-month to bombard Japan by sea and air, through into August. The USN reserves its right to finish off the Imperial Japanese Navy and in aircraft strikes on Kure destroys battleship *Haruna*, battleship/carriers *Ise* and *Hyuga*, carrier *Amagi* and several carriers under construction. Late on the 29th, after delivering atomic bomb components to Tinian, US cruiser *Indianapolis* is sunk by a Japanese submarine in the Philippine Sea.

AUGUST

As US Third Fleet and the British Pacific Fleet continue their bombardment of Japan, the Royal and Dominion Navies win their last Victoria Cross of World War 2. ✣ Lt Robert Gray RCNVR, Corsair fighter-bomber pilot with *Formidable's* 1841 Squadron, presses home his attack on shipping in Onagawa harbour, northeastern Honshu, on the 9th. Under heavy fire, he sinks his target before crashing in flames, and is posthumously awarded the Victoria Cross.

Japan — Final Defeat . . .

Although Japan's cities and production facilities are being devastated by the strategic bombing offensive and now by Third Fleet warships laying off her shores, her navy and merchant marine are annihilated, and remaining overseas conquests are isolated and under attack, she is not beaten. There is therefore no let-up in the planning and execution of the campaigns to bring the war to a final conclusion. In South East Asia, Adm Mountbatten prepares to land in Malaya, and the Americans plan to invade the southern island of Kyushu in the autumn and Honshu around Tokyo early in 1946. US casualties alone of a million or more are expected. Then, in a matter of days, all the planning comes to nought:

6th — *B-29 Superfortress* Enola Gay, *flying from Tinian, drops the first atomic bomb on Hiroshima. The equivalent of 20,000 tons of TNT kills 80,000 people.*

8th — *Russia declares war on Japan and next morning invades Manchuria, overwhelming the Japanese forces there.*

9th — *The second A-bomb is detonated over Nagasaki and over 40,000 die.*

15th — *After days of internal argument, Emperor Hirohito over-rides the politicians and military and broadcasts to announce Japan's unconditional surrender — VJ-Day.*

27th — *Ships of Third Fleet under Adm Halsey start to arrive in Tokyo Bay and anchor within sight of Mount Fuji. Representatives of the British Pacific Fleet and Dominion Navies include* Duke of York *(flying the flag of Adm Fraser),* King George V, Indefatigable, *cruisers* Newfoundland *and the RNZN* Gambia *and two RAN destroyers. They are later joined by Australian cruisers* Shropshire *and* Hobart.

29th — *Adm Nimitz as C-in-C, Pacific, flies in; followed by Gen MacArthur, C-in-C, South West Pacific, and future overlord of Japan.*

SEPTEMBER

. . . and Surrender

2nd — *On the quarterdeck of the US battleship* Missouri, *Gen MacArthur accepts Japan's surrender on behalf of all the Allied powers.*

Amongst the signatories of the surrender document are Adm Sir Bruce Fraser for Great Britain, Gen Blamey for Australia, Col Moore-Cosgrove for Canada, Air Vice Marshal Isitt for New Zealand and, for the United States, Adm Nimitz.

As ships of the Royal and Dominion Navies repatriate Allied prisoners of war and transport food and supplies throughout South East Asia, other surrenders follow during the next few days, including:

6th — On board light carrier *Glory* off Rabaul, the surrender of the Bismarck Archipelago, New Guinea and the Solomons, taken by Australian Gen Sturdee. Local surrenders in this area take place on Australian warships.

12th — South East Asia is surrendered to Adm Mountbatten at a ceremony in Singapore.

16th — After arriving at Hong Kong in cruiser *Swiftsure*, Rear-Adm C. H. J. Harcourt accepts the Japanese surrender there.

BIBLIOGRAPHY

Although numerous older and more recent books on the war were referred to and used for additional cross-checking and background, only the main sources of published information are listed below. In all cases concerning RN losses, information available from the Naval Historical Branch was used as the final arbiter.

Warship Details and Loss Data

Conway's *All the World's Fighting Ships, 1922-1946*, Conway Maritime Press, 1980.

Couhat, Jean Labayle, *French Warships of World War II*, Ian Allan Ltd, 1978.

Fraccaroli, Aldo, *Italian Warships of World War II*, Ian Allan Ltd, 1978.

Lenton, H. T. and J. J. Colledge, *Warships of World War II*, Ian Allan Ltd, 1973.

Silverstone, Paul H, *US Warships of World War 2*, Ian Allan Ltd, 1982.

Taylor, J. C, *German Warships of World War II*, Ian Allan Ltd, 1977.

Janes Fighting Ships, various editions, Sampson Low, Marston.

Naval Events and Background, Including Additional Loss Data

Costello, John and Terry Hughes, *The Battle of the Atlantic*, William Collins, 1977.

Cunningham of Hyndhope, Admiral of the Fleet Viscount, *A Sailor's Odyssey*, Hutchinson & Co, 1951.

Dull, Paul S, *A Battle History of the Imperial Japanese Navy (1941-1945)*, Patrick Stephens, 1978.

King, Ernest J. and Walter Muir Whitehill, *Fleet Admiral King, A Naval Record*, Eyre and Spottiswoode, 1953.

Reynolds, Clark, *Command of the Sea*, Robert Hale, 1976.

Rohwer, J. and G. Hummelchen, *Chronology of the War at Sea*, 2 volumes, Ian Allan Ltd, 1972.

Roskill, Captain S. W, *The Navy at War 1939-1945*, Collins, 1964.

Roskill, Captain S. W, *The War at Sea, Volumes 1, 2 and 3, Parts I and II*, HMSO, 1954 to 1961.

Warner, Oliver, *Battle Honours of the Royal Navy*, G. Philip, 1956.

Winton, John, *The Victoria Cross at Sea*, Michael Joseph, 1978.

Military and Political Background

Argyle, Christopher, *Chronology of World War II*, Exeter Books, 1980.

Churchill, Winston S, *The Second World War*, 6 volumes, Cassell & Co, 1948 to 1954.

Goodenough, Simon, *War Maps, World War II from September 1939 to August 1945*, MacDonald and Co, 1982.

Lewin, Ronald, *Ultra goes to War*, Hutchinson, 1978.

Liddell Hart, Basil, *History of the Second World War*, Cassell & Co, 1970.

Young, Brigadier Peter, Editor, *The Almanac of World War II*, Hamlyn, 1981.

APPENDICES

1 ROYAL AND DOMINION NAVIES: ANALYSIS OF MAJOR WARSHIP LOSSES

Total Strengths and Losses

	I Strength as at 3 September 1939	II Commissioned up to 14 August 1945	(a) Total I + II	LOSSES (b) Prewar ships	In total
Battleships and battlecruisers	15	5	20	4	5
Fleet and escort carriers	7	58(c)	65	5	10
Cruisers	66	35	101	24	34
of which: Australian	6	1	7	3	3
Canadian	–	2	2	–	–
New Zealand	2	1	3	–	–
Destroyers	184	277	461	94	153
of which: Australian	5	13	18	3	4
Canadian	6	29	35	4	7
Submarines	60	178	238	34	76
Totals	332	553	885	161	278
of which: Australian	11	14	25	6	7
Canadian	6	31	37	4	7
New Zealand	2	1	3	–	–

Notes
(a) Includes ships lost, transferred from the US Navy and later returned, transferred from the Royal and Dominion Navies to Allies, captured from the Axis, and old vessels scrapped before war's end.
(b) Royal and Dominion Navies only. Includes ships badly damaged and not repaired or fully re-commissioned.
(c) Includes two escort carriers manned by RCN.

Losses by Year, including not repaired

	1939	1940	1941	1942	1943	1944	1945	Total
Capital ships	1	–	4	–	–	–	–	5
Fleet and escort carriers	1	1	2	3	1	1	1	10
Cruisers	–	3	11	13	4	3	–	34
of which: Australian			1	2				3
Destroyers	3	37	22	51	18	20	2	153
of which: Australian			1	3				4
Canadian		2		2	1	2		7
Submarines	1	24	11	19	13	5	3	76
Totals	6	65	50	86	36	29	6	278
of which: Australian			2	5				7
Canadian		2		2	1	2		7
Ocean escorts (a)	–	6	11	14	9	27	12	79
of which: Australian			1	1				2
Canadian			2	2	2	6	2	14
Indian		1		1				2

Notes
(a) Includes sloops, corvettes, frigates and cutters, but *not* fleet and sloop minesweepers and armed merchant cruisers.

Losses by Theatre

	Atlantic	Europe	Mediterranean	Indian and Pacific Oceans
Capital ships	1	1	1	2
Fleet and escort carriers	4	3	2	1
Cruisers	4	4	20	6
of which: Australian				3
Destroyers	23	53	67	10
of which: Australian			2	2
Canadian	5	2		
Submarines	3	23	45	5
Totals	35	84	135	24
of which: Australian			2	5
Canadian	5	2		
Ocean escorts	38	23	13	5
of which: Australian			1	1
Canadian	9	4	1	
Indian				2

Responsibility for Loss

	German	Italian	Japanese	French	Other (a)	Unknown
Capital ships	3	–	2	–	–	–
Fleet and escort carriers	8	–	1	–	1	–
Cruisers	20	6	5	–	3	–
Destroyers	114	15	8	1(b)	15	–
Submarines (c)	24	37	4	–	6	5
Totals	169	58	20	1	25	5

Notes
(a) Includes accidental explosion and fire, collision with Royal Navy or Allied ships, deliberately expended and marine loss due to grounding or weather.
(b) French shore batteries.
(c) Submarines 'presumed' or 'possibly' lost due to various causes have been allocated to the Axis power most likely to have been responsible.

Cause of Loss

	Surface forces	Submarine	Mines	Aircraft	Shore defences	Marine accident (and unknown)
Capital ships	1	2	–	2	–	–
Fleet and escort carriers	1	7	–	1	–	1
Cruisers	8	9	2	12	–	3
Destroyers	22	33	26	55	2	15
Submarines	29	5	26	7	–	4(+5)
Totals	61	56	54	77	2	23(+5)

2 AXIS NAVIES: LOSSES IN TOTAL AND DUE TO ROYAL AND DOMINION NAVIES

German Navy — All Major Warships

	1939	1940	1941	1942	1943	1944	1945	Total
Capital ships, including pocket battleships	1	–	1	–	1	1	3	7
of which RN	1	–	1	–	1	–	–	3
Cruisers	–	3	–	–	–	–	3	6
of which RN	–	2	–	–	–	–	–	2
Raiders	–	–	3	3	1	–	–	7
of which RN	–	–	3	1	–	–	–	4
Destroyers (a)	–	12	–	4	2	7	2	27
of which RN	–	12	–	3	1	2	–	18
Submarines	9	22	35	86	237	242	149	780
of which RN	9	17	28½	34	61	85	41	275½
Totals	10	37	39	93	241	250	157	827
of which RN	10	31	32½	38	63	87	41	302½

Notes
(a) Excludes large torpedo boats and ex-enemy destroyers designated 'TA' by German Navy.

German Navy — U-boat Loss Summaries

	1939	1940	1941	1942	1943	1944	1945	Total
Total losses	9	22	35	86	237	242	149	780
Theatres								
Atlantic	5	12	27	69	202	111	16	441
Europe	4	10	3	3	10	98	132	261
Mediterranean	–	–	5	14	23	26	–	68
Indian Ocean	–	–	–	–	2	7	1	10
Forces responsible								
Royal and Dominion Navies including Allied Navies with Royal Navy	9	17	28½	34	61	85	41	275½
of which:								
Australian	–	–	1	–	½	–	–	1½
Canadian	–	–	1	4½	4	11	3	23½
Indian	–	–	–	–	–	½	–	½
South African	–	–	–	–	–	–	1	1
Dutch	–	–	1	–	–	1	–	2
French	–	–	–	½	2½	½	–	3½
Greek	–	–	–	–	½	–	–	½
Norwegian	–	–	½	1	–	1	–	2½
Polish	–	–	–	–	½	½	–	1
RAF including Dominion and Allied Squadrons	–	1	2½	27½	91	72	50	244
US Forces including Allies	–	–	–	18½	72	44	41	175½
Russian Forces	–	–	1	–	1	4	6	12
Other causes including scuttling	–	4	3	6	12	37	11	73
Total losses	9	22	35	86	237	242	149	780

Notes
Sources vary on the cause of loss of some U-boats. This together with the difficulty of sharing responsibility when two or more forces were involved means that some of the 'scores' will be somewhat arbitrary. Nonetheless the main trends and periods of involvement are clear. U-boats scuttled in the closing days of the war are not included.

Italian Navy — up to and including 8 September 1943

	1940	1941	1942	1943	Total
Battleships	1	–	–	–	1
of which RN	1	–	–	–	1
Cruisers	1	6	3	2	12
of which RN	1	6	2	–	9
Destroyers (a)	8	14	8	13	43
of which RN	8	10	4	6	28
Submarines	20	18	22	25	85
of which RN	12	14	17	13	56
Totals	30	38	33	40	141
of which RN	22	30	23	19	94

Note
(a) Excludes torpedo boats and destroyer escorts.

Japanese Navy

	1941	1942	1943	1944	1945	Total
Capital ships	–	2	1	4	4	11
Aircraft carriers	–	6	1	12	2	21
Cruisers	–	6	2	24	9	41
of which RN	–	–	–	1	3	4
Destroyers	4	18	34	61	18	135
Submarines	3	16	28	53	27	127
of which RN	–	2½	2½	3	–	8(a)
Totals	7	48	66	154	60	335

Note
(a) Royal Navy — 4; Australian — 2; Indian — ½; New Zealand — 1½.

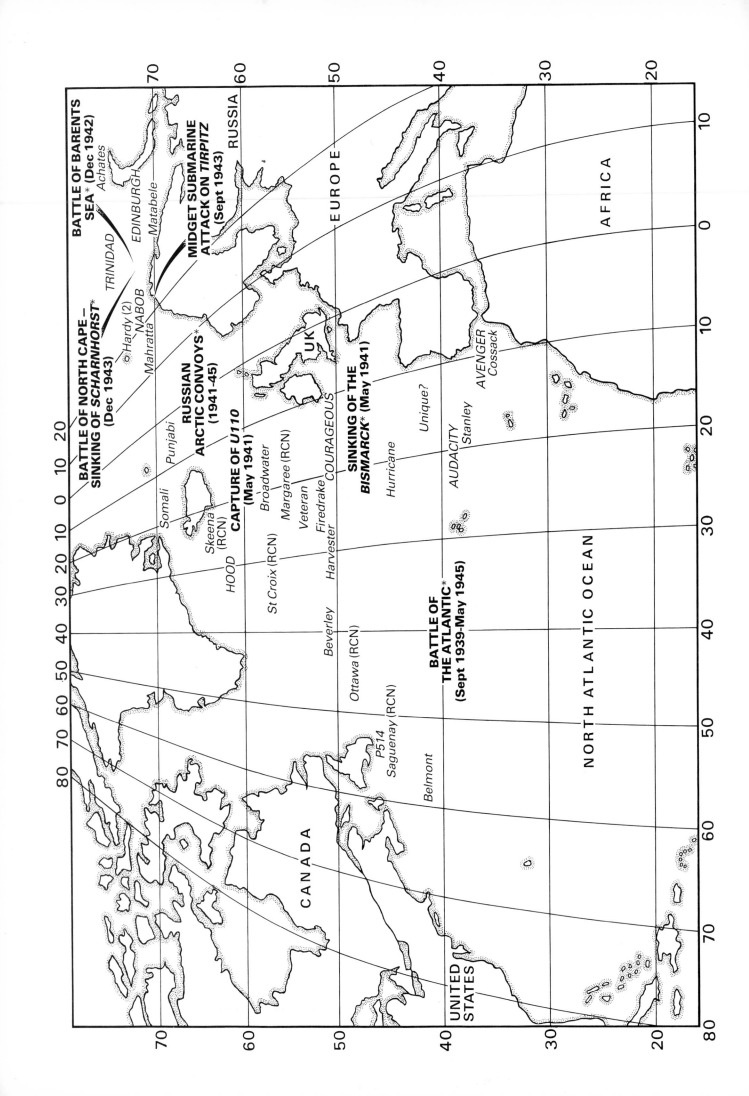

BATTLE OF BARENTS SEA * (Dec 1942)

Achates

BATTLE OF NORTH CAPE – SINKING OF *SCHARNHORST* * (Dec 1943)

EDINBURGH

Matabele

TRINIDAD

MIDGET SUBMARINE ATTACK ON *TIRPITZ* (Sept 1943)

RUSSIA

Hardy (2)

NABOB

Mahratta

Punjabi

RUSSIAN ARCTIC CONVOYS * (1941-45)

Somali

EUROPE

Skeena (RCN)

UK

CAPTURE OF U110 (May 1941)

Broadwater

HOOD

Margaree (RCN)

St Croix (RCN)

Veteran

Firedrake

COURAGEOUS

Harvester

SINKING OF THE *BISMARCK* * (May 1941)

Beverley

Hurricane

Unique?

AVENGER

Cossack

AUDACITY

Stanley

Ottawa (RCN)

BATTLE OF THE ATLANTIC * (Sept 1939-May 1945)

AFRICA

P514

Saguenay (RCN)

Belmont

CANADA

NORTH ATLANTIC OCEAN

UNITED STATES

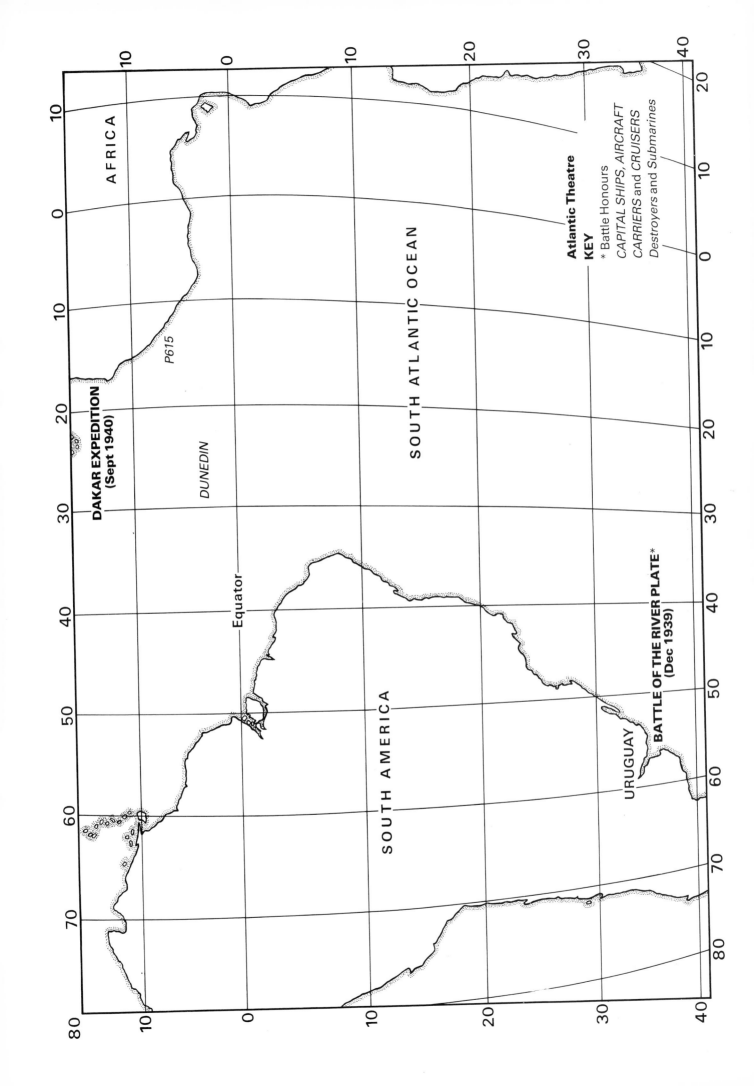

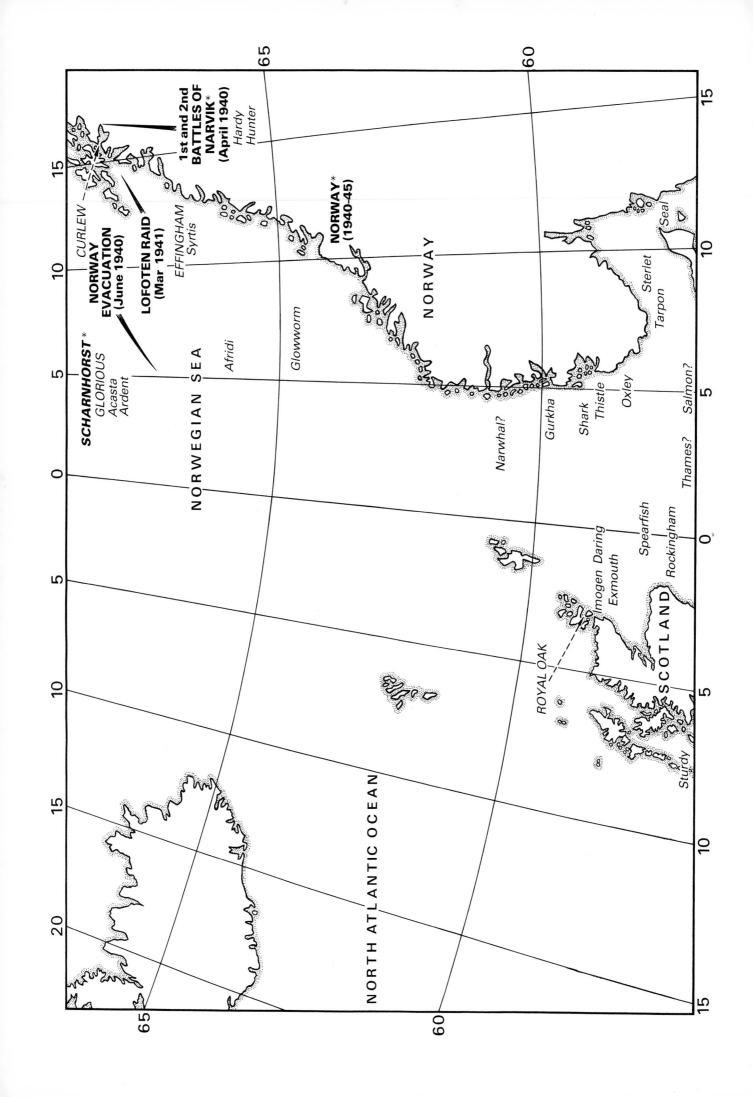

CURLEW

1st and 2nd
BATTLES OF
NARVIK*
(April 1940)
Hardy
Hunter

NORWAY
EVACUATION
(June 1940)

LOFOTEN RAID
(Mar 1941)

EFFINGHAM
Syrtis

NORWAY*
(1940-45)

SCHARNHORST*
GLORIOUS
Acasta
Ardent

NORWAY

NORWEGIAN SEA

Afridi

Glowworm

Narwhal?

Gurkha

Shark

Thistle

Oxley

Salmon?

Thames?

Spearfish

Rockingham

Imogen Daring
Exmouth

ROYAL OAK

SCOTLAND

Sturdy

Sterlet

Tarpon

Seal

NORTH ATLANTIC OCEAN

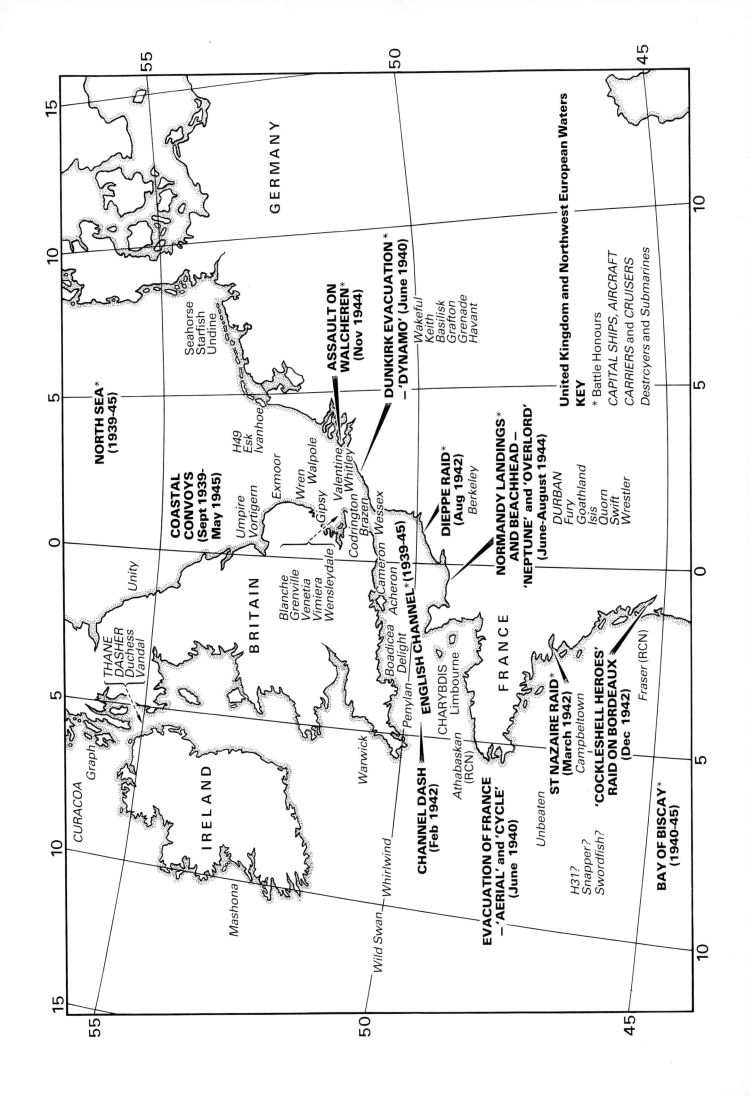

GERMANY

NORTH SEA *
(1939-45)

Seahorse
Starfish
Undine

ASSAULT ON
WALCHEREN *
(Nov 1944)

DUNKIRK EVACUATION *
– 'DYNAMO' (June 1940)

Wakeful
Keith
Basilisk
Grafton
Grenade
Havant

COASTAL
CONVOYS
(Sept 1939-
May 1945)

H49
Esk
Ivanhoe

Umpire
Vortigern
Exmoor
Wren
Walpole
Gipsy
Valentine
Codrington Whitley
Brazen
Cameron Wessex

United Kingdom and Northwest European Waters

KEY

* Battle Honours
CAPITAL SHIPS, AIRCRAFT
CARRIERS and CRUISERS
Destroyers and Submarines

Unity

DIEPPE RAID *
(Aug 1942)

Berkeley

NORMANDY LANDINGS *
AND BEACHHEAD –
'NEPTUNE' and 'OVERLORD'
(June-August 1944)

DURBAN
Fury
Goathland
Isis
Quorn
Swift
Wrestler

BRITAIN

Blanche
Grenville
Venetia
Vimiera
Wensleydale

Boadicea
Delight

Acheron

ENGLISH CHANNEL * (1939-45)

THANE
DASHER
Duchess
Vandal

CURACOA
Graph

Penylan

CHARYBDIS
Limbourne

FRANCE

IRELAND

Warwick

CHANNEL DASH
(Feb 1942)

Athabaskan
(RCN)

ST NAZAIRE RAID *
(March 1942)

Campbeltown

'COCKLESHELL HEROES'
RAID ON BORDEAUX
(Dec 1942)

Fraser (RCN)

Wild Swan

Whirlwind

EVACUATION OF FRANCE
– 'AERIAL' and 'CYCLE'
(June 1940)

Unbeaten

H31?
Snapper?
Swordfish?

BAY OF BISCAY *
(1940-45)

Mashona

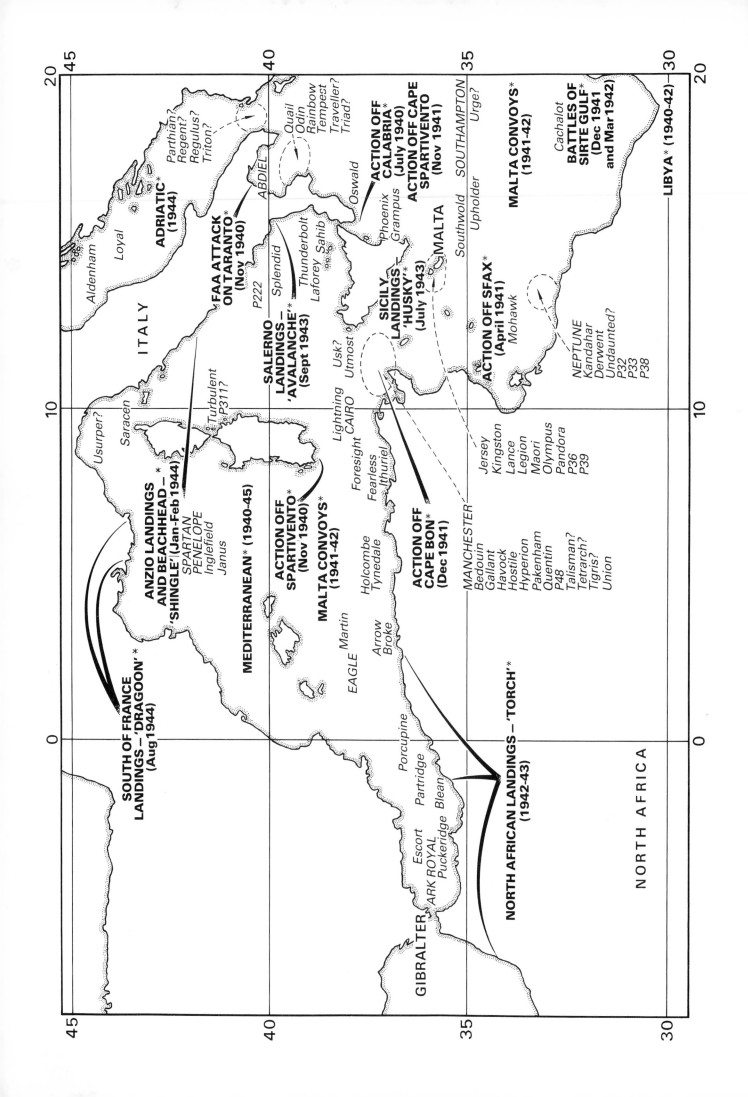

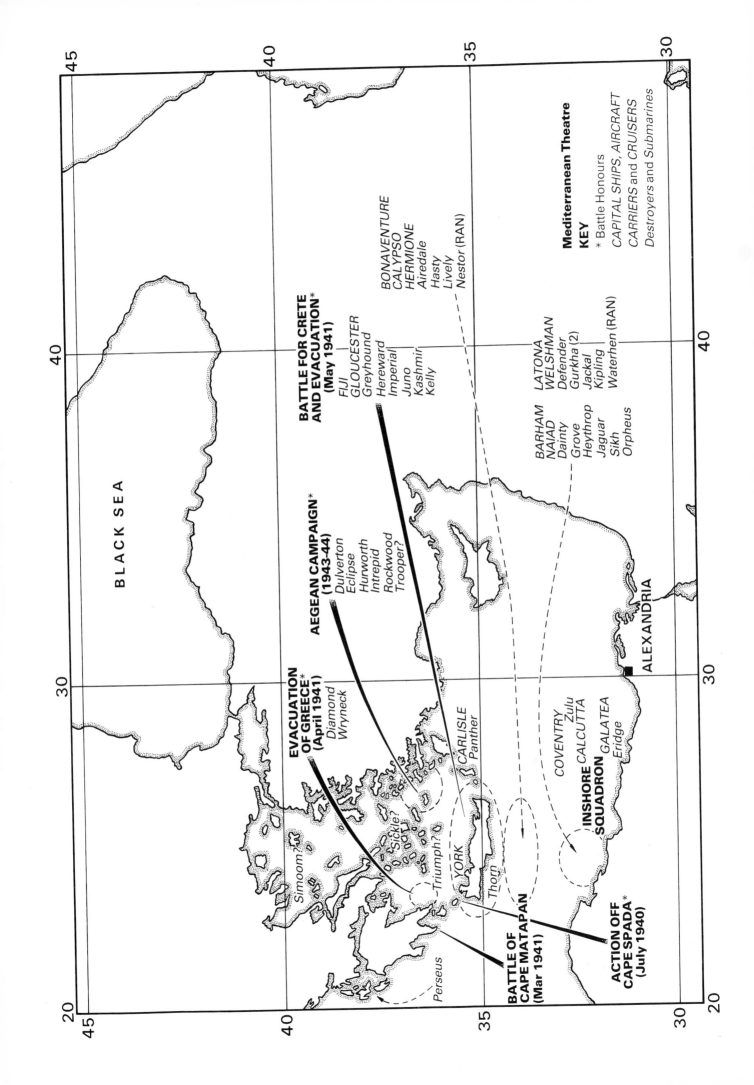

BLACK SEA

**EVACUATION
OF GREECE*
(April 1941)**
*Diamond
Wryneck*

AEGEAN CAMPAIGN*
(1943-44)
*Dulverton
Eclipse
Hurworth
Intrepid
Rockwood
Trooper?*

**BATTLE FOR CRETE
AND EVACUATION***
(May 1941)
*FIJI
GLOUCESTER
Greyhound
Hereward
Imperial
Juno
Kashmir
Kelly*

*BONAVENTURE
CALYPSO
HERMIONE
Airedale
Hasty
Lively
Nestor (RAN)*

Simoom?

Sickle?

Triumph?

Thorn

YORK

*CARLISLE
Panther*

**BATTLE OF
CAPE MATAPAN**
(Mar 1941)

Perseus

**ACTION OFF
CAPE SPADA***
(July 1940)

COVENTRY
Zulu
CALCUTTA
GALATEA
Eridge

**INSHORE
SQUADRON**

*BARHAM
NAIAD
Dainty
Grove
Heythrop
Jaguar
Sikh
Orpheus*

*LATONA
WELSHMAN
Defender
Gurkha (2)
Jackal
Kipling
Waterhen (RAN)*

ALEXANDRIA

**Mediterranean Theatre
KEY**
* Battle Honours
*CAPITAL SHIPS, AIRCRAFT
CARRIERS and CRUISERS
Destroyers and Submarines*

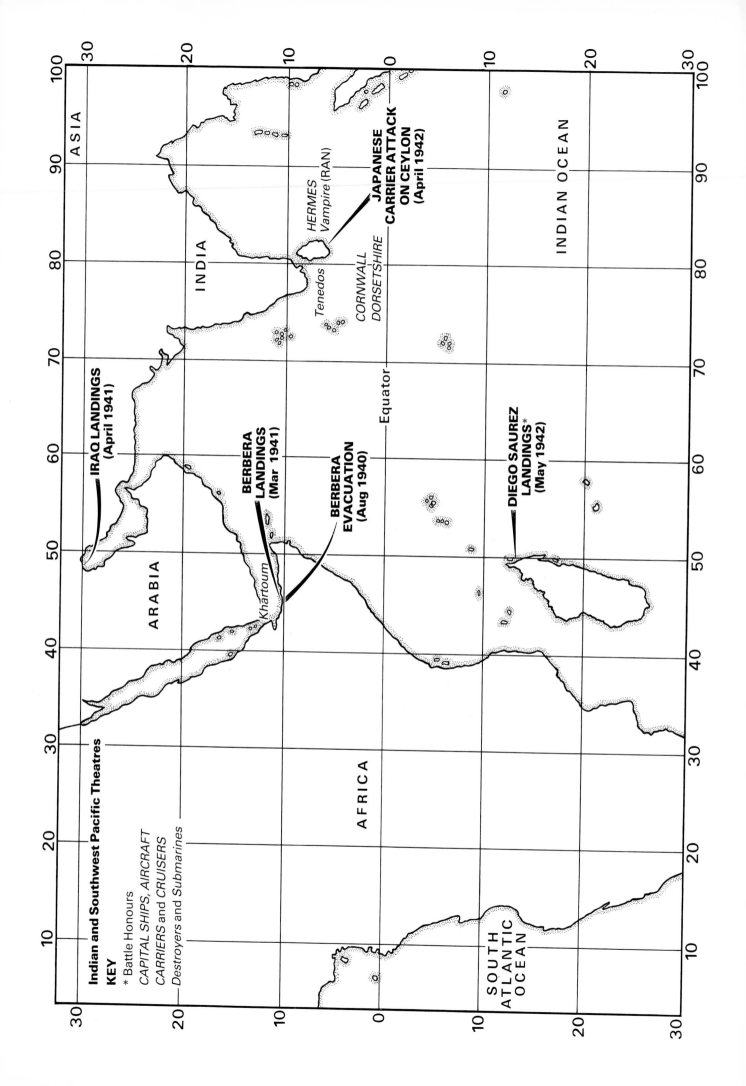

Indian and Southwest Pacific Theatres
KEY

* Battle Honours
CAPITAL SHIPS, AIRCRAFT
CARRIERS and CRUISERS
— Destroyers and Submarines

ASIA

INDIA

INDIAN OCEAN

HERMES
Vampire (RAN)

JAPANESE
CARRIER ATTACK
ON CEYLON
(April 1942)

Tenedos

CORNWALL
DORSETSHIRE

IRAQ LANDINGS
(April 1941)

ARABIA

BERBERA
LANDINGS
(Mar 1941)

BERBERA
EVACUATION
(Aug 1940)

Khartoum

Equator

DIEGO SAUREZ
LANDINGS*
(May 1942)

AFRICA

SOUTH
ATLANTIC
OCEAN

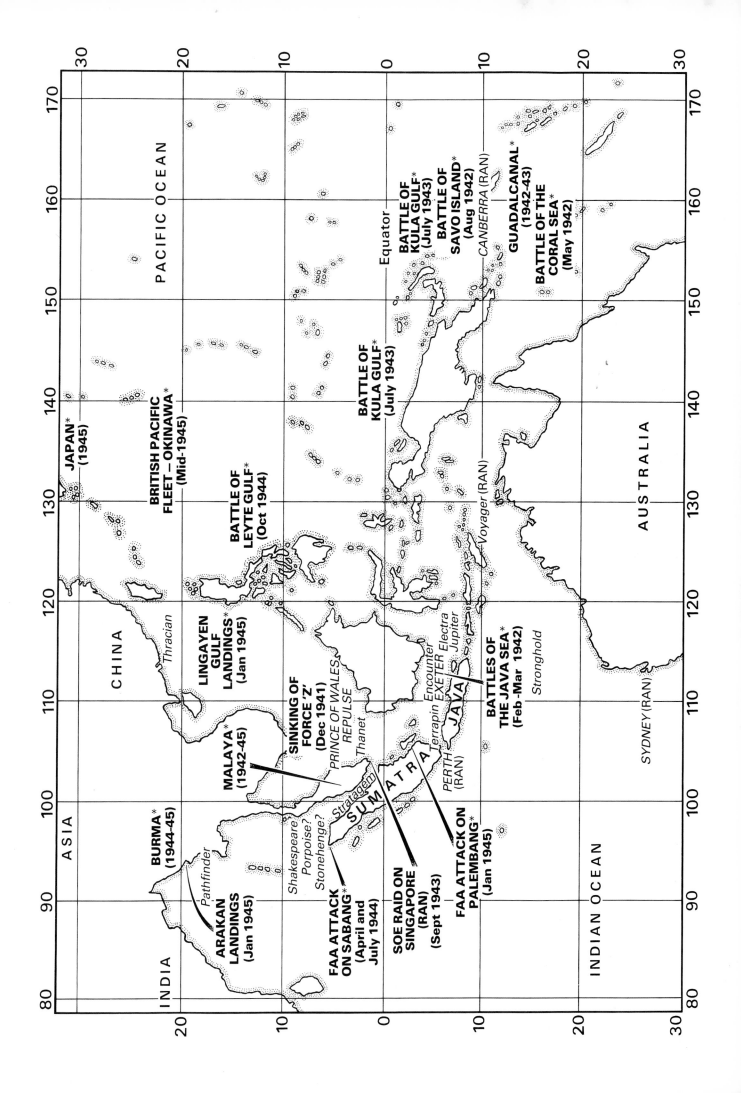

INDEX

Major Royal and Dominion Navy Warships Lost or Damaged

(including Allied warships serving under Royal Navy)

Cornwall, CA 73
Cossack, DD 56
Courageous, CV 12
Coventry, CL 16, 35, 85
Culver, cutter 64
Cumberland, CA 30
Curacoa, CL 19, 88
Curlew, CL 21

Dainty, DD 41
Daring, DD 16
Dasher, CVE 102
Defender, DD 53
Delhi, CL 93, 163
Delight, DD 26
Denbigh Castle, cor 162
Derwent, DD 103
Diamond, DD 45
Dido, CL 49
Dorsetshire, CA 73
Dragon, Pol/CL 140
Duchess, DD 14
Dulverton, DD 123
Dundee, sloop 30
Dunedin, CL 58
Dunvegan Castle, AMC 28
Durban, CL 67, 140

Eagle, CV 83
Eclipse, DD 121
Edinburgh, CL 72, 74
Effingham, CL 21
Egret, sloop 114
Electra, DD 67
Encounter, DD 69
Erica, cor 101
Eridge, DE 85
Escort, DD 29
Esk, DD 28
Exeter, CA 14, 67, 69
Exmoor, DD 40
Exmouth, DD 16

Fearless, DD 53
Fiji, CL 30, 49
Firedrake, DD 94
Fleur de Lys, cor 56
Foresight, DD 83
Forfar, AMC 34
Formidable, CV 49, 173
Fraser, Can/DD 24
Frobisher, CL 146
Fury, DD 141

Galatea, CL 30, 62
Gallant, DD 73
Gardenia, cor 93
Gipsy, DD 13
Gladiolus, cor 56
Glasgow, CL 35, 141
Glavkos, Gr/SS 73
Glorious, CV 24
Gloucester, CL 27, 39, 49
Glowworm, DD 18
Goathland, DE 142
Godetia, cor 30
Goodall, fr 166
Gould, fr 132
Grafton, DD 21
Grampus, SS 23
Graph, SS 132
Grenade, DD 21
Grenville, DD 16
Greyhound, DD 49
Grimsby, sloop 47
Grom, Pol/DD 20
Grove, DE 77
Gurkha, DD 18
Gurkha (2), DD 65

H.31, SS 60
H.49, SS 32
Hardy, DD 19
Hardy (2), DD 128
Hartland, cutter 91
Harvester, DD 102
Hasty, DD 79
Havant, DD 22
Havock, DD 73
Hector, AMC 73

Hereward, DD 49
Hermes, CV 73
Hermione, CL 79
Heythrop, DE 69
Hobart, Aus/CL 111
Holcombe, DE 126
Hollyhock, cor 73
Hood, BC 48
Hostile, DD 29
Hunter, DD 19
Hurricane, DD 124
Hurst Castle, cor 150
Hurworth, DE 121
Hussar, MS 146
Hyperion, DD 35

Ibis, sloop 93
Illustrious, CV 39, 167
Imogen, DD 26
Imperial, DD 49
Indefatigable, CV 167
Indomitable, CV 58, 83, 113, 173
Indus, Ind/sloop 73
Inglefield, DD 131
Intrepid, DD 119
Isaac Sweers, Dutch/DD 93
Isis, DD 142
Itchen, fr 116
Ithuriel, DD 93
Ivanhoe, DD 28

Jackal, DD 75
Jaguar, DD 71
Janus, DD 129
Jastrzab, Pol/SS 74
Jersey, DD 47
Jervis Bay, AMC 32
Juno, DD 49
Jupiter, DD 67

Kandahar, DD 62
Kashmir, DD 49
Keith, DD 22
Kelly, DD 49
Kent, CA 31
Kenya, CL 83
Khartoum, DD 25
King George V, BB 74
Kingston, DD 73
Kipling, DD 75
Kite, sloop 144
Kujawiak, Pol/DE 79

Laforey, DD 133
Lagan, fr 116
Lance, DD 73
Lapwing, sloop 164
Lark, sloop 162
Latona, ML 57
Laurentic, AMC 32
Lawford, fr 140
Leander, NZ/CL 111
Leda, MS 86
Legion, DD 71
Levis, Can/cor 54
Lightning, DD 103
Limbourne, DE 120
Lively, DD 75
Liverpool, CL 33, 77
Louisburg, Can/cor 101
Loyal, DD 153
Loyalty, MS 146

Mahratta, DD 130
Malaya, BB 42
Manchester, CL 53, 83
Manners, fr 160
Maori, DD 67
Margaree, Can/DD 32
Marigold, cor 95
Martin, DD 93
Mashona, DD 48
Matabele, DD 64
Mohawk, DD 45
Montbretia, Nor/cor 90
Mourne, fr 141

Nabob, CVE 144
Naiad, CL 49, 69
Narwhal, SS 28

Nelson, BB 14, 55, 140
Neptune, CL 62
Nestor, Aus/DD 79
Newcastle, CL 79
Newfoundland, CL 113
Niger, MS 80
Nigeria, CL 83
Norfolk, CA 17, 124
Nubian, DD 49

O.13, Dutch/SS 24
Odin, SS 23
Olympus, SS 75
Orion, CL 49
Orkan, Pol/DD 120
Orpheus, SS 23
Orzel, Pol/SS 24
Oswald, SS 29
Ottawa, Can/DD 86
Oxley, SS 12

P., submarines
P.32, 53
P.33, 53
P.36, 73
P.38, 67
P.39, 71
P.48, 96
P.222, 96
P.311, 96
P.514, 76
P.615, 102
Pakenham, DD 105
Pandora, SS 73
Panther, DD 121
Parramatta, Aus/sloop 59
Parthian, SS 115
Partridge, DD 96
Pathan, Ind/sloop 25
Pathfinder, DD 163
Patroclus, AMC 32
Penelope, CL 19, 62, 121, 131
Penylan, DD 94
Penzance, sloop 28
Perseus, SS 61
Perth, Aus/CL 49, 69
Phoebe, CL 55, 88
Phoenix, SS 29
Picotee, cor 54
Pink, cor 141
Pintail, sloop 50
Polyanthus, cor 116
Porcupine, DD 95
Porpoise, SS 161
Prince of Wales, BB 48, 61
Puckeridge, DE 115
Punjabi, DD 74

Quail, DD 139
Queen Elizabeth, BB 62
Queen Olga, Gr/DD 119
Quentin, DD 95
Quorn, DE 146

Rainbow, SS 33
Rajputana, AMC 44
Ramillies, BB 75
Rawalpindi, AMC 13
Regent, SS 105
Regina, Can/cor 146
Regulus, SS 35
Renown, BC 18
Repulse, BC 61
Resolution, BB 30
Rockingham, DD 150
Rockwood, DE 123
Royal Oak, BB 13

Saguenay, Can/DD 90
Sahib, SS 105
St Croix, Can/DD 116
Salamander, MS 146
Salmon, SS 26
Salopian, AMC 46
Salvia, cor 62
Samphire, cor 99
Saracen, SS 115
Scotstoun, AMC 22
Scylla, CL 141
Seahorse, SS 16

Seal, SS 20
Shakespeare, SS 161
Shark, SS 20
Shawinigan, Can/cor 154
Sheffield, CL 68
Sickle, SS 139
Sikh, DD 85
Simoom, SS 123
Sirius, CL 121
Skeena, Can/DD 152
Slinger, CVE 130
Snapdragon, cor 96
Snapper, SS 40
Somali, DD 86
Southampton, CL 13, 39
Southwold, DE 71
Spartan, CL 129
Spearfish, SS 28
Spikenard, Can/cor 66
Splendid, SS 105
Squirrel, MS 174
Stanley, DD 60
Starfish, SS 16
Sterlet, SS 19
Stonehenge, SS 133
Stratagem, SS 155
Stronghold, DD 69
Sturdy, DD 32
Suffolk, CA 19
Sussex, CA 30, 174
Svenner, Nor/DD 141
Swift, DD 141
Swordfish, SS 32
Sydney, Aus/CL 58
Syrtis, SS 132

Talisman, SS 85
Tarpon, SS 19
Teme, Can/fr 164
Tempest, SS 67
Tenedos, DD 73
Terrapin, SS 171
Tetrarch, SS 57
Thames, SS 67
Thane, CVE 160
Thanet, DD 65
Thistle, SS 19
Thorn, SS 83
Thracian, DD 61
Thunderbolt, SS 103
Tigris, SS 103
Traveller, SS 96
Trentonian, Can/cor 162
Triad, SS 33
Trinidad, CL 68, 74
Triton, SS 35
Triumph, SS 65
Trooper, SS 121
Turbulent, SS 103
Tweed, fr 128
Tynedale, DE 126

Uganda, CL 119
Umpire, SS 52
Unbeaten, SS 88
Undaunted, SS 47
Undine, SS 16
Union, SS 53
Unique, SS 88
Unity, SS 20
Upholder, SS 73
Urge, SS 73
Usk, SS 47
Usurper, SS 121
Utmost, SS 93

Valentine, DD 21
Valiant, BB 62, 145
Valleyfield, Can/fr 136
Vampire, Aus/DD 73
Vandal, SS 100
Venetia, DD 32
Vervain, cor 162
Vestal, MS 174
Veteran, DD 86
Victorious, CV 83, 173
Vimiera, DD 64
Voltaire, AMC 44
Vortigern, DD 68

Voyager, Aus/DD 87

Wakeful, DD 21
Walney, cutter 91
Walpole, DD 160
Warspite, BB 49, 119, 140
Warwick, DD 130
Waterhen, Aus/DD 51
Welshman, ML 101
Wensleydale, DD 156
Wessex, DD 21
Weyburn, Can/cor 100
Whirlwind, DD 26
Whitley, DD 21
Wild Swan, DD 76
Windflower, Can/cor 60
Woodpecker, sloop 130
Wren, DD 26
Wrestler, DD 140
Wryneck, DD 45

Yarra, Aus/sloop 69
York, CA 41

Zinnia, cor 54
Zulu, DD 85

Major Axis Warships Lost or Damaged due to the Royal and Dominion Navies

Acciaio, It/SS 113
Admiral Graf Spee, Ger/pocket BB 14
Admiral Hipper, Ger/CA 18, 96
Adua, It/SS 55
Airone, It/TB 33
Albatros, It/TB 57
Alcione, It/TB 61
Aldebaran, It/TB 57
Alfieri, It/DD 43
Altair, It/TB 57
Anfitrite, It/SS 41
Anton Schmitt, Ger/DD 18
Aquilone, It/DD 31
Ariel, It/TB 33
Armando Diaz, It/CL 41
Artigliere, It/DD 33
Ascari, It/DD 103
Ascianghi, It/SS 113
Ashigara, Jap/CA 173
Asteria, It/SS 101
Atlantis, Ger/raider 58
Attendolo, It/CL 85
Aviere, It/DD 96
Avorio, It/SS 101

Baleno, It/DD 45
Bande Nere, It/CL 71
Baracca, It/SS 54
Bartolomeo Colleoni, It/CL 29
Berillo, It/SS 33
Bernd von Arnim, Ger/DD 19
Bianchi, It/SS 52
Bismarck, Ger/BB 48
Bolzano, It/CA 53, 85
Bombardiere, It/DD 99
Borea, It/DD 31
Bronzo, It/SS 113

Caio Duilio, It/BB 35
Cantore, It/TB 85
Capponi, It/SS 43
Caracciolo, It/SS 61
Carducci, It/DD 43
Castore, It/TB 109
Chinotto, It/TB 43
Ciclone, It/DE 103
Cigno, It/TB 105
Climene, It/TB 105
Cobalto, It/SS 83
Conte di Cavour, It/BB 35